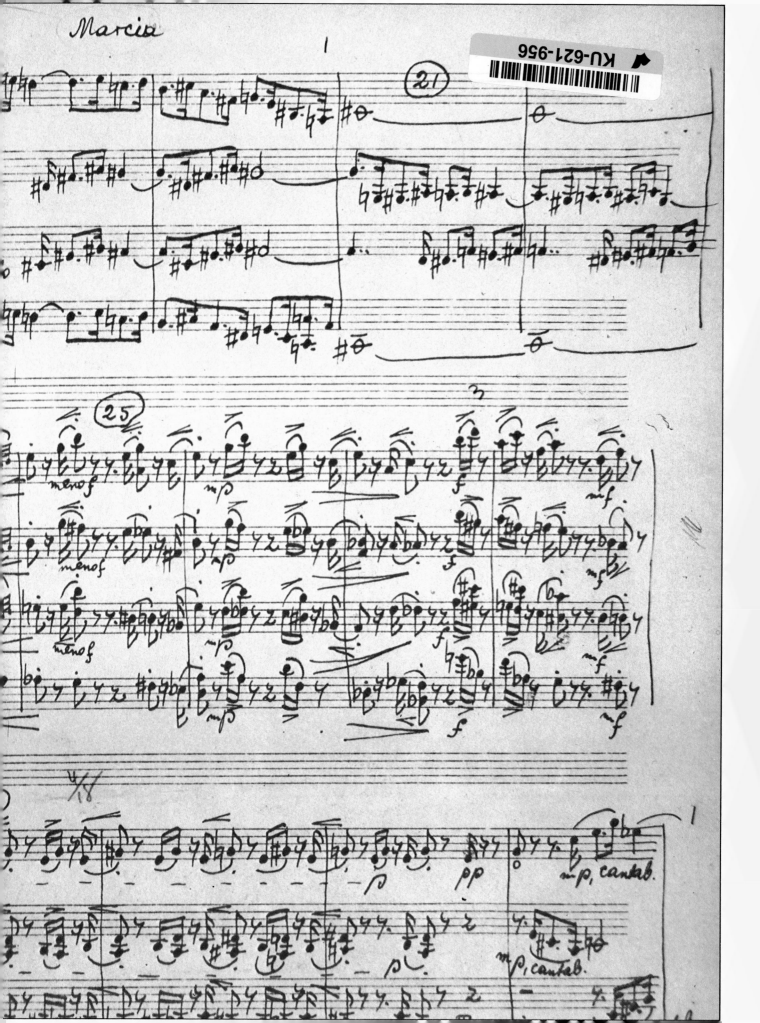

Marcia

THE GRAMOPHONE GUIDE TO
CLASSICAL COMPOSERS

THE
GRAMOPHONE GUIDE TO
CLASSICAL
COMPOSERS

Lionel Salter

PEERAGE BOOKS

First published in Great Britain in 1978 by
Salamander Books Limited

This edition published in 1984 by
Peerage Books
59 Grosvenor Street
London W1

© 1978 Salamander Books Limited

ISBN 0 907408 92 3

Credits

Editor: Trisha Palmer
Designers: Nick Buzzard and Roger Hyde
Artwork: Will Rowlands and Michael Whittlesea
            (© Salamander Books Ltd)
Fold-out: Text by Peter Gammond,
            illustrated by Olivia Beasley
            (© Salamander Books Ltd)
Photography: Michael Stannard (jacket); Bruce Scott
Printed in Hong Kong

Acknowledgements

The publishers would like to give special thanks to
HMV Ltd of Oxford Street, London, who kindly
supplied record sleeves for photography where these
were unavailable from the record companies listed
below, and to Boosey and Hawkes Music Publishers Ltd
for their help in supplying manuscripts.

We would also like to thank the following record
companies who gave their permission to use record
sleeves as illustrations in this book:

CBS Records   Lyrita Recorded Edition
CRD (Continental Record   Phonogram Ltd
   Distributors Ltd)   Pye Records Ltd
Decca Record Company Ltd   RCA Ltd
Deutsche Grammophon   Saga Records Ltd
EMI Records Ltd   Selecta (London)

The Author

The composers' biographies have been written by Lionel Salter, who has been a critic with *Gramophone* for 30 years and is a musician whose exceptional experience and range are widely recognised. A harpsichordist, pianist and conductor, he has made frequent broadcasts, a number of records and has performed in some 15 countries. He also has a reputation as a musicologist, with editions of several 17th- and 18th-century works to his credit. A former editor of the BBC *Music Guides,* he was also programme editor of the Edinburgh Festival in Scotland for five years and of the annual Promenade concerts in London's Albert Hall for eight. He has contributed to many symposia and encyclopedias (including the *Britannica* and the new *Grove*), and written three books, of which *Going to a Concert* has sold over 70,000 copies. He long ago lost count of the number of record sleeve and programme notes he has written and of song translations he has made. For many years he held a succession of senior posts in the BBC, including those of Head of TV Music, Head of Opera and finally Assistant Controller of Music.

Publisher's Note

The recommended recordings in this book have been compiled by the editorial team of *Gramophone.* The US catalogue numbers and labels have been added by Salamander Books Ltd, and every care has been taken to make sure these numbers are up to date at the time of going to press. However, American readers are advised to consult catalogues and their local record dealer for the latest information.

The record listings show details of soloists (where appropriate), orchestra and conductor; where other works are included on the same record, these are given in italics. The UK catalogue number, date of review in *Gramophone* and label are followed where relevant by the US number and label; an asterisk denotes that this information applies to both countries.

Note to the 1984 edition

Some of the older records listed in this volume may not now be on sale. Readers who wish to obtain these recordings are advised to try their local record library.

Nearly all of us acquire a knowledge of the musical repertory in the most astonishingly haphazard fashion, picking up works by chance hearings, either on radio or records or from live performances, and the elements of surprise and delight in such casual encounters are not to be minimised. When buying records, we mostly begin with works that have already caught our fancy, so as to savour them more fully at our leisure, but after that there comes a time for more conscious or methodical explorations. Where to branch out?

Some guidance to the flood of new discs that pours forth every month can be found in record reviews; but apart from there being endless duplications, the choice of works available, though bewilderingly large, is dictated by what the record companies, and their artists, decide on. Listeners who have gained pleasure from some work are logical in wanting to sample others by the same composer (a surer and more musical method than following the same artist), and the purpose of the present book is to give an insight into the career, output and personality (yes, they were real people, not just names in textbooks and catalogues) of 134 composers, and to offer recommendations of recordings of their works. These recommendations have been based on the opinions of the critics—some of the most experienced in the world—who write regularly in the monthly magazine *Gramophone*.

It will at once be seen that this is a selective, not a comprehensive, book. The composers included are known

to interest the majority of music lovers, but to forestall any outcry at omissions it must be explained that some composers who merited a place by their status had to be left out because they were not represented by altogether recommendable recordings in the current catalogue as at May 1978 (the date limit adopted here, which obviously is several months before publication). The appearance of new and better versions of listed works, the disappearance of present versions, or the addition of further recommendations, may be monitored by referring to *Gramophone* each month, which will keep readers abreast of the current position.

Inevitably there are bound to be divergences of opinion over performances (and even over technical quality), and the very last thing any sensible reviewer wants—or expects—is to be taken as gospel, so the wisdom of attempting to establish a "best version" of all works (which often tells one as much about the critic as about the performance) is highly questionable. In this book accordingly, several versions are frequently listed where by general consent they are outstanding, and the reader's final choice must be a personal one: no significance should be attached to the order in which recommendations appear.

Gramophone   L.S. (1978)

ISAAC ALBÉNIZ
(b. Camprodón, Catalonia, 1860; d. Cambo-les-Bains 1909)

Although youthful musical prodigies have appeared in every generation, few have been so precocious or led so adventurous an early career as Albéniz. He first came before the public as a pianist at the age of four in Barcelona; at seven he performed in Paris and started writing music. Declared too young for admission to the Conservatoire there, he went to Madrid to study, but at the age of nine ran away and gave concerts in various Spanish towns. To escape being sent home he took ship for Costa Rica, played throughout the USA and returned via England to become, at the age of 14, a pupil at the Leipzig Conservatory. Returning penniless to Spain, he had the good fortune to obtain a grant from the king enabling him to study in Brussels; but at 18 he managed to fulfil his childhood ambition of taking lessons in Budapest from Liszt ❯, whose influence on his style was very considerable.

After touring extensively (including in his programmes small pieces of his own with a Spanish flavour, such as the now famous *Tango*), he tried to settle down to teaching; but this proved uncongenial, and in 1890 he went to Paris to study composition seriously with Dukas ❯. A wealthy English banker with a hankering for writing librettos offered him a handsome allowance in return for his setting them to music; but the Arthurian cycle which was his patron's pride and joy fizzled out, and their only joint operatic success was *Pepita Jiménez* (1896).

It is as one of the earliest figures in the Spanish musical renaissance at the turn of the nineteenth century that Albéniz claims attention. His copious output for the piano, for which he wrote with great facility, includes a large number of pieces in mainly Andalusian idiom, most of which have justifiably been forgotten; but his fame rests on the virtuoso piano suite entitled *Iberia* (1909), which consists of twelve impressions of various parts of Spain, reflecting the rhythms and harmonies of popular music. To some extent the influence of the French school is apparent in these masterly and colourful evocations, though their over-elaborately decorated texture is characteristic of Albéniz's own exhibitionist personality, abetted by Liszt's teaching.

Left: *Isaac Albéniz, a musical prodigy in his early years, whose most famous work, the piano suite* Iberia, *was completed in the year of his death.*

IBERIA; NAVARRA; CANTOS DE ESPANA
☐ Larrocha
SXL6586-7 (10/73) Decca

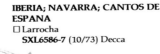

TOMMASO ALBINONI
(b. Venice 1671; d. there 1751)

Although Albinoni received a thorough musical training and his works were enthusiastically received both by the public, inside and outside Italy, and by fellow-musicians —J. S. Bach ❯ studied them closely and based three of his own fugues on movements from them—he was for many years at pains to describe himself as an "amateur composer of violin music and a Venetian"; by this he meant that he indulged his activities as a composer and performer purely for his own pleasure and did not accept money for them. (His fellow-citizen and contemporary Alessandro Marcello was similarly an amateur.) However, at the age of 40 he seems to have been obliged to change his status, and he is referred to as directing a "singing school of renown". In the last decade of his life he appears to have produced no music at all.

His works include over 50 operas for the teeming theatrical life of Venice, the earliest great operatic centre, trio and duo sonatas, and concertos (in a style linking Corelli ❯ with Vivaldi ❯) which were in avid demand; he received many pressing requests for concertos from Dutch publishers. His quartet symphonies were forerunners of the true quartet form of half-a-century later. He is chiefly represented on record by his concertos for violin and for oboe, which not only show a true understanding of instrumental technique and a fluent invention (one of his admirers spoke of his "rage to compose") but make delightful listening. Beware of the often-played *Adagio for strings and organ*, a spurious modern confection which travesties his style.

OBOE CONCERTOS—OP. 7 NOS. 3 AND 6
☐ Sutcliffe, Virtuosi of England, Davison/*Vivaldi*
CFP163 (7/71) Classics for Pleasure,

OBOE CONCERTO OP. 9 NO. 8;
VIOLIN CONCERTO OP. 9 NO. 1;
DOUBLE OBOE CONCERTO OP. 9 NO. 3; VIOLIN CONCERTO OP. 10 NO. 8; ADAGIO (arr. Giazotto)
☐ Holliger, Driehuys, Michelucci, I Musici
6580 001 (6/72) Phonogram

THOMAS AUGUSTINE ARNE
(b. London 1710; d. there 1778)

For some reason people persist in speaking of "Dr Arne", rather as if there were something special which set him apart from other composers with honorary degrees. His father, who had intended him for the law, was opposed to his studying music; but he took violin lessons surreptitiously, taught singing to his sister Susanna (later to become celebrated as the tragic actress Mrs Cibber, who took part in the première of Handel's *Messiah*), and by his early twenties had his first opera produced, with his sister in the title-role. Other stage works quickly followed, and in 1738 he was engaged to compose music for an adaptation at Drury Lane Theatre, London, of Milton's *Comus*. Its melodic charm immediately attracted notice, and Arne followed this up two years later with a fine masque to Congreve's *Judgment of Paris*. At the same time the masque *Alfred* was performed in Clivedon, the Prince of Wales's residence, to celebrate the anniversary of the accession of a Hanoverian monarch: this concluded with a patriotic air, *Rule Britannia*, which has since become almost a second national anthem in England, usually sung in a weakened version of the original. Arne's songs for revivals of Shakespeare's *As You Like It* and *The Tempest* have also become part of the English vocal heritage (though again often in corrupt forms).

Meanwhile Arne had been busy as an associate of David Garrick in the management of Drury Lane and as the composer of innumerable elegant but trifling songs for the London pleasure gardens at Vauxhall, Ranelagh and Marylebone. His comedy *Thomas and Sally* and the delightful ballad opera *Love in a village* were written for Covent Garden; but between these he produced there an experiment—a serious opera in English after the Italian model, with recitative instead of dialogue. This work, *Artaxerxes*, which was far more ornate in style than his other music, achieved an enormous success which endured for over half a century.

After the death of Handel ≫ in 1759, the year when Arne received his doctorate, he turned for the first time to oratorio, and his dramatic *Judith* was the first English oratorio in which a female chorus was employed. His instrumental works—overtures, concertos and sonatas—have a continuing freshness and grace, though they are lightweight beside those of Handel, who overshadowed him in London for the greater part of his life.

SYMPHONIES 1-4
□ Bournemouth Sinfonietta/ Montgomery/*S. Wesley: Sym. in D*
CSD3767 (3/76) EMI/HMV
4041 HNH
OVERTURES 1-8
□ Academy of Ancient Music/Hogwood
DSL0503 (11/74) L'Oiseau-Lyre*

Left: *Arne's doctorate was an honorary one from Oxford.*

Below: *Arne's 1745 arrangement of the National Anthem.*

Right: *Caricature of Arne by Bartolozzi, from the National Portrait Gallery.*

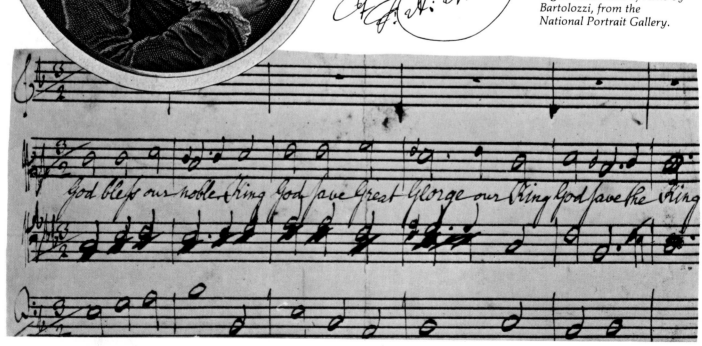

MALCOLM ARNOLD
(b. Northampton 1921)

The bluff, breezy personality of this composer—who had several years' invaluable practical experience as a trumpeter in the London Philharmonic and BBC Symphony orchestras and also won the Cobbett Composition Prize and a Mendelssohn Scholarship which allowed him a year in Italy—is reflected in the exuberance and boisterous humour of much of his music. Blessed with an enviable technical facility, he has devoted much of his energy to writing film scores, which besides their financial return have brought him an Oscar for *Bridge on the River Kwai* and an Ivor Novello award for *Inn of the Sixth Happiness*; but he has also composed a very large number of concert works, many of which are characterised by a directness of utterance and an unaffected pleasure in providing entertainment. The virtuosity of his instrumentation, combined with a sparkling wit, may be heard in the overtures *Beckus the Dandipratt* (which first made his name) and *Tam O'Shanter*, the *English dances* and *Scottish dances*, and in a different medium the *Shanties* for wind quintet and the brass quintet. His overt dislike of pomposity has sometimes led to his being accused of jokiness, though such themes as the "cream-puff tune" (as it has been called) in the Guitar Concerto's first movement are disarming; and that he can be totally serious is evidenced by, for example, the Concerto for two violins.

BRASS QUINTET (1961)
☐ Philip Jones Brass Quintet/*Dodgson; Salzedo; Ewald*
  ZRG655 (11/70) Decca Argo∗
SYMPHONY NO. 5
4 CORNISH DANCES
PETERLOO OVERTURE
☐ CBSO/Arnold
  ASD2878 (5/73) EMI/HMV
GUITAR CONCERTO
☐ Bream, Melos/Arnold/*Giuliani*
  SB6826 (4/70) RCA
  LSC-2487 RCA
3 SHANTIES FOR WIND QUINTET (1952)
☐ London Wind Quintet
  SPA396 (8/75) Decca
  5326 Argo

Right: *Two studies of Malcolm Arnold in rehearsal.*

CARL PHILIPP EMANUEL BACH
(b. Weimar 1714; d. Hamburg 1788)

In his own day this second son of Johann Sebastian Bach ❯ achieved a wider renown than his great father, who was his only teacher in composition and keyboard playing, and whom he venerated, although in his own style he reacted against learned counterpoint. From a very early age he showed remarkable talent, but being left-handed he was hampered in playing the violin and concentrated instead on the harpsichord. He studied law for a time, but then became cembalist to the Crown Prince of Prussia, who in 1740 succeeded to the throne and is known to history as Frederick the Great. The monarch was an enthusiastic flautist, though distinctly conservative and unadventurous in his tastes, and Carl Philipp had to accompany him in the same flute concertos several times a week for 27 years, a job made even more irksome by the king's poor sense of rhythm, to which Bach's artistic conscience would not allow him to pander. His witty but caustic tongue earned him the displeasure of his master, who did not care for his music either—though by this time two sets of keyboard sonatas and a brilliant treatise on keyboard playing had spread his fame, and Frederick was certainly aware of his talent. On the death of his godfather Telemann ❯ in 1767 he at last managed to get away from Potsdam and succeed him as director of music for the city of Hamburg—one of the plum appointments in the whole of Germany. His chief duty (rather as his father's had been in Leipzig, where he had unsuccessfully applied to follow him) was to provide and direct the music in the city's principal churches and to give concerts for the municipality; and his twenty years' activities there brought him much honour.

Left: *C P E Bach was the most original genius of the family.*

Carl Philipp codified the foundations of piano technique and established the form of the three-movement sonata and symphony; but beyond that, his music pointed forward not only to the "storm and stress" of Haydn » who, like Mozart » and Beethoven », declared an admiration for him, but even to early romanticism. Far from being smoothly "galant", like that of his youngest brother Johann Christian », some of his music (e.g. the *Fantasies*) is strikingly, even quirkily, original, capturing the spirit of the improvisations with which he so impressed his hearers; it contains dramatic brilliance, expressive harmonies, bold and unexpected modulations, instrumental recitatives and disconcertingly abrupt contrasts of dynamics and mood that mirrored changing emotions in a way no previous composer had ever attempted.

CONCERTO IN E FLAT FOR HARPSICHORD, FORTEPIANO AND STRINGS
☐ Leonhardt Consort, VCM, Leonhardt/ J. C. Bach, W. F. Bach
  AW6 41210 (6/67) Telefunken
  641210 Telefunken
CONCERTO IN C MINOR FOR HARPSICHORD AND STRINGS, W43/4
☐ Malcolm, ASMF/Marriner
  SDD336 (11/72) Decca Ace of Diamonds
KEYBOARD WORKS
☐ (Sonatas: C major, W55/1; D minor, W57/4. Rondos: C major, W56/1; E major, W57/1; D minor, W61/4.

Fantasias: E flat major, W58/6; F major, W59/5).
Dreyfus (*fortepiano*)
  2533 327 (1/77) DG Archiv
MAGNIFICAT IN D MINOR, W215
☐ Palmer, Watts, Tear, Roberts, Choir of King's College, Cambridge, ASMF/Ledger
  ZRG853 (3/77) Decca Argo*
6 SYMPHONIES, W182
☐ **2.** ASMF/Marriner
  SDD336 (11/72) Decca Ace of Diamonds
4 SYMPHONIES, W183
☐ **1-4.** Little Orch. of London/Jones
  H71180 (11/72) WEA Nonesuch

JOHANN CHRISTIAN BACH
(b. Leipzig 1735; d. London 1782)

The youngest son of Johann Sebastian Bach was often known as the "English Bach" because of his twenty years' residence in London, where he was a central figure in musical life; among much else he founded, with his friend Abel, an important series of concerts which ran for 17 years, and he was associated in the building of the Hanover Square Rooms (for long the capital's chief concert hall). He had been educated first by his father and then by his elder brother Carl Philipp Emanuel » after which he had gone to Italy, where he had written church music and been appointed organist of Milan Cathedral. But the call of the stage lured him away, and the success of three operas by him in Turin and Naples led to his being invited to London in 1762 as composer to the Italian Opera at the King's Theatre.

The first of his seven operas there greatly pleased the fashionable audience and ran for nearly three months; as a result he was appointed music master to Queen Charlotte, consort of George III. Apart from visits to Mannheim and Paris for further operas, he spent the rest of his life in London, composing numerous songs, orchestral and instrumental pieces for his own concerts and for Vauxhall and the other pleasure gardens. When Mozart » visited London as a child of eight, Johann Christian befriended him, treated him with much kindness, and played duets with the child on his knee. His elegant, Italianate mellifluous style much influenced the boy, who took piano sonatas by him as a basis for his own first piano concertos.

J. C. Bach's short symphonies and concertos are notable for charm and grace rather than profundity. He popularised the then new pianoforte in London; his playing was described as "expressive", but his technique was apparently limited, so that his keyboard works were "such as ladies can execute with little trouble". His use of a double orchestra in some of the Op.18 symphonies harks back to a previous generation, but in the main his music points forward to Mozartian style.

JOHANN SEBASTIAN BACH
(b. Eisenach 1685; d. Leipzig 1750)

The Bach family, which flourished in Thuringia from the late sixteenth to the early nineteenth century, included so many musicians that the name became a professional appellation, and all musicians in that area were known simply as "Bachs". The greatest figure of this close-knit clan, and indeed one of the greatest figures in the whole history of music, was Johann Sebastian (of whose many children four became notable composers). Though he himself achieved a very considerable reputation in central Germany, both as a brilliant organist and as a composer, he never had an opportunity to travel further afield like his cosmopolitan contemporary Handel »; he was kept tied to posts at provincial courts and churches, where with incredible energy and industry he created a vast output to meet the practical needs of the moment.

At the court of Weimar (1708-17), for example, he composed church cantatas and the bulk of his numerous organ works. Then, as director of music to Prince Leopold of Anhalt-Cöthen, he wrote orchestral suites, concertos on the Italian model of Vivaldi » — the fifth of the set of six dedicated to the Margrave of Brandenburg is the earliest known concerto to feature a solo keyboard instrument — and secular instrumental works, in which his noble master was interested. For the education of his family and pupils he supplied much harpsichord music (with which he furthered the equal-temperament system of tuning, as in the two sets of preludes and fugues in all the major and minor keys known as the "48"). When, in 1723, he was appointed Cantor at St Thomas's Church in Leipzig he immediately set to and with astonishing application wrote five sets of cantatas for each Sunday and holy-day of the year; these musical meditations on the text of the Gospel of the day, shared between solo voices, a chorus which nearly always provided a final Lutheran hymn, and a small orchestra of varying constitution, contain a wealth of expressive devotional music which amply repays exploration. It was in Leipzig, too, that he created his monumental settings of the Passion, according to St John

CONCERTI FOR KEYBOARD AND ORCHESTRA, OP. 7
☐ Haebler *(fortepiano)*, Vienna Capella Academica/Melkus
☐ **1-3**
  6500 846 (4/75) Phonogram
☐ **6**
  6500 041 (1/74) Phonogram
CONCERTI FOR KEYBOARD AND ORCHESTRA, OP. 13
☐ Haebler *(fortepiano)*, Vienna Capella Academica/Melkus
☐ **1, 3, 6**
  6500 041 (1/74) Phonogram
☐ **2, 5**
  6500 847 (4/75) Phonogram
☐ **4**
  6500 846 (7/75) Phonogram
KEYBOARD SONATAS, OP. 17
☐ **1-4.** Haebler *(fortepiano)*
  6500 848 (5/75) Phonogram
SYMPHONIES, OP. 3 NOS. 1-6
☐ ASMF/Marriner
  6500 115 (7/72) Phonogram
SYMPHONIES, OP. 18
☐ Stuttgart CO/Munchinger
☐ **1, 3, 5**
  SXL6638 (6/74) Decca
☐ **2, 4, 6/Telemann: Don Quixote**
  SXL6755 (10/76) Decca

Left: *A Gainsborough portrait of Mozart's friend Johann Christian, the 'English' Bach.*

KING'S COLLEGE CHOIR, CAMBRIDGE
BACH: CANTATA NO.147, 'HERZ UND MUND' (including the chorale 'Jesu, Joy of Man's Desiring')
3 MOTETS, BWV 226, BWV 228, & BWV 230
ELLY AMELING · JANET BAKER · IAN PARTRIDGE · JOHN SHIRLEY-QUIRK
ACADEMY OF ST.MARTIN-IN-THE-FIELDS · DAVID WILLCOCKS

Right: *Engraving after a portrait of J S Bach painted two years before his death. He is holding a six-part canon composed in the previous year for a learned music society in Leipzig.*

and St Matthew, which gave a new dramatic dimension to the form. The Mass in B Minor, one of the supreme masterpieces in the whole literature of music, in its complete form dates from Bach's Leipzig years, though it is a composite work, some movements of which were drawn from earlier compositions. That Bach, a staunch Lutheran, should have written a Latin Mass (albeit far too long for liturgical use) is explained by the fact that it was offered to his Catholic sovereign, the Elector of Saxony.

In his early years Bach had been much influenced by Buxtehude » (to hear whom he had once walked 200 miles!) and other North German composers in his writing for organ, but his own achievements for that instrument, which now form the core of its repertoire, have eclipsed them: in particular his great and diverse development of the chorale prelude opened up new horizons. In various fields he raised music to great heights by his combination of contrapuntal virtuosity (most conspicuously in the *Musical Offering* for Frederick the Great, the *Goldberg Variations* written for his pupil Goldberg to play to his insomniac patron, and, especially, in the *Art of Fugue*) with rhythmic vitality, instrumental inventiveness, emotional intensity and often amazingly daring harmony (as in the *Chromatic Fantasia*). Nevertheless, even in his lifetime his work was criticised as being far too complex—he was frequently at loggerheads with church or civic authorities who did not appreciate his innovations, and whom he stubbornly resisted—as well as for being old-fashioned. Indeed, when he applied for the Leipzig post with which his name is chiefly associated, the authorities accepted him reluctantly only after two other, more forward-looking, candidates (one of whom was Telemann ») had withdrawn.

The character of music was radically changing from the polyphonic—of which style Bach marks the peak—to the homophonic, which was to reign supreme for the best part of a century; and during that period Bach's music fell into an oblivion from which it began to be rescued only when, in 1829, Mendelssohn » revived the *St Matthew Passion*.

Johann Sebastian Bach

ART OF FUGUE
☐ Lionel Rogg (organ)
SLS782 (10/69) HMV
S-3766 Angel
☐ *arr. Marriner/Davis.*
Marriner
6747 104 (10/75) Phonogram
6747 172 Philips

BRANDENBURG CONCERTI (Cpte)
☐ Wurtemberg Chamber/Faerber
TV34044-5S (3/66) Decca Turnabout*
☐ ASMF/Marriner
6700 045 (9/72) Phonogram*
☐ Virtuosi of England/Davison
CFP40010-1 (10/72) Classics for
Pleasure
S313/4 Vanguard
☐ ECO/Leppard
6747 166 (4/76) Phonogram*
☐ ECO/Britten
SXL6774-5 (8/76) Decca
2225 London
☐ Bath Festival CO/Menuhin
ASD327-8 (5/60) EMI/HMV
S-3787 Angel

CANTATA NO. 56. ICH WILL DEN KREUZSTAB GERNE TRAGEN
CANTATA NO. 82. ICH HABE GENUG
☐ Shirley-Quirk, ASMF/Marriner
SOL280 (5/65) L'Oiseau-Lyre
☐ Souzay/Berlin Bach Soloists/
Winschermann
SAL3767 (3/70) Phonogram

CANTATA NO. 92, ICH HAB IN GOTTES HERZ UND SINN;
CANTATA NO. 126, ERHALT' UNS, HERR, BEI DEINEM WORT
☐ Mathis, Reynolds, Schreier, Fischer-
Dieskau/Munich Bach Ch. and
Orch./Richter
2533 312 (7/76) DG Archiv*

CANTATA 147, HERZ UND MUND TAT UND LEBEN
☐ Ameling, Baker, Partridge, Shirley-
Quirk, Choir of King's College,
Cambridge, ASMF/Willcocks/*Motets*
HQS1254 (5/74) EMI/HMV
S-36804 Angel

CANTATA NO. 211: SCHWEIGT STILLE, PLAUDERT NICHT (COFFEE)
CANTATA NO. 212: MER HAHN EN NEUE OBERKEET (PEASANT)
☐ Hansmann, Equiluz, Egmond, VCM/
Harnoncourt
AF6 41359 (5/73) Selecta/Telefunken
641079 Telefunken

CHORALE PRELUDES
☐ Hurford (organ)
PHB673 (12/70) Abbey

CHRISTMAS ORATORIO (Cpte.)
☐ Ameling, Watts, Pears, Krause,
Lubeck Kantorei, Stuttgart Chamber
Orch./Munchinger
SET346-8 (12/67) Decca
1386 London
☐ Anon treble, Esswood, Equiluz,
Nimsgern, Vienna Boys' Choir,
Chorus Viennensis/VCM/
Harnoncourt
FK6 35022 (12/75) Selecta/Telefunken*

CHROMATIC FANTASIA AND FUGUE IN D MINOR, BWV903; ITALIAN CONCERTO IN F, BWV971; TOCCATA IN D, BWV912; FRENCH SUITE NO. 5 IN G, BWV816
☐ Malcolm
ECS788 (10/76) Decca Eclipse
6197 London

Left: *One of the chorale preludes from Bach's Orgel-
büchlein, in his own hand.*

CONCERTO IN D MINOR FOR 2 VIOLINS, BWV1043
☐ Grumiaux, Toyoda/New Philh./
Waart/*Vln. and Oboe Conc.;* *Vivaldi*
6500 119 (9/71) Phonogram*
☐ Bean, Sillito, Virtuosi of England/
Davidson/*Vln. Concs. in A minor, E*
CFP40244 (8/76)

CONCERTO IN D MINOR FOR VIOLIN AND OBOE, BWV10600
☐ Menuhin, Goossens/Bath Festival/
Handel, Vivaldi
ASD500 (11/62) EMI/HMV
☐ Grumiaux, Holliger/New Philh./
Waart/*Double Vln. Conc.; Vivaldi*
6500 119 (9/71) Phonogram
☐ Perlman, Black, ECO/Barenboim/
*Vln. Conc. in A minor; Vln. Conc. in
D minor*
ASD3076 (6/75) EMI/HMV

ENGLISH SUITES, BWV806-11
☐ Dreyfus
2533 164-6 (9-76) DG Archiv*
☐ Leonhardt
6709 500 (10/77) Phonogram

FRENCH SUITES NOS. 1-6, BWV812-7
☐ Gilbert
HMU438 (8/76) Rediffusion/Harmonia
☐ Leonhardt
6709 500 (10/77) Phonogram

GOLDBERG VARIATIONS, BWV988
☐ Leonhardt
AW6 41198 Selecta/Telefunken*

HARPSICHORD CONCERTOS
☐ 1-7. Malcolm, Menuhin Festival,
Menuhin
SLS5039 (5/76) HMV

ITALIAN CONCERTO
☐ Malcolm/*Chromatic Fantasia;
Fantasia in C min.; etc.*
SXLP30141 (5/72) EMI/HMV
6197 London

MAGNIFICAT
☐ Ameling, van Bork, Watts, Krenn,
Krause, Vienna Acad. Choir,
Stuttgart CO/Munchinger/*Cantata
No. 10*
SXL6400 (10/69) Decca
26103 London

MASS IN B MINOR (Cpte.)
☐ Ameling, Minton, Watts, Krenn,
Krause, Chorus/Stuttgart CO/
Munchinger
SET477-8 (3/71) Decca
1287 London
☐ Palmer, Watts, Tear, Rippon, Amor
Artis Chorale/ECO/Somary
VSD71190 (7/75) Pye Vanguard
71190 Vanguard

ORGAN WORKS
Toccata and Fugue in D min.;
Passacaglia in C min.; Preludes and
Fugues in A min. and D
☐ Chorzempa
6500 214 (2/71) Phonogram*
Toccata and Fugue in D min.; Pastoral
in F; Prelude and Fugue in G min.;
In dulci jubilo; Von Himmel hoch;
Nun freut euch; Ich ruf zu dir;
Herzlich tut mich; Valet will ich
☐ Walcha
2565 002 (4/72) DG Heliodor
Fantasia and Fugue in G min.;
Preludes and Fugues in E flat, F min.
and B min.
☐ Walcha
138958 (7/65) DG
Fantasia and Fugue in C min.,
BWV537, Fantasia and Fugue in G min.,
BWV542; Passacaglia in C min.,
BWV582, Toccata and Fugue in D
min., BWV565
☐ Rogg
EXP2 (1/65) Peerless Oryx
Prelude and Fugue in D major,
BWV532; Trio Sonata No. 2 in
C min., BWV526; Chorale Prelude, O
Lamm Gottes, BWV656; Pastorale in
F, BWV590
☐ Rogg
EXP51 (8/72) Peerless Oryx

Fantasia and Fugue in G minor,
BWV542; Fugue in D major, BWV577;
Prelude and Fugue in B minor,
BWV544; Toccata and Fugue in F
major, BWV540; Concerto No. 2 in
A minor after Vivaldi, BWV593
☐ Kynaston
CFP40241 (11/76) Classics for Pleasure

3 PARTITAS FOR SOLO VIOLIN; 3 SONATAS FOR SOLO VIOLIN
☐ Grumiaux
SAL3472-4 (12/69) Phonogram
☐ Suk
SLS828 (2/72) HMV

ST JOHN PASSION (Cpte.)
☐ Harper, Hill, Hodgson, Pears, Burgess,
Tobin, Thompson, Tear, Shirley-
Quirk, Howell, Wandsworth School
Choir, ECO/Britten
SET531-3 (7/72) Decca
13104 London

ST MATTHEW PASSION (Cpte.)
☐ Pears, Fischer-Dieskau, Berry, Casa,
Gedda, Kraus, Schwarzkopf, Evans,
Ludwig, Brown, Watts/
Hampstead Church Choir/Philh.
Orch. & Ch./Klemperer
SLS827 (6/72) HMV
☐ Ameling, Hoffgen, Pears, Wunderlich,
Prey, Krause, Blankenburg,
Messthaler, Stuttgart Chamber Orch./
Munchinger
SET288-91 (3/65) Decca

6 SONATAS FOR VIOLIN AND KEYBOARD
☐ Melkus, Dreyfus
2708 032 (8/76) DG*

SUITES (Cpte.)
☐ ASMF/Marriner
ZRG687-8 (9/71) Decca Argo*
☐ ECO/Leppard
6500 067-8 (4/72) Phonogram
7750 035 Philips

6 SUITES FOR SOLO CELLO
☐ Tortelier
SLS798 (3/71) HMV

VIOLIN CONCERTO IN A MINOR, BWV1041
☐ Michelucci/I Musici/*Conc. in E;
Double Conc.*
6580 021 (3/72) Phonogram
☐ Menuhin/Masters Chamber Orch./
Bach: Vln. Concs.
ASD346 (6/60) EMI/HMV
60258 Seraphim
☐ Perlman/ECO/Barenboim/*Vln. Conc.
in D minor; Vln and Oboe Conc.*
ASD3076 (6/75) EMI/HMV
S-37076 Angel
☐ Sillito/Virtuosi of England/Davison/
Conc. in E; Double Conc.
CFP40244 (8/76) Classics for Pleasure
☐ Melkus/Vienna Capella Academica/
Conc. in E; Double Conc.
2533 075 (11/71) DG Archiv*

VIOLIN CONCERTO IN E, BWV1042
☐ Menuhin/Orch./Menuhin/*Bach:
Vln. Concs.*
ASD346 (6/60) EMI/HMV
☐ Bean/Virtuosi of England/Davison/
Conc. in A minor; Double Conc.
CFP40244 (8/76) Classics for Pleasure
☐ Melkus/Vienna Academica/*Conc. in
A minor; Double Conc.*
2533 075 (11/71) DG Archiv

MILY BALAKIREV
(b. Nijni-Novgorod 1837; d. St Petersburg 1910)

He was the animator and mentor of a mid-nineteenth century group of Russian composers (Cui, Mussorgsky », Rimsky-Korsakov » and Borodin ») who became known as the "kuchka" or "mighty handful" and, inspired by the example of Glinka », were dedicated to the cause of musical nationalism. Balakirev, a talented pianist, was obliged by financial pressures to give up much of his time to teaching—in which his finicky and dictatorially didactic temperament found scope—and in 1862 became assistant director of the newly-founded Free School of Music in St Petersburg, where he conducted orchestral concerts at which works by members of his group and such composers as Berlioz », Schumann » and Liszt » were introduced. In that same year he spent some time in the Caucasus, where he was much influenced by exotic Circassian and Georgian melodic idioms; the first results of this were some songs and the "oriental fantasy" *Islamey*, a brilliant and colourful showpiece for piano demanding great technical virtuosity.

His ceaseless, close supervision of his disciples' work —he not only suggested ideas, themes and keys but constantly interfered in matters of detail, altering or re-composing passages which dissatisfied him—became tyrannical, and sooner or later they all fell out with him;

and by his heated championship of musical nationalism he aroused much opposition. At various times he suffered from severe depressions (the worst in 1871, when he had a complete breakdown and became a religious fanatic), so that work on his compositions was fitful, and his career as a conductor and, by this time, as director of the Free School was often interrupted, sometimes for long periods. In 1883, despite the hostility aroused by his tactlessness, he was appointed director of the Imperial Court Chapel; on retiring from this post eleven years later he threw himself into writing, completing the Symphony in C major he had begun 30 years earlier—which well exemplifies his powers of invention, his fine craftsmanship and mastery of structure. He also arranged a collection of Russian folksongs and composed a number of short piano pieces and his Lisztian piano sonata, the first movement of which, most originally, combines fugue with sonata form. His earlier symphonic poem *Thamar* is based on a barbaric legend by Lermontov; one of the melodies in his *Overture on three Russian themes* also appears in the finale of the Fourth Symphony of Tchaikovsky », who was a friend of his although not sharing his ideals.

ISLAMEY—ORIENTAL FANTASY
☐ Katchen/*Rachmaninov: Pno. Conc. 2*
 SDD181 (10/68) Decca Ace of
  Diamonds
 STS-15086 London
SYMPHONY NO. 1 IN C
☐ RPO/Beecham/*Borodin*
 SXLP30171 (10/74) EMI/HMV
 S-60062 Seraphim
THAMAR
☐ SRO/Ansermet/*Glazunov*
 ECS642 (6/72) Decca Eclipse

Left & right: *Mily Balakirev, who gave the impetus and lead to the 'mighty handful' of Russian nationalist composers who included Rimsky-Korsakov, Borodin, Cui and Mussorgsky.*

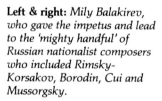

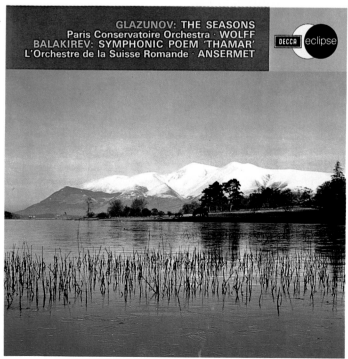

GLAZUNOV: THE SEASONS
Paris Conservatoire Orchestra · WOLFF
BALAKIREV: SYMPHONIC POEM 'THAMAR'
L'Orchestre de la Suisse Romande · ANSERMET
DECCA eclipse

BÉLA BARTÓK

(b. Nagyszentmiklós 1881; d. New York 1945)

Bartók's stature as one of the major figures in the music of the first half of the twentieth century transcends that which he earned as the greatest composer Hungary has produced, though his universality is deeply rooted in his nationalism. He was an eclectic who was able to absorb diverse new developments, welding them on to the classical tradition to forge an individual language which bridged idioms from Eastern and Western Europe. His music, for all its intellectual virtuosity, is at the same time spiritual and intensely emotional, in an unobvious way, but like much great art does not easily yield up its treasures at a first encounter.

A frail child, he was brought up by his mother, who scraped to enable him to study music in Pozsony (Bratislava), where he fell under the influence of his slightly older contemporary Dóhnanyi », a follower of Brahms », who was a frequent visitor to Hungary at that time. As a result, Bartók followed Dóhnanyi to Budapest, where he excelled as a pianist but remained unproductive as a composer until he was galvanised into activity by hearing a concert of works by Richard Strauss ». This allegiance however did not last long, and from 1905 he became immersed in research into genuine Hungarian, Rumanian and Bulgarian folk music (which had been neglected in favour of synthetic gipsy styles), and in company with Kodály » collected and arranged a vast amount of this material, whose irregular rhythms and

Below: *Béla Bartók, Hungary's greatest composer and one of the leading musical figures of the first half of this century.*

non-diatonic melodies, which suggested dissonant or bitonal harmonies to him, left a deep and lasting impression on his own creative style.

His music met with considerable opposition, and it was not until 1918, with the success of his brooding but powerful opera *Bluebeard's castle*, that he began to attract attention—though mostly abroad, for in Hungary he was viewed askance politically; even so, his expressionist ballet *The miraculous mandarin* was widely banned because of its erotic and violent subject. Nevertheless, his *Dance suite* was commissioned to commemorate the fiftieth anniversary of the union of Buda with Pest, and Bartók himself declared that this marked a watershed in his development. His progression from Brahms, Liszt », Debussy » and Strauss to a tough expressionism was now to be balanced by a movement through neo-classicism, as in the First Piano Concerto, to romanticism. The increasing Nazification of Hungary drove Bartók to leave his native country, where he received but grudging recognition, for the USA, which he had already visited as a pianist. The strain of making ends meet there, with only a modest two-year research grant from Columbia University and constant concert-giving to alleviate his financial straits, took toll of his never robust health; from 1943 he lived in straitened circumstances on little more than his wartime-

reduced royalties plus a few commissions, such as for the Concerto for orchestra, and a Viola Concerto he did not live to finish. Bartók's works written in America, particularly the witty *Concerto for orchestra* and the engaging Third Piano Concerto, are his most accessible and have become repertoire classics; but he had been gradually moving towards a mellower, more direct idiom after the impressionistic 1936 *Music for strings, percussion and celesta* (in which Stravinsky's » influence is discernible and which, like the Third Piano Concerto, contains one of Bartók's mysteriously beautiful "night music" movements) —most notably in the 2nd Violin Concerto and the high-spirited *Divertimento for strings* which, like all his orchestral music, is scored with great subtlety. His large output for piano runs the gamut from his percussive, dissonant concert works to the simplicities of his folk-inspired children's pieces (as in the *Mikrokosmos* collection); but without doubt his greatest legacy is the six string quartets, the most masterly contributions to the medium between Beethoven » and Shostakovich ». Highly charged emotionally, and extremely exacting to play, they illustrate Bartók's stylistic progress—but Nos 3 and 4, the most austere, uncompromising and experimental, are best left until his more accessible works have been fully digested.

PIANO CONCERTO NO. 1 IN A
☐ Bishop-Kovacevich/LSO/C. Davis/
Conc. 3
9500 043 (7/76) Phonogram∗
PIANO CONCERTO NO. 3 IN E
☐ Katchen/LSO/Kertesz/*Ravel*
SXL6209 (9/66) Decca
☐ Ranki/Budapest PO/Ferencsik/
Viola Conc.
SLPX11421 (3/76) Hungaroton/
Selecta
☐ Bishop-Kovacevich/LSO/C. Davis/
Conc. 1
9500 043 (7/76) Phonogram∗
QUARTETS 1-6
☐ Hungarian Quartet
2733 001 (10/74) DG Privilege
SVBX-593 Vox
☐ Juilliard Quartet
61118-20 (3/70) CBS Classics
D3S-717 Columbia
RUMANIAN FOLKDANCES
☐ I Musici/*Britten: Simple Sym.; Barber:
Adagio; Respighi: Ancient Airs and
Dances—Suite 3*
6580 045 (6/73) Phonogram
**SONATA FOR 2 PIANOS AND
PERCUSSION**
☐ Eden, Tamir, Holland, Fry/*Poulenc:
Dble. Pno. Son.*
SXL6357 (10/68) Decca
6583 London
VIOLIN CONCERTO NO. 2
☐ Perlman, LSO/Previn
ASD3014 (10/74) EMI/HMV
S-37014 Angel
☐ Chung/LPO/Solti
SXL6802 (4/78) Decca
THE WOODEN PRINCE—BALLET
☐ *Suite:* SWDR Orch./Reinhardt./
Mandarin
TV34086S (12/67) Decca Turnabout∗

Right: *Bartók's researches shed
a completely new light on the
true nature of Hungarian folk
music.*

Far left: *The beginning of the
second movement (Marcia) of
Bartók's 6th String Quartet
(composed in 1939).*

ARNOLD BAX
(b. London 1883; d. Cork 1953)

The "Celtic twilight" atmosphere which pervades much of Bax's music has misled some people into thinking of him as an Irish composer; but this was not the case, although he was strongly drawn to Ireland and its literature. Indeed, he himself published literary works under an Irish pseudonym, and his first orchestral piece, the charming *In the faery hills*, was based on a work by W. B. Yeats. A modest and diffident figure who shunned the public limelight, he was in private a quick thinker, a witty conversationalist, and brilliant pianist with a quite exceptional skill in sight-reading even the most complicated orchestral score at the piano. His enormous facility—his output in all fields, except opera, which he never attempted, was very large indeed—ironically dwindled after his appointment as Master of the King's Music in 1942 (he had been knighted five years previously); but another facet of his abundant invention is to be seen in the luxuriant texture and sensuous colouring of his music. This complexity of decoration has in fact sometimes proved a stumbling-block to his wider appreciation, though beneath the rich chromatic arabesques his thinking is fundamentally diatonic: similarly, his music often appears to be impressionistically rhapsodic, but its form is usually quite clear.

Bax described himself as "a brazen romantic, by which I mean that my music is the expression of emotional states", and his idiom remained remarkably constant and recognisable throughout the forty years of his composing career—deeply poetic and nostalgic, with occasional outbursts of almost aggressive energy. Behind many of his works lies a literary programme, though only rarely was this explicitly stated, as in *The garden of Fand* (a legend of the sea); others, such as *November woods*, *The tale the pine-trees knew* and the Debussyan *Tintagel*, his best-known work, may be described as mood-pictures.

Bax's splendid choral works, such as *Mater ora filium* and *This worldes joie*, and his many distinguished songs have recently been much neglected, as has his voluminous chamber music, which includes such undisputed masterpieces as the nonet and the sonata for viola and piano. The first of his three string quartets, like the third of his four piano sonatas, incidentally shows to what extent Bax could re-create the contours of Irish folksong. He wrote a quantity of short piano pieces besides the sonatas (which are more epic in character); but his reputation nowadays rests more on his orchestral music, particularly the seven symphonies, all written after 1920, which though seemingly diffuse at a first hearing are firmly cast in a three-movement mould. In these, where Bax's thought is at its most passionate and intense, there is frequent thematic inter-relationship between movements. The symphonies however differ widely in mood: the Second is imaginatively introspective, the Third ultimately achieves serenity after stress, and the Fifth (perhaps his finest and most direct-speaking), emerges triumphantly from the shadows.

PIANO WORKS
☐ Burlesque; Gopack; May night in the Ukraine; Romance; Sleepy head; Sonata No. 4 in G major: Loveridge
RCS26 (8/65) Lyrita
SYMPHONY NO. 2
☐ LPO/Fredman
SRCS54 (6/71) Lyrita
SYMPHONY NO. 5 IN C SHARP MINOR
☐ LPO/Leppard
SRCS58 (5/72) Lyrita
TINTAGEL: THE GARDEN OF FAND; NORTHERN BALLAD NO. 1; MEDITERRANEAN
☐ LPO/Boult
SRCS62 (10/72) Lyrita

Inset right: *Arnold Bax, the 'brazen romantic', at the age of 40, when he was working on his Second Symphony.*

Right: *The honours which fell on Bax ironically coincided with a marked decline in his hitherto voluminous output.*

22

LUDWIG VAN BEETHOVEN
(b. Bonn 1770; d. Vienna 1827)

While the standing and popularity of most other composers wax or wane in successive generations, Beethoven's towering stature has always claimed the allegiance both of musicians—who have recognised in him a creative spirit of genius who vastly expanded the form, vocabulary and emotional range of music, and epitomised the new age of liberal idealism after the French Revolution—and of the musical public, in whose hearts his stirring, subjective, passionately affirmative works have won an unshakeable place. Two generations of his family, which was of Flemish origin, had been in the service of the Elector of Cologne—his grandfather as *kapellmeister*, his father as a tenor singer—and it was therefore natural that, after his worthless father had attempted to exploit him as a child prodigy, he also should enter the Elector's employ, as harpsichordist, court organist, and subsequently viola-player in the opera orchestra. His brilliance at keyboard improvisation attracted the attention of various aristocrats, who helped him in his struggles to maintain his younger brothers and drunken father (who had been dismissed); and when his father died their introductions and support were invaluable to the young Beethoven when, in 1792, he moved to Vienna for good to study and to make his livelihood as pianist, teacher and composer.

There were many striking contradictions in Beethoven. Though ill-favoured, unkempt, blunt, conspicuously lacking in the social graces, and an ardent egalitarian, he enjoyed the company of numerous noble families (to whom the bulk of his music is dedicated) and frustratedly fell in love with several young ladies far above him in station. He was quick-tempered, aggressively self-assured and proud, but his vitality and genius won him many devoted friends. He rebelled against the old system of patronage, making his living as a freelance, and detested Napoleon for betraying republican principles and accepting the crown as Emperor (which caused him to slash out the original dedication to Napoleon of the *Eroica* Symphony), yet only a generous annuity from three noble patrons stopped him accepting the post of court *kapellmeister* to the French puppet kingdom in Westphalia. Despite the high-minded tone he adopted (for example expressing abhorrence of the "frivolity" of Mozart's comic operas) he had no scruples about cheating his publishers. He was a poor manager, and lived alone in squalor even when financially most successful; but a powerful factor in his distrust of people and prickly self-reliance was the deafness which began to afflict him before the age of 30.

He realised, with an anguish that brought him close to suicide, that this was incurable, and had to give up all thoughts of performing; but by 1819 he was totally deaf and could communicate with others only through a note-pad. What is truly remarkable is that his greatest masterpieces all come from this period. The sense of isolation and constriction, allied to his natural impatience and rebelliousness against curbs, often impelled him to make demands on voices and instruments then (and sometimes even now) considered excessive—the high tessitura of the chorus sopranos in the *Missa Solemnis*, the gambolling of

Right: *An impression by J D Böhm of Beethoven out walking.*

23

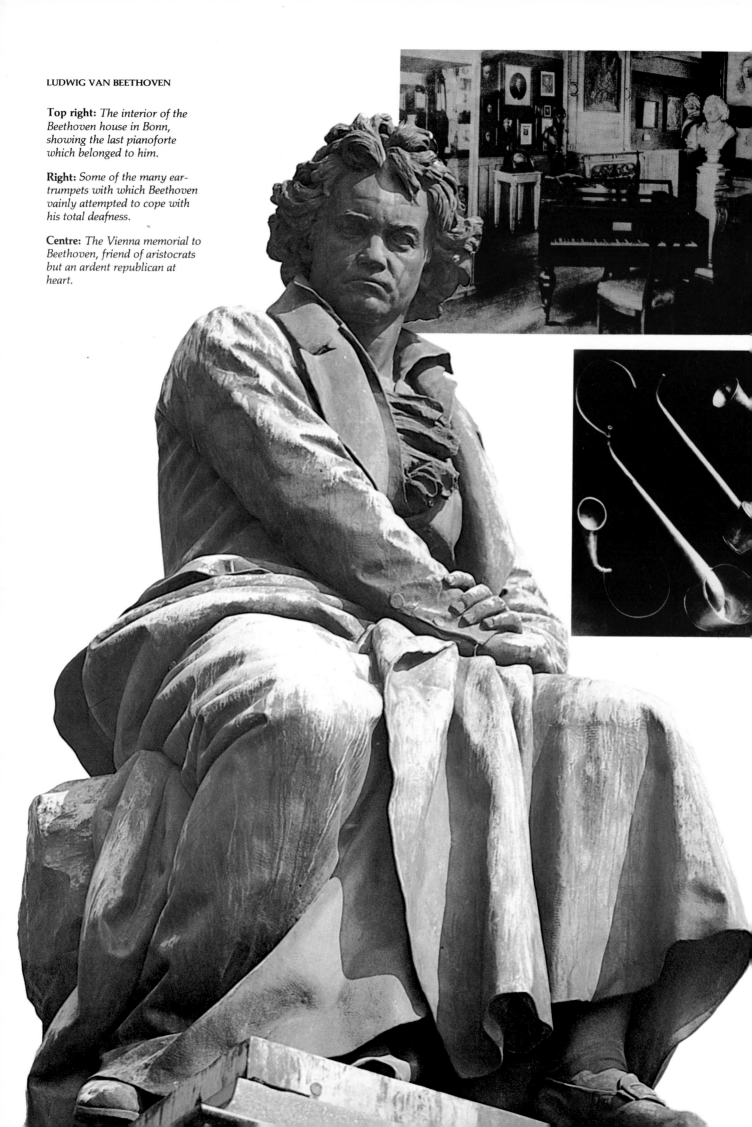

LUDWIG VAN BEETHOVEN

Top right: *The interior of the Beethoven house in Bonn, showing the last pianoforte which belonged to him.*

Right: *Some of the many ear-trumpets with which Beethoven vainly attempted to cope with his total deafness.*

Centre: *The Vienna memorial to Beethoven, friend of aristocrats but an ardent republican at heart.*

the double-basses in the scherzo of the Fifth Symphony, the jagged and desperately striving sonorities of the *Grosse Fuge* for string quartet, the Olympian thunder of the *Appassionata* and *Hammerklavier* piano sonatas are examples; it also made possible the metaphysical depths of his so-called "third period" late works, which seemed incomprehensible to most of his contemporaries. In some of their slow movements, such as those of the Ninth Symphony, the A minor string quartet and the Op.111 piano sonata, he attained a transcendental tranquillity which lies at the bounds of human experience.

The social idealism which informs much of his music is evident from his choice of subjects, which centre on the theme of liberty: *Fidelio*, his only opera—which underwent many vicissitudes—is a broadside aginst political oppression, and a celebration of courageous wifely devotion;

Goethe's *Egmont*, to which he wrote incidental music, is a drama of struggle against tyranny; a theme associated with the heroic Prometheus in an early ballet of his reappears in a set of piano variations and again for the finale of the *Eroica* Symphony; and the choral finale of the Ninth Symphony is a setting of Schiller's "Ode to Joy", a hymn to the brotherhood, and freedom, of man. Beethoven wrestled not only with concepts which lay far beyond the experience of his great predecessors Haydn » (with whom he had as a youth taken some abortive lessons) and Mozart », but with his actual material: he was a slow worker, and his habit was to jot down ideas in sketchbooks he always carried with him, to mull them over in his mind, and constantly to reshape and polish them until the original thought, often naive or banal, emerged as something striking and significant.

BAGATELLES
☐ 1-24. Brendel
   TV34077S (2/67) Decca Turnabout*
☐ 1-24. Bishop-Kovacevich
   6500 930 (1/76) Phonogram
CONCERTO IN D FOR VIOLIN AND ORCHESTRA
☐ Suk/NPO/Boult
   ASD2667 (3/71) EMI/HMV
   S-353 Vanguard
☐ D. Oistrakh, Philh./Cluytens
   SXLP30168 (11/74) EMI/HMV
☐ Grumiaux/ Concertgebouw/Davis
   6500 775 (3/75) Phonogram*
☐ Krebbers/Concertgebouw/Haitink
   6580 115 (2/76) Phonogram
☐ I. Oistrakh/VSO/D. Oistrakh
   GL25005 (10/76) RCA Gold Seal
CONCERTO IN C FOR VIOLIN, CELLO, PIANO AND ORCHESTRA
☐ Beaux Arts Trio/LPO/Haitink
   9500 382 (4/78) Phonogram
☐ D. Oistrakh, Rostropovich, Richter, Berlin PO/Karajan
   ASD2582 (9/70) EMI/HMV
   S-36727 Angel
EROICA VARIATIONS
☐ Curzon/*Schubert*
   SXL6523 (1/72) Decca
   6727 London
☐ Brendel
   TV34251DS (3/71) Decca Turnabout
FIDELIO
☐ *Cpte*. Ludwig, Vickers, Hallstein, Unger, Frick, Berry, Crass, Chorus, Philh./Klemperer
   SLS5006 (5/75) HMV
   S-3625 Angel
MASS IN C
☐ Ameling, Baker, Altmeyer, Rintzler, NP Chorus, NPO/Giulini
   ASD2661 (6/71) EMI/HMV
   S-36775 Angel
☐ Palmer, Watts, Tear, Keyte, St. John's College/ASMF/Guest
   ZRG739 (5/74) Decca Argo*
MISSA SOLEMNIS
☐ Soderstrom, Hoffgen, Kmentt, Talvela, NP Chorus, NPO/Klemperer
   SLS922 (7/66) HMV
   S-3679 Angel

☐ M. Price, Ludwig, Ochman, Talvela, Vienna State Opera Chorus, VPO/ Böhm
   2707 080 (6/75) DG*
☐ Janowitz, Ludwig, Wunderlich, Berry/ Vienna Singverein/Berlin PO/Karajan
   2726 048 (11/76) DG
   2707 030 DG
PIANO CONCERTOS (*Cpte.*)
☐ Ashkenazy/Chicago SO/Solti
   SXLG6594-7 (9/73) Decca
   2404 London
☐ Bishop-Kovacevich/BBC SO and LSO/Davis
   6747 104 (10/75) Phonogram*
☐ Brendel/LPO/Haitink
   6767 002 (11/77) Phonogram*
PIANO CONCERTO NO. 1 IN C MAJOR
☐ Kempff/Berlin PO/Leitner
   138774 (6/62) DG
☐ Katchen/LSO/Gamba/*Choral Fantasia*
   STS-15211 London
   SDD227 (4/70) Decca Ace of Diamonds
☐ Ashkenazy/Chicago SO/Solti/ *Sonata 8*
   SXL6651 (2/76) Decca
   6853 London
☐ Arrau/Concertgebouw/Haitink/ *Sonata 6*
   6580 122 (4/76) Phonogram
PIANO CONCERTO NO. 2 IN B FLAT MAJOR
☐ Kempff/Berlin PO/Leitner/*Conc. 4*
   138777 (9/62) DG
☐ Katchen/LSO/Gamba/*Conc. 4*
   SDD228 (4/70) Decca Ace of Diamonds
   STS-15212 London
☐ Bishop-Kovacevich/BBC SO/Davis/ *Conc. 4*
   6500 975 (2/76) Phonogram
☐ Ashkenazy/Chicago SO/Solti/*Son. 21*
   SXL6652 (1/76) Decca
   6854 London
PIANO CONCERTO NO. 3 IN C MINOR
☐ Kempff/Berlin PO/Leitner
   138776 (7/62) DG

☐ Bishop-Kovacevich, BBC SO/Davis/ *Pathetique Son.*
   6500 315 (1/73) Phonogram
☐ Ashkenazy/Chicago SO/Solti/*Son. 26*
   SXL6711 (11/75) Decca
   6855 London
☐ Arrau/Concertgebouw/Haitink
   6580 078 (6/76) Phonogram*
☐ A. Fischer/Bavarian State Orch./ Fricsay/Mozart: *Rondos*
   2548 238 (8/76) DG Heliodor
PIANO CONCERTO NO. 4 IN G MAJOR
☐ Kempff/Berlin PO/Leitner/*Conc. 2*
   138775 (9/62) DG
☐ Gilels/Philharmonia/Ludwig/*Mozart: Vln. Conc. 3*
   SXLP30086 (10/67) EMI/HMV
☐ Katchen/LSO/Gamba/*Conc. 2*
   SDD228 (4/70) Decca Ace of Diamonds
☐ Richter-Hasser/Philh. Orch./Kertesz
   CFP155 (12/73) Classics for Pleasure
☐ Ashkenazy, Chicago SO/Solti/ *Leonore Overture No. 3*
   SXL6654 (5/75) Decca
   6856 London
☐ Pollini/VPO/Bohm
   2530 791 (3/77) DG*
PIANO CONCERTO NO. 5 IN E FLAT MAJOR ('EMPEROR')
☐ Kempff/Berlin PO/Leitner
   138777 (5/62) DG
☐ Curzon/VPO/Knappertsbuch
   SPA334 (7/74) Decca
☐ Lill/Scottish National/Gibson
   CFP40087 (10/74) Classics for Pleasure
☐ Arrau/Concertgebouw/Haitink
   6580 094 (12/74) Phonogram
   6570 086 Philips Festivo
☐ Ashkenazy/Chicago SO/Solti/*Egmont Ov.*
   SXL6655 (5/75) Decca
   6857 London
PIANO QUINTET IN E FLAT, OP. 16
☐ Panhoffer/Vienna Octet
   SDD256 (10/70) Decca Ace of Diamonds
PIANO SONATA NO. 8 IN C MINOR, OP. 13 (PATHETIQUE)
☐ Rubinstein/*Moonlight and Les Adieux Sons.*
   SB6537 (6/63) RCA
   LSC-2654 RCA

☐ Serkin/*Moonlight and Appassionata Sons.*
   72148 (2/64) CBS
   MS-6481 Columbia
☐ Arrau/*Moonlight; Appassionata*
   6599 308 (5/74) Phonogram*
☐ Ashkenazy/*Waldstein; Les Adieux*
   SXL6706 (5/75) Decca
   6921 London
☐ Brendel/*Sonatas 18 & 19*
   9500 077 (12/76) Phonogram*
PIANO SONATA NO. 14 IN C SHARP MINOR, OP. 27 NO. 2 (MOONLIGHT)
☐ Barenboim/*Pathetique; Appassionata*
   HQS1076 (3/67) EMI/HMV
☐ Arrau/*Pathetique; Appassionata*
   6599 308 (5/74) Phonogram*
PIANO SONATA NO. 17 IN D MINOR, OP. 31 NO. 2 (TEMPEST)
☐ Bishop-Kovacevich/*Sonata No. 18*
   6500 392 (3/74) Phonogram*
PIANO SONATA NO. 21 IN C, OP. 53 (WALDSTEIN)
☐ Gilels/*Sonata No. 28*
   2530 253 (11/72) DG*
☐ Ashkenazy/*Pathetique; Les Adieux*
   SXL6706 (5/75) Decca
☐ Brendel/*Op. 110*
   6500 762 (11/75) Phonogram
PIANO SONATA NO. 23 IN F MINOR, OP. 57 (APPASSIONATA)
☐ Gilels/*Sonata No. 6*
   2530 406 (5/74) DG*
☐ Arrau/*Pathetique; Moonlight*
   6599 308 (5/74) Phonogram*
☐ Serkin/*Pathetique; Moonlight*
   72148 (2/64) CBS
   MS-6481 Columbia
☐ Rubinstein/*Son. in C, Op. 2 No. 3*
   SB6633 (6/66) RCA
   LSC 2812 RCA
☐ Ashkenazy/*Sonata No. 7*
   SXL6603 (10/73) Decca
   6821 London
PIANO SONATA NO. 24 in F# MINOR, OP. 78
☐ Arrau/*Sonata No. 29*
   6580 104 (11/75) Phonogram
   6833 145 Philips

His nine symphonies, his concertos (five for piano, one for violin—arguably the greatest in violin literature), his 16 string quartets and 32 piano sonatas, and his ten sonatas for violin and five for cello form the core of their respective repertoires and are constantly being recorded. The chamber music ranges from the relaxed directness of the early *Rondino* for wind and the Septet, through the masterly mid-period "Rasumovsky" quartets and the "Archduke" piano trio (each named for its dedicatee), to the profundities of the Op.131 and 132 quartets. Of the symphonies the most popular are No. 5, which progresses from dark drama to blazing triumph; the large-scale No. 3, the *Eroica*, already mentioned; No. 6, the *Pastoral*, which shows the composer's delight in nature and includes a programmatic element, although he insisted that it was "more the expression of feeling than depiction"; and the mighty No. 9, one of the world's loftiest works of art. With his individual combination of heroism, boisterous humour (as in his scherzos, a form he made very much his own), poetic lyricism (as in the slow movement of the Violin Concerto) and noble aspiration, Beethoven remains one of the giants of music.

PIANO SONATA NO. 25 IN G, OP. 79
☐ Gilels/*Sonatas Nos. 26-27*
  2530 589 (12/75) DG∗
PIANO SONATA NO. 26 IN E FLAT, OP. 81a (LES ADIEUX)
☐ Barenboim/*Op. 49 No. 1; Op. 111*
  HQS1088 (6/67) EMI/HMV
☐ Brendel/*Piano Conc. No. 3*
  TV34207S (5/68) Decca Turnabout
☐ Ashkenazy/*Pathetique; Waldstein*
  SXL6706 (5/75) Decca
☐ Gilels/*Sonatas Nos. 25, 27*
  2530 589 (12/75) DG∗
PIANO SONATA NO. 27 IN E MINOR, OP. 90
☐ Gilels/*Sonatas Nos. 25-26*
  2530 589 (12/75) DG∗
☐ Brendel/*Sonatas 6 & 30*
  9500 076 (11/76) Phonogram∗
PIANO SONATA NO. 28 IN A, OP.101
☐ Gilels/*Sonata No. 21*
  2530 253 (11/72) DG∗

PIANO SONATA NO. 29 IN B FLAT, OP. 106 (HAMMERKLAVIER)
☐ Brendel/ *Sonata, Op. 78*
  6500 764 (6/75) Phonogram∗
☐ Brendel
  TV34112DS (1/70) Decca Turnabout
  34392 Turnabout
☐ Arrau/*Sonata No. 24*
  6580 104 (11/75) Phonogram
  6833 145 Philips
PIANO SONATA NO. 30 IN E, OP. 109
☐ Kempff/*Sonata No. 29*
  138 944 (3/68) DG
☐ Pollini/*Sonata No. 31*
  2530 645 (5/76) DG∗
☐ Brendel/*Sonatas 6 & 27*
  9500 076 (11/76) Phonogram∗
PIANO SONATA NO. 31 IN A FLAT, OP. 110
☐ Kempff/*Op. 111*
  138 845 (3/68) DG
☐ Ashkenazy/*Sonata No. 32*
  SXL6630 (8/74) Decca
  6843 London

☐ Bishop-Kovacevich/*Op. 111*
  6500 764 (6/75) Phonogram
☐ Brendel/*Sonata No.21*
  6500 762 (11/75) Phonogram
☐ Pollini/*Sonata No. 30*
  2530 645 (5/76) DG∗
PIANO SONATA NO. 32 IN C MINOR, OP. 111
☐ Barenboim/*Op. 49 No. 1; Les Adieux*
  HQS1088 (6/67) EMI/HMV
☐ Kempff/*Op. 110*
  138 945 (3/68) DG
☐ Brendel/*Appassionata*
  6500 138 (6/71) Phonogram∗
☐ Ashkenazy/*Op. 110*
  SXL6630 (8/74) Decca
  6843 London
☐ Bishop-Kovacevich/*Op. 110*
  6500 764 (6/75) Phonogram
PIANO TRIO NO. 6 IN B FLAT OP. 97 (ARCHDUKE)
☐ Szeryng, Fournier, Kempff
  2530 147 (4/72) DG∗

SEPTET IN E FLAT, OP. 20
☐ Vienna Octet
  SDD200 (8/69) Decca Ace of Diamonds
  STS-15361 London
☐ Melos Ens/*Duo in C*
  HQS1286 (2/73) EMI/HMV
SONATAS FOR CELLO AND PIANO (Cpte.)
☐ Chuchro, Panenka/*Variations for cello and piano*
  MS1091-3 (1/73) Supraphon
STRING QUARTETS
☐ *Cpte.* Hungarian Quartet
  SLS857 (9/73) HMV
STRING QUARTETS, OP. 18
☐ Amadeus Quartet
  2733 002 (11/74) DG Privilege
☐ Juilliard Quartet
  77362 (12/76) CBS
STRING QUARTET IN F, OP. 18 NO. 1
☐ Quartetto Italiano/*Op. 18 No. 3*
  6500 181 (2/73) Phonogram
☐ Gabrieli Quartet/*Op. 18 No. 2*
  SDD478 (4/76) Decca Ace of Diamonds
  STS-15398 London
STRING QUARTET IN G, OP. 18 NO. 2
☐ Quartetto Italiano/*Op. 18 No. 4*
  6500 646 (6/76) Phonogram
☐ Gabrieli Quartet/*Op. 18 No. 1*
  SDD478 (4/76) Decca Ace of Diamonds
  STS-15398 London
STRING QUARTET IN D, OP. 18 NO. 3
☐ Quartetto Italiano/*Op. 18 No. 1*
  6500 181 (2/73) Phonogram
STRING QUARTET IN C MINOR, OP. 18 NO. 4
☐ Quartetto Italiano/*Op. 18 No. 2*
  6500 646 (6/76) Phonogram
STRING QUARTETS, OP. 59 NOS. 1-3; OP. 74; OP. 95
☐ Vegh Quartet
  EX6 35041 (8/76) Selecta/Telefunken∗
STRING QUARTET IN F, OP. 59 NO.1
☐ Hungarian Quartet
  HQS1159 (8/68) EMI/HMV
STRING QUARTET IN E MINOR, OP. 59 NO. 2
☐ Hungarian Quartet
  HQS1160 (8/68) EMI/HMV
STRING QUARTET IN C, OP. 59, NO. 3
☐ Hungarian Quartet/*Op. 74*
  HQS1161 (8/68) EMI/HMV
STRING QUARTET IN E FLAT, OP. 74
☐ Quartetto Italiano/*Op. 95*
  6500 180 (10/72) Phonogram
☐ Weller Quartet/*Op. 95*
  SDD309 (1/72) Decca Ace of Diamonds
STRING QUARTET IN F MINOR, OP. 95
☐ Hungarian Quartet/*Op. 59 No. 2*
  HQS1160 (8/68) EMI/HMV
☐ Quartetto Italiano/*Op. 74*
  6500 180 (10/72) Phonogram∗
☐ Weller Quartet/*Op. 74*
  SDD309 (1/72) Decca Ace of Diamonds
STRING QUARTETS, OP. 127, 130, 131, 132, 135; GROSSE FUGE
☐ Vegh Quartet
  FK6 35040 (10/74) Selecta/Telefunken∗
STRING QUARTET IN E FLAT, OP. 127
☐ Quartetto Italiano/*Op. 135*
  SAL3703 (4/69) Phonogram

STRING QUARTET IN B FLAT, OP. 130
☐ Quartetto Italiano/*Grosse Fuge*
SAL3780 (4/70) Phonogram
STRING QUARTET IN C SHARP MINOR, OP. 131
☐ Quartetto Italiano
SAL3790 (4/70) Phonogram
STRING QUARTET IN A MINOR, OP. 132
☐ Quartetto Italiano
SAL3638 (9/68) Phonogram
STRING QUARTET IN F, OP. 135
☐ Quartetto Italiano/*Op. 127*
SAL3703 (4/69) Phonogram
SYMPHONIES NOS. 1-9 AND OVERTURES
☐ Philh/Klemperer
SLS788 (5/70) HMV
SH-3619 Angel
☐ Chicago SO/Solti
11BB188-96 (9/75) Decca
CS-P9 London
☐ Leipzig Gewandhaus/Masur
6747 135 (9/75) Phonogram
☐ Berlin PO/Karajan
2740 172 (10/77) DG★
SYMPHONIES NOS. 1-9
☐ VPO/Bohm
2740 115 (11/72) DG
SYMPHONY NO. 1 IN C
☐ Berlin PO/Karajan/*Sym. 2*
2531 001 (4/77) DG
☐ Berlin PO/Jochum/*Sym. 8*
2538 074 (12/71) DG Privilege
☐ ASMF/Marriner/*Sym. 2*
6500 113 (5/72) Phonogram★
☐ Bavarian RSO/Jochum/*Sym. 8*
2548 224 (4/76) DG Heliodor
SYMPHONY NO. 2 IN D
☐ Berlin PO/Karajan/*Sym. 1*
2531 001 (4/77) DG
3300 456 DG
☐ Berlin PO/Cluytens/*Egmont Ov.*
CFP193 (5/72) Classics for Pleasure
☐ ASMF/Marriner/*Sym. 1*
6500 113 (5/72) Phonogram★
SYMPHONIES NOS. 3, 5 AND 7
☐ Philh/Klemperer/*Overtures; Grosse Fuge*
SLS873 (5/74) HMV
SYMPHONY NO. 3 IN E FLAT (EROICA)
☐ Berlin PO/Karajan
2531 003 (4/77) DG
☐ VPO/Schmidt-Isserstedt
JB6 (1/78) Decca
☐ BPO/Cluytens
CFP203 (8/72) Classics for Pleasure
☐ VPO/Bohm
2530 437 (9/74) DG★
☐ NYPO/Bernstein
61902 (11/77) CBS
☐ Concertgebouw/Jochum
6580 137 (11/76) Phonogram
6570 088 Philips Festivo
SYMPHONY NO. 4 IN B FLAT
☐ VPO/Schmidt-Isserstedt/*Consecration of the House*
JB7 (1/78) Decca Jubilee
☐ Berlin PO/Karajan
2531 004 (4/78) DG
☐ Berlin PO/Cluytens/*Overtures*
CFP40001 (12/72) Classics for Pleasure
SYMPHONY NO. 5 IN C MINOR
☐ Berlin PO/Karajan
2531 005 (4/78) DG
☐ VPO/C. Kleiber
2530 516 (6/75) DG★
☐ Berlin PO/Cluytens/*Sym. No. 8*
CFP40007 (12/72) Classics for Pleasure
☐ Bavarian RSO/Jochum/*Fidelio Ov.*
2548 255 (1/77) DG Heliodor
SYMPHONY NO. 6 IN F (PASTORAL)
☐ VPO/Bohm
2530 142 (2/72) DG
☐ NPO/Giulini
ASD2535 (3/70) EMI/HMV
S-36684 Angel
☐ Berlin PO/Cluytens
CFP40017 (2/73) Classics for Pleasure
☐ Berlin PO/Maazel
2548 205 (11/75) DG Heliodor

SYMPHONY NO. 7 IN A
☐ RPO/Davis
SXLP20038 (6/62) EMI/HMV
S-37027 Angel
☐ Berlin PO/Karajan
2531 007 (4/78) DG
☐ VPO/Schmidt-Isserstedt/*Leonore 3*
JB4 (9/77) Decca Jubilee
☐ Berlin PO/Cluytens
CFP40018 (3/73) Classics for Pleasure
☐ Chicago SO/Solti/*Coriolan Ov.*
SXL6764 (6/76) Decca
☐ VPO/Kleiber
2530 706 (9/76) DG★
SYMPHONY NO. 8 IN F
☐ Berlin PO/Karajan/*Sym. 9*
2707 109 (3/77) DG
☐ VPO/Abbado/*Schubert*
SXL6418 (1/73) Decca
☐ Berlin PO/Cluytens/*Sym. No. 5*
CFP40007 (12/72) Classics for Pleasure
☐ VPO/Schmidt-Isserstedt/*Sym. 5*
JB5 (9/77) Decca Jubilee
☐ Berlin PO/Jochum/*Sym. 1*
2548 224 (4/76) DG Heliodor
SYMPHONY NO. 9 IN D MINOR (CHORAL)
☐ Tomova-Sintov, Baltsa, Schreier, van Dam, Vienna Singverein, Berlin PO/Karajan
2707 109 (3/77) DG
☐ Lorengar, Minton, Burrows, Talvela, Chicago SO/Solti
6BB121-2 (11/72) Decca
☐ Sutherland, Horne, King, Talvela, V. St. Op. Chor., VPO/Schmidt-Isserstedt
JB1 (9/77) Decca Jubilee
☐ Brouwenstein, Meyer, Gedda, Guthrie, St. Hedwig's Cath. Choir, Berlin PO/Cluytens
CFP40019 (8/73) Classics for Pleasure
S-60079 Seraphim
☐ Sutherland, Procter, Dermota, Van Mill, Chorus, SRO/Ansermet
SPA328 (3/75) Decca
THIRTY-THREE VARIATIONS ON A WALTZ OF DIABELLI
☐ Brendel
TV34139S (7/68) Decca Turnabout★
☐ Bishop-Kovacevich
SAL3676 (1/69) Phonogram
VIOLIN SONATAS NOS. 1-10
☐ Perlman, Ashkenazy
D92 D5 (3/78) Decca
VIOLIN SONATA NO. 5 IN F, OP. 24 (SPRING)
☐ Grumiaux/Arrau/*Sonata 1*
9500 055 (5/76) Phonogram
☐ Perlman/Ashkenazy/*Sonata 4*
SXL6736 (7/76) Decca
2501 London
VIOLIN SONATA NO. 9 IN A, OP. 47 (KREUTZER)
☐ Perlman/Ashkenazy/*Sonata 2*
SXL6632 (2/75) Decca
6845 London

Above right: *Beethoven obliterated the dedication to Bonaparte of the 'Eroica'.*

Right: *Beethoven was swarthy and short in stature.*

VINCENZO BELLINI
(b. Catania 1801; d. nr. Paris 1835)

Bellini's gentle, uncomplicated, exquisitely lyrical music was the exact counterpart of this sensitive young Sicilian's nature. Though he lacked the ebullience and sparkle of his slightly older contemporaries Rossini ≫ and Donizetti ≫, and certainly did not possess their rapidity and fluency of composition, his operas (he wrote little else) are by no means always languishing or devoid of drama, nor is his harmony always as conventional as is sometimes imagined. His melodies have a sensuously romantic cast, but behind them lies a Mozartian purity, and they were admired by Chopin ≫ and—of all unlikely people—Wagner ≫. The fact that Bellini's works call for, and offer unrivalled opportunities to, star singers has meant that, economics being what they are, they are more frequently encountered on records than in the theatre. In particular his very high tenor parts, which were written for Rubini, present a formidable challenge today.

An Italian nobleman paid for him to study at the Naples Conservatory; and while there he had the good fortune that his first opera, performed by fellow-students, was heard by the very influential Barbaia, manager of several opera-houses, including the great San Carlo in Naples and La Scala in Milan. The young composer was offered a commission for a work for Naples, and when this made a good impression he was invited to write *Il Pirata* for Milan: with its graceful and uncluttered writing for the voice (a reaction against the over-florid style then prevailing) it proved a great success and quickly made its way to other European cities. In 1831 his two masterpieces were both produced in Milan—*La Sonnambula* and *Norma*, the former a sentimental, idyllic showpiece for a lyric soprano, the latter more weighty, combining pathos with grandeur. On Rossini's recommendation he was invited to compose *I Puritani*, a quasi-historical opera, for Paris: it is burdened by a poor libretto (which, like his rival Donizetti's *Lucia di Lammermoor* of the same year, contains a "mad scene" for the heroine), but Bellini's orchestration has some deft touches, and the work's more extended scope suggests a development which was unfortunately nipped in the bud when he died at 33.

CONCERTINO FOR OBOE AND STRINGS IN E FLAT
☐ Lord/ASMF/Marriner/*Concert*
   SOL277 (4/65) L'Oiseau-Lyre
☐ Holliger, Bamberg SO/Maag/*Saliene; Cimarosa; Donizetti*
   139152 (11/66) DG*
NORMA
☐ Caballe, Cossotto, Domingo, Raimondi, Ambrosian Op. Chorus/LPO/Cillario
   SER5658-60 (11/75) RCA
   LSC-6202 RCA
IL PIRATA
☐ Caballe, Marti, Cappuccilli, Raimondi/ Rome RO/Gavazzeni
   SLS953 (9/71) HMV
   S-3772 Angel
LA SONNAMBULA
☐ Sutherland, Monti, Corena/Maggio Musicale Fiorentino/Bonynge
   SET239-41 (2/63) Decca
   1365 London

Left: *Vincenzo Bellini, one of the many composers whose developing careers were tragically and prematurely cut short. Yet in his one decade of production, four or five of his ten operas became famous throughout Europe and were welcomed as vehicles by the greatest singers of the period.*

ALBAN BERG
(b. Vienna 1885; d. there 1935)

Berg's is certainly the most approachable, and possibly the most likely to endure, of all the music written by the pupils of Schoenberg » or even by their revered master himself (to whom Berg dedicated three of his best works). As a boy from a cultivated Viennese family he had already written a large quantity of highly emotional, almost neurotic, songs which reveal his sensitivity to literary quality, before meeting Schoenberg and enthusiastically following his comprehensively thorough and strict tuition for six years. He discarded his youthful efforts and acknowledged as his first mature compositions the *Seven early songs*, which were influenced by Mahler », and the Piano Sonata. The works of the next few years—the String Quartet, the Altenberg songs and the Three Orchestral Pieces—reveal an increasingly dramatic content, mostly of broodingly melancholy mood; then there was a long period of gestation until the completion in 1921 of *Wozzeck*, one of the outstanding landmarks in twentieth-century opera. Its psychopathic subject is aptly reflected in its expressionist style and atonal idiom (it should be remembered that Schoenberg's theories of dodecaphony, basing a work on a "tone-row" of "twelve notes related only to each other", found expression for the first time only in 1923, so that *Wozzeck* is not a 12-tone work but freely atonal—although the powerful orchestral interlude in the last act is firmly in D minor). It utilises Schoenberg's *Sprechstimme* (speech-song) techniques, and structurally each of its fifteen scenes is cast in a definite formal mould—scherzo, rondo, fantasia and fugue, and so on. Unpromising as all this may seem, in fact the opera is imbued with a deep compassion for the wretched and an imaginative lyric intensity which never fail to move listeners.

Berg had to wait four years for *Wozzeck* to be produced on the stage (Berlin 1925), but it then caused a furore and made the composer world-famous. After it he turned again to chamber music: the *Chamber concerto* for piano, violin and 13 wind instruments, and the *Lyric suite* for string quartet—both illustrating, as had the orchestration of *Wozzeck*, his remarkable ear for sonorities; and it was in part of the latter that for the first time he used the 12-tone technique to which he was then always to adhere. His procedures however were less rigid and abstract than Schoenberg's, and far less austere than those of his fellow-pupil Webern. A strong vein of romanticism is conspicuous almost throughout his music, and it is this humanity which makes it more accessible to the ordinary listener; in his supreme masterpiece, the 1935 Violin Concerto—written, unusually for him, very rapidly, under the compulsion of a vivid sense of tragedy at the untimely death of an 18-year-old girl—the basic "row" contains consonant tonal elements which make possible the introduction of a Carinthian folksong and, to over-whelming emotional effect, a Bach chorale. The sheer beauty and rapt sense of poetry of this concerto, which reconciles dodecaphony with traditional tonality, make it the ideal work from which to approach Berg's music.

CHAMBER CONCERTO
☐ Kozina, Straus/Prague CE/Pesek/
  *Stravinsky: Symphonies of Wind
  Instruments*
  50679 (10/67) Rediffusion/Supraphon
LULU
☐ Lear, Johnson, Dicks, Driscoll,
  Fischer-Dieskau/Berlin Op/Bohm
  2709 029 (7/68) DG∗
LYRIC SUITE FOR STRING QUARTET
☐ Alban Berg Qt/*String Quartet*
  AS6 41301 (12/74) Selecta/Telefunken∗
STRING QUARTET, OP. 3
☐ Alban Berg Qt/*Lyric Suite*
  AS6 41301 (12/74) Selecta/Telefunken∗

VIOLIN CONCERTO
☐ Suk/Czech PO/Ancerl/*Bach: Cantata
  No. 60*
  50804 (8/68) Rediffusion/Supraphon
☐ Menuhin/BBC SO/Boulez/*Bartok:
  Rhapsodies*
  ASD2449 (3/69) EMI/HMV
WOZZECK
☐ Lear, Fischer-Dieskau, Wunderlich,
  Melchert, Stolze, Kohn/Berlin
  Op/Bohm
  2707 023 (12/65) DG∗

Right: *Alban Berg.*

LENNOX BERKELEY
(b. Oxford 1903)

The facile description of Berkeley's music as "Gallic" which has dogged him throughout his career has blinded many and prevented them seeing the serious core beneath the elegant, fastidious surface. Yet he is of partly French descent and studied the language, which he speaks like a native, at Oxford; if the term "Gallic" is taken as short-hand for those qualities of lucidity, restraint and refinement which characterise the finest French composers, the description is apt enough. The fact that Berkeley, on the recommendation of Ravel », began his musical studies in Paris under Nadia Boulanger, absorbing from her a Stravinsky-flavoured piquancy (akin to that of Poulenc », to whose memory he later dedicated his *Ronsard sonnets*), gave his work an initial slant which set it apart from that of most of his English contemporaries.

He first attracted attention in the early 1940s with his transparent-textured *Serenade* for strings, First Symphony and *Divertimento* for chamber orchestra: these were followed by such chamber works as the Violin Sonatina, String Trio, Viola Sonata and Piano Sonata (he has always written graceful and polished music for this instrument, including two concertos and one for two pianos). Apart from the witty one-act farce *A dinner engagement*, his operas have not held the stage; but his songs attain distinction, with a sympathetic feeling for the voice and great sensibility towards the poetic stimuli. Religious texts have called forth his deepest responses, and the mystical *Four poems of St Teresa of Avila* and the finely-moulded *Stabat Mater* for six solo voices and 12 instruments are outstanding in this regard; the later large-scale *Magnificat* represents a *rapprochement* with the English festival choral tradition.

Berkeley has been particularly prolific in the chamber music field, to which he has made valuable contributions. He was knighted in 1974.

Above: *Berlioz at the age of 57 (from an early photograph).*

CONCERTO FOR 2 PIANOS AND ORCHESTRA
☐ Beckett, McDonald/LPO/Del Mar/
  Symphony No. 1
  SRCS80 (11/75) Lyrita
  4017 HNH

Below: *A recent picture of Sir Lennox Berkeley.*

PARTITA; DIVERTIMENTO IN B FLAT; SERENADE FOR STRINGS; SINFONIA CONCERTANTE (Exc)
☐ LPO/Berkeley
  SRCS74 (9/75) Lyrita
4 RONSARD SONNETS
☐ Pears/London Sinfonietta/Berkeley/
  Bedford; Lutoslawski
  HEAD3 (5/74) Decca Headline
SEXTET FOR CLARINET, HORN AND STRING QUARTET
☐ Music Group of London/*Sonatina;
  A. Bush*
  ZRG749 (10/74) Decca Argo
SONATINA FOR VIOLIN AND PIANO
☐ Bean, Parkhouse/*Sextet; A. Bush*
  ZRG749 (10/74) Decca Argo
SYMPHONY NO. 1
☐ LPO/Del Mar/*Concerto*
  SRCS80 (11/75) Decca Argo

BEATRICE ET BENEDICT
☐ Cantelo, Veasey, Watts, Mitchinson,
  Cameron, Shirley-Quirk/St Anthony
  Singers/LSO/Davis
  SOL256-7 (2/63) L'Oiseau-Lyre*
BENVENUTO CELLINI
☐ Eda-Pierre, Gedda, Massard, Soyer,
  Herincx, Cuenod, Bastin/Covent
  Garden Chorus & Orch/Davis
  6707 019 (3/73) Phonogram
LA DAMNATION DE FAUST
☐ Veasey, Gedda, Bastin, Ambrosian
  Singers, Wandsworth School Boys'
  Choir, LSO/Davis
  6703 042 (1/74) Phonogram*
L'ENFANCE DU CHRIST— ORATORIO
☐ Pears, Fleet, Frost, Rouleau, Morison,
  Cameron, St. Anthony Singers,
  Goldsbrough Orch./Davis
  SOL60032-3 (7/61) L'Oiseau-Lyre
GRANDE MESSE DES MORTS
(Requiem)
☐ Dowd, Wandsworth School Boys'
  Choir, LSO and Chorus/Davis
  6700 019 (9/70) Phonogram*
☐ Tear/CBSO and Chorus/Fremaux
  SLS 982 (9/75) HMV
  S-3814 Angel

HAROLD IN ITALY, OP. 18
☐ Menuhin/Philh./C. Davis
  ASD537 (8/63) EMI/HMV
  S-36123 Angel
☐ McInnes/French Nat. Orch./
  Bernstein
  ASD3389 (11/77) EMI/HMV
  S-37413 Angel
LES NUITS D'ETE—SONG CYCLE
☐ Baker, NPO/Barbirolli/*Ravel:
  Scheherazade*
  ASD2444 (2/69) EMI/HMV
  S-36505 Angel
ORCHESTRAL WORKS: ROMAN CARNIVAL OVERTURE; HAMLET— FUNERAL MARCH; DAMNATION DE FAUST—ORCHESTRAL PIECES; BENVENUTO CELLINI—OVERTURE; LES TROYENS—ROYAL HUNT AND STORM
☐ CBSO/Fremaux
  ASD3080 (8/75) EMI/HMV
OVERTURES; LE ROI LEAR; LES FRANCS-JUGES; ROMAN CARNIVAL; WAVERLEY; LE CORSAIRE
☐ LSO/Davis
  SAL3573 (10/66) Phonogram
  835367 Philips

HECTOR BERLIOZ

(b. La Côte-St André, nr. Grenoble, 1803; d. Paris 1869)

"They tell me", said the King of Prussia amiably, "that you are the composer who writes for 500 musicians". "Your Majesty has been misinformed", quipped Berlioz, "I sometimes write for only 450". On the strength of a handful of works, the image of the composer who wrote monumentally for extravagant forces lives on: his *Requiem* calls for four brass bands besides a colossal orchestra, including eight sets of timpani, and a large chorus, the *Te Deum* for a triple chorus with orchestra, the *Symphonie funèbre et triomphale* for massed military bands. But all these were conceived for public ceremonies on a grand scale, the last-named for open-air performance; and though Berlioz could build up apocalyptic climaxes (for example in the *Tuba mirum* and *Judex crederis* of the *Requiem*), he often scored with restraint. Undeniably his leanings were towards the grandiose: his *Symphonie fantastique*, a revolutionary work in which for the first time a composer's fantasised private life was translated into orchestral terms, using to that end the structural device of an *idée fixe*, was given a long and barely coherent sequel, *Lélio*, for narrator, chorus and orchestra; his greatest opera, *Les Troyens*, inspired by his love of Virgil and of Shakespeare, takes five hours to perform — giving anti-Berliozians (conveniently forgetting the case of Wagner ») an excuse for not attempting it. On the other hand, the whole oratorio *L'Enfance du Christ* is of a delicacy and transparency which led to the accusation that he had changed his style ("No", retorted Berlioz, "only the subject has changed"); and the song-cycle *Les Nuits d'été* shows him at his most exquisitely poetic.

Two contradictions lie at the heart of this eccentric and flamboyant personality (who not altogether surprisingly struck the genteel and correct Mendelssohn » as a talentless *poseur*). He was the archetypal Romantic self-dramatising artist: the *Symphonie fantastique* was an attempt publicly to pillory a Shakespearian actress who had rejected his love (but with whom he was later to contract a disastrous marriage); he seriously set out to shoot another girl who had jilted him; and he eagerly identified himself with the picturesque Byronic central figure of the quasi viola concerto *Harold in Italy* commissioned by Paganini » and with the brooding Faust of his frenetic half-cantata, half-opera *La Damnation de Faust*. Yet side by side with his desire for sensationalism was a passionate love of classicism in its broadest sense — the music of Gluck » and the works of Shakespeare, on whom he repeatedly drew (the opera *Beatrice and Benedict*, the *Romeo and Juliet* "dramatic symphony", the *King Lear* overture and *La mort d'Ophélie* for voice and orchestra). He had received a somewhat sketchy musical education — which helps to account for his unorthodox, but effective, harmony and his often curiously loose structure — and had little instrumental talent (he could play only the guitar and the flute); yet he had an unparallelled genius for orchestration, of which nearly all his work can furnish examples of startling originality and beauty. He wrote a *Traité d'instrumentation* which is a classic textbook on the subject; he was also a trenchant and witty music critic whose *Memoirs* and *Evenings in the orchestra* make compulsive reading.

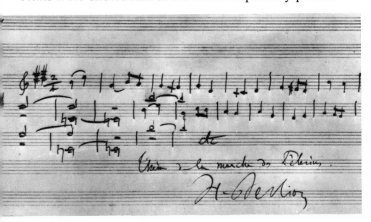

Above: *Theme from Berlioz's Harold in Italy.*

OVERTURES: LE CARNAVAL ROMAIN; BEATRICE ET BENEDICT; LE CORSAIRE; BENVENUTO CELLINI; LES FRANCS-JUGES
☐ LSO/Previn
  ASD3212 (6/76) EMI/HMV
  S-37170 Angel
ROMEO AND JULIET SYMPHONY
☐ Kern, Tear, Shirley-Quirk, Alldis Choir, LSO/Davis
  6700 032 (12/68) Phonogram
  839716/7 Philips
  Orch. sections only
☐ Chicago SO/Giulini
  ASD2606 (12/70) EMI/HMV
  S-36038 Angel
☐ LSO/Davis
  6580 052 (1/73) Phonogram
SYMPHONIE FANTASTIQUE, OP. 14
☐ LSO/Boulez
  72704 (2/69) CBS
  M-30587 Columbia
☐ French Nat. Orch./Bernstein
  ASD3397 (11/77) EMI/HMV
☐ Concertgebouw/Davis
  6500 774 (3/75) Phonogram★
☐ Berlin PO/Karajan
  2530 597 (3/76) DG★

☐ Sydney SO/Otterloo
  GL25012 (10/76) RCA Gold Seal
☐ French Nat. RO/Martinon
  ASD3263 (10/76) EMI/HMV
  S-37138 Angel
SYMPHONIE FUNEBRE ET TRIOMPHALE
☐ LSO/Davis/*Hamlet Funeral March*
  SAL3788 (3/70) Phonogram
  802913 Philips
TE DEUM
☐ Tagliavini, Wandsworth School Boys' Choir, LSO and Chorus/Davis
  SAL3724 (7/69) Phonogram
  839790 Philips
LES TROYENS
☐ Veasey, Vickers, Lindholm, Glossop, Bainbridge, Soyer, Howells, Thau, Davis/Covent Garden Opera Chorus & Orch./Davis
  6709 002 (5/70) Phonogram★

Above: *Berlioz conducting (as seen by Gustave Doré).*

LEONARD BERNSTEIN
(b. Lawrence, Mass., 1918)

Like most energetic individuals of abundantly varied gifts, Berstein has not been without his detractors, who view his versatility with a suspicion not untinged with envy. Certainly his range is prodigious: apart from composing, he is phenomenally successful as a conductor (an international career which was launched, in the best showbiz tradition, by his standing in for the indisposed Bruno Walter on a coast-to-coast broadcast), was for some years a university professor of music and has always been an excellent pianist, besides being highly articulate as a "communicator" (both lecturer and writer). Conservative distrusts are deepened by the facts that much of the popularisation he has undertaken has been through the mass-medium of television and that his own music not only constantly crosses the tracks between the concert-hall and the Broadway/Hollywood scene but has won huge acclaim, and rich financial rewards, from the latter.

The truth is that Bernstein's facility and technical brilliance as a composer are the results of a sound grounding and a naturally quick intelligence: as one fellow-composer has somewhat wistfully put it, "there seems to be nothing he cannot do". His first major work (contemporary with his leap to fame as a conductor) was his *Jeremiah* Symphony, whose last movement is an emotional setting, in Hebrew, for mezzo-soprano of a passage from the Lamentations: he was later to return to Jewish inspirations in his Third Symphony (in memory of President Kennedy), the *Chichester Psalms*, and the 1974 Jerome Robbins ballet *The Dybbuk*. Except for the last of these, in which the influence of Stravinsky ≫ is dominant, Bernstein's "serious" music—which also includes the ballet *Fancy free*, a Second Symphony (for piano and orchestra) based on Auden's "Age of Anxiety", a *Serenade* for violin and orchestra, the one-act chamber opera

Trouble in Tahiti, the full-scale sparkling theatre piece *Candide*, and a highly controversial theatrical Mass in more than questionable taste—is extremely eclectic in idiom, embracing Copland ≫-like American "outdoor" elements and jazz (even, in the Mass, pop), and served up with great vitality. There are times when his material only just bears the weight of the structure built upon it, and certainly he is apt to wear his heart very much on his sleeve; but his natural self-assurance carries him through. His rhythmic vivacity and orchestral virtuosity are even more to the fore in his entertainment music—the musicals *On the town*, *Wonderful town* and especially *West Side Story* (a smash hit with the most sophisticated and brilliant score in the entire *genre*), and the Oscar-winning film *On the waterfront*.

Bottom: *Like Mahler, Bernstein is a conductor-composer.*

Below: *Bernstein's conducting is characterised by fervour.*

CHICHESTER PSALMS
☐ King's College Choir, Cambridge/
Britten: Choral works
ASD3035 (12/74) EMI/HMV
S-37119 Angel
MASS
☐ Titus/choirs, bands and orchestra/
Bernstein
77256 (4/72) CBS
SYMPHONY NO. 1 (JEREMIAH))
☐ Merriman/St Louis SO/Bernstein/
Facsimile
SMA7002 (12/75) RCA
WEST SIDE STORY
☐ Original Broadway cast
31491 (4/74) CBS
S-32603 Columbia
☐ Original film soundtrack
70006 CBS

WEST SIDE STORY—DANCES; ON THE WATERFRONT—SYMPHONIC SUITE
☐ NYPO/Bernstein
61096 (9/69) CBS Classics
MS-6251 Columbia

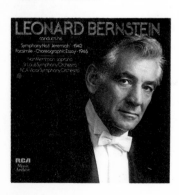

FRANZ BERWALD
(b. Stockholm 1796; d. there 1868)

Rarely heard in the concert-hall, and neglected in his native country almost until the beginning of the present century, Berwald's music has made its headway in the world principally through the medium of records; and he is now recognised not only as the outstanding Swedish composer of the nineteenth century and his country's first symphonist but as a writer of great freshness, individuality and skill. A member of a large family of musicians, he followed the example of his father and uncle by becoming a violinist in the Royal Orchestra (of which a cousin was appointed conductor in succession to Franz's teacher, and which his younger brother was later to lead). At the same time he was editing a musical journal and writing his first compositions, but receiving little encouragement he decided to seek his fortune abroad. In Berlin he could not get two operas he wrote there performed, and turned aside from music to design remedial medical appliances and to direct an orthopaedic institute for six years. He then went to Vienna, Paris and Salzburg, writing operas and symphonies, applied unsuccessfully for various musical posts in Sweden, and, greatly disappointed, again left the musical scene for a decade to manage a glass factory and undertake other commercial enterprises (meanwhile writing numerous newspaper articles). Not until 1864 did he receive the recognition of being elected a member of the Academy of Music, and only in the very last year of his life did he, for a brief period, hold an appointment as professor of composition at the Stockholm Conservatory.

It was undoubtedly the originality of his style that hindered his acceptance for so long—indeed, his best orchestral work, the *Sinfonie Singulière*, had to wait 60 years for performance; but today his chamber music and symphonies charm by their unusual melodic contours, their wit, their daring harmonies and modulations (sometimes recalling Schubert »), their Weberian romanticism, their unexpected instrumentation (rather akin to that of Berlioz »), and not least their unconventional form. The early Septet shares with the vigorous *Sinfonie Singulière* of 1845 a plan which has the scherzo enclosed within the slow movement; and this is carried further in the almost Chinese-box construction of the String Quartet in E flat, where this slow-scherzo-slow sandwich is itself inserted into the first movement. His A minor Quartet, like some of his other works, contains a chromaticism which links Berwald with Spohr ». (In his European travels he may well have come across music of the composers just mentioned.) The two delightful piano quintets, the second dedicated to Liszt » who had praised it, are each conceived as a whole, the component sections divided only by changes of key signature; and both draw material from orchestral tone-poems which this unlucky but un-discouraged composer never had the chance to hear played.

PIANO QUINTET NO. 1 IN C MINOR
PIANO QUINTET NO. 2 IN A
□ Vienna Philharmonic Quintet
 SDD448 (6/75) Decca Ace of Diamonds
SYMPHONY NO. 3 IN D
SYMPHONY NO. 4 IN E FLAT
□ LSO/Ehrling
 SXL6374 (11/78) Decca

Left: *Berwald received almost nothing but discouragement for nearly 60 years, and twice abandoned music altogether to work in industry and commerce; yet he is now recognised as Sweden's leading 19th-century composer.*

GEORGES BIZET
(b. Paris 1838; d. nr. there 1875)

If Fate has a more cruel trick than to withhold her favours from an artist throughout his career, it is to make lavish promises in his youth only to dash them in maturity. At the outset Fate certainly smiled on Bizet: born into a musical family which encouraged his leanings, he entered the Paris Conservatoire, by special dispensation, at the age of nine, rapidly became an excellent pianist and score-reader, and won prizes in all directions. He started to compose from the age of 12, and a month after his 17th birthday completed a Symphony in C (much influenced by Rossini » and his teacher Gounod ») whose high spirits, sparkling colouring and classical clarity are altogether delightful—it nevertheless was put aside by the young musician, left unconsidered in a pile of manuscripts after his death, and first performed 80 years after its composition! The following year he was joint winner of a prize for a one-act operetta, *Le Docteur Miracle*, offered by Offenbach », and then won the prestigious Prix de Rome, enabling him to spend three happy years in the Roman capital.

Nevertheless he became a prey to self-questioning and doubts, and was of an excitable, ironic temperament which took reverses badly. His career, centred on the theatre, met with little but disappointments. *The Pearl Fishers*, a lyrical opera set in the Orient, but with a conventional plot, was coolly received, and a later exotic subject, *Djamileh*, was a total failure; the production of *Don Rodrigue* was indefinitely shelved when the Paris Opéra was burnt down; and several other opera projects were started but left unfinished. Even *The fair maid of Perth* (ineptly based on Scott), though much praised, attained less than twenty performances, owing to a run of illness in the cast and financial difficulties in the management. Yet Bizet's characterisation, melodic invention and orchestral skill are frequently striking; and these qualities are even more in evidence in his atmospheric incidental score to Daudet's *L'Arlésienne*, which is a model of its kind both dramatically and musically. With Bizet's usual ill fortune, however, audiences and the literary set alike resented the music to the play, and the music critics ignored it.

There had been a Spanish vogue in Paris even before Napoleon III took a Spanish bride, and Bizet probably had this in mind when he began work on *Carmen*. It was repeatedly held up by casting difficulties, by the shocked objections of the directors of the Opéra-Comique to the heroine's immorality and, particularly, to her murder on stage, and by the uncooperative attitude of the orchestra and chorus, who declared parts of it impossible to perform; and even when it was eventually produced the realism of this vivid masterpiece provoked a cold reaction from the public and the press, which led to the management having to give away tickets, while the music, unbelievably, was variously labelled colourless, undramatic and lacking in melody. (*Carmen* is usually performed today with the original spoken dialogue replaced by recitatives, written by Bizet's friend Guiraud, which weaken the story-line.) Acutely depressed by his lack of success, Bizet became obsessed with thoughts of death, and died of a throat infection three months after the première of *Carmen* without the slightest premonition that it was to prove one of the most beloved mainstays of the operatic repertoire throughout the world.

Above: *Bizet about the time of the composition of* Carmen.

L'ARLESIENNE
□ *Suites 1 & 2* RPO/Beecham/*Carmen*
  HQS1108 (12/67) EMI/HMV
□ *Suite 1.* New Philh/Munch/*Carmen*
  SDD492 (9/76) Decca Ace of Diamonds
  21023 London

CARMEN
□ *Cpte.* Price, Freni, Corelli, Merrill,
  Vienna State Opera Chorus,
  VPO/Karajan
  SER5600-2 (11/71) RCA
  LSC-6199 RCA
□ *Cpte.* De Los Angeles, Micheau,
  Gedda, Blanc, Chorus/French
  National Radio Orch./Beecham
  SLS5021 (2/76) HMV
  S-3613 Angel
□ *Cpte.* Troyanos, Te Kanawa,
  Domingo, van Dam/Alldis
  Choir/LPO/Solti
  D11D3 (10/76) Decca
  13115 London

□ *Suites 1 & 2.* New. Philh./Munich/
  L'Arlesienne
  SDD 492 (9/76) Decca Ace of Diamonds
□ *Suite 1,* French Nat. Radio
  Orch./Beecham/*L'Arlesienne*
  HQS1108 (12/67) EMI/HMV

JEUX D'ENFANTS—SUITE
□ Scottish National/Gibson/*Ravel: Ma
  Mere; Saint-Saens: Carnival*
  CFP40086 (6/75) Classics for Pleasure
□ Paris Cons./Martinon/*Ibert; Saint-
  Saens*
  ECS782 (8/76) Decca Eclipse
  STS-15093 London

SYMPHONY IN C
□ NYPO/Bernstein/*Prokofiev; Dukas*
  61071 (5/69) CBS Classics
  MS-7159 Columbia
□ ASMF/Marriner/*Prokofiev*
  ZRG719 (12/73) Decca/Argo∗
□ Paris Orch/Barenboim/*Jolie fille; Patrie*
  ASD3277 (10/76) EMI/HMV

ARTHUR BLISS
(b. London 1891; d. there 1975)

The not uncommon progression from *enfant terrible* to respected pillar of the Establishment could scarcely be better exemplified than by the case of Bliss. After an orthodox training which was cut short by the 1914-18 war, in which he served with distinction, he first made his name with works of a vigorously experimental nature such as *Madam Noy* and *Rout* (in which a soprano voice is used as an instrument along with the other ten in the ensemble)—both of which featured in early festivals of the International Society for Contemporary Music—and with the satirical *Conversations* for quintet. For the last 22 years of his life he held the post of Master of the Queen's Music, having been knighted three years previously, in 1950.

In fact his early iconoclastic phase was short-lived, for already by his 1922 *Colour Symphony* he had moved towards a broad, openly romantic style (diatonic but with pungent sub-Stravinskian dissonances) in which a certain grandiloquence was apparent—a trait even more marked later in the Piano Concerto written for the 1939 New York World Fair. Following the *Colour Symphony* he seemed to find pleasure in closer-knit construction, and produced some chamber works which were both lively and deeply poetic, notably the Oboe Quartet (1927) and Clarinet Quintet (1931), the exquisite idyllic *Pastoral* for chorus and orchestra, the *Serenade* for baritone and orchestra, and a large-scale symphony for orator, chorus and orchestra, *Morning heroes*, which served to lay the ghosts of his war years. All these last three works selected texts drawn from a variety of sources. By common consent Bliss's finest orchestral composition, highly characteristic in its muscular, sturdy extroversion, is the *Music for strings* (written for the 1935 Salzburg Festival), which is in the line of descent from Elgar's » *Introduction and Allegro*. In the same year his score for the film *Things to come* won wide popularity. This was to mark the beginning of a series of compositions for specific ends: the *Kenilworth* suite as a National Brass Band Festival test piece, the dramatic *Checkmate* for the Vic-Wells Ballet, the piano concerto already mentioned, and two further ballets—*Miracle in the Gorbals* and *Adam Zero*. He later wrote two operas—*The Olympians* for Covent Garden and *Tobias and the Angel* for BBC Television—though these proved too conservative in idiom to satisfy the younger generation which by then had overtaken him.

Bliss: Music for Strings
Howells: Concerto for String Orchestra

London Philharmonic Orchestra
Sir Adrian Boult

(A) COLOUR SYMPHONY
☐ LSO/Bliss/*Elgar: Falstaff*
  ECS625 (7/71) Decca Eclipse
HYMN TO APOLLO
☐ LSO/Bliss
  SRCS55 (8/71) Lyrita
MORNING HEROES
☐ Westbrook (orator) Liv. Phil.
  Choir/RLPO/Groves
  SAN365 (3/75) EMI/HMV Angel
MUSIC FOR STRINGS
☐ LPO/Boult/*Howells: Concerto*
  ASD3020
**PASTORAL (LIE STREWN THE
WHITE FLOCKS)**
☐ Michelow/London CO/Morris/
  Knot of Riddles
  TPLS13036 (11/70) Pye/Virtuoso
PRAYER TO THE INFANT JESUS
☐ Ambrosian Singers/Ledger
  SRCS55 (8/71) Lyrita
**ROUT FOR SOPRANO AND
ORCHESTRA**
☐ Woodland/LSO/Bliss
  SRCS55 (8/71) Lyrita
**SERENADE FOR BARITONE AND
ORCHESTRA**
☐ Shirley-Quirk/LSO/Bliss
  SRCS55 (8/71) Lyrita
**(THE) WORLD IS CHARGED WITH
THE GRANDEUR OF GOD**
☐ Ambrosian Singers/LSO/Bliss
  SRCS55 (8/71) Lyrita

Above: *Bliss at the time he first made his name.*

Left: *Bliss when Master of the Queen's Music.*

SCHELOMO
☐ Rostropovich/French National Orch/
  Bernstein/*Schumann: Cello Conc.*
  ASD3334 (3/77) EMI/HMV
  S-37256 Angel
VIOLIN CONCERTO
☐ Menuhin/Philh/Kletzki
  SXLP30177 (3/75) EMI/HMV
  Concert Classics
  S-36192 Angel

Left: *Whether in Switzerland,*
Belgium, Germany, France
or the USA, Bloch's music
always retained its Jewish
character.

ERNEST BLOCH
(b. Geneva 1880; d. Portland, Oregon, 1959)

Though there have been numerous Jewish composers, nearly all have been content to be assimilated into the culture of their country of residence: not so with Bloch, whose restless life seems to have militated against him putting down roots. He was born in Switzerland, studied in Brussels, Frankfurt and Munich, lived for a while in Paris, returned to Geneva and lectured on musical aesthetics, visited the USA as a ballet conductor and while there became successively a professor in New York, director of the Cleveland Institute of Music and director of the San Francisco Conservatory, returned to live in Switzerland, with visits to France and Italy, and finally in 1938, as war clouds gathered in Europe, settled in America and taught at Berkeley, California. For the most part his music is consciously Jewish in character—not just through the use of exotic-sounding intervals, and certainly not through any quotation of traditional Hebrew music (whose authenticity he questioned): in his own words, "It is the Jewish soul that I feel vibrating

throughout the Bible that interests me: the freshness and naiveté, the violence, the savage love of justice, the despair, the sorrow and immensity, the sensuality". The very titles of his works bear witness to this deep-seated preoccupation: the *Trois poèmes juifs* for orchestra, the powerful *Schelomo* rhapsody for cello (his most frequently played work), the *Israel* symphony, the *Baal Shem* suite for violin, the *Sacred Service*, and many more.

But Bloch's significance is far from being purely racial: the passionate intensity of his writing, which tends to be rhapsodic and colourful, would be striking in any case, both where the idiom contains something of the Oriental, as in the first Violin Sonata and the highly emotional Violin Concerto, and elsewhere, as in the early opera *Macbeth*, the orchestral pieces *America* and *Helvetia*, and in his chamber music (perhaps the summit of his achievement), which includes five string quartets and a magnificently dark Piano Quintet.

LUIGI BOCCHERINI
(b. Lucca 1743; d. Madrid 1805)

It is ironical that to the general public Boccherini's name suggests only a much-played Minuet (which in fact comes from his E major String Quintet, Op.13 No.5), when he was so enormously prolific that music seemed to pour out of him: he wrote, for example, 155 quintets, 102 string quartets, 60 trios and much more chamber music, besides operas, oratorios, church music, 20 symphonies and four cello concertos. It is again ironical that the Cello Concerto in B flat which is most frequently played is a grotesquely over-romanticised conflation of two different works. Yet the delicacy and melodiousness even of the favourite Minuet are quite representative of his elegantly expressive style, which resembles that of his contemporary Haydn » but without his depth.

He was taught the cello by his father, a bass player, and rapidly made a considerable reputation as a soloist, particularly in Paris, where he became all the rage and publishers vied with each other to issue his compositions; and on the recommendation of the Spanish ambassador there he went to Spain (which strongly influenced his music, as it had influenced that of Domenico Scarlatti ») as composer and *virtuoso di camera* to the Infante Don Luis, restricted to writing only for his master. On the Infante's death twelve years later, he became, for the next decade, chamber composer to Frederick William II of Prussia; but his health was deteriorating, and though he came for a time under the patronage of Lucien Bonaparte, his fortunes also declined, and after eking out a precarious living writing and arranging for wealthy amateur guitarists, he died in utter poverty.

GUITAR QUINTETS—NO. 4 IN D;
NO. 7 IN E MINOR; NO. 9 IN C
□ Yepes/Melos Qt
2530 069 (4/71) DG*
STRING QUINTET IN E, OP. 13 NO. 5
□ Kehr, Bartels, Sichermann, Braunholz,
Herbruch/*String Quintet, Op. 47/1*
TV34094S (5/67) Decca Turnabout
STRING QUINTET IN C, OP. 37 NO. 7
□ ASMF/Marriner/*Mendelssohn: Octet*
ZRG569 (5/68) Decca Argo*
**STRING QUINTET IN A MINOR, OP.
47 NO. 1**
□ Kehr, Bartels, Sichermann, Braunholz,
Herbruch/*String Quintet, Op. 13/5*
TV34094S (5/67) Decca Turnabout*

Left: *For over a quarter of a century Boccherini lived in Spain, which coloured his music and led him to write much for the guitar; but we have yet to rediscover the full wealth of his chamber music.*

ALEXANDER BORODIN
(b. St Petersburg 1833; d. there 1887)

As was the case with the other members of the "kuchka" gathered by Balakirev » under his tutelage, music to Borodin was not his primary occupation: he was an analytical chemist of international experience and repute, whose time was much taken up with his duties as professor of chemistry, and later as an administrator, in the Medical Academy of St Petersburg. Brought up privately by his mother, the wife of a well-to-do doctor, he was gifted in languages and showed a cultivated amateur's interest in music which was quickened when he fell in love with an excellent pianist who opened his eyes to Liszt » and Schumann », and whom he eventually married. He had already composed a few chamber works, including a piano quintet, but when, in 1862, he met Balakirev he was fired to write a symphony and a number of songs, several of which are of the first rank. Learning by the experience of hearing his work performed, he began work on a second symphony, interspersing his writing of this with bursts of energy devoted to an opera on the subject of the 12th-century Prince Igor. Both these, together with other operatic projects never completed, often had to be left while Borodin got on with his hospital work; the B minor Symphony was finished by 1875, but when the promise of a performance suddenly materialised the two middle movements could not be found and had to be re-scored. This symphony, later revised to lighten the orchestration, is now a firm favourite, with its vivid first movement and ebulliently syncopated scherzo.

Work on composition continued to be desultory, and though the fiery and exciting *Polovtsian dances* and other isolated numbers from *Prince Igor* were successfully performed at concerts by Rimsky-Korsakov », who constantly tried to urge and assist him, the opera still remained to be completed and edited after his death by Rimsky-Korsakov and his pupil Glazunov »—the brilliant overture was written by the former from recollections of hearing Borodin play it on the piano. Meanwhile Borodin's reputation as a musician was making headway in western Europe through the championship of Liszt, to whom he dedicated the programmatic orchestral piece *In the steppes of Central Asia*. Like the Tartar music in *Prince Igor* and the Second Symphony, this has a strongly Oriental turn of phrase which was in his blood, for his real father was a Georgian prince. Nearly all his music is marked by original ideas and piquant harmony: the Second String Quartet from which comes the slightly over-sweet celebrated *Nocturne* is perhaps the least characteristic of his major works.

A. Borodine.

IN THE STEPPES OF CENTRAL ASIA
☐ Parish Orch./Rostropovich/*Mussorgsky; Glinka; Rimsky-Korsakov*
ASD3421 (2/78) EMI/HMV
S-37464 Angel
PIANO QUARTET IN C MINOR
☐ Vienna Octet/*Mendelssohn: Sextet*
SDD410 (3/74) Decca Ace of Diamonds
PRINCE IGOR—POLOVSTIAN DANCES
☐ RPO & Ch./Beecham/*Balakirev: Sym. 1*
SXLP30171 (10/74) EMI/HMV Concert Classics

Above: *A distinguished chemist, Borodin as a musician owed much to the example and the encouragement of Liszt.*

☐ Orch. de Paris/Rozhdestvensky/ *Mussorgsky; Rimsky-Korsakov*
ESD7006 (9/76) EMI/HMV
S-36889 Angel
STRING QUARTET NO. 2 IN D
☐ Gabrieli Quartet/*Dvorak: Qt. 6*
CFP40041 (8/73) Classics for Pleasure
☐ Quartetto Italiano/*Dvorak: Qt. 6*
SAL3708 (5/69) Phonogram
☐ Borodin Quartet/*Shostakovich*
ECS795 (3/77) Decca Eclipse
STS-15046 London
SYMPHONY NO. 2 IN B MINOR
☐ Suisse Romande/Ansermet/*Sym. 3; Prince Igor Ov.*
ECS576 (3/71) Decca Eclipse
STS-15149 London
☐ Bournemouth SO/Brusilow/*Balakirev; Rimsky-Korsakov*
ASD3193 (7/76) EMI/HMV
SYMPHONY NO. 3 IN A MINOR
☐ Suisse Romande/Ansermet/*Sym. 2; Prince Igor Ov.*
ECS576 (3/71) Decca Eclipse
STS-15149 London
☐ LPO/Lloyd-Jones/*Mussorgsky; Rimsky-Korsakov*
6580 053 (6/72) DG

Left: *Alexander Borodin, photographed in 1885.*

PIERRE BOULEZ
(b. Montbrison 1925)

Most familiar to the public as an international conductor with a fantastically acute ear and a formidable intellect, whose lucid presentation of difficult contemporary works has materially contributed to their acceptance and understanding, Boulez is also a tireless "animator" and himself a leading composer of today's *avant garde*, despite his increasingly prolonged thought, hesitation and critical consideration before setting down even a few bars on paper. A pupil of Messiaen », he adheres rigorously to serial techniques, which he applies to every aspect of music—melody, harmony, rhythm, instrumentation etc; yet at the same time, in accordance with the ideas of the poet Mallarmé, who has dominated his thinking, the very complexity of his art leads to deliberate ambiguities, and he has included in his structures an element of chance and choice which once taken, however, is thenceforth strictly controlled. Nor is his music coldly objective and mathematical in effect: on the contrary, it is alternately delicate and violent in expression, with the most fastidious ear for novel sonorities.

Apart from his first two piano sonatas, the second of which stretches keyboard virtuosity to new limits, the earliest work to be representative of him is the cantata *Le Soleil des eaux* (1948); but his reputation was firmly established with another cantata, for voice and chamber ensemble, six years later, *Le Marteau sans maître*. This has already become a contemporary classic, and the seductive quality of its glinting metallic sounds has succeeded in fascinating many listeners unable to comprehend either the stylised verse or the musical idiom. Since that time Boulez has been ever more reluctant to publish his works or even to recognise a finalised version for them: he has made some, such as the Third Piano Sonata, susceptible to alternative readings, extensively altered some, such as the large-scale Mallarmé triptych *Pli selon pli*, and left others as "works in progress".

LE MARTEAU SANS MAITRE
☐ Minton, Musique Vivante Ens./Boulez/
Livre
73213 (2/74) CBS
M-32160 Columbia
PLI SELON PLI
☐ Lukomska, Bergmann, Stingl, d'Alton/
BBC SO/Boulez
72770 (1/70) CBS
M-30296 Columbia
LE SOLEIL DES EAUX
☐ Nendick, McDaniel, Devos, BBC
Chorus & SO/Boulez
ZRG756 (4/76) Decca Argo∗

Left: *Orchestras respect Boulez for his truly remarkable ear.*

Below: *Pierre Boulez conducting the BBC Symphony Orchestra at a 1973 Promenade Concert in the Royal Albert Hall.*

WILLIAM BOYCE
(b. London 1710; d. there 1779)

London was the central point of Boyce's entire life: he was born and died there, and was buried in St Paul's Cathedral, where as a boy he had been a chorister; and during his career held various important organist posts in London churches, including that of St Michael's, Cornhill. He was for many years a composer to the Chapel Royal and a conductor of the Three Choirs Festival, and for the last 24 years of his life was Master of the King's Music. In this last capacity he composed a number of Odes for the king's birthday and for New Year; but he also wrote incidental music for a dozen or so stage plays (from which were drawn the eight attractive and ever-fresh symphonies), twelve trio-sonatas which gained great popularity and were also pressed into service as theatre act-tunes, and a number of secular choral works besides a large quantity of church music (including 60 anthems). A man of gentle nature, never known (in Charles Wesley's words) "to speak a vain or ill-natured word, either to exalt himself or depreciate another", he was a serious scholar, and towards the end of his life, when he was becoming very deaf, published a famous three-volume collection of cathedral music by English composers of the previous two centuries.

SYMPHONIES NOS. 1-8
☐ Wurttemberg CO/Faerber
TV34133S (2/68) Decca Turnabout∗
TRIO SONATAS— NO. 2 IN F; NO. 8 IN E FLAT; NO. 9 IN C; NO. 12 IN G
☐ Latchem, Brown, Ryan, Lumsden
ORYX1729 (6/70) Peerless/Oryx∗

Right: *The opening of the 4-part verse* Te Deum *in A major by William Boyce.*

Below: *In his old age Boyce, Master of the King's Music, became extremely deaf.*

JOHANNES BRAHMS
(b. Hamburg 1833; d. Vienna 1897)

It seems barely credible today, when Brahms's symphonies
and other works form part of the very core of the concert
repertoire, that in the edition of Grove's Dictionary
published only 50 years ago a writer should worry that
the finale of his Fourth Symphony might be too difficult
to follow even by "students who are fairly familiar with
the movement" and should comment that his Violin
Concerto—one of the greatest and most profound ever
written for the instrument, and one which every concert
violinist needs to be able to play—"offers rare
opportunities to a player who can cope with its
difficulties". Seeking for the grit within these pearls, it is
undeniable that the spaciousness and seriousness of
much of Brahms's music, sober in its orchestral colouring,
is of a maturity which may make its greatest appeal to the
thoughtful; but his rhythmic vigour and broad sweeping
melodic lines, and the warmth of his lyricism, do not
need a connoisseur for their appreciation. Brahms is
recognised as particularly satisfying in that below the
richly romantic emotional surface lie very solid classical
foundations.

He was born into a humble family and quickly showed
gifts as a pianist: nevertheless he had to support himself

Above: *Brahms about the time he composed his* German Requiem.

Below: *A photograph of Brahms taken in his sixties.*

by playing in sailors' dives—an experience which caused a disillusionment with women which coloured his whole life. A concert tour with a Hungarian violinist led not merely to the composition of his popular *Hungarian dances* but, more importantly, to a meeting with the eminent violinist Joachim, who was to become a lifelong friend. Through him Brahms had valuable introductions to Liszt » (whose admiration he did not reciprocate) and Schumann », to whom, and to whose wife Clara, he became deeply devoted.

After his energetic early piano works and first piano concerto (which incidentally reveal how big his hands were) he concentrated on large-ish chamber works—such as the two sextets, the piano quartets, the Horn Trio and the Piano Quintet (which, as was often the case with him, had undergone various changes of instrumentation)—and choral works, including the *German Requiem* (written after his mother's death, but with Schumann's death also in his mind) and the *Alto Rhapsody*—before feeling himself ready to tackle a symphony. His orchestral music had so far been confined to two *Serenades*, written in the short period when he had held a part-time appointment as musical director to the court of Detmold. He was later

ACADEMIC FESTIVAL OVERTURE
☐ Halle/Loughran/*Haydn Var; Tragic Ov.; Alto Rhapsody*
  CFP40064 (10/74) Classics for Pleasure
☐ LPO/Boult/*Sym. 4*
  ASD2901 (6/73) EMI/HMV
  S-37034 Angel
ALTO RHAPSODY
☐ Baker/Alldis Choir/LPO/Boult/*Sym. 2*
  ASD2746 (12/71) EMI/HMV
  S-37032 Angel
☐ Greevey/Halle Choir/Halle/ Loughran/*Academic Festival Ov.; Tragic Ov.; Haydn Var.*
  CFP40046 (10/74) Classics for Pleasure
☐ Baker/Alldis Choir/LPO/Boult/ *R. Strauss; Wagner*
  ASD3260 (9/76) EMI/HMV
  S-37199 Angel
BALLADES, OP. 10
☐ Rubinstein/*Rhapsodies; Piano Pieces (exc.)*
  SB6845 (7/71) RCA
  LSC-3186 RCA
☐ Gilels/*Fantasies, Op. 116*
  2530 655 (7/76) DG*

Right: *This memorial by Ilse Conrat was unveiled in the Vienna central cemetery in 1903.*
Below: *As a young man Brahms was obliged to play in taverns as well as concert halls.*

BRAHMS

1833 - 1897

to be, briefly, conductor of a ladies' choir in Hamburg and then of the Singakademie in Vienna before becoming, for three years, director of the Gesellschaft der Musikfreunde in Vienna. With the giant shadow of Beethoven » hanging over him, he in fact deliberated over his first symphony for nearly twenty years before completing it: right to the last minute he hesitated, turning aside to compose the *Variations on a theme of Haydn*.

Once completed, the First Symphony was quickly followed by the Second: then came various piano and smaller chamber works, the Violin Concerto (dedicated to Joachim) and the enormously expansive Second Piano Concerto. The Third and Fourth symphonies, like the First and Second, were written in quick succession: the Fourth is the epitome of Brahms's strength and nobility of style, into which a certain terseness was now creeping, as the Double Concerto for violin and cello and the *Four serious songs* make clear. His last few works, like the masterly Clarinet Quintet, breathe a mellow autumnal beauty. Except for oratorio and opera, Brahms greatly enriched almost every *genre* of music; but between the intimacy of feeling of his late piano pieces and the extroversion of his youthful sonatas lies as large a gap as between the deeply expressive quality of his numerous *lieder* and the gruff exterior and caustic tongue he presented to the world.

CELLO SONATA NO. 2 IN F, OP. 99
☐ Starker, Katchen/*Piano Trio No. 2*
SXL6589 (6/73) Decca
6814 London
CLARINET QUINTET IN B MINOR, OP. 115
☐ Stahr, Berlin Octet/*Dvorak: Bagatelles*
6500 453 (11/73) Phonogram
☐ Boskovsky/Vienna Oct./*Wagner*
SDD249 (9/70) Decca Ace of Diamonds
CLARINET SONATAS NO. 1 IN F MINOR, NO. 2 IN E FLAT, OP. 120
☐ de Peyer, Barenboim
ASD2362 (5/68) EMI/HMV
S-60302 Seraphim
DOUBLE CONCERTO IN A MINOR
☐ D. Oistrakh, Rostropovich, Cleveland/Szell/*Dvorak*
ASD3312 (5/77) EMI/HMV
S-36032 Angel
☐ Suk, Navarra, Czech PO/Ancerl
SUAST50573 (4/66) Supraphon
☐ Francescatti, Fournier/Columbia SO/ Walter/*Alto Rhapsody; Song of Destiny*
61428 (3/74) CBS Classics
☐ Ferras, Tortelier, Philh./Kletzki/ *Gluck: Iphigenie en Aulide Ov.*
CFP40081 Classics for Pleasure
☐ D. Oistrakh, Fournier/Philh/ Galliera/*Tragic Ov.*
SXLP30185 (9/75) EMI/HMV
S-35353 Angel
FANTASIES, OP. 116
☐ Katchen/*Op. 76*
SXL6118 (9/64) Decca

A GERMAN REQUIEM
☐ Schwarzkopf, Fischer-Dieskau, Philh. Chorus, Philh./Klemperer/*Tragic Ov.; Alto Rhapsody*
SLS821 (8/72) HMV
S-3624 Angel
HORN TRIO IN E FLAT, OP. 40
☐ Perlman, Tuckwell, Ashkenazy/ *Franck: Vln. Son.*
SXL6408 (5/69) Decca
6628 London
HUNGARIAN DANCES NOS. 5, 6, 7, 1 13, 19, 21
☐ VPO/Reiner/*Dvorak*
SPA377 (5/76) Decca
STS-15009 London
HUNGARIAN DANCES (TWO-PIANO VERSION)
☐ W. and B. Klein
TV350685 (4/67) Decca Turnabout
34068 Turnabout
LIEBESLIEDER
☐ Gachinger Kantorei/Rilling/*Neue Liebeslieder*
TV34277S Decca Turnabout
PIANO CONCERTO NO. 1 IN D MINOR
☐ Curzon/LSO/Szell
SXL6023 (12/62) Decca
6329 London
☐ Arrau/Philh./Giulini
CFP40028 (5/74) Classics for Pleasure
S-60264 Seraphim
☐ Barenboim/New Philh./Barbirolli/ *Conc. 2*
SLS874 (5/74) HMV

Below: *To the end of his life Brahms lived a bachelor existence in furnished rooms, surrounded by his books and music.*

□ Gilels/Berlin PO/Jochum
2530 258 (12/73) DG*
□ Katchen/LSO/Monteux/*Ballade 3*
SPA385 (7/75) Decca
STS-15209 London
PIANO CONCERTO NO. 2 IN B FLAT
□ Gilels/Chicago SO/Reiner
CCV5042 (7/59) Camden Classics
VICS-1026 RCA
□ Arrau/Philh./Giulini
CFP40034 (6/73) Classics for Pleasure
S-60052 Seraphim
□ Barenboim/New Philh./Barbirolli/
Conc. 1
SLS874 (5/74) HMV
□ Gilels/BPO/Jochum
2530 259 (6/74) DG*
□ Anda/Berlin PO/Fricsay
2538 256 (11/74) DG Privilege
PIANO QUARTET NO. 1
□ Gilels, Amadeus Quartet
2530 133 (11/71) DG*
PIANO QUINTET IN F MINOR OP. 34
□ Eschenbach/Amadeus Quartet
139 397 (8/69) DG*
PIANO SONATA NO. 3 IN F MINOR,
OP. 5
□ Katchen/*Scherzo*
SXL6228 (6/66) Decca
6482 London
□ Curzon/*2 Intermezzi*
SDD498 (12/76)
STS-15272 London
PIANO TRIO NO. 1 IN B, OP. 8
□ Suk, Katchen, Starker/*Piano Trio 3*
SXL6387 (5/69) Decca
PIANO TRIO NO. 2 IN C MAJOR,
OP. 87
□ Suk, Katchen, Starker/*Cello Sonata
No. 2*
SXL6589 (6/73) Decca
6814 London

PIANO TRIO NO. 3 IN C MINOR,
OP. 101
□ Katchen, Suk, Starker/*Piano Trio 1*
SXL6387 (5/69) Decca
6611 London
RHAPSODIES, OP. 79
□ Rubinstein/*Ballades; Piano Pieces (exc.)*
SB6845 (7/71) RCA
LSC-3186 London
STRING SEXTET NO. 2 IN G, OP. 35
□ Berlin Philharmonic Ens.
SAL3763 (3/70) Phonogram
TRAGIC OVERTURE
□ Halle/Loughran/*Haydn Var.,
Academic Festival Ov.; Alto Rhapsody*
CFP40064 (10/74) Classics for Pleasure
□ Dresden Staatskapelle/Sanderling/
Sym. 2
SB6875 (6/73) RCA
□ Concertgebouw/Haitink/*Sym. 3*
6500 155 (3/71) Phonogram*
□ Berlin PO/Kempe/*Sym. 3*
SXLP30100 (5/68) EMI/HMV
VARIATIONS ON A THEME OF
HAYDN (ST. ANTONI CHORALE)
□ LSO/Monteux/*Elgar*
SPA121 (6/71) Decca
STS-15188 London
□ Halle/Loughran/*Academic Festival
Ov.; Alto Rhapsody; Tragic Ov.*
CFP40046 (10/74) Classics for Pleasure
□ Dresden Staatskapelle/Sanderling/
Sym. 2
SB6877 (11/73) RCA
□ Berlin PO/Karajan/*Sym. 3*
138 926 (1/65) DG*
□ Concertgebouw/Haitink/*Sym. 2*
6500 375 (7/75) Phonogram*
□ LSO/Jochum/*Elgar: Enigma Vars.*
2530 580 (12/75) DG*

SYMPHONIES 1-4
□ Berlin PO/Karajan
2721 076 (7/74) DG
2721 002 DG
□ LPO & LSO/Boult/*Academic Festival
Ov.; Tragic Ov.; Alto Rhapsody*
SLS5009 (5/75) HMV
□ Halle/Loughran
CFP40096/40219/40237/40084
□ Berlin PO/Abbado
2530 125 (10/71) DG
SYMPHONY NO. 3 IN F
□ Berlin PO/Kempe/*Tragic Overture*
SXLP30100 (5/68) EMI/HMV
□ Berlin PO/Karajan
138 926 (1/65) DG
□ Concertgebouw/Haitink/*Tragic Ov.*
6500 155 (2/71) Phonogram
□ Dresden Staatskapelle/Sanderling/
Haydn Variations
SB6877 (4/75) RCA
□ Halle/Loughran/*Hung. Dances, 1,
3, 19*
CFP40237 (7/76) Classics for Pleasure
SYMPHONY NO. 4 IN E MINOR
□ LPO/Boult/*Academic Festival Ov.*
ASD2901 (6/73) EMI/HMV
S-37034 Angel
□ Dresden Staatskapelle/Sanderling
SB6879 (2/74) RCA
□ Halle/Loughran
CFP40084 (10/74) Classics for Pleasure
□ VPO/Kertesz
SXL6678 (1/76) Decca
□ Philh./Klemperer
SXLP30214 (8/76) EMI/HMV
VARIATIONS ON A THEME BY
HANDEL, OP. 24
□ Klien/*Rhapsody 2; Piano Pieces (exc.);
Waltzes (exc.)*
TV34165S (2/69) Decca Turnabout*

□ Bishop-Kovacevich/*Piano Pieces (exc.)*
SAL3758 (12/69) Phonogram
□ Vazsonyi/*Piano Pieces*
TPLS13035 (11/70) Pye/Virtuoso
VARIATIONS ON A THEME BY
PAGANINI, OP. 35
□ Katchen/*Variations on a theme by
Handel*
SXL6218 (4/66) Decca
STS-15150 London
VIOLIN CONCERTO IN D MAJOR
□ Krebbers/Concertgebouw/Haitink
6580 087 (4/75) Phonogram
□ Menuhin, Berlin PO/Kempe
SXLP30186 (6/75) EMI/HMV
□ Perlman/Chicago SO/Giulini
ASD3385 (11/77) EMI/HMV
□ D. Oistrakh, Cleveland/Szell
ASD2525 (9/73) EMI/HMV
S-36033 London
VIOLIN SONATA NO. 1 IN G
VIOLIN SONATA NO. 2 IN A
VIOLIN SONATA NO. 3 IN D MINOR,
OP. 108
□ Suk, Katchen
SXL6321 (1/68) Decca
6549 London
WALTZES, OP. 39
□ *Exc.* Klien/*Handel Vars; Piano Pieces
(exc.)*
TV34165S (2/69) Decca Turnabout*
34165 Turnabout

[signature: Johannes Brahms]

Above: *Brahms's whole attitude at the piano suggests breadth.*

SERENADE NO. 1 IN D MAJOR,
OP. 11
□ LSO/Kertesz
SXL6340 (5/68) Decca
6567 London
□ Concertgebouw/Haitink
9500 322 (2/77) Phonogram*
SERENADE NO. 2 IN A, OP. 16
□ LSO/Kertesz/*Dvorak: Wind Serenade*
SXL6368 (2/69) Decca
6594 London
STRING QUARTET NO. 1 IN C
MINOR, OP. 51 NO. 1
□ Melos Quartet/*String Quartet No. 3*
2530 344 (11/73) DG
STRING QUARTET NO. 2 IN
A MINOR, OP. 51 NO. 2
□ Weller Quartet/*Quartet No. 1*
SDD322 (4/72) Decca Ace of Diamonds
STS-15245 London
STRING QUARTET NO. 3 IN B
FLAT, OP.
□ Melos Quartet/*String Quartet No. 1*
2530 345 (11/73) DG

SYMPHONY NO. 1 IN C MINOR
□ LPO/Boult
ASD2871 (4/73) EMI/HMV
□ Berlin PO/Karajan
138924 (11/64) DG
□ Halle/Loughran
CFP40096 (3/75) Classics for Pleasure
□ Berlin PO/Bohm
2535 102 (7/75) DG Privilege
□ LSO/Horenstein
GL25001 (10/76) RCA Gold Seal
7028 Quintessence
□ Philh./Klemperer
SXLP30217 (12/76) EMI/HMV
SYMPHONY NO. 2 IN D MAJOR
□ Berlin PO/Karajan
138925 (11/64) DG
□ VPO/Kertesz
SXL6676 (2/75) Decca
□ LPO/Boult/*Alto Rhapsody*
ASD2746 (12/71) EMI/HMV
S-37032 Angel
□ Dresden Staatskapelle/Sanderling
SB6876 (6/73) RCA

BENJAMIN BRITTEN
(b. Lowestoft 1913; d. Aldeburgh 1976)

Precociously gifted and immensely prolific, Britten began to study composition while still a schoolboy and later worked with John Ireland ≫ at the Royal College of Music in London, after which he set out to earn a living by writing music for the theatre, for documentary films and for radio dramas, where his facility attracted professional notice and the backing of a publisher. Called upon in a hurry to provide a new work for a string orchestra visiting the 1937 Salzburg Festival, he won a great success with the inventive and witty *Variations on a theme of Frank Bridge* (his first teacher). He had already felt a strong pull towards word-setting, both for chorus and for solo voice (particularly that of his lifelong companion, the tenor Peter Pears), exhibiting, then and later, a remarkable literary eclecticism in several languages and conspicuous technical virtuosity in his large output. A violin concerto, his first string quartet, a *Sinfonia da Requiem* in memory of his parents, the *Michelangelo sonnets*, the choral *Hymn to St Cecilia* and *A Ceremony of carols* were written while he was in the USA at the start of the war. He returned with a grant from the Koussevitzky Music Foundation to write an opera, and established a world-wide reputation with *Peter Grimes*, which was produced in 1945 and promptly hailed as marking a new era in English opera.

It was the start of a long string of stage works during the remaining 30 years of his life. Several of these were designed for a chamber orchestra, for presentation by his own English Opera Group: *The Rape of Lucretia*, the comedy *Albert Herring*, the children's opera *The little sweep*, the eerie *Turn of the screw*, the three church parables, written in stylised form and drawing on elements from plainsong and Japanese Noh plays, and the highly compressed *Death in Venice*. A recurrent theme in his operas is that of the flawed hero—Grimes, Billy Budd (in the full-scale opera of that name, based on Melville), Albert Herring, Owen Wingrave (the central character of an opera for TV). Two further operas should be mentioned—*Gloriana* and *A Midsummer night's dream*, which catches the magic atmosphere of Shakespeare's play to an extraordinary degree—as well as *Noyes fludde* for children, introducing several novel but simple sound effects, and the ballet *Prince of the pagodas* (the first indication of his interest in Oriental music which was eventually to blossom in the church parables).

Britten held no appointments and did not have to resort to teaching, preferring to live and work among a small entourage of friends in the little East Coast town of Aldeburgh, where in 1948 he founded an annual Festival

BILLY BUDD
☐ Glossop, Pears, Langdon, Drake, Kelly, Brannigan, Ambrosian Singers, LSO/Britten
SET379-81 (9/68) Decca
1390 London

(The) BURNING FIERY FURNACE—parable
☐ Pears, Drake, Shirley-Quirk, Tear, Dean, EOG/Britten
SET356 (12/67) Decca
1163 London

CEREMONY OF CAROLS
☐ St. John's College Choir, Cambridge/ G. Guest/*Carols*
SPA/A164 (11/65) Decca

CURLEW RIVER—parable
☐ Pears, Blackburn, Shirley-Quirk, Drake, Webb, Ens/Britten
SET301 (1/66) Decca
1156 London

HOLY SONNETS OF JOHN DONNE
☐ Pears, Britten/*Songs and Proverbs*
SXL6391 (5/69) Decca
26099 London

LES ILLUMINATIONS
☐ Pears, ECO/Britten/*Serenade*
SXL6449 (9/70) Decca
26161 London
☐ Harper/Northern Sinfonia/Marriner/ *Serenade*
SXLP30194 (1/76) EMI/HMV
S-36788 London

(A) MIDSUMMER NIGHT'S DREAM
☐ Deller, Harwood, Pears, Hemsley, Veasey, Harper, Shirley-Quirk, Watts, Brannigan, Children's Choirs, LSO/Britten
SET338-40 (5/67) Decca
1385 London

ON THIS ISLAND—song cycle
☐ Tear, Ledger/*Sonnets of Michelangelo; Winter Words*
HQS1310 (4/74) EMI/HMV

Far left: *Benjamin Britten was an excellent pianist, accompanist and conductor.*
Left: *A page of Britten's MS score of* Pastoral, *from his 1943* Serenade *for tenor, horn and strings.*

at which works by himself and his circle were performed and attracted devoted audiences. No other musician has ever had so many of his works recorded so shortly after their composition; and this undoubtedly added greatly to their wide dissemination. A handful of them have achieved special popularity—the *Serenade* for tenor, horn and strings, the *Spring Symphony* (a verse anthology for solo voices, chorus and orchestra, in a Mahlerian symphonic mould), the *War Requiem* (which movingly intermingles verse by war poets with the Requiem text) written for the opening of the new Coventry Cathedral, and above all the *Young person's guide to the orchestra*, a brilliant set of variations on a theme of Purcell composed for a film demonstrating the various instruments of the modern orchestra. Six months before his death Britten was awarded a life peerage.

PETER GRIMES
☐ Pears, Watson, Pease, Nilsson, Brannigan, Evans, Lanigan, Cov. Gdn. Orch./Britten
SXL2150-2 (10/59) Decca
1305 London
☐ *Four Sea Interludes; Passacaglia,* LSO/Previn/*Sinfonia de Requiem*
ASD3154 (3/74) EMI/HMV
S-37142 Angel
PHANTASY QUARTET FOR OBOE, VIOLIN, VIOLA AND CELLO
☐ Craxton, Gabrieli Quartet
SDD497 (6/77) Decca Ace of Diamonds
PIANO CONCERTO
☐ Richter/ECO/Britten/*Violin Conc.*
SXL6512 (8/71) Decca
6723 London
THE PRODIGAL SON—parable
☐ Pears, Shirley-Quirk, Drake, Tear, EOG/Britten & Tunnard
SET438 (6/70) Decca
1164 London

(The) RAPE OF LUCRETIA
☐ Harper, Pears, Shirley-Quirk, Luxon, Drake, Baker, Bainbridge, ECO/Britten
SET492-3 (6/71) Decca
1288 London
SERENADE FOR TENOR, HORN AND STRINGS
☐ Pears, Tuckwell/LSO/Britten/*Les Illuminations*
SXL6449 (9/70) Decca
26161 London
☐ Tear, Civil/Northern Sinfonia/ Marriner/*Les Illuminations*
SXLP30194 (1/76) EMI/HMV
S-36788 Angel
SIMPLE SYMPHONY FOR STRINGS
☐ ECO/Britten/*Frank Bridge; Delius; Elgar; Purcell*
SXL6405 (6/69) Decca
☐ RPO/Sargent/*Britten: Purcell Var.; Walton; Facade (exc.)*
SXLP30114 (12/68) EMI/HMV
SINFONIA DA REQUIEM
☐ New Philh./Britten/*Sym. for Cello*
SXL6641 (7/74) Decca
☐ LSO/Previn/*Peter Grimes (exc.)*
ASD3154 (3/76) EMI/HMV
S-37142 Angel
SONGS AND PROVERBS OF WILLIAM BLAKE
☐ Fischer-Dieskau, Britten/*Holy Sonnets*
SXL6391 (5/69) Decca
26099 London
7 SONNETS OF MICHELANGELO
☐ Tear, Ledger/*On this Island; Winter Words*
HQS1310 (4/74) EMI/HMV
SPRING SYMPHONY
☐ Vyvyan, Procter, Pears, Chorus, Cov. Gdn. Orch./Britten
SXL2264 (5/61) Decca
25242 London
STRING QUARTETS—NO. 1, OP. 25; NO. 2 IN C, OP. 36
☐ Allegri Quartet
SXL6564 (6/73) Decca
STS-15303 London
SYMPHONY FOR CELLO AND ORCHESTRA
☐ Rostropovich/ECO/Britten/*Sinfonia da Requiem*
SXL6641 (7/74)
VARIATIONS ON A THEME OF FRANK BRIDGE
☐ ECO/Britten/*Young Person's Guide*
SXL6450 (9/70) Decca
6671 London
☐ Bath Fest. Orch./Menuhin/*Tippett*
SXLP30157 (10/73) EMI/HMV
☐ ASMF/Marriner/*Butterworth*
ZRG860 (11/76) Decca Argo
VIOLIN CONCERTO
☐ Lubotsky/ECO/Britten/*Piano Conc.*
SXL6512 (8/71) Decca
6723 London
☐ Friend/LPO/Pritchard/*Serenade*
CFP40250 (2/77) Classics for Pleasure
WAR REQUIEM
☐ Vishnevskaya, Pears, Fischer-Dieskau, Bach Choir, Highgate School Choir, LSO Chorus, Melos Ens., LSO/Britten
SET252-3 (5/63) Decca
1255 London
WINTER WORDS
☐ Tear, Ledger/*On this Island; Sonnets of Michelangelo*
HQS1310 (4/74) EMI/HMV
YOUNG PERSON'S GUIDE TO THE ORCHESTRA
☐ Baker (narrator)/New Philh./ Leppard/*Prokofiev*
CFP185 (1/72) Classics for Pleasure
☐ Previn (narrator), LSO/Previn/ *Prokofiev*
ASD2935 (12/73) EMI/HMV
☐ LSO/Britten/*Bridge Variations*
SXL6450 (9/70) Decca
6671 London
☐ BBC SO/Sargent/*Simple, Sym., Walton: Facade*
SXLP30114 (12/68) EMI/HMV

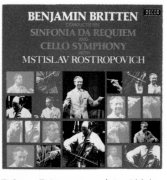

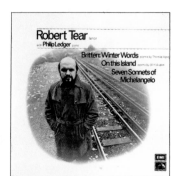

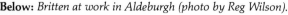

Below: *Britten at work in Aldeburgh (photo by Reg Wilson).*

MAX BRUCH
(b. Cologne 1838; d. nr. Berlin 1920)

If Bruch's shade is saddened by the fact that his three operas, three symphonies, dozen chamber works and great quantities of choral music have all disappeared into limbo, perhaps it is some consolation that three or four of his *concertante* works have held a place in the repertoire, and that one of them—the G minor Violin Concerto, the first of three for that instrument—remains a firm favourite with players and audiences alike. Its flow of warmly emotional ideas, its effective writing for the violin and its overall craftsmanship command both affection and respect; but in all that Bruch wrote his touch was equally sure and his technique unobtrusively polished. The far less known Second Violin Concerto again shows the melodic beauty which he was able to summon up so easily.

On the strength of his overt romanticism and his impassioned free arrangement for cello and orchestra of *Kol Nidrei* (his second most popular work), he is often thought of as a Jewish composer; but this was not so, and he several times drew on other kinds of traditional music—notably German and Welsh folksongs and, in the brilliant *Scottish Fantasy* for violin and orchestra, Scots tunes. Unusually, he was not himself an instrumentalist, though he wrote for all instruments with complete understanding, but he had a considerable reputation as a conductor, both in Germany and in England, where for three years he directed the Liverpool Philharmonic Society.

Below: *Though Max Bruch was no instrumentalist, he wrote brilliantly and gracefully for the violin and cello, and was a successful conductor.*

SCOTTISH FANTASY, OP. 46 FOR VIOLIN AND ORCHESTRA
☐ Chung/RPO/Kempe/*Violin Conc. 1*
  SXL6573 (11/72) Decca
☐ D. Oistrakh/LSO/Horenstein/
  Hindemith: Vln. Conc.
  SDD465 (6/76) Decca Ace of Diamonds
  6337 London
☐ Campoli/LPO/Boult/*Mendelssohn*
  ECS775 (8/76) Decca Eclipse
  STS-15015 London
☐ Perlman/New Philh./Lopez-Cobes/
  Violin Conc. 2
  ASD3310 (6/77) EMI/HMV
  S-37210 Angel

VIOLIN CONCERTO NO. 1 IN G MINOR, OP. 26
☐ Suk/Czech PO/Ancerl/*Mendelssohn*
  SUAST50546 (8/66) Supraphon
☐ Stern, Philadelphia/Ormandy/*Lalo*
  MS-7003 Columbia
☐ Perlman/LSO/Previn/*Mendelssohn: Vln. Conc. in E minor*
  ASD2926 (1/74) EMI/HMV
  S-36963 Angel
☐ Chung/RPO/Kempe
  Scottish Fantasy
  SXL6573 (11/72) Decca
  6795 London
☐ Morini/Berlin RSO/Fricsay/
  Glazunov
  2548 170 (11/75) DG Heliodor

VIOLIN CONCERTO NO. 2 IN D MINOR, OP. 44
☐ Perlman/New Philh./Lopez-Cobos/
  Scottish Fantasy
  ASD3310 (6/77) EMI/HMV
  S-37210 Angel

ANTON BRUCKNER

(b. Ansfelden, Upper Austria, 1824; d. Vienna 1896)

If Schubert's "Great" C major Symphony moved Schumann ❯ to write of its "heavenly length", it is fascinating to speculate on what he would have said about the symphonies of Bruckner, which follow and greatly expand the Schubertian tradition in a peculiarly Austrian atmosphere of leisurely spaciousness. The unhurried simple grandeur of his "cathedrals in sound", as they have been called, has been likened by non-Brucknerians to Lewis Carroll's "reeling, writhing and fainting in coils"; but paradoxically their length is made to seem even greater in the cut versions urged upon him by well-meaning friends, to which he agreed in the hopes of making his works more acceptable but which only upset their proportions. (These are fortunately less commonly played nowadays than the originals.)

To appreciate Bruckner's music one needs to understand the man. He came from humble Catholic peasant stock, and was himself deeply devout and almost incredibly gauche: his appearance, in baggy trousers deliberately too short for his legs (to have more freedom

Below: Bruckner at his piano, two years before his death. He habitually wore the peasant costume seen here.

Right: Anton Bruckner in 1885, the year when his Seventh Symphony brought him his first real success.

MASS NO. 2
☐ Schutz Choir/Philip Jones Brass Ens./Norrington
  ZRG710 (12/73) Decca Argo∗
SYMPHONY NO. 4 IN E FLAT
☐ Philh./Klemperer
  SXLP30167 (7/74) EMI/HMV
  S-36245 Angel
☐ Concertgebouw/Haitink
  6599 729 (12/74) Phonogram
☐ VPO/Bohm
  6BB171-2 Decca
  2240 London
☐ Berlin PO/Jochum
  2535 111 (8/75) DG Privilege∗
☐ LSO/Kertesz
  SDD464 (3/76) Decca Ace of Diamonds
  STS-15289 London
☐ Berlin PO/Karajan
  2530 674 (10/76) DG∗
SYMPHONY NO. 5 IN B FLAT
☐ Concertgebouw/Haitink
  6700 055 (6/72) Phonogram
SYMPHONY NO. 7 IN E
☐ Concertgebouw/Haitink/*Te Deum*
  SAL3624-5 (9/67) Phonogram
☐ Berlin PO/Karajan/*Wagner: Siegfried Idyll*
  2707 142 (4/77) DG
  2707 102 DG
SYMPHONY NO. 8 IN C MINOR
☐ Concertgebouw/Haitink
  6700 020 (10/70) Phonogram
☐ Berlin PO/Karajan
  2707 085 (5/76) DG∗
☐ Berlin PO/Karajan
  SXDW3024 (5/76) EMI/HMV Concert Classics
SYMPHONY NO. 9 IN D MINOR
☐ Berlin PO/Karajan
  139011 (6/69) DG∗
☐ Concertgebouw/Haitink
  SAL3575 (10/66) Phonogram
☐ Chicago SO/Barenboim
  2530 639 (4/76) DG∗
TE DEUM
☐ Soloists, Netherlands Radio Ch./ Concertgebouw/Haitink/*Sym. 7*
  6700 038 (9/67) Phonogram
  802759 Philips
☐ Soloists/Vienna Singverein/Berlin PO/Karajan/*Mozart*
  2530 704 (2/77) DG∗

when playing the organ) and always in far too large a collar, was bizarre. And as a result of his rustic upbringing he was extremely naive: for example, he tipped the distinguished conductor Hans Richter after rehearsing one of his symphonies. His hero-worship of Wagner » (to whom he dedicated his Third Symphony, which emptied the hall at its première, and whose death inspired the *Adagio* of his Seventh Symphony, in which for the first time he included Wagner tubas in his orchestra) was so extreme that he fell on his knees before him at their first meeting, and would never sit in his presence.

A slow developer, Bruckner had started his adult life as a village schoolmaster-cum-organist, but his gifts in the latter capacity, particularly in the art of improvisation, took him from the monastery of St Florian to the post of organist at Linz Cathedral, and later to extensive concert tours. With immense earnestness he studied strict methods of composition, and wrote several works for chorus, and his first Mass, before seriously attempting the symphonic form at the age of just over 40 (like Brahms »). He moved to Vienna, and apart from later appointments as a professor at the Conservatory there as a Court organist and as a lecturer at the University, he gave the rest of his life to composition. There were eventually eight symphonies, plus an early one he had himself called, with a typical lack of self-confidence, "No. 0"; his Ninth was left unfinished.

His country background influenced the cut of his melodies, especially the *Ländler*-like scherzos; and the *tremolando* with which he often began a symphony, apart from showing the influence of Beethoven's Ninth, lends it a romantic haze from which his themes emerge as from a meditative communion with Nature. His orchestration, like that of Franck », proclaims his allegiance to the organ. But special contributions of his to the symphony as a form were his introduction of extra subjects in the exposition and the merging of development and recapitulation, and the building-up of the finale from elements in previous movements (as in Nos. 5, 7 and 8). The large-scale *Te Deum*, composed about the time of the Seventh Symphony, represents the peak of his liturgical music.

FERRUCCIO BUSONI
(b. Empoli 1866; d. Berlin 1924)

Like his younger contemporary Rachmaninov », Busoni suffered from a tug-of-war in his life between his international career as one of the greatest pianists of his day (and as a conductor) and his activities as a composer. Unlike him, however, Busoni's music has appealed chiefly to connoisseurs, and he never expected otherwise: "all art is aristocratic", he declared. The intellectual character of much of his work does make it something of an acquired taste; yet his early compositions such as the *Comedy overture* and the violin sonatas are immediately attractive, showing an Italianate warmth (like his piano playing, which was characterised by the classically-minded as "ultra-romantic" but which all agreed had at the same time a visionary grandeur and an interpretative perception all his own), and his greatest masterpiece, the opera *Doktor Faust*, completed after his death by a pupil, is deeply impressive.

He also felt an inner tug-of-war about his nationality. His mother had been a pianist of German descent; after a cosmopolitan career—touring as a child prodigy in Austria and Italy, and then teaching in Helsingfors, Moscow and the New England Conservatory in Boston—he settled by choice in Berlin. His great musical allegiances were to Bach », the inspiration of his elaborate *Fantasia contrappuntistica*, and Liszt », the obvious influence behind his huge piano concerto (which also calls for a male chorus); and he wrote the texts of all his own operas in German—the one-act *Arlecchino* and *Turandot* are both marked by quirky, sardonic humour. Yet at heart he considered himself Italian, like his father, and his brief and abortive directorship of the Liceo Filarmonico in Bologna where as a boy of 15 he had become the youngest member since Mozart », proved a bitter disappointment to his hopes of revitalising musical life in his own country.

Above: *Ferruccio Busoni.*

BERCEUSE ELEGIAQUE
☐ New Philh./Prausnitz/*Dallapiccola;
  Wolpe*
  ZRG757 (5/76) Decca Argo∗
FANTASIA CONTRAPPUNTISTICA
☐ Lorenzi, Gorini (pianos)
  HM314 Rediffusion

PIANO CONCERTO
☐ Ogdon, Alldis Choir, RPO/
  Revenaugh/*Doktor Faust—two
  studies*
  SLS776 (1/68) HMV
VIOLIN SONATA NO. 2
☐ Granat, Gray/*Paderewski: Violin
  Son.*
  DSM1004 (2/76) Rediffusion/Desmar∗

DIDERIK BUXTEHUDE
(b. Helsingör 1637; d. Lübeck 1707)

Little is known of the early life of this Danish composer, a pupil of his father, who had been an organist in Helsingör (Elsinore) for many years; but at the age of 31 he secured the important post of organist at the Marienkirche in Lübeck. As was not uncommon in those days, in taking over the post he also, as one of the conditions, married his predecessor's daughter; but when he sought to impose the same condition on his own successor, Handel » and others withdrew their applications.

He made Lübeck a Mecca for German musicians both by his own splendid playing (Bach » for example tramped 200 miles to hear him) and by the evening concerts for organ, chorus and orchestra he instituted and which took place each year on the five Sundays before Christmas. His quasi-oratorio *The Last Judgment*, which introduces personifications of righteous and wicked souls and three of the deadly sins, was designed to be spread over the five *Abendmusiken* in 1683. As one of the principal North German composers, Buxtehude influenced many musicians beside Bach, particularly in the fields of cantatas and organ toccatas, chaconnes and fantasias. He was one of the first to demand a virtuoso technique on the pedals.

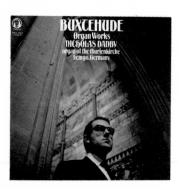

ORGAN MUSIC
    Canzonettas—E minor; G minor; Ciacona in E minor; Chorale Preludes—Gott der Vater; Nun lob mein Seel; Magnificat I tono; Preludes and Fugues—A minor; F; Toccata and Fugue in D minor.
☐ Danby
TPLS13041 (6/71) Pye-Virtuoso
ORGAN MUSIC
    Preludes and Fugues—A minor; B; F; E sharp; D; G minor. Canzona in C. Canzonettas in E minor; D minor; C. Chorale Preludes—Ach Herr, mich armen; Ach Gott und Herr; Jesus Christus, unser Heiland; Komm, heiliger Geist; Vater unser; Ein feste Burg; Es ist das Heil; Christ unser Herr; Mensch, willst du leben; Durch Adams Fall; Te deum laudamus; Auf meinem lieben Gott; Nimm von uns; Ciacona in C minor.
☐ Chapius
EX6 35308 (5/77) Selecta Telefunken
642001 Telefunken

Below: *A cantata written by Buxtehude in tablature.*

WILLIAM BYRD
(b. ? Lincolnshire 1543; d. Stondon, Essex, 1623)

Numerous literary references bear witness to the fame and esteem surrounding this sixteenth-century English composer, who excelled in all branches of composition: one poem declares that his

> "greater skill and knowledge dothe excelle all at this tyme
> and far to strange countries abroade his skill dothe shyne;
> famous men be abroad and skilful in the arte . . .
> but in Ewroppe is none like to our Englishe man".

A cultivated but austere and litigious man "naturally disposed to gravitie and pietie", he seems to have studied under Thomas Tallis » and was appointed organist of Lincoln Cathedral at the age of 20: nearly ten years later he went to London to share the post of organist to the Chapel Royal with his old master. Together they held a licence from Queen Elizabeth giving them, to the resentment of other printers, a virtual monopoly for printing music for 21 years—though even this seems not to have satisfied them. The first fruit of their licence was the collection of 34 *Cantiones sacrae* (Latin motets) dedicated to the Queen, each composer contributing half. Remarkably, Byrd continued to hold his Chapel Royal post, and indeed composed much music for the Reformed English Church, although he himself was a practising Catholic and wrote three great Masses which, along with his Anglican *Great Service*, are considered his masterpieces. Among his other works, many of which also attest to his mastery of expressive polyphony, were collections of *Psalmes, Sonets and Songs of Sadnes and Pietie*, which were madrigalian in style, like his *Songs of sundrie natures* (though this volume also contains seven penitential psalms treated metrically); two sets of *Gradualia* containing over 100 motets, and two further sets of *Cantiones sacrae*; a quantity of music for virginals and for viols, in both of which fields he was a pioneer—his keyboard variations and his fantasias for viols are outstanding; a number of English anthems, canons and rounds; solo songs, both sacred and secular, with lute or viols; and dramatic songs for stage plays.

WILLIAM BYRD
Mass in three parts
Mass in four parts

THE CHOIR OF
KING'S COLLEGE, CAMBRIDGE
Director   David Willcocks

CANTIONES SACRAE
(jointly with Tallis)
☐ Cantores in Ecclesia/Howard
  SOL311-3 (12/69) L'Oiseau-Lyre
MASS FOR 3 VOICES
☐ St. Margaret's Singers/Hickox/
  Mass for four voices
  RL25070 (6/77) RCA
☐ King's College Choir/Willcocks/
  Mass for four voices
  ZRG5362 (11/63) Decca Argo∗
MASS FOR 4 VOICES
☐ St. Margaret's Singers/Hickox/
  Mass for three voices
  RL25070 (6/77) RCA
☐ King's College Choir/Willcocks/
  Mass for three voices
  ZRG5362 (11/63) Decca Argo∗
MY LADYE NEVELLS BOOKE
☐ Hogwood
  D29D4 (1/77) Decca∗

Above: *'Since singing is so good
a thing, I wish all men would
learne to sing', wrote William
Byrd.*

53

EMMANUEL CHABRIER
(b. Ambert, Puy-de-Dôme, 1841; d. Paris, 1894)

One might not expect an ardent admirer of Wagner »— one who carried a score of *Tristan and Isolde* with him everywhere—to be notable for his gleeful wit and verve; but such was the case with Chabrier, who showed early musical talent but whose parents, with typical French bourgeois prudence, persuaded him to treat music as a hobby. He dutifully studied law and became a civil servant, but associated with poets, musicians and painters (incidentally building up a collection of impressionist pictures which included Manet's "Bar aux Folies-Bergères") and composed in his spare time—notably two operattas, *L'Etoile* and *Une Education manquée*.

But immediately afterwards, in 1880, he was overwhelmed by the experience of hearing *Tristan* at Bayreuth, and resigned his post to devote his life to music. Ten charming *Pièces pittoresques* for piano were followed by the work which brought him immediate fame, the ebullient orchestral rhapsody *España*, which to this day has rightly remained a popular favourite. He became chorus-master to Lamoureux, acquiring valuable practical experience which was later to bear fruit in his enchanting *Ode to Music* for female voices and orchestra. Under the spell of Wagner he produced an unsuccessful

tragic opera, *Gwendoline*, which received only two performances in Brussels before the management there went bankrupt; then, his natural comic vein re-asserting itself, came the delightful three-act comedy *Le Roi malgré lui*—which met with equally bad luck, as the theatre caught fire after the third performance. His irrepressible high spirits are evident not only from some of his songs (written late in the single decade of his career as a professional composer), which have a drollery that was to influence Satie », Poulenc » and Milhaud », and from the brisk and vivacious *Marche joyeuse* (scored, like everything of Chabrier's, with originality, vivid but delicate colouring and impeccable artistic taste), but from the snook he permitted himself to cock at his beloved *Tristan* in the shape of a *Quadrille* for piano duet on themes from the opera.

ESPANA—RHAPSODY
☐ CBSO/Fremaux/*Ravel; Dukas; Saint-Saens; Debussy*
ASD3008 (9/74) EMI/HMV
☐ LSO/Argenta/*Rimsky-Korsakov; Granados; Moszkowski*
ECS797 (6/77) Decca Eclipse
6006 London
ESPANA; SUITE PASTORALE; MARCHE JOYEUSE; LE ROI MALGRE LUI (exc.)
☐ SRO/Ansermet
JB10 (6/78) Decca Jubilee
6438 London
3 VALSES ROMANTIQUES
☐ Kyriakou, Klien/*Milhaud; Scaramouche; Faure: Dolly; Souvenirs de Munich; Ravel: Ma mere l'oye*
TV34234S (11/70) Decca Turnabout

Left: *Chabrier at the piano. A candid and revealing sketch by one of his many artist friends.*

ERNEST CHAUSSON
(b. Paris 1855; d. Limay, nr. Mantes, 1899)

Chausson came to music late, not beginning to study with Massenet » at the Paris Conservatoire until he was 25 and then becoming a private pupil of Franck ». A slow and meticulous writer, he was fortunate enough to have private wealth, but his extremely self-deprecating and sensitive nature prevented him from making use of this for the furtherance of his own works. His stage music, which includes an opera, *Le Roi Arthus*, heavily indebted to Wagner's *Tristan and Isolde*, is not important, but many of his songs are among the most exquisite in the repertoire of the French *mélodie*, and the orchestral song-cycle *Poème de l'amour et de la mer*, which employs Franck's cyclical technique, is heard less often than it deserves. It is however by his instrumental works that Chausson is chiefly remembered. There is a poetic Concerto for the curious medium of violin, piano and string quartet, and an emotional but somewhat flaccid symphony modelled on that by his teacher Franck; but Chausson is best represented by the *Poème* for violin and

orchestra, a typically sensuous and melancholy work which has endeared itself to artists and audiences alike. His career was prematurely cut short when he was killed in a bicycle accident on his own estate.

POEME DE L'AMOUR ET DE LA MER
☐ Angeles, Lamoureux, Orch./ Jacquillat/*Canteloube: Songs of the Auvergne*
ASD2826 (3/73) EMI/HMV
S-37897 Angel
POEME FOR VIOLIN AND ORCHESTRA
☐ Milstein/Philh./Fistoulari/*Saint Saens*
SXLP30159 (5/74) EMI/HMV
S-36005 Angel
☐ Perlman/Paris Orch/Martinon/ *Ravel; Saint-Saens*
ASD3125 (1/76) EMI/HMV
S-37118 Angel
SYMPHONY IN B FLAT
☐ Suisse Romande, Ansermet/*Franck: Eolides*
SXL6310 (1/68)
STS-15294 London

FRYDERYK CHOPIN
(b. Zelazowa Wola, nr. Warsaw, 1810; d. Paris 1849)

For the universal recognition he commands as one of the supremely great writers for the piano, an instrument he invested with a new poetry, and for the imperishable affection of players and listeners, Chopin has had to pay a high price—a novelettishly distorted view of his personality and life, cavalier treatment of his texts (on whose exactitude he set great store) by exhibitionist pianists, numerous silly legends and nicknames attached to some of the works, and a widespread misunderstanding both of their nature and, even, of the style in which they should be performed.

With very few exceptions, all his music was for piano (even the exceptions, such as the early Piano Trio, the songs and a cello sonata, include the keyboard), and most of it was written for himself to play. As a pianist, and as an improviser, he was everywhere the object of almost unqualified admiration, not merely by impressionable young ladies, although they abounded, but by Europe's leading musicians; yet he had been virtually self-taught. He had shown a precocious aptitude for music, publishing his first little pieces at the age of seven, and, like the young Mozart », had been made much of in aristocratic salons. But his father, a teacher of French,

wisely saw that he received a solid musical grounding at the Warsaw Conservatoire.

Meetings with visiting celebrities, and concerts in Vienna, where his Polish-flavoured works created an instant impression, broadened his musical horizons. During a more extended concert tour in 1830, Warsaw fell to the Russians, and Chopin decided to settle in Paris, in whose artistic life he quickly became a fashionable figure. Within the elegant, reserved dandy whose brilliant gifts of mimicry amused his friends, however, lay strong, often violent, feelings, intolerance, and a vulnerable sensitivity which were allowed an outlet only in sarcasm. It was not long before his health, never robust, began to cause some anxiety, and on its account his betrothal to the daughter of family friends was broken off: it was further undermined by a sojourn in Majorca with the masterful woman novelist George Sand, with whom he then formed a liaison (her accounts of their life are full of romantic inventions). He dropped out of public music-making, devoting himself to composition and frequenting influential circles: the *affaire* with George Sand dragged on for ten years altogether, and by the time it broke up, after prolonged emotional upsets, he was a fatally sick and mentally exhausted man with only two years to live.

His principal teacher had felt that Chopin should be

Below: *The house and garden at Zelazowa Wola, near Warsaw, where Fryderyk Chopin was born in 1810.*

Left: *Chopin shortly before his death.*

ANDANTE SPIANATO AND GRANDE POLONAISE; NOCTURNE IN B, OP. 62 NO. 1; SCHERZO IN E, OP. 54; POLONAISE—FANTASIA, OP. 61
☐ Ax
   ARL1 1569 (9/76) RCA*
BALLADES (Cpte.)
☐ Ashkenazy/*Nouvelles Etudes*
   SXL6143 (3/65) Decca
   6422 London
☐ Frankl/*Fantaisie in F minor*
   TV34217S (7/69) Decca Turnabout
   34271 Turnabout
BARCAROLLE
☐ Barenboim/*Chopin: shorter piano works*
   ASD2963 (5/74) EMI/HMV
CELLO SONATA
☐ Du Pre, Barenboim/*Franck: Cello Sonata*
   ASD2851 (2/73) EMI/HMV
   S-36937 Angel
ETUDES, OP. 10 AND OP. 25
☐ Pollini
   2530 291 (11/72) DG*
☐ Ashkenazy
   SXL6710 (12/75) Decca
   6844 London
☐ *Exc.* Perlemuter/*Nocturnes*
   REB153 (1/74) BBC
IMPROMPTUS (Cpte.)
☐ Rubinstein
   SB6649 (3/66) RCA
☐ Vasary/*Etudes; Ballades*
   2726 014 (3/74) DG

writing operas: certainly the exquisitely embroidered *bel canto* melodic lines characteristic of his music show an affinity with the Italian operas current in Warsaw in his youth, but his instinctive understanding of the piano's textures, as in his Studies, and imaginative realisation of its poetic possibilities, as in the Nocturnes and Mazurkas, were idiomatic to the instrument. His beautifully expressive melodies, and the rhythms of his idealised Polish dances (in the Mazurkas and heroic Polonaises), exercise their spell on all music-lovers; but of equal fascination to musicians are the romantic chromaticism of his harmony, the subtle part-writing (particularly in the later works, when his lifelong love of Bach », whose "48" he knew by heart, had been fortified by a study of Cherubini's contrapuntal teachings), and his individual sense of colour and of form. The notion (nurtured on the popularity of the Preludes and Waltzes) that he was only a miniaturist is exploded by such works as the concertos, the sonatas in B flat minor and B minor, the rhapsodic Ballades and Scherzos, the F minor Fantaisie and the Barcarolle; but though his playing frequently astonished his hearers by its intensity, it was its lightness and grace that captivated them; the grandiose effects of some star performers are utterly alien to his art.

Above: *At the age of 20 Chopin settled in France for good.*

Below: *Memorial to Chopin in the grounds of his birthplace.*

MAZURKAS
(Cpte.) Rubinstein
  SB6702-4 (5-7/67) RCA
  LSC-6177 RCA
□ *(Cpte.)* Ronald Smith
  SLS5014 (5/75) HMV
□ Michelangeli
  2530 236 (6/72) DG*
NOCTURNES
□ *(Cpte.)* Rubinstein
  SB6731-2 (2/68) RCA
  LSC-7050 RCA
□ Exc. Perlemuter/*Etudes*
  REB153 (1/74)
PIANO CONCERTO NO. 1 IN E MINOR
□ Pollini, Philh./Kletzki
  SXLP30160 (6/74) EMI/HMV
  S-60066 Seraphim
□ Arrau/LPO/Inbal
  6500 255 (6/72) Phonogram*

□ Gilels/Philadelphia/Ormandy
  72338 (7/65) CBS
  Y-32369 Odyssey
□ Askenase/The Hague PO/Otterloo/ *Krakowiak*
  2548 066 (10/75) DG/Heliodor
PIANO CONCERTOS NOS. 1 AND 2; KRAKOWIAK; FANTASY ON POLISH AIRS
□ Ohlsson/Polish Radio Nat. SO/ Maksymiuk
  SLS5043 (4/76) HMV
PIANO CONCERTO NO. 2 IN F MINOR
□ Rubinstein, Philadelphia Orch./ Ormandy/*Fantasy on Polish Airs*
  SB6797 (8/69) RCA
□ Ashkenazy/LSO/Zinman/*Ballade 3; Nocturne 17; Scherzo 3; Barcarolle*
  SXL6693 (4/74) Decca
PIANO WORKS
□ (Ballades; Mazurkas; Nocturnes; Polonaises; Andante spianato and Grande polonaise; Impromptus; Fantaisie-Impromptu; Scherzi; Sonatas 2 and 3; Waltzes; Barcarolle; Nouvelles-Etudes; Bolero; Fantaisie in F Minor; Berceuse; Tarantelle) Rubinstein
  SER5692 (12 discs) (12/73) RCA
POLONAISE FANTAISIE, OP. 61; MAZURKA IN A MINOR, OP. 17 NO. 4; ETUDE IN G FLAT, OP. 10 NO. 5; WALTZ IN A MINOR, OP. 34 NO. 2; POLONAISE IN A FLAT, OP. 53
□ Horowitz
  72969 (9/72) CBS
POLONAISE IN A FLAT, OP. 61; ANDANTE SPIANATO AND GRANDE POLONAISE IN E FLAT; IMPROMPTUS NOS. 1-3; FANTAISIE IMPROMPTU IN C SHARP MINOR
□ Rubinstein
  SB6649 (3/66) RCA
POLONAISES 1-16
□ Frankl
  TV34254-5S (10/69) Decca Turnabout
□ *1-7.* Pollini
  2530 659 (12/76) DG*
PRELUDES
□ Arrau
  6500 622 (6/75) Phonogram*
□ *1-24.* Pollini
  2530 550 (12/75) DG*
□ *1-24.* Perahia
  76422 (1/76) CBS
RECITALS:
BALLADE NO. 1 IN G MINOR; SCHERZO NO. 2 IN B FLAT MINOR; PRELUDE NO. 25 IN C SHARP MINOR; SCHERZI 1-4
□ Ashkenazy/*Barcarolle in F; Prelude Op. 45*
  SXL6334 (4/68) Decca
SONATA NO. 2 IN B FLAT MINOR; NOCTURNES, OP. 15, NOS. 1 AND 2; MAZURKA, OP. 59 NO. 2; GRANDE VALSE BRILLANTE
□ Vasary/*Waltzes*
  2726 029 (8/74) DG
SONATA NO. 2 IN B FLAT MINOR
□ Perahia/*Son. 3*
  76242 (7/74) CBS
  M-32780 Columbia
□ Argerich/*Andante spinato; Scherzo 2*
  2530 530 (6/75) DG*
□ Ashkenazy/*Nocturnes 4 and 5; Mazurka 37; Waltz 1*
  SXL6575 (11/72) Decca
SONATA NO. 3 IN B MINOR
□ Perahia/*Son. 2*
  76242 (7/74) CBS
  M-32780 Columbia
VALSE BRILLANTE
□ Ashkenazy
  SXL6575 (11/72) Decca
WALTZES
□ *1-17.* Vasary/*Scherzi*
  2726 029 (8/74) DG
□ *1-14.* Rubinstein
  SB6600 (2/65) RCA
□ *1-14.* S. Askenase
  2548 146 (4/74) DG Heliodor

Below: *Chopin's characteristically neat manuscript: a page from the finale of his Piano Sonata in B minor.*

AARON COPLAND
(b. Brooklyn, N.Y., 1900)

Though Ives » may have preceded him in establishing a specifically American idiom, Copland was the first American composer of serious music in this century to make an impact on the world at large, and all his adult life has occupied a foremost place in musical activities in the USA—not only as composer but as conductor, lecturer, author, festival organiser and musical administrator—in the course of which he has received very numerous honours.

After initial studies in New York, he went to France at the age of 21 and worked for three years with Nadia Boulanger, who on his return was the soloist in his *Symphony for organ and orchestra*. He was the first composer to be awarded a Guggenheim Fellowship, and in 1930 won an RCA Victor award for a *Dance symphony* hurriedly put together from a previous ballet. In this, the 1925 *Music for the theater* and the Piano Concerto of the following year, he employed jazz idioms treated with a Stravinskian pungency; but the vitality and rhythmic vigour which these displayed were soon to be deflected into other channels. Chief among these were works with an "open-air" flavour, sometimes making use of rural folk-music or cowboy songs, such as the ballets *Billy the Kid*, *Rodeo* and the highly evocative *Appalachian Spring*, and the folk opera *The tender land* (1954), and works in which Latin-American styles figured, like the rhythmically ingenious *El Salón México* (1936) and the Clarinet Concerto.

For the most part Copland's works are characterised by a striking economy and transparency of texture, which has made for immediate accessibility when they were intended for functional purposes: his film scores for *Our town* and *The red pony*, for example, have a rare charm, and the poetic *Quiet city*, also derived from a film, has a touchingly tender atmosphere. At other times (as in his Piano Sonata) he has favoured a harsh, austere idiom; and between the two lie such thoughtful but approachable works as his Third Symphony.

Left & above: *Two portraits of Aaron Copland.*

APPALACHIAN SPRING
□ LSO/Copland/*Lincoln Portrait*
  72872 (6/72) CBS
  M-30649 Columbia
□ Philadelphia/Ormandy/*Billy the Kid*
  LSB4018 (7/71) RCA
□ Los Angeles PO/Mehta/*Bernstein; Gershwin*
  SXL6811 (9/76) Decca
BILLY THE KID
□ NYPO/Bernstein/*Rodeo*
  72411 (4/61) CBS
  MS-6175 Columbia
□ LSO/Copland/*Rodeo*
  72888 (2/71) CBS
  M-30114 Columbia
□ Philadelphia/*Appalachian Spring*
  LSB4018 (7/71) RCA
QUIET CITY
□ ASMF/Marriner/*Ives; Cowell; Barber; Creston*
  ZRG845 (7/76) Decca Argo∗
RODEO
□ NYPO/Bernstein/*Billy the Kid*
  72411 (4/61) CBS
  MS-6175 Columbia
□ 4 Dances only. LSO/Copland/*Billy the Kid*
  72888 (2/71) CBS
  M-30114 Columbia
SYMPHONY NO. 3
□ NYPO/Bernstein/*Harris: Symphony 3*
  61681 (6/76) CBS Classics
  MS-6594 Columbia

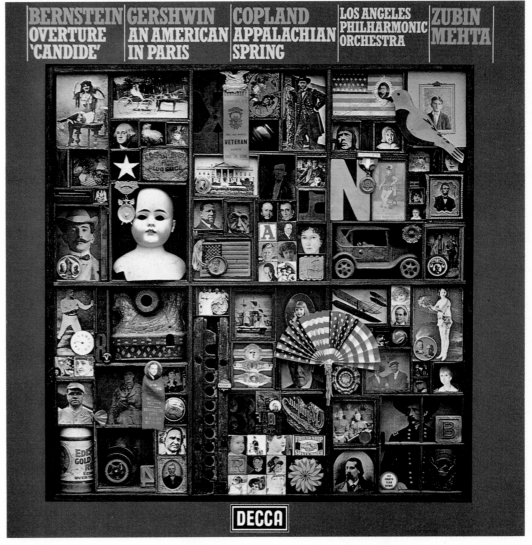

ARCANGELO CORELLI
(b. Fusignano 1653; d. Rome 1713)

Born of a good family, this courteous and cultured musician spent the greater part of his life in Rome, where for about twenty years he directed the regular Monday concerts at the palace of Cardinal Ottoboni which were a focal point of the musical life of the city, and where he was held in the highest esteem; but his fame both as violinist and composer was widespread throughout Europe. His works were published in Antwerp, Amsterdam, Paris and London as well as in Italy: numerous violinists later to be famous came to study with him; and he repeatedly refused invitations from other noble patrons to leave Rome and enter their service, though he did direct performances by an orchestra of 150 players in the Roman palace of Queen Christina of Sweden. When at long last he visited Naples, then the operatic centre of Italy, to play with Alessandro Scarlatti, he was slighted by the King and returned, much mortified, to find that a newcomer seemed to have supplanted him in the public's favour: he was so dejected by all this that he went into a decline.

He was buried in the Pantheon near Raphael—an apt choice since he had associated with the leading painters of his own day and had formed a valuable collection of pictures.

His dignified, elegantly fashioned writing, which featured sequential progressions and chains of suspensions, was channelled into two forms: the baroque trio-sonata and solo sonata, and the four- or five-movement *concerto grosso* (the forerunner of the modern concerto) which contrasted a small solo group of two violins and a cello with the full body of strings. His slow movements in particular have a gentle beauty which relies on the singing quality of the violin that he himself cultivated in his playing; but in the solo sonatas the melodic line of these adagios would have been expected to be embellished according to the conventions of the time.

CONCERTI GROSSI, OP. 6
☐ ASMF/Marriner
ZRG773-5 (9/74) Decca Argo∗
NOS. 1, 8, 9 & 12 ONLY
☐ Naples Scarlatti/Gracis
2533 124 (5/73) DG Archiv Production
VIOLIN SONATAS, OP. 5
☐ Melkus, Dreyfus
2533 132-3 (10/75) DG Archiv Produktion

Right: *Details from a painting after Carlo Maratti of Corelli, one of the greatest names in the history of the violin and virtual creator of the concerto grosso. He influenced the young Handel and was the teacher of such virtuosi as Geminiani and Locatelli.*

Above: *Title-page to the second edition of Corelli's violin sonatas, one of the pillars of string literature.*

FRANÇOIS COUPERIN

(b. Paris 1668; d. there 1733)

Known even in his own lifetime as "le Grand", the appellation serves not only to distinguish François from the rest of the numerous Couperin dynasty (some twelve of whom, over two centuries, were musicians, and at least four composers) but to indicate his renown and the general admiration in which he was held. (Bach » for example studied his works and copied some out.) At the age of eleven he inherited from his father, who had himself inherited it from his brother Louis, the post of organist at St Gervais, which, after putting in Lalande as his deputy, he took over six years later and held for nearly 40 years before passing it on to his cousin Nicolas (whence it was handed down in turn to two more generations of Couperins). After the publication of two organ Masses (versets to alternate with the plainsong of the Ordinary, plus an organ solo at the Offertory), Louis XIV nominated him one of the directors of music of the royal chapel, which included some of the finest instrumentalists of the day, in 1693, following this up the next year by an appointment as harpsichord tutor to the royal children, and two years later ennobled him.

In his capacity as composer to the king he wrote motets, the passionate *Leçons de ténèbres* which are considered the peak of his church music, a series of *Concerts royaux* for the court's Sunday concerts, and, over the years, well over 200 harpsichord pieces, which were published in 27 loosely-organised *ordres* or suites. Couperin was much concerned to try to reconcile the divergent French and Italian styles then current, and this found expression not only in *L'Apothéose de Corelli* and *L'Apothéose de Lully*, which were published together under the significant title *Les Goûts réunis*, but also in *Les Nations*, which consisted of French suites together with Italian trio-sonatas (a form he took over from Corelli »). His music also blends flexible counterpoint and rich harmonic thinking, employing emotional suspensions and inner chromaticisms. But perhaps his chief legacy to posterity lies in his refined and charming harpsichord pieces, almost all of which have fanciful titles and which represent a great diversity of styles—dance forms, chaconnes and passacailles (such as the great B minor example in Ordre No.8 or *L'Amphibie* in No.24), rondeaux, satirical or burlesque pieces, pastorals and character portraits. In this gallery, as in his own personality, urbanity, melancholy and ironic wit are fascinatingly combined.

Left: *An engraving of François Couperin, 'organiste de la chapelle du Roy', in the last decade of his life.*

APOTHEOSE DE LULLY
☐ ECO/Leppard/*Charpentier: Medée*
  SOL300 (10/67) L'Oiseau-Lyre
LIVRES DE CLAVECIN
Book 1-Ordre 4; Book 2-Ordre 6, 11;
Book 3-ordre 13, 18; Book 4-Ordre 24, 26, 27
☐ Dreyfus (harpsichord)/*L'Art de toucher le clavecin*
  EK6 35276 (1/76) Selecta/Telefunken
MESSE PROPRE POUR LES COUVENTS
MESSE SOLENNELLE POUR LES PAROISSES
☐ Weir (organ)
  4BBA1011-2 (6/73) Decca
LES NATIONS
☐ Jacobean Ens.
  OLS137-8 (1/72) L'Oiseau-Lyre

COUPERIN
APOTHÉOSE DE LULLY
CHARPENTIER
SUITE FROM THE OPERA MÉDÉE

ENGLISH CHAMBER ORCHESTRA
RAYMOND LEPPARD

L'OISEAU-LYRE

CLAUDE DEBUSSY
(b. St. Germain-en-Laye 1862; d. Paris 1918)

The adjective "impressionist", borrowed from the art of painting, is commonly applied to Debussy's music. Although he himself disliked the term, his references to the scintillating play of light (eg in writing of his orchestral *Nocturnes*, which have been likened to Whistler's paintings) reveal an uncommon visual sensibility, and his lifelong love of fluid orchestral colours, flexible rhythm, vague tonality, and even of piano tone which should create the illusion of an instrument "without hammers", was very much in accord with the impressionists' outlook. Equally important, however, was the influence of literary symbolists such as Mallarmé, Baudelaire, Verlaine (whose mother-in-law, a pupil of Chopin », had been his first piano teacher) and Maeterlinck, whose *Pelléas et Mélisande* he turned, after ten years' work, into a lyric drama whose quasi-naturalistic word-setting and orchestral and emotional reticence make it a landmark in operatic development.

As a student at the Paris Conservatoire he had rebelled against orthodox harmony teaching but had managed to win the Prix de Rome at his third attempt, although his self-indulgent temperament and dislike of routine impelled him to leave Rome after only two of the prescribed three years. One cause of his restlessness may have been that his current mistress, to whom he dedicated his first set of *Fêtes galantes*, was still in Paris: Debussy's hedonistic and sensual nature was later to be responsible for a hectic love-life which resulted in the attempted suicide of his first wife when he eloped with another woman. In his twenties he had undergone a variety of musical influences—the Russians, particularly Mussorgsky », the Javanese *gamelang* he heard at the 1889 Exposition Universelle, and above all Wagner », under whose spell he fell (like many of his compatriots), only to shake himself free later: during the 1914 war, indeed, when he published the three instrumental sonatas written in an unusually elliptical and finely-chiselled style, he assertively described himself on their title-pages as "musicien français".

It is, however, his compositions in the twenty years between 1893, the year of his string quartet and the

CHILDREN'S CORNER SUITE
☐ Michelangeli
   2530 196 (12/71) DG∗
ESTAMPES; MAZURKA; DANSE BOHEMIENNE; MASQUES; IMAGES; TARANTELLE STYRIENNE; D'UN CAHIER D'ESQUISSES
☐ Frankl
   TV37023S (7/72) Decca Turnabout
ETUDES 1-12
☐ Jacobs
   H71322 (9/76) WEA/Nonesuch∗
ETUDES—BOOKS 1 AND 2; L'ISLE JOYEUSE
☐ Frankl
   TV37025S (7/72) Decca Turnabout
IMAGES—BOOKS 1 AND 2; NOCTURNE; LA PLUS QUE LENTE; LA BOITE A JOUJOUX
☐ Frankl
   TV37026S (7/72) Decca Turnabout
IMAGES (1. Gigues, 2. Iberia, 3. Rondes de printemps)
☐ Boston SO/Tilson Thomas/*Prelude*
   2530 145 (5/72) DG
JEUX
☐ NPO/Boulez/*Prelude, La Mer*
   72533 (6/67) CBS
   MS-7361 Columbia
☐ SRO/Ansermet/*Nocturnes; Danse*
   ECS816 (4/78) Decca Eclipse
   STS-15022 London
LA BOITE A JOUJOUX
☐ SRO/Ansermet/*Dukas*
   SDD293 (11/71) Decca Ace of Diamonds
LA MER
☐ Berlin PO/Karajan/*Prelude; Ravel*
   138 923 (3/65) DG∗
☐ NYPO/Boulez/*Prelude a l'Apres-midi d'un faune; Jeux*
   72533 (7/67) CBS
☐ Philh./Giulini/*Nocturnes*
   SXLP30146 (8/72) EMI/HMV
   S-35977 Angel
☐ Concertgebouw/Haitink/*Prelude a l'Apres-midi d'un faune; Clarinet Rhapsody; Marche ecossaise*
   9500 359 (4/78) Phonogram
NOCTURNES (1, Nuages, 2. Fetes, 3. Sirenes)
☐ Chorus/Philh./Giulini/*La Mer*
   SXLP30146 (8/72) EMI/HMV
   Concert Classics
   S-35977 Angel
☐ Chorus/New Philh./Boulez/*Printemps; Clarinet Rhapsody*
   72785 (4/71) CBS

Left: *Debussy charted a quite new course in music.*

evocative *Prélude à l'Après-midi d'un faune* (there were originally to have been two other sections besides the Prelude to go with Mallarmé's poem), and 1913, when he wrote *Jeux* for Diaghilev's Russian Ballet, for which Debussy is best remembered and which so powerfully affected the course of music. He loosened the hold of traditional harmony by employing "forbidden" progressions and unrelated chords, leaving dissonances unresolved, and making extensive use of the whole-tone and pentatonic scales and of the old church modes. His piano music, particularly the *Estampes* and the two books of *Préludes* (whose imaginative titles were added *after* they were composed) and of *Images*, called for a new palette of keyboard colours, including a new pedal technique. Apart from works already mentioned, his compositions for orchestra include two other masterpieces—the large-scale *La Mer*, which despite its wonderfully impressionistic sound-painting has an underlying classical structure, and the second orchestral *Image* entitled *Ibéria*, which, like the piano *La Puerta del Vino* and *Soirée dans Grenade*, captures an authentic Spanish atmosphere although he had spent only a single day across the Spanish border.

Above: *Debussy at 22, when he won the first Prix de Rome.*

☐ Chorus/SRO/Ansermet/*Jeux; Danse*
  ECS816 (4/78) Decca Eclipse
☐ NE Cons. Chorus/Boston SO/Abbado/ *Ravel*
  2530 038 (12/70) DG★
ORCHESTRAL WORKS
☐ Berceuse heroique; La boite a joujoux; Children's Corner Suite; Danses sacree et profane; Fantaisie for piano and orchestra; Images; Jeux; Khamma; La mer; Marche ecossaise; Nocturnes; Petite Suite; La plus que lente; Prelude a l'Apres-midi d'un faune; Printemps; Clarinet Rhapsody; Saxophone Rhapsody; Le Roi Lear; Tarantelle styrienne
☐ National ORTF/Martinon
  SLS893 (2/75) (5 discs) HMV
  S-37064 Angel
PELLÉAS ET MELISANDE
☐ Soderstrom, Shirley, Minton, McIntyre, Ward, Covent Garden Op/Boulez
  77324 (10/70) CBS
  MS-30119 Columbia
PRELUDES—COMPLETE
☐ Kars
  3BB107-8 (11/71) Decca
☐ *Book 1 only. Rev.*
  SAGA5391 (3/75) Saga
PRELUDE A L'APRES-MIDI D'UN FAUNE
☐ Berlin PO/Karajan/*La Mer, Ravel*
  138923 (3/65) DG★
☐ New Phil./Boulez/*La Mer; Jeux*
  72533 (7/67) CBS
  MS-7361 Columbia
☐ LSO/Monteux/*Nocturnes; Ravel*
  SDD425 (9/74) Decca Ace of Diamonds
  STS-15356 London
☐ SRO/Ansermet/*La Mer; Petite Suite; etc.*
  SPA231 (6/72) Decca
☐ Concertgebouw/Haitink/*La Mer; Clarinet Rhapsody; Marche ecossaise*
  9500 359 (4/78) Phonogram
☐ Strasbourg PO/Lombard/*Faure; Ravel; Roussel*
  STU70889 (1/76) RCA/Erato
PRINTEMPS
☐ New Philh./Boulez/*Nocturnes; Clarinet Rhapsody*
  72785 (4/71) CBS

PROSES LYRIQUES
☐ Gomez, Constable/*Berlioz; Bizet*
  SAGA5388 (1/75) Saga
RHAPSODY FOR CLARINET
☐ de Peyer, New Philh./Boulez/ *Nocturnes; Printemps*
  72785 (4/71) CBS
SONATA FOR CELLO AND PIANO
☐ Rostropovich, Britten/*Britten, Schumann*
  SXL2298 (1/62) Decca
  6237 London
SONATA FOR FLUTE, VIOLA AND HARP
☐ Melos Ens./*Ravel; Roussel; Ropartz*
  SOL60048 (9/62) L'Oiseau-Lyre★
SONATA FOR VIOLIN AND PIANO
☐ Hasson, Isador/*Faure: Son. 1*
  CFP40210 (6/75) Classics for Pleasure
☐ Wallez/Rigutto/*Faure; Ravel*
  7174 (8/76) Selecta/French Decca
STRING QUARTET IN G MINOR
☐ Quartetto Italiano/*Ravel*
  SAL3643 (5/68) Phonogram
  835361 Philips
☐ Parrenin Qt./*Ravel*
  HQS1231 (10/70) EMI/HMV
  2103 Connoisseur Society
SUITE BERGAMASQUE
☐ Adni/*Recital*
  HQS1262 (5/72) EMI/HMV
SUITE BERGAMASQUE; HOMMAGE A HAYDN; VALSE ROMANTIQUE; LE PETIT NEGRE; BERCEUSE HEROIQUE; CHILDREN'S CORNER SUITE; POUR LE PIANO
☐ Frankl
  TV37024S (7/72) Decca Turnabout

LÉO DELIBES
(b. St Germain du Val 1836; d. Paris 1891)

So great an admirer of Delibes was Tchaikovsky » that he declared his own *Swan lake* ballet music to be "poor stuff" measured against the former's *Sylvia*: indeed, he went further and wrote in a letter that the Frenchman was a composer of talent with whom the "dry *routinier*" contemporary Germans (presumably Brahms » and Wagner ») were not to be compared. Delibes was in fact the first to raise the standard of ballet music from the low level into which it had sunk. He had been a pupil at the Paris Conservatoire of Adolphe Adam, the composer of the ballet *Giselle* and of several light operas, who secured him a job as *répétiteur* at the Théâtre Lyrique at the age of 17: this immediately spurred him to compose operettas, of which he produced about fifteen in as many years.

In his late twenties he was appointed a *répétiteur*, then a chorus-master, at the Opéra, and started to write ballets. The two acts he contributed to *La Source* were so successful—they were later used on their own under the title *Naïla*—that he was promptly invited to compose a complete ballet by himself. The result was the delightful comedy *Coppélia* (1870), whose wealth of elegant melody and delicately coloured orchestration made it an instant popular favourite; and it has so remained with ballet companies throughout the world ever since. The larger-scale mythological ballet *Sylvia*, six years later, was regarded by some ballet critics of the time as too symphonic, but the suite extracted from it has certainly kept its place in the concert repertoire. Delibes's operas have not held the stage, except (in France) *Lakmé*: this followed the fashion of the time in choosing an exotic setting, a faintly absurd India under English rule, and contains much charming music but is remembered mainly by the "Bell Song", a favourite with coloratura sopranos.

Above: *Delibes rescued ballet music from its lowly state.*

COPPELIA
□ *Cpte.* Minneapolis SO/Dorati
6780 253 (11/75) Phonogram
2-77004 Mercury
□ *Exc.* Berlin PO/Karajan/*Chopin*
2535 189 (1/77) DG Privilege
COPPELIA (exc.); SYLVIA (exc.)
□ SRO/Ansermet
SPA314 (7/74) Decca
6185 London

LAKME .
□ Sutherland, Vanzo, Clement, Sinclair, Berbie/Monte Carlo Opera/Bonynge
SET387-9 (5/69) Decca
1391 London

Right: *Poster for the Paris première of* Sylvia, *1876.*

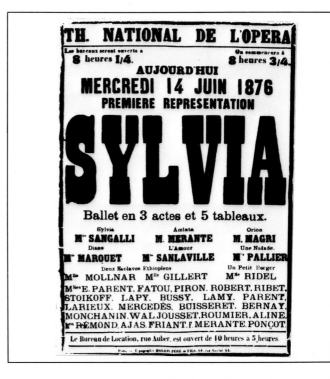

FREDERICK DELIUS
(b. Bradford 1862; d. Grez-sur-Loing 1934)

Delius presents the curious case of a composer whose music is recognisably and essentially English — "Shelley, Wordsworth and Keats could not call forth the magic of the English landscape with greater certitude", one musician has declared — yet who left England at the age of 21 to avoid going into his father's wool business, briefly emigrated to Florida (where he neglected his orange plantation for music), went to study desultorily in Leipzig for a couple of years, and then spent the remaining 46 years of his life in seclusion in France, where his work remained, and still remains, almost unknown. Moreover, most of his compositions received their first performance not in his native England, which was slow to appreciate them, but in Germany. Living aloof from the world as he did, his music would not have made its way in England without the indefatigable and redoubtable championship of Sir Thomas Beecham, whose performances captured their subtle and elusive character with astonishing empathy; and fortunately several of his unrivalled recordings are still current. Delius also owed much to the devotion of a young musician, Eric Fenby, who was so appalled to learn that the composer, though mentally alert, had become blind and paralysed (in which condition he spent the last decade of his life) that in 1928 he went to live with him as his amanuensis and in impossibly difficult conditions — Delius's sufferings intensified his egotism, his impatience and his acid tongue — laboriously took down several compositions from dictation.

By temperament, strengthened by his haphazard musical education, Delius had no use for orthodox harmonic or contrapuntal procedures. Intent largely on the expression of poetic pantheistic meditations, he favoured a sensuously impressionistic idiom, rich in texture, with fluid chromatic harmonies (although essentially tonal), for which he usually demanded a very large orchestra: there is little rhythmic variety in his work, and for structural purposes he frequently relied on more or less overt variation form (as in the well-known *Brigg Fair*, and the nostalgic *Appalachia* for chorus and orchestra, both based on folksongs). In mood his music ranges from the gently idyllic, as in *On hearing the first cuckoo in Spring*, to the ecstatic, as in the Violin Concerto and *Song of the high hills*, often imbued with a sense of regretful yearning, as in his masterpiece *Sea-drift*. His Nietzschean choral works *A Mass of Life* and *Requiem* are vehicles for his rationalist philosophy. His operas, though never successful on the stage, are well suited to the gramophone, and the rapturous *Walk to the Paradise Garden*, an interlude from *A Village Romeo and Juliet*, is the perfect epitome of his individual style.

APPALACHIA
☐ Ambrosian Singers/Halle/Barbirolli/ *Brigg Fair*
   ASD2635 (2/71) EMI/HMV
   S-36756 Angel
BRIGG FAIR; SONG BEFORE SUNRISE; MARCHE CAPRICE; ON HEARING THE FIRST CUCKOO IN SPRING; SUMMER NIGHT ON THE RIVER; SLEIGH RIDE; FENNIMORE AND GERDA (INTERMEZZO)
☐ RPO/Beecham
   ASD357 (8/60) EMI/HMV
CELLO CONCERTO
☐ Du Pre/RPO/Sargent/*Elgar: Cello Conc.*
   ASD2764 (3/72) EMI/HMV
(A) DANCE RHAPSODY NO. 2
☐ RPO/Beecham/*Florida Suite; Over the hills and far away*
   HQS1126 (4/68) EMI/HMV

IN A SUMMER GARDEN; HASSAN (INTERMEZZO AND SERENADE); A SONG BEFORE SUNRISE; LA CALINDA; ON HEARING THE FIRST CUCKOO IN SPRING; SUMMER NIGHT ON THE RIVER; LATE SWALLOWS
☐ Halle/Barbirolli
   ASD2477 (7/68) EMI/HMV
   S-36588 Angel
KOANGA
☐ Lindsey, Allister, Erwen, Holmes, Herincx, Estes/Alldis Choir/Groves
   SLS974 (6/74) HMV
MASS OF LIFE
☐ Harper, Watts, Tear, Luxon/LPO & Choir/Groves
   SLS958 (3/72) HMV
   S-3781 Angel
PARIS
☐ RLPO/Groves/*Eventyr: Dance Rhapsody No. 1*
   ASD2804 (8/72) EMI/HMV
   S-36870 Angel
A VILLAGE ROMEO AND JULIET
☐ Harwood, Tear, Shirley-Quirk, Luxon, Mangin/Alldis Choir/RPO/Davis/ *Talk by Fenby*
   SLS966 (2/73) HMV
   S-3784X Angel
VIOLIN SONATAS NOS. 1-3
☐ Holmes, Fenby/*Talk by Fenby*
   UNS258 (5/73) Unicorn

Right: *The blind and paralysed Delius towards the end of his life. Painting by Ernest Procter, from the National Portrait Gallery.*

ERNÖ DOHNÁNYI
(b. Pozsony 1877; d. New York 1960)

Though of the same generation as his compatriots Bartók » and Kodály », Dohnányi took no part in their quest for roots in genuine Hungarian folk music and had little sympathy with their aims, giving his allegiance firmly to the orthodox German tradition of Brahms »: indeed, he even preferred to use the German version of his name, which appears as Ernst von Dohnányi on most of his published compositions. He was educated musically in his native town, now called Bratislava, and in Budapest; at the age of 20 he won a prize for his first symphony and made his début as a pianist in Berlin and Vienna, being hailed at once as a player of the first rank. He toured extensively, with great success, in Europe, England and the USA, taught in Berlin for seven years, became director of the Budapest Conservatory in 1919 and director of the Hungarian Radio in 1931. After the Second World War he found himself in bad political odour and left Hungary for good, settling first in Argentina and then in the USA, where he spent the final decade of his life.

His music, without being particularly distinctive, is always notable for its fine craftsmanship and mellifluousness; and there is often — as in the Brahmsian *Rhapsody in C* for piano and his most popular work, the *Variations on a nursery song* for piano and orchestra, which contains the most elaborate leg-pull and deliberate bathos in the repertory — an element of somewhat Teutonic humour. Among his other works which are heard from time to time are a melodious orchestral *Suite in F sharp minor*, a short orchestral suite entitled *Symphonic minutes*, a suite from the ballet *The Veil of Pierrette*, a very Brahmsian violin sonata and a *Serenade* for string trio. His few attempts to create a nationalist Hungarian atmosphere, as in the *Ruralia Hungarica* suite, are, for all their surface attraction, pale beside the genuine article emanating from his contemporaries.

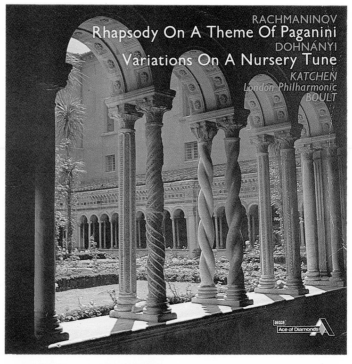

VARIATIONS ON A NURSERY SONG FOR PIANO AND ORCHESTRA
☐ Katchen, LPO/Boult/*Rachmaninov; Rhapsody*
   SDD428 (10/74) Decca Ace of Diamonds
☐ Ortiz/New Philh./Koizumi/ *Rachmaninov; Rhapsody*
   ASD3197 (6/76) EMI/HMV
   S-37178 Angel
☐ Siki/Seattle SO/Katims/*Suite*
   TV4623S (2/77) Decca Turnabout★
   34623 Turnabout
SUITE IN F SHARP MINOR
☐ Seattle SO/Katims/*Variations*
   TV34623S (2/77) Decca Turnabout★

Left: *Pianist, conductor, composer, educationist and radio administrator, Dohnányi was more German in his allegiances than Hungarian.*

GAETANO DONIZETTI
(b. Bergamo 1797; d. there 1848)

Even among composers renowned for their facility and speed Donizetti, a musician of uncommon amiability and modesty (unlike his rival Bellini »), occupies a special place: in the 25 years of his active career he produced nearly 70 operas, often at the rate of three a year. The entertainingly farcical one-act operetta *Il Campanello*, for example, was written (libretto as well as music) in nine days; on a larger scale and in more serious style, the last act of *La Favorite* — one of his very finest — took only a few hours! It is true that subtleties of harmony in his work are few, but his melodic freshness and stage sense, particularly his dramatic irony, are striking; his instrumentation is more original than is usually recognised, as is his structure, and his technical fluency is illustrated by such examples as the masterly sextet in *Lucia di Lammermoor*.

He had in fact received a sound musical training, and after a successful début in Venice as an operatic composer at the age of 21 (actually with his fourth stage work) he was invited by theatres in all the chief operatic centres in Italy to compose for them, and produced 30 works in twelve years. In 1830 he won European fame with *Anna Bolena* — a work of astonishingly mature design — in Milan: its libretto presents rather less garbled history (and geography) than do many of his romantic tragedies. Like all his principal works, it was tailored to the star singers of his time, to whom it offered superb opportunities for the vocal display demanded by the public. A particular vehicle for such pyrotechnics was the "mad scene" for the heroine, as in *Lucia di Lammermoor* and *Linda di Chamounix* — a feature later to become the subject of parody; but the scene of the distracted Anne Boleyn in prison is of an altogether less conventional and superficial kind.

The ensuing five years brought forth several notable dramatic operas, including *Lucrezia Borgia* (to which Victor Hugo, author of the play on which it was based, later objected), *Maria Stuarda* and *Lucia di Lammermoor*, as well as the delightful rustic comedy *L'Elisir d'amore*. A brush with the Neapolitan censors caused him to transfer his activities to Vienna (where he was appointed a composer to the court, for which he wrote a *Miserere* and *Ave Maria*) and Paris, the scene of his triumphs with *La Fille du régiment* and *La Favorite* (both in 1840) and, three years later, *Don Pasquale*, one of the great comic masterpieces of the repertoire.

Left: *Donizetti's romantic tragedies were far more numerous than his comedies, but much his most popular opera today is the sparkling* Don Pasquale.

Below: *Fantasias on Donizetti's operas abounded.*

DON PASQUALE *(Cpte.)*
☐ Sciutti, Oncina, Mercuriali, Krause, Corena, Vienna State Opera Chorus and Orch./Kertesz
SET280-1 (4/65) Decca
1260 London
☐ Maccianti, Benelli, Basiola, Mariotti/ Maggio Musicale Fiorentino Chorus and Orch./Gracis
2705 039 (2/75) DG Privilege
LA FILLE DU REGIMENT *(Cpte.)*
☐ Sutherland, Sinclair, Pavarotti, Malas, Covent Garden/Bonynge
SET372-3 (11/68) Decca
1273 London
L'ELISIR D'AMORE *(Cpte.)*
☐ Domingo, Cotrubas, Wixell, Evans, Covent Gdn/Pritchard
79210 (11/77) CBS
LUCIA DI LAMMERMOOR *(Cpte.)*
☐ Sutherland, Milnes, Pavarotti, Ghiaurov, Covent Garden/Bonynge
SET528-30 (5/72) Decca
13103 London

☐ Sutherland, Cioni, Merrill, Siepi/ Maggio Musicale Fiorentino/Pritchard
GOS663-5 (1/76) Decca Ace of Diamonds
1327 London
MARIA STUARDA *(Cpte.)*
☐ Sutherland, Tourangeau, Pavarotti, Soyer/Bologna Teatre Communale Ch. and Orch./Bonynge
D2D3 (6/76) Decca
13117 London

PAUL DUKAS
(b. Paris 1865; d. there 1935)

To the musical world at large Dukas is a "one-work" composer, the work in question being his brilliant orchestral scherzo based on Goethe's ballad *The Sorcerer's apprentice*: although this hugely popular piece is essentially programmatic, it is equally satisfying on its own terms as music, making its effect by its rhythmic vitality and vivid scoring. In fact, Dukas left a very small output to posterity, not so much because he came late to music and because his published works, with the exception of the 1911 *La Péri* (a concert work conceived for dancing), occupied a mere fifteen years of his life, as because his extreme self-criticism led him to destroy most of his compositions—not just those of this youth but a large number from his maturity. All his life he was a very acute and perceptive professional critic for a number of musical periodicals, and his intellectual integrity would not allow him to release any works of his own which did not meet his exacting and perfectionist standards: he preferred to act as a stimulating mentor to his pupils, who included Albéniz » and Messiaen» and who held him in reverence and affection.

He had been a fellow-student with Debussy » at the Paris Conservatoire, and showed a predilection for dramatic subjects with some early overtures, including one to Corneille's *Polyeucte*: in 1897 his three-movement Symphony in C, a romantic work of classical poise which proclaimed its roots in Franck », was performed, and *The Sorcerer's apprentice* started on its triumphant progress.

A monumental piano sonata of Beethovenian weight and ancestry, and a more elegant piano *Variations, interlude et final* on a theme by Rameau » (some of whose stage works he edited), plus a handful of songs and instrumental pieces, make up the tally of his works except for his opera *Ariane et Barbe-bleue*. Musicians as unlike in their tastes as Sir Thomas Beecham and Bruno Walter, among others, have declared this darkly symbolic but luminous-textured and beautifully orchestrated work, for which Maeterlinck himself fashioned the libretto from his play, one of the finest lyric dramas of the early twentieth century, worthy to be placed beside Debussy's *Pelléas et Mélisande*.

Right: *A single work by Dukas is hugely popular at the expense of others equally fine.*

LA PERI
☐ Czech PO, Almeida/*Sorcerer's Apprentice; Polyeucte Ov.*
110 1560 (7/76) Rediffusion/Supraphon
(The) SORCERER'S APPRENTICE
☐ Israel PO/Solti/*Rossini: Boutique*
SPA374 (9/75) Decca
☐ CBSO/Fremaux/*Ravel; Chabrier; Saint-Saens; Debussy*
ASD3008 (9/74) EMI/HMV
☐ SRO/Ansermet/*Honegger, Ravel*
SXL6065 (2/64) Decca
6367 London
☐ LPO/Weller/*Symphony*
SXL6770 (6/76) Decca
6995 London

SYMPHONY IN C
☐ Paris ORTF/Martinon/*Ariane et Barbe-bleue; Honegger: Pastorale d'ete*
ASD2953 (7/74) EMI/HMV
2134 Connoisseur Society
VARIATIONS, INTERLUDE AND FINALE ON A THEME BY RAMEAU
☐ Johannesen
STGBY671 (11/74) Decca Vox

72

ANTONIN DVOŘÁK
(b. Nelahozeves, nr. Prague, 1841; d. Prague 1904)

Like Schubert ≫, Dvořák was one of the great "naturals" of music—a seemingly inexhaustible spring of melody and delightful invention bubbled out of him through-out his career: the fact that many of his most spontaneous-sounding ideas were very carefully worked out and polished does not detract from the freshness of their impact. Dvořák has always made an immediate appeal by reason of his uncomplicated sincerity, his combination of abounding vitality with an innocent tenderness, his charming orchestral colouring, and his sense of poetry and of the sunny open-air atmosphere of Nature. The rustic Bohemian landscape in which he had spent his childhood (he was one of the large family of a village innkeeper and butcher) was an ever-present element in his music, and it was indeed by this that he first caught the ear of the outside world; but what has assured his place in music-lovers' affections is the basic optimism of his works, notwithstanding a strong vein of autumnal nostalgia.

After studying in a neighbouring small town and then in Prague, Dvořák earned his living for nine years as a viola player in the Czech Provisional Theatre in Prague, composing prolifically in his spare time but not showing

Below: *Dvořák in 1886, two years after his first English visit.*

Above: *Dvořák's manuscript title-page and opening of the* Slavonic Dances.

CARNIVAL OVERTURE
☐ LSO/Kertesz/*Scherzo capriccioso; In Nature's realm; Othello*
   SXL6348 (7/68) Decca
CELLO CONCERTO IN B MINOR
☐ Tortelier/Philh./Sargent
   SXLP30018 (12/63) EMI/HMV
☐ Rostropovich/BPO/Karajan/ *Tchaikovsky*
   139 044 (10/69) DG*
☐ Rostropovich/RPO/Boult
   SXLP30176 (1/75) EMI/HMV
   S-60136 Seraphim
☐ Harell/LSO/Levine
   ARL1 1155 (2/76) RCA*
MASS IN D, OP. 86
☐ Christ Church Cathedral Choir, Oxford/Preston
   ZRG781 (12/74) Decca Argo*
PIANO QUARTETS—No. 1 in D; No. 2 in E flat
☐ Trampler, Beaux Arts Trio
   6500 452 (1/74) Phonogram
PIANO QUINTET IN A, OP. 81
☐ Curzon/VPO Quartet/*Schubert*
   SDD270 (4/71) Decca Ace of Diamonds
PIANO TRIO NO. 4 IN E MINOR (DUMKY)
☐ Czech Trio/*Novak: Pno. Trio*
   111 1089 (11/74) Rediffusion/Suprapho
☐ Smetana Piano Trio/*Suk; Elegy*
   111 0234 (7/75) Rediffusion/Supraphon
☐ Yuval Piano Trio/*Smetana*
   2530 594 (3/76) DG*
RUSALKA *(Exc.)*
☐ *O silver moon:* Streich, Berlin RIAS/ Gaebel/*Recital*
   136011 (3/59) DG
SCHERZO CAPRICCIOSO
☐ LSO/Kertesz/*Carnival Ov.; In Nature's realm; Othello*
   SXL6348 (7/68) Decca
SERENADE IN D MINOR, OP. 44
☐ Netherlands Wind Ens/Waart/ *Gounod; Schubert*
   6500 163 (5/71) Phonogram

his work to any but his closest associates. However, by 1873, when he had unexpected success with a patriotic cantata, he had given up his job and devoted himself entirely to composition and teaching. Up till then there had been a recognisably Wagnerian tinge to his music, notably in the Third and Fourth Symphonies (it should be explained that the now current numbering of the symphonies follows their chronological order); but now Dvořák began to acknowledge the strength of his Bohemian heritage and to adopt national dance-forms such as the furiant and polka, as well as the Ukrainian *dumka* form—a melancholy movement with quick interludes. The innocently happy String Serenade and the Fifth Symphony (whose pastoral atmosphere and woodwind birdsong—which was to become one of his fingerprints—still owe something to Wagnerian forest music) date from the year in which he was awarded a State grant, but the real change in his fortunes came when Brahms », struck by his *Moravian duets*, used his good offices to find him a publisher and befriended him. Brahms's influence is to be heard in his next symphony (No. 6); but Dvořák, highly conscious of his nationality, resisted his publisher's attempts to Germanise his first name and held firmly to Czech folk sources in such works as the piano-duet *Slavonic dances*, *Legends* and the *Hussite* overture.

Increasingly widespread success—the *Slavonic dances* created a furore throughout Europe—eventually brought a new serenity to Dvořák's music. In 1884 he made the first of numerous visits to England, a country which enormously helped to spread his renown and strengthen his financial status: his *Stabat Mater* there led the way to several further commissions, such as the unusually taut and virile Symphony No.7 in D minor (almost certainly his finest) and the cantata *The Spectre's bride*, and to first performances there of the lyrical G major Symphony (No.8) and

the *Requiem*. In 1891 he became a professor at the Prague Conservatory (and ten years later its director), but after only a year he sought and obtained leave to take up the directorship of the National Conservatory of Music in New York. In the USA, where he also spent some time in the Czech colony in Spillville, Iowa, he listened with interest to Indian and Negro themes, but his music in fact shows an intensified yearning for his native country. To that period belong his last symphony, whose great popularity is partly due to the accident of its having a title, *From the New World;* the now so-called "American" String Quartet; the splendid String Quintet in E flat; and the Cello Concerto (unquestionably the greatest work for that medium in the whole repertory of music), the long sunset glow of whose coda, where Dvořák seems unable to tear himself away from his meditations, is very typical. After his return home almost his only compositions were a series of symphonic poems, marked by highly imaginative orchestration, on rather grisly Czech legends, and three further operas (taking his total up to ten), including the only one to make any headway outside Czechoslovakia, the tragic fairy-tale *Rusalka*.

□ LSO/Kertesz/*Brahms*
  SXL6368 (2/69) Decca
  6594 London
SERENADE FOR STRINGS IN E
□ ASMF/Marriner/*Grieg: Holberg Suite*
  ZRG670 (11/70) Decca Argo⋆
□ LSO/Davis/*Symphonic Vars*
  SAL3706 (2/69) Phonogram
□ Hamburg RO/Schmidt-Isserstedt/
  Tchaikovsky; Serenade
  2548 121 (4/75) DG Heliodor
□ ASMF/Marriner/*Tchaikovsky:*
  Serenade
  ZRG848 (7/76) Decca Argo⋆
□ ECO/Leppard/*Tchaikovsky*
  9500 105 (3/77) Phonogram⋆
□ ECO/Kubelik/*Smetana: Má Vlast (excs)*
  2538 313 (7/74) DG Privilege
SLAVONIC DANCES OP. 46 (1-8); OP.
72 (9-16)
□ *1-16:* Czech PO/Neumann/*Czech*
  Suite; Wood Dove; Slav Rhapsodies
  FT6 35075 (12/72) Selecta/Telefunken⋆
□ *1-16:* Cleveland/Szell/*Carnival Ov./*
  Smetana: Bartered Bride (excs)
  78299 (8/76) CBS
  MS-7208 Columbia
□ *1-16:* Czech PO/Neumann
  PFS4396 (12/77) Decca Phase 4
□ *1-8:* Bavarian RSO/Kubelik/*Scherzo*
  2530 466 (11/75) DG⋆
□ *9-16:* Bavarian RSO/Kubelik/*My*
  Home Ov.
  2530 593 (12/75) DG⋆
□ *1, 3, 8, 9, 10:* Israel PO/Kertesz/
  Smetana
  SPA202 (8/72) Decca
□ *1, 3, 8, 9, 10:* VPO/Reiner/*Brahms*
  SPA377 (5/76) Decca
SLAVONIC DANCES, OP. 46 & 72;
LEGENDS, OP. 59 (FOR TWO
PIANOS)
□ Lesek, Leiskova
  111 1301-2 (7/75) Rediffusion/
  Supraphon
STRING QUINTET IN E FLAT
□ Vienna Octet/*String Sextet*
  SDD315 (3/72) Decca Ace of Diamonds
  STS-15242 London
STRING QUARTET NO. 6 IN F
(AMERICAN)
□ Quartetto Italiano/*Borodin Qt. 2*
  SAL3708 (5/69) Phonogram
□ Janacek Quartet/*Qt. Op. 34*
  SDD250 (2/71) Decca Ace of Diamonds
□ Gabrieli Quartet/*Borodin*
  CFP40041 (8/73) Classics for Pleasure
□ Prague String Quartet/*Qt. No. 7*
  2530 632 (4/76) DG
STRING SEXTET IN A
□ Vienna Octet/*String Quintet*
  SDD315 (3/72) Decca Ace of Diamonds
  STS-15242 London
SYMPHONY NO. 5 IN F, OP. 76
□ LSO/Kertesz/*My Home*
  SXL6273 (3/67) Decca
SYMPHONY NO. 6 IN D, OP. 60
□ Berlin PO/Kubelik
  2530 425 (12/74) DG⋆
□ RPO/Groves
  ASD3169 (5/76) EMI/HMV
SYMPHONY NO. 7 IN D MINOR,
OP. 70
□ LSO/Kertesz
  SXL6115 (10/64) Decca
□ Berlin PO/Kubelik
  2530 127 (10/71) DG⋆
□ LSO/Monteux
  ECS779 (7/76) Decca Eclipse
  STS-15157 London
□ Concertgebouw/C. Davis
  9500 132 (2/77) Phonogram⋆
SYMPHONY NO. 8 IN G, OP. 88
□ LSO/Kertesz/*Scherzo*
  SXL6044 (7/63) Decca
□ VPO/Karajan
  SDD440 (2/75) Decca Ace of Diamonds
  6443 London
□ BPO/Kubelik
  139181 (3/67) DG⋆
SYMPHONY NO. 9 IN E MINOR, OP. 95
□ LSO/Kertesz/*Othello*
  SXL6291 (11/67) Decca

□ Berlin PO/Karajan
  138922 (1/64) DG⋆
□ VPO/Kertesz
  SPA87 (10/70) Decca
  STS 15101 London
□ Philh./Giulini/*Carnival Ov.*
  SXLP30163 (7/74) EMI/HMV
  S-60045 Seraphim
□ Berlin PO/Kubelik
  2530 415 (9/74) DG⋆
□ New Philh./Dorati
  PFS4128 (1/68) Decca Phase 4
  21025 London
SYMPHONIC VARIATIONS, OP. 78
□ LSO/Davis/*Serenade in E minor*
  SAL3706 (2/69) Phonogram
VIOLIN CONCERTO IN A MINOR
□ Suk/Czech PO/Ancerl/*Romance*
  50026 (5/62) Rediffusion/Supraphon
□ Perlman/LPO/Barenboim/*Romance*
  ASD3120 (10/75) EMI/HMV
  S-37069 Angel

Right: *Czech music reached*
the world through Dvořák.

No 2.

To my friend
Granville Bantock.

Titolo originale voll poter esser Score

"Pomp and circumstance"

Military Marches

Edward Elgar.

No 1 in D Major   (Quick march)
No 2 in A minor, (Quick march.)
No 3.
4.
5.
6.

Edward Elgar.
Birchwood Lodge
nr Malvern.

EDWARD ELGAR
(b. Broadheath, nr. Worcester, 1857; d. Worcester 1934)

The characterisation of Elgar's music as "epitomising the Edwardian era" is not inapposite, although two of his major works precede Edward VII's accession, but this by no means tells the whole story. Against the broad, opulent canvases of uninhibited emotionalism, the confidently expansive mood, the frequent use of the direction *nobilmente*, the exuberance which could spill over into brashness (as in the *Cockaigne* overture and, still more, in the *Pomp and circumstance* marches) must be set lyrical and intimate works like the elegiac Cello Concerto or the delicate *Serenade for strings*. It cannot be denied, also, that Elgar was guilty of writing pot-boilers and banal "occasional" works, and that his solo songs show little sensitivity to the quality or rhythm of words; but many of his lightweight miniatures have an engaging wistful charm. He was, in fact, a more complex character than might appear, and even his critics cannot gainsay his status as the greatest English composer of the turn of the century.

Left: *Title-page of Elgar's score of a popular march.*

Below: *Elgar always remained a countryman at heart.*

EDWARD ELGAR

He received little formal musical education, but learned to play the organ, bassoon and violin and assimilated a good deal in his father's music shop and from local amateur activities. Disappointed in his ambition to become a solo violinist, he played in orchestras, picked up practical experience with diverse amateur organisations and as an organist at the local Roman Catholic church, where he succeeded his father, and began to compose. Encouraged by his wife (his social superior) he turned his thoughts to more ambitious works, and after some initial frustrations attracted attention when, at the age of 33, his romantic overture *Froissart* (which already showed the mastery of orchestral writing which was to be one of his strengths) was played at the Three Choirs Festival. This led to a number of choral works, of rather conventional character, at Worcester and elsewhere, including the oratorio *Caractacus* for Leeds, before his first great triumph in 1899, the *Variations on an original theme* (called "Enigma" not because each variation delineated one of his friends, who were soon identified, but because

Left: *Elgar's own recordings of his works, though inevitably dated in sound quality, are much to be treasured.*

Below: *Elgar's work-desk in the study of his birthplace in Worcestershire, now kept as a museum.*

Elgar declared the theme to be a counter-melody to another whose identity he never divulged and which has provoked endless inconclusive speculation). He followed this up immediately with the oratorio *The Dream of Gerontius*, based on Cardinal Newman's poem (a copy of which he had been given as a wedding present a decade earlier); and though the first performance in Birmingham was a disaster, the work aroused tremendous enthusiasm in Germany and called forth a tribute from Richard Strauss » to "the first English progressive musician".

The wider recognition this sparked off led to his being invited to write a *Coronation ode* (for which a tune in the first *Pomp and circumstance* march was fitted out with words to become the celebrated *Land of hope and glory*), to a knighthood in 1904, and the following year to a chair of music specially created for him in the University of Birmingham. Meanwhile he had written two oratorios— *The Apostles* and *The Kingdom*—of a projected trilogy which was never completed: their contemplative, rather than dramatic, nature has impeded their general acceptance, though the latter is considered by some to be at least the equal of the far more popular *Gerontius*. But this was the start of a phase in which he produced a whole series of

major works—the tautly incisive *Introduction and Allegro* for strings, the two vast-scale symphonies (the first of which achieved about 100 performances in its first year), the long and intensely heartfelt Violin Concerto, and the brilliantly programmatic "symphonic study" *Falstaff*.

The First World War took the gilt off the gingerbread of the militaristic swagger of his early works, and after it he produced little more than some chamber music and the touchingly beautiful Cello Concerto. With the death of his wife he lost all urge to compose: he was appointed Master of the King's Music in 1924, but nothing further of any consequence came from his pen except the *Severn Suite* as a test piece for a brass-band festival.

(The) APOSTLES
☐ Armstrong, Watts, Tear, Luxon, Grant, Case/LPO and Choir/Boult/ *Illustrated talk by Boult*
SLS976 (11/74) HMV
2094 Connoisseur Society
☐ Zukerman/LPO/Barenboim
76528 (11/76) CBS
☐ Menuhin/LSO/Elgar (rec. 1932)
HLM7107 (4/77) EMI/HMV
☐ Chung/LPO/Solti
SXL6842 (10/77) Decca

CONCERTO IN E MINOR FOR CELLO AND ORCHESTRA
☐ Tortelier, LPO/Boult/*Introduction and Allegro; Serenade*
ASD2906 (9/73) EMI/HMV
S-37029 Angel
☐ Du Pré/LSO/Barbirolli/*Sea Pictures*
ASD655 (12/65) EMI/HMV
☐ Du Pre/Philadelphia/Barenboim/ *Enigma*
76529 (11/76) CBS
M-34530 Columbia

Below: *Elgar at work on one of his orchestral scores.*

EDWARD ELGAR

(The) DREAM OF GERONTIUS
☐ Watts, Gedda, Lloyd, Alldis Choir,
LPO Choir, New Philh./Boult
SLS987 (5/76) HMV
FALSTAFF
☐ New Philh./A. Davis/*Enigma
Variations*
SRCS77 (9/75) Lyrita
**IN THE SOUTH—OVERTURE,
OP. 50**
☐ Bournemouth SO/Silvestri/*Vaughan
Williams*
ESD7013 (10/76) EMI/HMV
**INTRODUCTION AND ALLEGRO
FOR STRINGS**
☐ London Sinfonia/Barbirolli/*Elgar,
Vaughan Williams*
ASD521 (5/63) EMI/HMV
S-36101 Angel
☐ ECO/Britten/*Bridge; Britten;
Delius; Purcell*
SXL6405 (6/69) Decca
6618 London
☐ LPO/Boult/*Cello Conc.; Serenade*
ASD2906 (8/73) EMI/HMV
S-37029 Angel

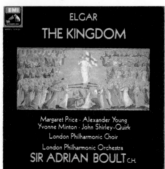

(The) KINGDOM
☐ Price, Minton, Young, Shirley-Quirk/
LPO and Choir/Boult
SLS939 (4/69) HMV
2089 Connoisseur Society
MINIATURES
☐ Minuet; May-Song; Rosemary;
Romance for bassoon and orch;
Sevillana; Mazurka; Serenade
mauresque; Contrast; Serenade
lyrique; Mina
Northern Sinfonia/Marriner
ESD7009 (11/76) EMI/HMV
**OVERTURES: COCKAIGNE;
FROISSART; IN THE SOUTH;
OVERTURE IN D MINOR (HANDEL
ORCH. ELGAR)**
☐ LPO/Boult
ASD2822 (9/72) EMI/HMV
OVERTURE, COCKAIGNE
☐ Philh./Barbirolli/*Enigma*
ASD548 (11/63) EMI/HMV
S-36120 Angel
**POMP AND CIRCUMSTANCE
MARCHES NOS. 1-5, OP. 39**
☐ New Philh./Barbirolli/*Elegy; Sospiri;
Froissart Ov.*
ASD2292 (12/66) EMI/HMV
S-36403 Angel
☐ RPO/Del Mar/*Enigma*
2535 217 (10/76) DG Privilege
SEA PICTURES
☐ Baker/LSO/Barbirolli/*Cello Conc.*
ASD655 (12/65) EMI/HMV

SERENADE IN E MINOR
☐ Sinfonia of London/Barbirolli/
*Introduction and Allegro; Vaughan
Williams*
ASD521 (5/63) EMI/HMV
S-36101 Angel
☐ LPO/Boult/*Cello Conc.; Introduction
and Allegro*
ASD2906 (8/73) EMI/HMV
S-37029 Angel
SYMPHONY NO. 1 IN A FLAT
☐ LPO/Solti
SXL6569 (8/72) Decca
6789 London
☐ LPO/Boult
ASD3266 (4/77)
S-37240 Angel
☐ SNO/Gibson
LRL1 5130 (9/76) RCA

SYMPHONY NO. 2 IN E FLAT
☐ LPO/Boult
SRCS40 (10/68) Lyrita
S-37218 Angel
☐ LPO/Solti
SXL6723 (6/75) Decca
6941 London
☐ LPO/Boult
ASD3266 (10/76) EMI/HMV
SEVERN SUITE
☐ Grimethorpe Colliery Band/Howarth/
Bliss, Holst, Ireland
SXL6820 (5/77) Decca

**VARIATIONS ON AN ORIGINAL
THEME (ENIGMA)**
☐ Philh./Barbirolli/*Cockaigne*
ASD548 (11/63) EMI/HMV
S-36120 Angel
☐ LSO/Monteux/*Brahms*
SPA121 (6/71) Decca
☐ LSO/Boult/*Vaughan Williams*
ASD2750 (11/71) EMI/HMV
☐ LPO/Haitink/*R. Strauss: Don Juan*
6500 481 (3/75) Phonogram*
☐ LSO/Jochum/*Brahms: Haydn Vars.*
2530 586 (12/75) DG*
☐ RPO/Del Mar/*Pomp & Circumstance
Marches 1-5*
2535 217 (10/76) DG Privilege
☐ LPO/Barenboim/*Cello Conc.*
76529 (11/76) CBS
M-34530 Columbia
**THE WAND OF YOUTH—SUITES
NOS. 1-2, CHANSON DE NUIT,
CHANSON DE MATIN, BAVARIAN
DANCES**
☐ LPO/Boult
ASD2356 (3/68) EMI/HMV

MANUEL DE FALLA
(b. Cadiz 1876; d. Alta Gracia, Argentina, 1946)

Incomparably the greatest of the Spanish composers of the early twentieth century, Falla succeeded in stamping his music with an unmistakably Spanish character without falling into the cliché-ridden style of the nationalist movement's lesser lights; and his subtle sense of orchestral sonorities removes it altogether from their facile travel-poster coloration. He studied with Felipe Pedrell, the musician chiefly responsible for the belated renaissance of music in Spain, who had a profound effect on his pupils by his advocacy of a study of the country's folk-music and its early composers. In 1905 Falla won a prize awarded by the Madrid Academy of Fine Arts with his opera *La Vida breve*, in which the colourful background is of more significance than the action; but no production followed, and the work received its première eight years later—outside Spain. In 1907 he went to Paris, where he lived for seven years, and was befriended by Debussy », Dukas » and Ravel ».

The intensely atmospheric *evocación* of his music following this period, in which the Andalusian side of his heredity gained from his association with impressionism but was balanced by a naturally concise and clean-cut style, is evidenced in the 1915 ballet *El Amor brujo* ("Wedded by witchcraft"), the symphonic impressions for piano and orchestra called *Nights in the gardens of Spain*, and the spirited, amusing and ever-fresh ballet *The Three-cornered hat*, produced in its final form by Diaghilev in 1919.

But then a marked change to a drier, more incisive style came over his music with the *Fantasia Bética* for piano and the little opera *Master Peter's puppet show* (on an episode from *Don Quixote*), which reveals the influence of the neo-classic movement headed by Stravinsky ». Falla had by this time moved to Granada, where he organised a festival of the traditional *canto jondo* of Andalusia and wrote the highly concentrated concerto for harpsichord and five instruments whose slow movement is a quint-essential expression of his religious mysticism. He had always been so fastidious and self-critical a composer that his output remained small; but around the age of 50 his ascetic nature caused him increasingly to withdraw from society and virtually to cease writing. Disturbed by political developments in Spain in the early 1930s, he retired first to Majorca and then, in 1940, to Argentina: in his last twenty years he worked desultorily on a large-scale cantata, *L'Atlàntida*, which however he left unfinished at his death.

EL AMOR BRUJO
☐ De Los Angeles, Philh./Giulini/
Three-Cornered Hat
SXLP30140 (8/72) EMI/HMV Concert
Classics
HARPSICHORD CONCERTO
☐ Kipnis/NYPO/Boulez/*Three-Cornered
Hat*
76500 (8/76) CBS
M-33970 Columbia
MASTER PETER'S PUPPET SHOW
☐ Bermejo, Munguia, Torres/Spanish
Nat Orch/Argenta/*El Amor Brujo*
SDD134 (2/66) Decca Ace of Diamonds
**NIGHTS IN THE GARDENS OF
SPAIN**
☐ Rubinstein, Philadelphia/Ormandy/
Saint-Saens: Pno. Conc. 2
SB6841 (12/70) RCA
LSC-3165 RCA
☐ Soriano/Paris Cons./Burgos/*La
vida breve (exc.): El amor (exc.);
Turina*
SXLP30152 (11/72) EMI/HMV
Concert Classics

PIANO WORKS (Fantasia Betica;
Homenaje a Paul Dukas; Serenata
Andaluza; Vals Capricho)
☐ Achucarro
TRL1 7073 (12/76) RCA
SEVEN SPANISH POPULAR SONGS
☐ Berganza, Lavilla/*Spanish song recital*
SDD324 (10/72) Decca Ace of
Diamonds
(The) THREE CORNERED HAT
☐ Cpte. Berganza/SRO/Ansermet
SDD321 (4/72) Decca Ace of
Diamonds
☐ Cpte. De Los Angeles,
Philh./Frühbeck de Burgos
SXLP30187 (2/76) EMI/HMV
Concert Classics
S-36235 Angel
☐ Suites 1 and 2 only: Philh./Giulini/*El
Amor Brujo*
SXLP30140 (8/72) EMI/HMV
Concert Classics

Right: *Manuel de Falla.*

GABRIEL FAURÉ
(b. Pamiers, Ariège, 1845; d. Paris 1924)

It has been well said of Fauré that the intimate spirit of chamber music permeates all his work: he was the very personification of that coolly reticent, cultivated, delicately lyrical style which is regarded as typically French. From his teacher Saint-Saëns ≫, to whom he acknowledged his indebtedness, he derived the classical outlook he maintained throughout his life, unaffected either by Wagnerism or impressionism; and though the influence of Schumann ≫ is discernible in his early works, such as the warm-hearted Piano Quartet No.1, it was transmuted and much refined. Curiously enough, he wrote no organ music although for most of his life he was an organist — at Rennes, later as Widor's assistant at the important Paris church of St Sulpice, and finally at the Madeleine (after nearly twenty years there as choirmaster) in 1896. That same year he was appointed professor of composition at the Paris Conservatoire, of which institution he became director just under ten years later: he retained this post until 1920, when the increasing deafness from which he had suffered for many years caused him to resign. His gentle good nature and kindliness had endeared him to his numerous pupils, who included Ravel ≫ and many other leading composers; some of them assisted him in the orchestration of his works — a task in which, again rather curiously, he took little interest.

He first made his mark with a number of songs of exquisite sensibility, notable for the long-spun melodic lines and subtly daring harmonic progressions which were to be characteristic of him: even such early examples as *Après un rêve* and *Lydia* are among the most elegant examples of French song-writing. From these he moved into chamber music: his first violin sonata however — which might be thought reminiscent of Franck's ≫ except that the latter's was written a decade later — found only a publisher not prepared to pay him either a fee or any royalties (a rapacious treatment also meted out—by another publisher—to his two piano quartets). His piano music, cast in small poetic forms, albeit of classical structure, and mostly labelled *Barcarolle*, *Impromptu* or *Nocturne*, began to appear in 1883 and, for all its evident roots in Chopin ≫, has an unmistakably individual texture. The lovely and serene *Requiem*, one without the terrors of the Last Judgment, was written in 1887. Then Fauré's thoughts began to turn towards to stage: he wrote incidental music for two plays in Paris, including *Shylock*, before being invited to do the same for the London production of Maeterlinck's *Pelléas et Mélisande* (four years before the appearance of Debussy's opera on that play). Only after that did he venture into the field of opera, significantly taking his subjects from Hellenic mythology—*Prométhée* and *Pénélope*. His later songs and such works as the second violin sonata, the two cello sonatas and the piano trio are marked by a greater sobriety, even austerity, of style.

Above: Gabriel Fauré at the age of 50, sketched by Sargent.

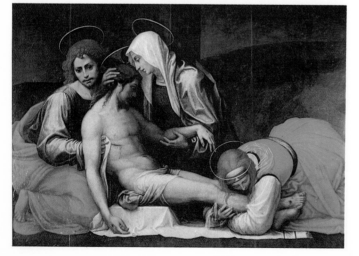

FAURÉ REQUIEM
KING'S COLLEGE CHOIR, CAMBRIDGE
NEW PHILHARMONIA ORCHESTRA
John Carol Case & Robert Chilcott (TREBLE)
DAVID WILLCOCKS

BALLADE FOR PIANO AND ORCHESTRA
☐ Ogdon/CBSO/Fremaux/*Litolff: Scherzo; Saint-Saens: Carnival*
ASD2753 (2/72) EMI/HMV
527 Klavier
FANTAISIE FOR PIANO AND ORCHESTRA
☐ Larrocha/LPO/Fruhbeck de Burgos/ *Ravel*
SXL6680 (11/74) Decca
6878 London
PAVANE, OP. 50
☐ Edinburgh Festival Chorus, Paris/Barenboim/*Requiem*
Q4ASD3065 (6/75) EMI/HMV
Quadraphonic
S-37077 Angel
PELLEAS ET MELISANDE—SUITE; MASQUES ET BERGAMASQUES; PENELOPE—PRELUDE
☐ SRO/Ansermet/*Debussy*
SDD388 (7/74) Decca Ace of Diamonds
6227 London
☐ *Pelleas only:* Strasbourg PO/ Lombard/*Debussy; Ravel; Roussel*
STU70889 (1/76) RCA/Erato
PIANO QUARTET NO. 1 IN C MINOR
☐ Pro Arte Piano Quartet/*Piano Trio*
SOL289 (8/66) L'Oiseau-Lyre

PIANO TRIO IN D MINOR
☐ Pro Arte Piano Quartet/*Piano Quartet No. 1*
SOL289 (8/66) L'Oiseau-Lyre
REQUIEM, OP. 48
☐ Chilcott, Case/NPO/Willcocks/ *Pavane*
ASD2358 (3/68) EMI/HMV
☐ Clement, Huttenlocher, Chorus, Berne SO/Corboz
STU70735 (6/73) RCA/Erato
SONATAS FOR CELLO AND PIANO: NO. 1 IN D MINOR, NO. 2 IN G MINOR
☐ Tortelier/Heidsieck/*Cello and piano works*
ASD3153 (3/76) EMI/HMV
SONGS: Chanson d'amour; Barcarolle; En priere; Poeme d'un jour; Apres un reve; Nell; Le secret; Clair de lune
☐ I. Partridge/J. Partridge/*Duparc: Songs*
SHE524 (2/76) Pavilion/Pearl
SONGS: La bonne chanson, Op. 61; Three songs, Op. 23; Cinq melodies, Op. 58; Fleur jetee, Op. 39 No. 2; Les roses d'Ispahan, Op. 39 No. 4
☐ Palmer/Constable
ZRG815 (8/76) Decca Argo
☐ Souzay/Baldwin/*Duparc*
HQS1258 (6/72) EMI/HMV
VIOLIN SONATA NO. 1
☐ Hasson/Isador/*Debussy: Violin Son.*
CFP40120 (7/75) Classics for Pleasure

CHORALE NO. 2 IN B MINOR
PIECE HEROIQUE
☐ Simon Preston/*Messiaen, Widor*
ZRG5339 (3/63) Decca Argo
PIANO QUINTET IN F MINOR
☐ Curzon, Vienna Philh. Quartet
SDD277 (10/71) Decca Ace of
Diamonds
PRELUDE, ARIA ET FINALE
PRELUDE, FUGUE ET VARIATION
☐ Crossley
DSL08 (5/76) L'Oiseau-Lyre
PSYCHE
☐ Czech PO/Fournet
50674 (9/67) Rediffusion/Supraphon
SONATA IN A FOR VIOLIN AND
PIANO
☐ Perlman, Ashkenazy/*Brahms: Horn
Trio*
SXL6408 Decca
6628 London

SYMPHONIC VARIATIONS FOR
PIANO AND ORCH.
☐ Curzon/LPO/Boult/*Grieg, Litolff*
SXL2173 (2/60) Decca
☐ Larrocha, LPO/Fruhbeck de
Burgos/*Khachaturian*
SXL6599 (6/73) Decca
6818 London
☐ R. Casadesus, Philadelphia/Ormandy/
Symphony
61356 (10/73) CBS Classics
SYMPHONY IN D MINOR
☐ Paris Orch./Karajan
ASD2552 (9/70) EMI/HMV
S-36729 Angel
☐ Philadelphia/Ormandy/*Sym.
Variations*
61356 (10/73) CBS Classics
☐ Dresden Staatskapelle/Sanderling
2548 132 (10/75) DG Heliodor
☐ Berlin RSO/Maazel
2535 150 (4/76) DG Privilege
☐ RCA Victor SO/Boult
GL25004 (10/76) RCA Gold Seal

Left: *The devout César Franck.*

CÉSAR FRANCK
(b. Liège 1822; d. Paris 1890)

Few composers' lives have been less eventful than that of this deeply religious, unworldly organist, who was so beloved by his pupils: indeed, almost the only disturbance to his placid, hard-working existence was on his wedding day, during the 1848 revolution, when in order to reach the church he and his bride had, with the help of amused insurgents, to be helped over a barricade.

He was born of Flemish stock and studied in his native Liège and then in Paris, where his father was anxious for him to become a piano virtuoso; but the political turmoil of the time was not conducive to such a life. Though he tried for a while to reach a compromise with his own desires to compose by writing showy piano fantasias, his natural bent showed itself in a biblical eclogue; and with his marriage he broke away altogether from paternal pressures. He made a habit of rising every morning at 5.30 and writing for a couple of hours before becoming immersed in his teaching. He was organist at a couple of smaller Paris churches before being appointed in 1858 to St Clotilde, where he had previously been choir-master; in 1872 he became organ professor at the Conservatoire, where he upset his fellow professors not only by his naive candour but by helping his organ students in composition

with embarrassing success. The public's almost complete indifference to his music and the lack of official recognition, though it irked his pupils, seemed not to worry him: in his modest way he was not even put out by poor performances on the rare occasions when his works were given at all. It is characteristic that when he won his first real success (at the age of 68!) with his String Quartet, he mildly remarked, "You see, the public is beginning to understand me".

Though Franck's output was uneven and included some banal and over-sentimental pieces, his last ten years saw the creation of nearly all his best works. These include the impassioned *Prélude, chorale et fugue* for piano, which shows the influence of Liszt » (who was so overcome by the brilliance of his organ extemporisation that he compared him with Bach »); the imaginative and mysterious *Les Djinns* for piano and orchestra, which he followed up with the romantic *Variations symphoniques* for the same combination; the Violin Sonata, whose finale provides one of the best-known canons in musical literature; the contemplative *Psyché* and the expansive Symphony, which like many of his works is in cyclic form, and whose inclusion of a cor anglais deeply agitated the diehards; and the three organ chorales.

ROBERTO GERHARD
(b. Valls, nr.Tarragona, 1896; d. Cambridge 1970)

Gerhard began to study music seriously only at the age of 19, in Barcelona, after a false start in commercial life in Switzerland. He took piano lessons from Granados » and composition from Pedrell (who had taught Falla »), before becoming for five years a pupil of Schoenberg » in Vienna and Berlin. In the early 1930s he taught at the Escola Normal in Barcelona, was appointed music librarian at the Biblioteca Central there, edited much eighteenth-century Catalan music and took an active part in musical administration. On the defeat of the Republicans in the Spanish Civil War he first stayed in Paris and then, in 1939, settled in self-imposed exile in Cambridge, where he spent the last 30 years of his life quietly composing, with occasional lecturing visits to the USA.

A musician of penetrating intellect and of cultivated literary and philosophical tastes, he was for many years appreciated only by a minority; but it can confidently be asserted that he is the only post-Falla Spanish composer of the front rank. The Spanish character of his music shines through his use of Schoenbergian dodecaphony (which theory he extended to rhythmic parameters, as in his Second Symphony); but his employment of serialism was highly personal, relying often on a recognisable harmonic basis and always on a singularly acute ear and original mind. It was typical of him that he should urge people to *listen* to music rather than look at it in a score or analyse it.

He first attracted attention as a composer in pre-war meetings of the International Society for Contemporary Music; but the bulk of his work, and certainly the best of it, dates from his days in England. *Don Quixote*, expanded from a concert suite into a ballet, and the lighter-weight Andalusian ballet *Alegrías* were followed in 1948 by the opera *The Duenna*, a sparkling and eclectic score combining neo-classic pastiche, Spanish dance-rhythms and atmospheric dodecaphony. A kaleidoscopic First Symphony intervened in a series of concertos, successively for violin, piano and harpsichord, in the 1950s; then his interest in electronics, which had been fanned by a number of brilliantly craftsmanlike and evocative incidental music scores for radio, theatre and films, led to the Third Symphony and *The Plague* (based on Camus), where tape is used in conjunction with the orchestra. A final cycle of chamber works with zodiacal titles—*Gemini*, *Leo* and *Libra*—had autobiographical connotations.

GEORGE GERSHWIN
(b. Brooklyn, N.Y., 1898; d. Hollywood 1937)

Coming from a humble home and showing no special interest in music until his teens, Gershwin had piano lessons for only three years before becoming, at the age of sixteen, a song-plugger for a firm of popular music publishers. While thus employed, he started to write musical shows and songs (winning a huge commercial success with *Swanee*), but hankered after more ambitious compositions. His chance came in 1924 when the bandleader Paul Whiteman commissioned *Rhapsody in blue* for piano (to be played by Gershwin himself, a tirelessly self-indulgent pianist) and orchestra: its then novel crossing of jazz with diluted Liszt caused so much stir that he was promptly asked to write a "real" concerto for the New York Symphony Society. Whether or not it is true that his first reactions were to look up the word "concerto" in a musical dictionary and buy a book on orchestration (for *Rhapsody in blue* had been scored by one of Whiteman's arrangers), he certainly took some lessons in orchestration; and the Concerto shows an advance in technique, though still some uncertainty over large-scale construction.

It is not entirely without significance that his best extended works came when he finally severed his dependance on the piano as a participating instrument; he reached a new level with the more symphonic *American in Paris* (whose splendid broad blues tune scandalised the earnestly progressive International Society for Contemporary Music) and, particularly, the 1935 Negro opera *Porgy and Bess*. In these, as well as in the stream of immensely successful musical shows and, later, films he produced from the mid-1920s (many to his brother Ira's lyrics), his distinctive invention and inbuilt feeling for melodic contour, coupled with a natural ebullience and sincerity of sentiment, lifted him far out of the class of his light music contemporaries.

ASTROLOGICAL SERIES—GEMINI;
LEO; LIBRA
□ London Sinfonietta/Atherton
 HEAD11 (8/77) Decca Headline
CONCERTO FOR ORCHESTRA
□ BBC SO/Del Mar/*Rawsthorne: Sym. 3*
 ZRG553 (3/68) Decca Argo
DON QUIXOTE—DANCES
□ BBC SO/Dorati/*Sym. 1*
 ZRG752 (10/74) Decca Argo∗
SYMPHONY NO. 1
□ BBC SO/Dorati/*Don Quixote*
 ZRG752 (10/74) Decca Argo∗
SYMPHONY NO. 4
□ BBC SO/C. Davis/*Violin Concerto*
 ZRG701 (2/72) Decca Argo∗
VIOLIN CONCERTO
□ Neaman/BBC SO/C. Davis/*Sym. 4*
 ZRG701 (2/72) Decca Argo∗

Left: *Roberto Gerhard, the most
distinguished of modern Spanish
composers, who spent the last 30
years of his life in self-imposed
exile in Cambridge.*

AMERICAN IN PARIS
□ St. Louis SO/Slatkin/*Porgy and
 Bess—Suite: Promenade*
 TV37081S (7/75) Decca Turnabout
 SVBX 5132 Vox
□ LSO/Previn/*Piano Conc.; Rhapsody
 in Blue*
 ASD2754 (11/71) EMI/HMV
 S-36810 Angel
□ Los Angeles PO/Mehta/*Bernstein;
 Copland*
 SXL6811 (11/71) Decca
 7031 London

Left: *Gershwin hit the jackpot
early on with Swanee.*
Above: *Gershwin, the authentic
voice of urban America.*

□ NYPO/Thomas/*Rhapsody*
 76509 (2/77) CBS
 XM-34205 Columbia
**CONCERTO IN F FOR PIANO AND
ORCHESTRA**
□ Previn/LSO/*American in Paris;
 Rhapsody in Blue*
 ASD2754 (11/71) EMI/HMV
 S-36810 Angel
□ Siegel/St. Louis SO/Slatkin/*Porgy
 and Bess—Suite; American in Paris*
 TV37080S (7/75) Decca Turnabout
 SVBX 5132 Vox
□ Szidon, LPO/Downes/*Bernstein:
 West Side Story*
 2535 210 (8/77) DG Privilege
PRELUDES NOS.1-3
□ Watts/*Song book; Rhapsody in Blue*
 76508 (9/76) CBS
 M-34221 Columbia

PORGY AND BESS
□ *(Cpte.)* White, Mitchell, Boatwright,
 Quivar/Cleveland Ch. and
 Orch./Maazel
 SET609-11 (4/76) Decca
 13116 London
**'FOR GEORGE AND IRA'—A
SELECTION OF SONGS**
□ Frances Gershwin (with piano
 accompaniment)
 SH208 (9/74) EMI/World Records
RHAPSODY IN BLUE
□ Katchen/LSO/Kertesz/*Prokofiev;
 Ravel*
 SXL6411 (5/70) Decca
□ Previn/LSO/*Piano Conc.; American
 in Paris*
 ASD2754 (11/71) EMI/HMV
 S-36810 Angel

□ Siegel/St. Louis SO/Slatkin/*Second
 Rhapsody; I got rhythm*
 TV37082S (7/75) Decca Turnabout
 SVBX 5132 Vox
□ Gershwin/Columbia Jazz Band/
 Thomas/*American*
 76509 (2/77) CBS
 XM-34205 Columbia
□ Watts (piano solo version)/*Preludes;
 Song book*
 76508 (9/76) CBS
 M-34221 Columbia
SONGBOOK
□ Watts/*Preludes; Rhapsody in Blue*
 76508 (9/76) CBS
 M-34221 Columbia

ALEXANDER GLAZUNOV
(b. St Petersburg 1865; d. Paris 1936)

Out of Glazunov's abundant output, the handful of his compositions that has remained in the repertoire is characterised by a broad and relaxed mellifluousness, a romantic warmth (which can verge on the sentimental), and accomplished craftsmanship of a very high order. Some of his eight symphonies and the early symphonic poem *Stenka Razin* are heard occasionally, but much his most popular works are the attractive Violin Concerto of 1904—which presents great technical challenges even to virtuoso players—and his ballet *The Seasons*. In denigrating his music as "academic" and "bourgeois", Soviet authorities express their disapproval of his having left Russia in 1928 to live in Paris and their disappointment that, as it has been expressed, he turned out to be "a Russian composer of music rather than a composer of Russian music".

Yet he had started off meteorically. On the recommendation of Balakirev ≫ he was accepted at the age of 15 as a private pupil by Rimsky-Korsakov ≫, and within eighteen months, thanks to his natural talent, aided by a phenomenal musical memory, had completed his course of composition; when Balakirev conducted the 16-year-old boy's first symphony it was hailed as showing outstandingly precocious maturity. But despite his training and his later occasional use of exotic material, Glazunov was drawn less towards the Russian nationalists than to the Germanic classical tradition, at least in the matter of musical form, with the result that as time passed his works seemed increasingly conservative. At the age of 40 he became director of the St Petersburg Conservatory, where he had already been a professor, and his administrative duties greatly slowed down his production. These responsibilities became still more onerous after the Revolution, when he reorganised the Leningrad Conservatory; and virtually nothing more came from his pen until the Saxophone Concerto, written in the last year of his life.

RAYMONDA
□ Bolshoi Theatre Orch/Svetlanov
  SLS826 (8/72) HMV
  S-40172 Melodiya/Angel
THE SEASONS, OP. 67—BALLET SUITE
□ PCO/Wolff/*Balakirev*
  ECS642 (6/72) Decca Eclipse
  STS-15108 London
VIOLIN CONCERTO IN A MINOR
□ Heifetz/RCA Orch./Hendl./*Bruch*
  LSB4061 (6/72) RCA
  LSC4011 RCA
□ Morini/Berlin RSO/Fricsay/*Bruch*
  2548 170 (11/75) DG Heliodor

Left: *A portrait of Alexander Glazunov by Ilya Repin, from the Russian State Museum, Leningrad. In that city he was director of the Conservatoire for 22 years: this diverted a great deal of his energy from composition.*

MIKHAIL GLINKA
(b. Novospasskoye, Smolensk, 1804; d. Berlin 1857)

The current dearth of recommendable recordings of Glinka's music, and its rare appearance in the concert-hall, should not lead us to suppose that, beyond its seminal influence both on the Russian nationalist school and on Tchaikovsky ≫, it is lacking in intrinsic merit. It is true that all his life Glinka was something of a rich dilettante (though eventually with a very sound technique), but he was much more than an interesting historical figure. In his childhood, spent on his father's country estate, he had been entranced by the folk music of the peasants; and when, after desultory studies and a few years in cultivated St Petersburg society, he travelled in Italy for his delicate health and came into contact with its leading operatic composers, the idea struck him of writing a truly national Russian opera.

He undertook a short but concentrated course of study in Berlin and then, returning to St Petersburg, composed his patriotic opera *Ivan Susanin* at speed (far outpacing his librettist): after some initial resistance, it was produced in 1836 in the presence of the imperial family (who persuaded him to change the title to *A Life for the Tsar*). Its freshness and its original combination of Italian lyrical grace with national-type Russian and Polish music (to point up the dramatic conflict between the two sides) won general approval, apart from some aristocratic sneers at its "coachmen's music". During the next couple of years, while he was choirmaster to the Imperial Chapel, he started on a second opera, *Ruslan and Ludmila;* but poor health and marital upsets delayed its completion. When it was produced in 1842 it failed to please, though in fact it was musically superior, and its fantastic subject and employment of Persian, Turkish and Tartar themes were to have a powerful influence on Balakirev ≫ and his circle.

The disappointed composer went off on a visit to Paris, where he was consoled when Berlioz ≫, whom he much admired, praised his originality and turned his thoughts towards purely orchestral music. Travelling on to Spain, he was fascinated by its folk music, which he subsequently turned to good use in *A Night in Madrid* and the *Jota aragonesa*. In the course of the further European wanderings with which he passed his time he wrote the popular *Kamarinskaya*, based on a traditional Russian wedding dance.

RUSLAN AND LUDMILA—OVERTURE
□ LSO/Solti/*Borodin, Mussorgsky*
  SXL6263 (2/67) Decca
  6785 London
□ Berlin PO/Solti/*Borodin, Mussorgsky*
  SPA257 (7/73) Decca
  6944 London

Below: *The monument to Glinka in Smolensk.*

CHRISTOPH WILLIBALD GLUCK

(b. Erasbach, nr. Neumarkt, 1714; d. Vienna 1787)

The son of one of the Elector of Bavaria's foresters, Gluck at first received a sketchy musical education in Prague, which he supplemented only in his mid-twenties when he was taken to Italy as a member of a nobleman's orchestra. There he heard much opera and, after studying for four years with Sammartini, an enormously prolific and accomplished composer, began himself to write operas after the traditional Italian model: in four years some ten were produced with fair success in Milan and other northern Italian cities. He then travelled to Paris, where he met Rameau », and to London, where his skill as a performer on the glass harmonica met with more appreciation than did a couple of operas he hastily wrote there—London, after all, was in thrall to Handel », then at the height of his powers. Handel was critical, though not unfairly or unkindly, of Gluck's lack of counterpoint; and his advice that he should adopt a more direct style did not go unheeded.

After touring extensively with an itinerant opera company, Gluck married a wealthy banker's daughter in Vienna and became director of a nobleman's orchestra: he had the good fortune so to please the Emperor with one of his stage pieces that this led to his appointment as musical director to the court. For the Imperial Opera he wrote half a dozen formal Italian works, and then, when the fashion changed, adroitly switched to light operas in French (one of which, *La Rencontre imprévue*, influenced Mozart's » *Abduction from the Seraglio*): his ballet *Don Juan* also dates from this time. But under the influence of literary collaborators Gluck was trying to turn away from the stiff conventions and stock artificialities which had dominated opera.

His *Orfeo ed Euridice* (1762) was strikingly original in its straightforward presentation of the story, without subplots, and achieved a greater continuity and more homogeneous texture by doing away with *secco* recitative (i.e. declamation to harpsichord accompaniment). Its static, even statuesque, quality was to be typical of Gluck's new style, which aimed at the nobility and grandeur of Greek classicism. He followed this up with *Alceste*, in which he developed his reformist theories of "dramatic truth" (for example, the overture broke with tradition by setting the mood of the subsequent drama) and deliberately sought to do away with the florid ornamentation introduced to pander to the vanities of singers: the whole function of the music, Gluck declared, was to serve the poetry. After a further work, *Paride ed Elena*, in which he sought an even greater simplicity, he went in 1773 to Paris, where his former pupil Marie Antoinette was now Dauphine. Stimulated by the imagination and superior powers of construction of French librettists, he produced in rapid succession *Iphigénie en Aulide*, whose first scene is one of his finest; *Orphée*, a revised version of *Orfeo*, but now with a tenor hero instead of a castrato; a revision of *Alceste* with extra choruses and ballets; *Armide*, in which, unusually, Gluck successfully portrayed passion and sensuous charm; and his masterpiece, *Iphigénie en Tauride*, whose overture depicts the storm about to engulf Orestes' ship.

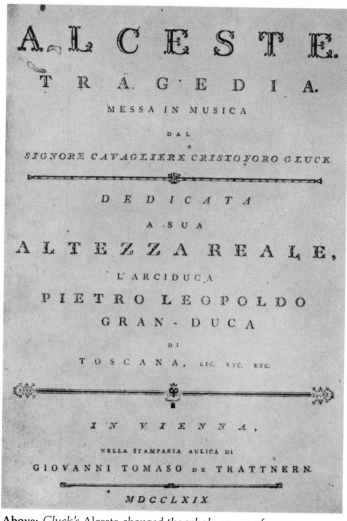

Above: *Gluck's* Alceste *changed the whole course of opera.*

DON JUAN—BALLET
☐ ASMF/Marriner
  SXL6339 (1/69) Decca
  STS-15169 London
OPERATIC ARIAS
☐ (**Alceste**— Divinites du Styx. **Armide** —Le perfide Renaud. **Iphigenie en Aulide**—Vous essayez en vain; Adieu, Conservez dans votre ame. **Orfeo ed Euridice**—Che puro ciel; Che faro senza Euridice. **Paride ed Elena**—

Spiagge amate; Oh, del mio dolce ardor; Le belle imagini; Di te scordarmi. **Le Rencontre Imprevue**— Bel inconnu; Je cherche a vous faire) Baker/ECO/Leppard
9500 023 (10/76) Phonogram*
ORFEO ED EURIDICE
☐ *Cpte.* Verrett, Moffo, Raskin/Virtuosi di Roma/Fasano
  SER5539-41 (9/66) RCA
  LSC-6169 RCA

Right: *Gluck, who brought about reforms in Italian opera.*

CHARLES GOUNOD
(b. Paris 1818; d. St Cloud 1893)

The phenomenal popularity of *Faust* for the first 70 years or so of its existence—it was far and away the most frequently performed opera in the repertory, thanks largely to the succession of star singers who made it a vehicle for their art—had two consequences: it eventually produced an inevitable reaction, so that on the few occasions when the work is now given it seems the embodiment of outdated sentimentalism, and, viewed in conjunction with his heavily effortful oratorios and his vast quantities of dull religious music, it obscures Gounod's natural gift for lightweight music of real charm. Drama was never his strong point, but he possessed a natural vein of elegant melody, not to be judged by his saccharine *Ave Maria* obbligato to Bach's C major Prelude; his vocal writing, particularly in his numerous songs, is always grateful, and he had a sure and delicate hand in orchestration. The *Petite symphonie* for wind, for example, is an enchanting and surprising work to come from a 70-year-old composer absorbed in religious mysticism.

He was born into an artistic family, studied at the Paris Conservatoire, and while in Italy as a result of winning the Prix de Rome became deeply interested in the music of Palestrina ». Returning home, he was called to study for the priesthood, and only at the last moment did he decide not to be ordained but to devote himself to music. He gained valuable experience as conductor for eight years of the Orphéon choral society (and during his later five-year residence in London he founded a choir which ultimately became the Royal Choral Society).

In France at that time the only real field of activity for a composer was the opera, and after two unsuccessful attempts at the grandiose style associated with Meyerbeer, Gounod found his true level in 1858 with the delightful and amusing *Le Médecin malgré lui*. The following year

Faust, a much diluted treatment of Goethe, appeared and was hailed as an important development in *opéra comique* (only ten years later was it turned into a "grand opera" by removing the dialogue and adding a ballet). The gentle lyricism of his *Philémon et Baucis* could not compensate for its feeble libretto, and his next success was the pastoral *Mireille*, which shows his lightness of touch. *Roméo et Juliette*, though graceful, emasculated Shakespeare's passionate drama, and Gounod's remaining operas stretched his talents unduly.

FAUST
- □ *Cpte.* Sutherland, Corelli, Bacquier, Ghiarov/Ambrosian Singers/LSO/ Bonynge
  SET327-30 (1/67) Decca
  1433 London
FAUST—BALLET MUSIC
- □ Covent Garden/Solti
  SPA373 (11/61) Decca
- □ Berlin PO/Karajan/*Offenbach: Gaîte Parisienne*
  2530 199 (5/72) DG*
PETITE SYMPHONIE IN B FLAT FOR WIND INSTRUMENTS
- □ Netherlands Wind Ens./De Waart/ *Dvorak, Schubert*
  6500 163 (5/71) Phonogram

Left: *The organ here looming over Gounod symbolizes the sacred works (now mostly forgotten) to which he devoted so much of his energies.*

PERCY GRAINGER
(b. Melbourne, 1882; d. New York, 1961)

The unpretentious good humour, verve and rhythmic vitality of Grainger's music—nearly all of it arrangements of folksongs or pieces owing much to folk influences—was typical of the man himself. Characteristic of his sturdy independence of mind was his determined use, despite some ridicule, of English indications of speed and dynamics (eg "louden lots" instead of *crescendo molto*, or "chippy" for *staccato*): his tireless athleticism, such as in his trick of throwing a ball high over a house and rushing through the building to catch it on the other side, found musical expression in the heartiness of some of his treatments, which however are always notable for their imaginative craftsmanship.

A piano prodigy first taught by his mother, at the age of ten he gave a series of concerts in Melbourne which enabled him to study first in Frankfurt and then with Busoni ≫ in Berlin. In 1900 he settled in England, making a great reputation as a recitalist and, subsequently, as an exponent of Grieg's ≫ piano concerto. His meeting with Grieg was of significance in that it set him to the energetic collection of folksongs, first in England and then in various parts of the globe (it was he who drew the attention of his friend Delius ≫ to the tune "Brigg Fair"): it also started him composing, with "titbits" such as *Mock Morris*, although he was entirely self-taught in this regard.

In 1914 Grainger went to the USA, and when America entered the war enlisted in the army, quickly being made an instructor in the Army Music School. In 1919 he became an American citizen, and later was for several years head of the music department in the Washington Square College of New York University. He was a good talker, full of individual ideas and not afraid of being thought a crank, and among other things invented a foot-operated device for turning pages on the music-stand of a piano.

HANDEL IN THE STRAND: MOLLY ON THE SHORE: COUNTRY GARDENS: SHEPHERD'S HEY: IRISH TUNE FROM COUNTY DERRY: MOCK MORRIS
☐ Light Music Soc. Orch/Dunn/ *Gardiner; Gibbs; Quilter; Toye*
TWO295 (4/70) EMI/Studio 2
PIANO WORKS
☐ Country Gardens; Irish tune from County Derry; Molly on the Shore; Nordic Princess; Lullaby; Over the Hills and Far Away; Handel in the Strand; Walking Tune; Knight and Shepherd's Daughter; Shepherd's Hey; Sailor's Song; Eastern Intermezzo/Nell *(Faure)*, Love walked in; The man I love *(Gershwin)*
Adni
HQS1363 (11/76) EMI/HMV
VOCAL AND CHAMBER WORKS
☐ Bold William Taylor; The Duke of Marlborough—fanfare; I'm seventeen come Sunday; Let's dance gay in green meadow; Lisbon; Lord Maxwell's goodnight; The lost lady found; My Robin is to the greenwood gone; The pretty maid milkin' her cow; Scotch Strathspey and Reel; Shallow Brown; Shepherd's Hey; The sprig of thyme; There was a pig went out to dig; Willow, willow
Pears, Shirley-Quirk, Ambrosian Singers/ECO/Britten and Tunnard
SXL6410 (10/69) Decca

Left: *A thoroughly practical musician, Grainger readily 'dished up' his folk settings as 'twosomes', 'room music' or for other combinations.*

91

ENRIQUE GRANADOS
(b. Lérida 1867; d. at sea 1916)

Like his slightly older contemporary and fellow-Catalan, Albéniz ≫ Granados was primarily a pianist; and though he wrote seven operas and some orchestral music, it is principally by his piano music that his is remembered. He studied composition in Barcelona with Pedrell (as Falla ≫ was later to do), and after further piano lessons in Paris, returned to Barcelona, where he made his début in 1890. Shortly afterwards he presented his *Spanish dances* to the public, and rapidly gained a considerable reputation as a pianist in Spain and France. His first opera, *María del Carmen*, was produced in Madrid; at the turn of the century he founded the Society of Classical Concerts, which he conducted during its short existence, and, more importantly, a piano school which he directed until his death and which produced a number of distinguished artists.

His masterpiece, the two books of *Goyescas*, was first played in 1911. These seven pieces, based on Goya's paintings and tapestries depicting eighteenth-century life in Madrid, are notable for their poetic quality and a mannered elegance which does not exclude passionate feeling, as in the haunting *Maiden and the nightingale*, the best-known of the set: there is often a tendency to diffuseness, but the piano texture is markedly less cluttered than that of Albéniz. Granados's absorption in the eighteenth-century spirit is also seen in his pithy and often highly emotional *Tonadillas*, songs "in the old style"; a late set of songs, the *Canciones amatorias*, are however entirely romantic in conception. He expanded the *Goyescas* into an opera which was accepted for production in Paris in 1914 but which, owing to war conditions, instead received its première in New York two years later. It was while returning home from this that Granados was drowned when the ship in which he was travelling was torpedoed by a German submarine.

Above: *Granados, the interpreter* par excellence *of the Madrid of Goya's time.*

GOYESCAS
☐ Miranda/*Soler: Sonatas*
  SAGA5343-4 (3/74) Saga
☐ Rajna
  CRD1001-2 (5/74) CRD
**LA MAJA DOLOROSA
NOS. 1-3**
☐ Berganza/Lavilla
  2530 598 (12/75) DG
TWELVE SPANISH DANCES
☐ Rajna
  CRD1021 (7/76) CRD
TONADILLAS AL ESTILO ANTIGŪO
☐ Gomez/Constable
  SAGA5409 (2/76) Saga

EDVARD GRIEG
(b. Bergen, 1843; d. there, 1907)

The description of Grieg's music by Debussy ≫ as "like a pink bonbon filled with snow", though intended as a sneer, contains more than a grain of truth: Grieg was essentially a lyrical miniaturist, and he did combine romantic sweetness with a pronounced Nordic quality. He was certainly not, as is sometimes claimed, the first nationalist composer in Scandinavia, but he was the first to make an impact on a wide European audience. The modest technical demands of his short piano pieces have helped to popularise his chromatic harmonic idiom, with its fondness for open fifths and falling leading-notes, which reflects the folk styles of his native land.

He studied in Leipzig, where the Mendelssohn ≫ tradition was still powerful, but initial overwork brought on severe pleurisy, damaging his left lung and leaving him for the rest of his life in frail health. After graduation and a period in Copenhagen in which he received helpful advice from the Danish composer Gade, he fell under the influence of Rikard Nordraak (writer of the Norwegian national anthem), who turned his thoughts to nationalism—it should perhaps be explained that from 1814 to 1905 Norway was under Swedish rule—and more

Left: *Troldhaugen, Edvard Grieg's home near Bergen.*

CONCERTO IN A MINOR FOR PIANO AND ORCHESTRA
☐ Lupu, LSO/Previn/*Schumann*
   SXL6624 (2/74) Decca
   6840 London
☐ Katin/LPO/Pritchard/*Peer Gynt*
   CFP160 (8/71) Classics for Pleasure
☐ Bishop/BBC SO/Davis/*Schumann*
   6500 166 (3/72) Phonogram∗
☐ Solomon/Philh/Menges/*Schumann*
   CFP40255 (12/76) Classics for Pleasure
☐ Curzon/LSO/Fjelstad/*Litolff: Scherzo;
   Franck: Symphonic Variations*
   SXL2173 (2/60) Decca
HOLBERG SUITE, OP. 40
☐ ASMF/Marriner/*Dvorak*
   ZRG670 (11/70) Decca Argo∗
☐ Northern Sinfonia/Tortelier/*Elegiac
   Melodies, Tchaikovsky*
   ASD2954 (2/74) EMI/HMV
☐ Netherlands Chbr. Orch./Zinman/
   Tchaikovsky
   6580 102 (4/75) Phonogram∗
**HOLBERG SUITE OP. 40
LYRIC PIECES, OP. 43
BALLADE, OP.24**
☐ Klien
   TV34365S (8/72) Decca Turnabout
LYRIC PIECES
☐ *Cpte.* Daniel Adni
   SLS898 (12/74) HMV
LYRIC PIECES
☐ *Exc.* Gilels
   2530 476 (3/75) DG∗
**NORWEGIAN DANCES: LYRIC
SUITE: SIGURD JORSALFAR
(MARCH): PEER GYNT (EXCERPTS)**
☐ Halle/Barbirolli
   SXLP30254 (9/77) EMI/HMV Concert
   Classics
PEER GYNT—INCIDENTAL MUSIC
☐ Armstrong/Ambrosian Singers/Halle/
   Barbirolli
   TWO269 (9/69) EMI/Studio 2
   S-36531 Angel
☐ Stolte, Leipzig, Gewandhaus/
   Neumann
   6580 056 (6/72) Phonogram
   657 0017 Philips Festivo
PEER GYNT—SUITES NOS. 1 AND 2
☐ Berlin PO/Karajan/*Sigurd Jorsalfar*
   2530 243 (11/73) DG
☐ LPO/Pritchard/*Piano Conc.*
   CFP160 (8/71) Classics for Pleasure
☐ Philh./Susskind/*Symphonic Dances*
   SXLP30105 (7/68) Decca
☐ ECO/Leppard/*Norwegian Dances*
   9500 106 (11/76) Phonogram∗
☐ New Philh./A. Davis/*Songs*
   76527 (2/77) CBS

specifically to Norwegian folksong, to whose melodic turns of phrase Grieg's music is, in fact, more indebted than is generally realised.

He wrote a number of sensitive songs (including the popular *I love thee*) for his future wife, gave concerts entirely of Norwegian music, planned a Norwegian Academy of Music, was appointed conductor of the Christiania (Oslo) Philharmonic Society, and composed his piano concerto. This work, which was to make his reputation, aroused the enthusiasm of Liszt », who had already sent him a letter of encouragement on his First Violin Sonata. In 1874, thanks to a government grant, Grieg was enabled to give up his teaching and conducting (he had meanwhile founded another society to give choral works) and concentrate on composition. He had set poems by Norwegian writers, particularly Björnson, for whose *Sigurd Jorsalfar* he wrote incidental music, but his incidental music to *Peer Gynt* in 1876—for all that it is purely picturesque and captures nothing of Ibsen's bitter satire—spread his fame worldwide. He was then in his early thirties: the rest of his life was a story of European concert tours and accumulating honours from all sides. Among his later compositions, the most interesting, as pointing the way to possible future developments, were the *Slåtter* (peasant fiddle-tunes) for piano and the *Haugtussa* song-cycle.

Above: *As pianist and composer Grieg put Norway on the musical map, and popularised its folk idiom.*

93

GEORGE FRIDERIC HANDEL
(b. Halle, 1685; d. London, 1759)

The mere accident that Handel and J. S. Bach » were born within a month, and within 100 miles, of each other has often misled people into mentally bracketing these two musical giants together, although they were totally unlike in background, personality, upbringing, career and style, and they never met. Except for a single year while at the University of Halle, Handel was never employed by the church, to which Bach devoted most of his life, but centred his whole career on opera (a genre Bach had no opportunity to attempt); where Bach set only German and Latin texts, Handel set little but Italian and English, with next to nothing in German; Handel, a widely travelled man, enjoyed a European reputation and royal favour, and in 1726 changed his nationality to British; and unlike Bach's, his music continued to be treasured and performed in the generations after his death—with almost incalculable effects on numerous other composers, including Haydn » and Beethoven », and on English musical life generally.

Handel had taken up music against his father's wishes, and abandoned his law studies to become a violinist, later a harpsichordist, in the Hamburg opera house, where his first stage work, *Almira*, was produced when he was twenty. He then spent five years in Italy, where some church music (including a *Dixit Dominus*), Italian cantatas and operas were well received and he was made

much of by influential cardinals and nobles: this led to his appointment as *kapellmeister* to the Elector of Hanover. But first he went to London, where his *Rinaldo*, written in a fortnight and sumptuously produced, made the recently introduced Italian opera all the rage; and he returned the following year, when he found wealthy patrons and was granted a pension by Queen Anne. He had long overstayed his leave from Hanover, but when by an irony of fate his master became King George I of England it was not long before they were reconciled— though almost certainly not, as the legend has it, through the *Water music* he wrote to accompany a Thames water-party of the king's.

After a year in the service of the Duke of Chandos (who had amassed enormous riches as an unscrupulous Paymaster-General), during which he composed the "Chandos anthems", in 1720 Handel became a director of an operatic venture to which all fashionable Society flocked after the impact of his *Radamisto*. Over the next two decades he wrote a string of 27 operas (including *Ottone*, *Giulio Cesare*, *Rodelinda*, *Ariodante*, *Alcina* and *Berenice*), first for the so-called Royal Academy of Music, then with another company, after a stormy history of intrigues, rival singers' tantrums, audiences' fickleness and financial difficulties, exacerbated by the triumph of the iconoclastic *Beggar's Opera*. All these works of

ALCINA (OVERTURE: BALLET MUSIC)
□ ASMF/Marriner
ZRG686 (6/72) Decca Argo
AS PANTS THE HEART
□ Cantelo, Partridge/King's College Choir/ASMF/Willcocks/*Lord is my light*
ZRG541 (7/68) Decca Argo
CONCERTI GROSSI, OP. 3, NOS 1-6
□ Mainz CO/Kehr
TV34103S (5/68) Decca Turnabout★
□ ASMF/Marriner
ZRG5400 (9/64) Decca Argo★
CONCERTI GROSSI, OPP. 3 AND 6
□ Dart/ASMF/Marriner
SDDB294-7 (9/71)
CORONATION ANTHEMS FOR GEORGE II:
Zadok the Priest; The King shall rejoice; My heart is inditing; Let Thy hand be strengthened
□ King's College Choir/English Chamber Orch./Willcocks
ZRG5369 (12/63) Decca Argo
DIXIT DOMINUS
□ Donath, Koelman, Heynis, van Dolder, Hollestelle/NCVR Vocal Ens/ Amsterdam CO/Voorberg
6580 135 (3/77) Phonogram

Left: *Copy of Handel's* Ode for St Cecilia's Day *(1739).*

Right: *Thomas Hudson's portrait of Handel in 1749.*

Handel's were cast in the rigid mould of *opera seria*, in which subjects from history or classical mythology were arranged in a sequence of static arias, linked by recitative, designed for star singers (the hero always being a castrato).

His numerous worries made him severely ill, and during his convalescence an idea came to his energetic entrepreneurial mind. In 1732 the Bishop of London's ban on acted performances of sacred subjects in a theatre had obliged him to present a revival of his earlier masque *Esther* as an oratorio: now he decided, as the public had wearied of operatic artificialities and singers' squabbles, to strike out in a new direction. In 1739 he produced the intensely dramatic *Saul* and the monumental *Israel in Egypt* (nothing like whose succession of massive choruses had ever been heard): in 1742, in Dublin, he performed *Messiah*—not so much an oratorio as a sacred cantata—which after a rather cool initial reception in

London the following year was fallen upon rapturously and performed almost as a sacred rite from then on. (It is worth remembering, in view of the grandiose massed-choir performances of that much-mauled work, that the original forces numbered about 30 in the choir and the same in the orchestra—though when Handel could call upon large orchestral forces, as in the *Fireworks music* to celebrate the peace of Aix-la-Chapelle, he did so with gusto.) Later oratorios included *Samson*, *Judas Maccabaeus*, *Solomon* and (his last) *Jephtha*. Between the acts Handel would often play an organ concerto, in which he would improvise much of his solo part.

His combination of German contrapuntal fluency with Italian vocal grace and the English choral tradition derived from Purcell ❯ was unique; but to present-day listeners the appeal of Handel lies in his nobility, his unfailing melodic invention, his dramatic expressiveness and, very often, his striking sense of instrumental colour.

GIULIO CESARE
☐ *Excs.* Sutherland, Elkins, Horne, Sinclair/New SO/Bonynge
  SDD213 (4/70) Decca Ace of Diamonds

LET GOD ARISE
☐ Vaughan, Young, Robinson/King's College Choir/ASMF/Willcocks/*O praise the Lord*
  ZRG5490 (1/66) Decca Argo

LUCREZIA
☐ Baker/ECO/Leppard/*Operatic arias*
  6500 523 (10/74) Phonogram

LORD IS MY LIGHT
☐ Cantelo, Partridge/King's College Choir/ASMF/Willcocks/*As pants the heart*
  ZRG541 (7/68) Decca Argo

MESSIAH
☐ *Cpte.* Harper, Watts, Wakefield, Shirley-Quirk, LSO/Davis
  6703 001 (11/66) Phonogram
  SC71-AX300 Philips
☐ *Cpte.* Harwood, Baker, Esswood, Tear, Herincx, ECO/Mackerras
  SLS774 (3/67) HMV
  S-3705 Angel

☐ *Cpte.* Palmer, Watts, Davis, Shirley-Quirk, ECO and Chorus/Leppard
  STU70921-3 (2/76) RCA/Erato
  RL3-1426 RCA
☐ Ameling, Reynolds, Langridge, Howell/ASMF & Chorus/Marriner
  D18D3 (11/76) Decca*
☐ *Exc.* Mackerras
  HQS1244 (4/71) EMI/HMV
☐ *Exc.* C. Davis
  6833 050 (11/71) Phonogram

MUSIC FOR THE ROYAL FIREWORKS
☐ ECO/Leppard
  6500 369 (1/73) Phonogram*
☐ LSO (augmented)/Mackerras/*Concerto*
  ASD3395 (11/77) EMI/HMV
  S-37404 Angel

O PRAISE THE LORD WITH ONE CONSENT
☐ Vaughan, Young, Robinson/King's College Choir/ASMF/Willcocks/*Let God arise*
  ZRG5490 (1/66) Decca Argo

OBOE CONCERTOS NOS. 1-3
☐ Holliger/ECO/Leppard
  6500 240 (11/72) Phonogram*

ORGAN CONCERTOS—OPP. 4 AND 7; 'SET 2' NOS. 7-10
☐ Preston, Menuhin Fest./Menuhin
  SLS824 (6/72) HMV
☐ Alain, Paillard CO/Paillard
  STU71097 (5/78) RCA/Erato
☐ Malcolm/ASMF/Marriner
  D3D4 (9/76) Decca*
☐ *Opp.* 4 and 7 only. Richter, CO
  SDD470-2 (11/75) Decca Ace of Diamonds

OVERTURES
☐ Lotario, Esther, Admeto, Alcina, Orlando, Poro, Partenope, Ottone
☐ ECO/Leppard
  6599 053 (11/72) Phonogram*

SONATAS FOR FLUTE AND HARPSICHORD
☐ Graf/Daehler
  ORYX1712-3 (3/73) Peerless/Oryx*

WATER MUSIC
☐ Philomusica of London/Dart/*Harp and Lute Conc, Op. 4 6; Harp Conc, Op. 4/5; Conc., Gross in C*
  DPA597-8 (4/78)
☐ ECO/Leppard
  6500 047 (1/71) Phonogram*
☐ BPO/Kubelik
  2535 137 (3/76) DG Privilege
  138799 DG
☐ *Suite:* Schola Cantorum Basiliensis/Wenzinger/*Fireworks*
  2548 164 (11/75) DG Heliodor

Right: *Handel's will. He was buried in Westminster Abbey.*
Left: *Handel bequeathed this harpsichord to his amanuensis.*

In the Name of God Amen
I George Frideric Handel considering the
uncertainty of humane Life doe make this my Will in manner
following (viz) I give and bequeath unto my Servant
Peter le Blond my Cloths and Linnen and three
hundred Pounds Sterl and to my other Servants a
Years Wages I give and bequeath to Mr Christopher
Smith my large Harpsicord my Little House Organ
my Musick Books and five hundred Pounds Sterl
I give and bequeath to Mr James Hunter five
hundred Pounds Sterl I give and bequeath to my
Cousin Christian Gottlieb Handel of Coppenhagen
One hundred Pounds Sterl Item I give and
bequeath to my Cousin Magister Christian August
Rotth of Halle in Saxony One hundred Pounds Sterl
Item I give and bequeath to my Cousin the
Widow of George Taust Pastor of Gibichenstein
near Halle in Saxony three hundred Pounds Sterl
and to her Six Children each two hundred
Pounds Sterling All the rest and residue of
my Estate in Bank Annuitys or of what
or of whatsoever kind or nature I give and
bequeath unto my dear Neice Johanna Friderica
Floerchen of Gotha in Saxony (born Michaelsen
in Halle) whom I make my Sole Executrix of
this my last Will In Witness whereof I have
hereunto set my hand this 1. day of June
1750. George Frideric Handel

JOSEPH HAYDN
(b. Rohrau, Lower Austria, 1732; d. Vienna, 1809)

Only 50 years ago a distinguished University professor could fairly label Haydn "the inaccessible" because only a fraction of his extensive output had been published in reliable editions, and an even smaller part was performed. Today, thanks to the enthusiastic efforts of Haydn scholars, the bulk of his music has been carefully studied, re-edited and republished, many more works have been discovered, and there have been complete recordings of his symphonies and quartets, with the operas now being added to the catalogue. From all this a new perspective has been gained, its total effect being to heighten still more the stature of this great musical figure. Although not literally the "father of the symphony", as he has been called, nor of the string quartet (seeing that a few composers had previously written works of these sorts), his importance in the formation and development of both can scarcely be exaggerated. The ordinary listener, however, concerned more with the enjoyment and satisfaction to be derived from a composer's music than with his historical influence, can find in Haydn a wealth of spontaneous melody, a lucidity, a buoyant rhythmic vitality in which cheerfulness abounds, along with deeply expressive or dramatic movements, and an inexhaustible fount of original ideas for treating his material. Respected, honoured and held in affection by all, he was an unaffected and modest man with a positive attitude to life which gave his work a unique quality.

He was the son of a wheelwright in an Austrian border village where Croatian and Hungarian elements were strong, and the folksongs he heard in his childhood often seem to find an echo in his later music. At the age of six he was sent off to live with a stern relative who gave him musical instruction, and two years later he became a chorister in St Stephen's Cathedral, Vienna. An incorrigible prankster, he was dismissed at 17 when his voice broke, and scraped a living as accompanist and servant to a famous singing teacher, who assisted him in the composition studies he was assiduously undertaking on his own. He began to write piano sonatas in the C. P. E. Bach ≫ mould and string quartets for a minor nobleman's music parties. When he was 27 he was invited to direct the small private orchestra of a Bohemian Count, for which he wrote his first symphonies: these attracted the notice of Prince Paul Anton Esterházy, who took Haydn on as assistant *kapellmeister* in 1761 when the Count was obliged, for reasons of economy, to dismiss his musicians. The following year the Prince died and was succeeded by his brother Nicolaus, an enthusiast for the arts with a taste for luxury which earned him the title of "the Magnificent"; he built a sumptuous palace across the Hungarian border on the model of Versailles where Haydn, now in charge of his musical establishment (which included many first-rate players and singers), for the next 24 years was kept busily occupied composing orchestral and chamber music (including a vast quantity of pieces for the Prince's favourite instrument, the baryton), religious music for his chapel and operas for his theatre, as well as all kinds of special celebrations to entertain the constant stream of royal and noble guests.

Largely isolated as he was from the outside world (although his fame quickly spread far and wide), Haydn was thrown upon his own resources and, with his master's full encouragement, "compelled to be original", as he

himself said. He was able to experiment to his heart's content with instrumentation and form, and in the 50 or so quartets of this period he enormously developed the importance and independence of the lower parts and deepened the significance of the medium as a whole. (Mozart ≫ declared that it was from Haydn's example that he had learned how to write quartets, and in return Haydn was powerfully impressed by the work of his great junior.) Though in Haydn's hands the symphony acquired shape and depth, he treated it with astonishing diversity and adventurousness: movements were frequently constructed from a single theme without lack of variety, the slow introduction appeared, development sections were enormously strengthened, there was much humour (particularly in the Trios of the minuets, which frequently call on orchestral soloists) and supple contrapuntal skill. During the early 1770s Haydn's works went through a more dramatic and overtly emotional phase—his "Storm and stress" period: to this belong the "Trauer", "Farewell" and "Passione" symphonies (Nos. 44, 45 and 49) and the Op.20 ("Sun") quartets. After this his works achieved greater grace and nobility, as shown in the Op.33 quartets in

Above: *Haydn's harpsichord is preserved in Vienna.*

Above right: *Joseph Haydn at the age of sixty.*

which the minuets give way to scherzos, and the six symphonies (Nos. 82-87) written for Paris.

After the death of his sympathetic and appreciative master, Haydn was freer to move about. He paid two long visits to England, on each occasion writing six brilliant symphonies for performance in London, including such favourites as the "Surprise", the "Clock" and the "London" (Nos. 94, 101 and 104): he was feted and honoured everywhere, and was stunned by the revelation of Handel's » oratorios, which spurred him to compose *The Creation* and *The Seasons*. He had meanwhile written a series of six great Masses for the new Prince Esterházy; and among other masterpieces in the final flowering of his talent were the quartets of Op.64 (of which No. 4 is the "Lark") and particularly, Op.76, of which No. 3 contains variations on his Emperor's Hymn which became the Austrian national anthem, and which he played on his deathbed.

CELLO CONCERTO IN C
□ Rostropovich/English Chamber Orch./*Britten: Cello Conc.*
SXL6138 (12/64) Decca
6419 London
□ Rostropovich/ASMF/*Concerto in D*
ASD3255 (9/76) EMI/HMV
37193 Angel
CELLO CONCERTO IN D
□ Rostropovich/ASMF/*Concerto in C*
ASD3255 (9/76) EMI/HMV
37193 Angel
THE CREATION
□ Ameling, Krenn, Krause, Choir, VPO/ Munchinger
SET362-3 (4/68) Decca
1271 London
□ *(in English)*. Harper, Tear, Shirley-Quirk, King's College Choir, ASMF/Willcocks
SLS971 (6/74) HMV
HARPSICHORD CONCERTO IN D MAJOR
□ Malcolm/ASMF/Marriner
SXL6385 (10/69) Decca
HORN CONCERTO NO. 1 IN D
□ Tuckwell/ASMF/Marriner/*Trumpet Conc.; Organ Conc. 1*
ZK6 (1/77) Decca Argo
LIRA CONCERTOS
(No. 1 in C; No. 3 in G; No. 5 in F)
□ Ruf, Ens
TV34055S Decca Turnabout*

MASS NO. 11 IN B FLAT (SCHOPFUNGSMESSE)
□ Cantelo, Watts, Tear, Robinson/St John's College Choir/ASMF/Guest
ZRG598 (3/69) Decca Argo*
MISSA IN TEMPORE BELLI (PAUKENMESSE)
□ Cantelo, Watts, Tear, McDaniel, St. John's College Choir/ASMF/ Guest
ZRG634 (4/70) Decca Argo*
□ Morison, Thomas, Witsch, Kohn, Janacek/Bavarian Radio Ch. & Orch./ Kubelik
2548 229 (4/76) DG Heliodor

Above: *Haydn, after a contemporary London engraving.*

NELSON MISSA (MISSA IN ANGUSTIIS)
☐ Stahlmann, Watts, Brown, Krause, King's College Choir, LSO/Willcocks
ZRG5325 (12/62) Decca Argo*
ORLANDO PALADINO
☐ *Cpte.* Auger, Ameling, Killebrew, Shirley, Ahnsjo, Luxon, Trimarchi, Mazzieri, Carelli/Lausanne CO/ Dorati
6707 029 (9/77) Phonogram*
PIANO SONATAS
☐ McCabe
☐ Nos. 6, 10, 18, 33, 38, 39, 47, 50, 52, 60/*Fantasia in C; Variations in F minor*
HDN100-2 (10/75) Decca
STS-15343 London
☐ Nos. 9, 17, 31, 36, 43, 45, 46, 48, 54-6/*Arietta con Variazioni in A*
HDN103-5 (5/76) Decca
☐ Nos. 8, 18, 19, 26, 27, 34, 42, 44, 49/ *Adagio in F; Variations in C*
HDN106-8 (9/76) Decca
☐ Nos. 2, 3, 5, 7, 11, 13, 16, 19, 34, 40, 44, 49, 51, 58/*Capriccio in G*
HDN109-11 (4/77) Decca
PIANO TRIOS
Beaux Arts Trio

☐ Nos. 5, 10, 11
9500 327 (2/78) Phonogram*
☐ Nos. 7, 9, 12
9500 327 (8/77) Phonogram*
☐ Nos. 13, 16, 17
9500 053 (2/77) Phonogram*
☐ Nos. 14, 15
9500 034 (11/76) Phonogram*
☐ Nos. 18, 19, 22
6500 521 (6/74) Phonogram*
☐ Nos. 20, 24, 32
6500 522 (11/73) Phonogram*
☐ Nos. 21, 23, 28
6500 401 (3/73) Phonogram*
☐ Nos. 25-27
6500 023 (6/71) Phonogram*
☐ Nos. 29-31
6500 400 (3/73) Phonogram*
THE SEASONS
☐ Janowitz, Schreier, Talvela, Vienna Singverein, VSO/Böhm
2709 026 (11/67) DG*
☐ *(in English).* Harper, Davies, Shirley-Quirk, BBC SO and Chorus/C. Davis
6703 023 (4/69) Phonogram
839719-21 Philips
SINFONIA CONCERTANTE IN B♭
☐ Engl, Baranyai, Ozim, Racz/Philh. Hung./Dorati/*Mozart K364*
SDD445 Decca Ace of Diamonds
STS-15229/34 London
STRING QUARTETS NOS. 31-36, OP. 20; NOS. 63-68, OP. 64
☐ Aeolian Quartet
HDNT70-5 (5/76) Decca
STRING QUARTETS NOS. 37-42, OP. 33; NO. 43, OP. 42; NOS. 44-49, OP. 50
☐ Aeolian Quartet
HDNU76-81 (11/76) Decca
☐ 37-39. Weller Quartet
SDD278 (5/71) Decca
Ace of Diamonds
☐ 40-42. Weller Quartet
SDD279 (6/71) Decca
Ace of Diamonds

STRING QUARTETS NOS. 44-5, OP. 50 NOS. 1 AND 2
☐ Tokyo Quartet
2530 440 (7/74) DG
STRING QUARTETS NOS. 57-59, OP. 54; NOS. 60-62, OP. 55
☐ Aeolian Quartet
HDNS67-9 (11/75) Decca
STRING QUARTET NO. 74 NO. 3 STRING QUARTET NO. 77, OP. 76 NO. 2
☐ Alban Berg Quartet
AS641302 (1/75) Selecta
STRING QUARTETS NOS. 75-80, OP. 76; NOS. 81, 82, OP. 77; NO. 83, OP. 103
☐ Aeolian Quartet
HDNP57-60 (9/74) Decca
**SYMPHONIES
NOS. 1-104**
Philharmonia Hungarica/Dorati
☐ Nos. 1-19
HDNA1-6 (10/73) Decca
☐ Nos. 20-35
HDNB7-12 (4/73) Decca
STS-15257 London
☐ Nos. 36-48
HDNC13-18 (9/72) Decca
STS-15249 London

☐ Nos. 49-56
HDND19-22 (5/71) Decca
STS-15127 London
☐ Nos. 57-64
HDNE23-6 (1/71) Decca
STS-15131 London
☐ Nos. 65-72
HDN27-30 (9/70) Decca
STS-15135 London
☐ Nos. 73-81
HDNG31-4 (3/71) Decca
STS-15182 London
☐ Nos. 82-92; Sinfonia Concertante
HDNH35-40 (3/72) Decca
STS-15229 London
☐ Nos. 82-87
ECO/Barenboim
SLS5065 (10/76) HMV
☐ Nos. 93-104
Philharmonia Hungarica/Dorati
HDNJ41-6(9/74) Decca
STS-15319 London
SYMPHONY NO. 45 IN F SHARP MINOR (FAREWELL)
☐ LPO/Pritchard
CFP40021 (2/74) Classics for Pleasure
☐ Philh. Hung./Dorati/*Sym. 42*
SDD414 (7/74) Decca Ace of Diamonds
SYMPHONY NO. 82 IN C (BEAR)
☐ Philh. Hungarica/Dorati/*Sym. 83*
SDD482 (8/76) Decca Ace of Diamonds
SYMPHONY NO. 83 IN G MINOR (HEN)
☐ Philh. Hungarica/Dorati/*Sym. 82*
SDD482 (8/76) Decca Ace of Diamonds
SYMPHONY NO. 84 IN E FLAT
☐ Philh. Hungarica/Dorati/*Sym. 85*
SDD483 (8/76) Decca Ace of Diamonds
SYMPHONY NO. 85 IN B FLAT (QUEEN)
☐ Philh. Hungarica/Dorati/*Sym. 84*
SDD483 (8/76) Decca Ace of Diamonds
SYMPHONY NO. 86 IN D
☐ Philh. Hungarica/Dorati/*Sym. 87*
SDD484 (8/76) Decca Ace of Diamonds

SYMPHONY NO. 87 IN A
☐ Philh. Hungarica/Dorati/*Sym. 86*
 SDD484 (8/76) Decca Ace of
 Diamonds
SYMPHONY NO. 88 IN G
☐ Berlin PO/Jochum/*Sym. 99*
 2548 241 (10/76) DG Heliodor
SYMPHONY NO. 93 IN D
☐ Philh. Hungarica/Dorati/*Sym. 94*
 SDD500 (11/76) Decca Ace of
 Diamonds
 STS-15178 London
SYMPHONY NO. 94 IN G
(SURPRISE)
☐ LPO/Pritchard/*Sym. 103*
 CFP40269 (12/77) Classics for
 Pleasure
☐ Cleveland/Szell/*Sym. 93*
 61052 (4/69) CBS Classics
 MS-7006 Columbia
☐ LPO/Jochum/*Sym. 101*
 2530 628 (7/76) DG*
☐ Philh. Hungarica/Dorati/*Sym. 93*
 SDD500 (11/76) Decca Ace of
 Diamonds
 STS-15320 London
SYMPHONY NO. 95 IN C MINOR
☐ LPO/Jochum/*Sym. 96*
 2530 420 (12/74) DG*
☐ Philh. Hungarica/Dorati/*Sym. 96*
 SDD501 (11/76) Decca Ace of
 Diamonds
 STS-15320 London
SYMPHONY NO. 96 IN D
☐ RPO/Schonzeler/*Sym. 102*
 CFP40073 (7/74) Classics for Pleasure
SYMPHONY NO. 97 IN C
☐ Philh. Hungarica/Dorati/*Sym. 98*
 SDD502 (11/76) Decca Ace of
 Diamonds
 STS-15321 London

Left: *Title-page of three of
Haydn's symphonies published
1787 in Vienna.*

SYMPHONY NO. 98 IN B FLAT
☐ Berlin PO/Jochum/*Sym. 88*
 2548 241 (10/76) DG Heliodor
☐ Philh. Hungarica/Dorati/*Sym. 97*
 SDD502 (11/76) Decca Ace of
 Diamonds
 STS-15321 London
☐ Philh. Hungarica/Dorati/*Sym. 95*
 SDD501 (11/76) Decca Ace of
 Diamonds
SYMPHONY NO. 99 IN E FLAT
☐ LPO/Jochum/*Sym. 100*
 2530 459 (8/74) DG*
SYMPHONY NO. 100 IN G
(MILITARY)
☐ LPO/Jochum/*Sym. 99*
 2530 459 (8/74) DG*
SYMPHONY NO. 101 IN D (CLOCK)
☐ BPO/Karajan/*Sym. No. 83*
 ASD2817 (1/73) EMI/HMV
 S-36868 Angel
☐ LPO/Jochum/*Sym. 94*
 2530 628 (7/76) DG*
SYMPHONY NO. 102 IN B FLAT
☐ RPO/Schonzeler/*Sym. 96*
 CFP40073 (7/74) Classics for Pleasure
SYMPHONY NO. 103 IN E FLAT,
(DRUM ROLL)
☐ VPO/Karajan/*Sym. 104*
 SDD362 (5/73) Decca Ace of
 Diamonds
☐ LPO/Jochum/*Sym. 104*
 2530 525 (7/75) DG*
☐ LPO/Pritchard/*Sym. 94*
 CFP40269 (12/77) Classics for
 Pleasure
SYMPHONY NO. 104 IN D,
(LONDON)
☐ VPO/Karajan/*Sym. 103*
 SDD362 (5/73) Decca Ace of
 Diamonds
☐ LPO/Jochum/*Sym. 103*
 2530 525 (7/75) DG*
☐ Berlin PO/Karajan/*Schubert: Sym.*
 ASD3203 (9/76) EMI/HMV
 S-37058 Angel
TRUMPET CONCERTO IN E FLAT
☐ Howarth/St. James Orch./*S.
 Bedford/Mozart: Clarinet Conc.*
 CFP40046 (3/73) Classics for Pleasure
☐ Stringer/ASMF/Marriner/*Horn
 Conc. 1; Organ Conc. 1*
 ZK6 (1/77) Decca Argo
VERA COSTANZA
☐ *Cpte.* Norman, Donath, Ahnsjo,
 Ganzarolli, Trimarchi, Lovaas,
 Rolfe-Johnson/Lausanne CO/Dorati
 6703 077 (6/77) Phonogram*

Below: *Sketch for the chorus 'The
heavens are telling', from Haydn's
Creation.*

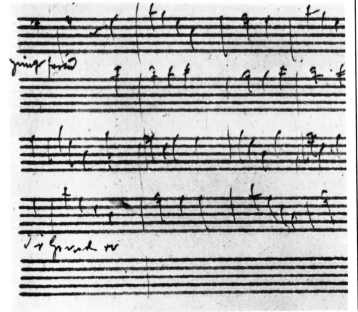

HANS WERNER HENZE
(b. Gütersloh, nr. Bielefeld, 1926)

Hailed in the 1950s and early 60s as the leading German opera composer of his day, Henze has since then devoted his considerable talents and fluency of invention to Marxist causes — which has caused some uncertainty in his very eclectic style and an evident barrier to his general acceptability. The seeds of revolt were laid at an early stage, however, when as a boy in the Nazi era he was conscripted into the army. He returned after the war, worked as a *répétiteur*, and became artistic director of the Wiesbaden Opera ballet; dancing left its influence on such works as his First Piano Concerto, his first opera *Boulevard Solitude* (an up-dating of the Manon Lescaut story) and his Third Symphony, as well as his actual ballets *Ondine* and *The Emperor's nightingale*. He was increasingly drawn to Italy, where lengthy residence mellowed the original asperities of his style, which had been formed on Schoenberg », though without the strictness of his followers, and on Stravinsky ». His highly extrovert early symphonies, which display a virtuoso technique, reveal this pull towards the Mediterranean (especially the Apollonian No.3, with its beautifully grave slow movement). The lyricism of his opera *King Stag* was paralleled by the vocal warmth of his *Five Neapolitan Songs* and the instrumental allure of his *Kammermusik*, and it later formed the basis for his Fourth Symphony; *Elegy for young lovers*, an opera to an English libretto, shows a similar romanticism; but after that Henze's style became tauter and more incisive, as in the very concentrated Fifth Symphony.

A double-bass concerto, the Double Concerto for oboe and harp, and *Muses of Sicily* (described as a "concerto for choir, two pianos, wind instruments and timpani") were all produced in 1966, and were followed by the Second Piano Concerto, which became the centre of an anti-Nazi demonstration and stung Henze to issue a declaration on the "importance of world revolution". The opera *The young lord* had already bitterly satirised German bourgeois pretensions; and the Sixth Symphony, written in Cuba, was specifically inscribed as "anti-bourgeois music" and quoted revolutionary songs. Political music-theatre became Henze's main interest, with *The Raft of the Medusa* (a protest against inhumanity, which ends with percussion hammering out the chant "Ho, ho, Ho-Chi-Minh!"), *El Cimarrón* (whose central character is a runaway slave) and *The tedious journey to Natascha Ungeheuer's apartment* (a fable of disillusion with political ideals).

**COMPASES PARA PREGUNTAS
ENSIMISMADAS**
☐ London Sinfonietta/Henze/*Violin
 Concerto*
 HEAD5 (11/74) Decca Headline*
IN MEMORIAM
☐ London Sinfonietta/Henze/
 Kammermusik
 DSL05 (11/75) L'Oiseau-Lyre*
KAMMERMUSIK
☐ Langridge, Walker/London
 Sinfonietta/Henze/*In Memoriam*
 DSL05 (11/75) L'Oiseau-Lyre*
VIOLIN CONCERTO NO. 2
☐ Langbein/London Sinfonietta/Henze/
 Compases
 HEAD5 (11/74) Decca Headline*

PAUL HINDEMITH
(b. Hanau 1895; d. Frankfurt 1963)

As a result of the eventual sweeping victories of the thinking of Schoenberg » and his followers, Hindemith's stock as an influence on 20th-century musical developments, once considered of major importance, has declined; but though only relatively few of his works have firmly established themselves (inevitably, in the case of so extremely prolific a composer), those that have bear witness to his extraordinary contrapuntal skill and lithe rhythmic energy. Some, such as his masterpiece the *Mathis der Maler* symphony, are also powerfully emotional under their athletic exterior; in other cases, as in the virtuosic *Symphonic metamorphoses on themes of Weber*, it is the sheer intellectual exuberance that is so stimulating.

His deep moral concern, throughout his life, with the artist's position in society almost certainly arose in the period of German demoralisation and febrile gaiety following the 1914-18 war, when he was first making his way in the world. He had left home at the age of 11 because of parental opposition to a musical career and played in cafés and cinemas to earn enough to enable him to study in Frankfurt—to such purpose that before he was twenty, he had become leader of the opera-house orchestra there. He acquired at least a competence on a very large number of instruments, which enabled him later to write with understanding for many that are not well catered for (even uncommon instruments like the heckelphone and trautonium). He left the Frankfurt Opera in 1923 to devote his time to playing viola in the Amar Quartet, which toured widely, and to composition, making a swiftly growing reputation at festivals of contemporary music. He also became famous as a solo violist.

His early compositions included, besides a number of instrumental works, several operas, either expressionist or studiedly "objective" and astringent (like the first version of *Cardillac* and the jape *Hin und zurück*); but in 1927, when he became a professor at the Music High School in Berlin, he sought to justify the composer's profession by declaring a policy of *Gebrauchsmusik*—"functional" music, mostly in a linear neo-classical idiom, designed for practical ends and for amateurs. This aroused a good deal of discussion, but in the early 1930s Hindemith, while retaining his desire to serve the community, adopted a new style notable not only for its increased textural clarity but for its deeper expressiveness. When the Nazis banned his music (objecting especially to the opera *Mathis der Maler*, which centred on the problem of the artist's role in society and which as a result was not produced until 1938, in Zurich) he acted for some time as music adviser to the Turkish government before quitting Europe in 1939 for the USA. He completed a treatise expounding his own theory of tonality based on harmonic tensions (exemplified in the piano preludes and fugues called *Ludus tonalis*) and became head of the music department at Yale, but in 1946 returned to Zurich to teach composition. Besides works already mentioned, his main contributions to the repertoire were the ballets *Nobilissima visione* and *The four temperaments*, various concertos (including six with chamber orchestra, each entitled *Kammermusik*), eight sonatas for wind instruments, and a series of works for different combinations entitled *Konzertmusik*.

HORN CONCERTO
☐ Brain/Philh./Hindemith/*R. Strauss*
  HLS7001 (3/72) EMI/HMV
LUDUS TONALIS
☐ Roggenkamp
  GSGC14150 (12/74) Pye Collector
MATHIS DER MALER—SYMPHONY
☐ Philadelphia/Ormandy/*Rachmaninov*
  61347 (3/73) CBS Classics
☐ LSO/Horenstein/*R. Strauss*
  RHS312 (8/73) Unicorn
  71307 Nonesuch
ORGAN SONATAS NOS. 1-3
☐ Preston
  ZRG663 (3/71) Decca Argo★
STRING QUARTET NO. 2 IN C
☐ Kreuzberger Quartet/*String Quartet 3*
  AW6 42077 Selecta/Telefunken

Above: *To Hindemith, practicality was a basic tenet.*

STRING QUARTET NO. 3 IN C
☐ Kreuzberger/*String Quartet 2*
  AW6 42077 Selecta/Telefunken
SYMPHONIC METAMORPHOSES ON THEMES OF WEBER
☐ LSO/Abbado/*Janáček: Sinfonietta*
  SXL6398 (5/69) Decca
  6620 London
☐ Cleveland/Szell/*Janáček*
  61367 (1/74) CBS Classics
VIOLIN CONCERTO IN D FLAT
☐ D. Oistrakh/LSO/Hindemith/*Bruch*
  SDD465 (6/76) Decca Ace of Diamond
  6337 London

GUSTAV HOLST
(b. Cheltenham 1874; d. London 1934)

More a "musician's musician" than his close friend Vaughan Williams », who was a fellow-student with him under Stanford at the Royal College of Music, Holst, the more intellectually enquiring and genuinely original of the two, never enjoyed the popularity of his contemporary, nor did he possess his common touch. Yet he had infinitely more practical experience, and was an entirely unassuming and understanding human being, intolerant only of sloppiness and pretension, and with a keen sense of humour, who in a lifetime of teaching (at two famous London schools, at Morley College and the Royal College of Music, and later in the USA) endeared himself to several generations of pupils. Like Vaughan Williams, he was able to shake himself free of Germanic traditions, though without being so completely immersed in English folksong.

His was an unusual mind, which prompted him even while a trombonist and *répétiteur* to the Carl Rosa Opera company and then organist at Covent Garden to learn Sanskrit so as to study Eastern poetry and philosophy, the first fruits of which were the sets of choral *Hymns from the Rig-Veda* and the exquisite chamber opera *Savitri* (1908). His eminently practical sense enabled him to write two successful suites for military band and the *St Paul's Suite* for the strings of the girls' school where he taught for nearly 30 years; but his strong vein of mysticism emerged in his most popular work, *The Planets* (which uses a large orchestra with vivid colours, and in which the terror of *Mars* and the awesome remoteness of *Saturn* and *Neptune* quite outweigh the heartiness of *Jupiter*), and even more in the dazzling vision of the choral *Hymn of Jesus* and in the

Below: *A portrait of Holst at work by Millicent Woodforde.*

Ode to death. The elasticity with which, in vocal settings, he had followed the rhythms of English words had led him to favour irregular patterns and unusual metrical units of five and seven, and these are apparent in the three major works just mentioned, as well as in the boisterous ballet music to his very funny parodistic opera *The perfect fool*.

A change to a more neo-classical, polytonal style in his works from the *Choral Symphony* onwards, though it coincided with a fall he suffered from a platform while conducting, was certainly the outcome of his search for an even greater clarity and precision of thought. The bleakness of the orchestral *Egdon Heath*, the mordancy of the two-violin concerto, the distant gaze of the song *Betelgeuse*, the concentration of the *Hammersmith* scherzo have never caught the public fancy, but they may represent the true core of Holst's individual utterance.

Above: *Throughout Holst's work ran a strong vein of mysticism, which however went hand in hand with a trenchant clarity of thought.*

Right: *Holst playing through the score of his opera* The Perfect Fool *at Covent Garden in 1923. It was conducted by Eugene Goossens (left).*

104

**BROOK GREEN SUITE; FUGAL
CONCERTO FOR FLUTE, OBOE
AND STRINGS; LYRIC MOVEMENT
FOR VIOLA AND STRINGS;
NOCTURNE FOR STRINGS; ST
PAUL'S SUITE**
☐ ECO/I. Holst
  SRCS34 (5/67) Lyrita
CHORAL PIECES
  (The Fields of sorrow; David's lament
  for Jonathan; Truth of all truth; Five
  choral folksongs; Dirge for two
  veterans; The homecoming; Hymn to
  Manas)
☐ Baccholian Singers
  CSD3764 (7/75) EMI/HMV
EGDON HEATH
☐ LSO/Previn/*Tale of the Wandering
  Scholar; Perfect Fool—ballet music*
  ASD3097 (9/75) EMI/HMV
THE PLANETS
☐ NPO/Boult
  ASD2301 (3/67) EMI/HMV
☐ LSO/Previn
  ASD3002 (7/74) EMI/HMV
  S-36991 Angel
☐ Bournemouth SO/Hurst
  CN2020 (9/76) Pickwick/Contour

☐ Philadelphia/Ormandy
  RL1797 (4/77) RCA
  ARL1-1797 RCA
SAVITRI
☐ Baker, Tear, Hemsley/ECO/I. Holst/
  Rig Veda
  ZNF6 (6/66) Decca Argo∗
**A SOMERSET RHAPSODY
HAMMERSMITH—PRELUDE AND
SCHERZO (1933-4)
BENI-MORA**
☐ LPO/Boult
  SRCS56 (5/72) Lyrita
**(The) TALE OF THE WANDERING
SCHOLAR**
☐ Burrowes, Tear, Rippon, Langdon/
  ECO/Bedford/*Egdon Heath; Perfect
  Fool—Ballet music*
  ASD3097 (9/75) EMI/HMV
**12 WELSH FOLKSONGS—
PARTSONGS**
☐ BBC Northern Singers/Wilkinson/
  Piano music
  LPB736 (5/76) Abbey

ARTHUR HONEGGER
(b. Le Havre 1892; d. Paris 1955)

Attempts to assess Honegger's position in the musical world have often been undermined by two accidents—his birth and education in France, although his parents were Swiss and his mind was much more attuned to German traditions, and his friendship with the other composers of the group known as "Les Six" (which actually was held together by little more than a journalist's label), whose Bright Young Things' irreverent jokiness, in the years immediately following the First World War, he never shared.

He received his musical education in Zurich and Paris, spending two years at the Conservatoire in each, and his earliest compositions show his absorption with Debussy » and Strauss »—although all his life he revered Bach » as his inspiration; but he later felt impressionism to be out of tune with the spirit of the times. In 1916 he was associated with his recent fellow-pupil Milhaud » in a group called "Les Nouveaux Jeunes" which was afterwards to form the basis of the so-called "Les Six"; but Honegger was at pains to stress that he was not, like the others, attracted to the music-hall and street fair but was intent on "chamber and symphonic music of the most serious kind". This was not to be read, however, as a declaration of austerity, as the charming 1920 *Pastorale d'été* revealed; but the two works of the following year—the "mime symphony" *Horace victorieux* and the "dramatic psalm" *Le Roi David*, which had a wildfire success and brought him fame—were marked by a tensile strength very characteristic of him. In 1923 his impression of a railway locomotive, *Pacific 231*, a *tour-de-force* of orchestral writing, created a sensation—"music of machines" was the latest fad—though Honegger was anxious for this to be heard not merely programmatically but as music in its own right.

The robustness of his style was seen again in the symphonic impression *Rugby*; but by the late 1930s a submerged vein of romanticism came to the surface to modify the sinewy quality of his writing, as in his other great success, *Joan of Arc at the stake*. Little is heard of his dozen operas and even more ballets, and his vast quantity of incidental music is likely to remain unknown (except for occasional re-screenings of the film *Pygmalion*), but whenever one of his concertos or symphonies is played there are always suspicions that Honegger has been undervalued.

CELLO CONCERTO
☐ Sadlo/Czech PO/Neumann/
  Shostakovich: Cello Conc. 1
  110 0604 Rediffusion/Supraphon
CONCERTO DA CAMERA
☐ Solum, Camden/English Sinfonia/
  Dilkes/*Ibert: Flute Conc; Jolivet: Flute Conc.*
  EMD5526 (5/76) EMI
PACIFIC 231
☐ CBSO/Fremaux/*Ibert: Divertissement; Poulenc: Les Biches; Satie: Gymnopédies*
  ASD2989 (5/74) EMI/HMV
PASTORALE D'ETE
☐ Paris ORTF/Martinon/*Dukas: Symphony; Ariane et Barbe-bleu (excs)*
  ASD2953 (7/74) EMI/HMV
(LE) ROI DAVID
☐ Danco, Montmollin, Hamel, Suisse Romande/Ansermet/*Ravel: Sheherazade; Melodies Hebraïques*
  GOS602-3 Decca
  STS-15155-6 London
SYMPHONY NO. 2
☐ Berlin PO/Karajan/*Sym. 3*
  2530 068 (7/73) DG
SYMPHONY NO. 3
☐ Berlin PO/Karajan/*Sym. 2*
  2530 068 (7/73) DG

Right: *To the public at large the name of Honegger is indelibly associated with his study* Pacific 231; *so that inevitably some enterprising photographer posed him on the footplate of an express—taking care not to show the number of wheels, which gave the work its title.*

JOHAN NEPOMUKA HUMMEL
(b. Pozsony 1778; d. Weimar 1837)

In the history of the piano Hummel holds a unique place; a player who enjoyed a brilliant reputation throughout Europe and whose powers of improvisation were considered even greater than those of his fellow-pupil and friend Beethoven », he forms a link between Mozart », in whose house he lived for two years as a young pupil, and Liszt », whose teacher was Hummel's pupil Czerny. His four operas and six ballets have long since been forgotten, but some of his abundant piano and chamber music—notable for its decorative elegance, facility and polish rather than depth of thought—survives and makes agreeable listening. In all his chamber works except his string quartets there is a piano part, which often has the lion's share (as in the virtuosic and enjoyable D minor Septet).

After making his début at the age of nine at one of Mozart's concerts, Hummel was taken by his father, a theatre conductor, on a lengthy concert tour in Germany, Denmark, England (where he stayed for a year, taking lessons from Clementi) and Holland, finally returning to Vienna, where he studied composition with Haydn » who had heard him play in London. In 1804 he became one of

Left: *The pianist and composer Hummel, once Mozart's pupil.*

Haydn's successors as *kapellmeister* at Esterháza, where he was instrumental in commissioning Beethoven's Mass in C, but was dismissed after seven years for neglecting his duties. He later took up similar appointments in Stuttgart and Weimar, also making extensive visits to St Petersburg, Paris and London, where he was, in 1833, conductor at the German Opera. An untidy, corpulent man of kindly disposition, he visited Beethoven (who had taken offence at the reception of his work in Esterháza) on his deathbed and valuably contributed to the dissemination of his symphonies by making piano-duet arrangements of them.

BASSOON CONCERTO IN F
☐ Zukerman/Wurtemberg CO/Faerber/
Piano Concertino
TV34348S Decca Turnabout
34348 Turnabout

CLARINET QUARTET IN E FLAT
☐ Music Party/*Crusell: Clarinet Quintet*
DSLO501 (11/74) L'Oiseau-Lyre*

PIANO CONCERTINO IN G
☐ Galling/Wurtemberg CO/Faerber/
Bassoon Conc.
TV34348S Decca Turnabout
34348 Turnabout

PIANO SONATAS: F SHARP MINOR; D
☐ Binns
DSLO530 (8/77) L'Oiseau-Lyre*

QUINTET IN E FLAT
☐ Melos Ens/*Septet*
SOL290 (5/66) L'Oiseau-Lyre

SEPTET IN D MINOR
☐ Melos Ens/*Quintet*
SOL290 (5/66) L'Oiseau-Lyre

TRUMPET CONCERTO IN E FLAT
☐ Andre/Berlin PO/Karajan/*L. Mozart; Telemann; Vivaldi—Trumpet Concs.*
ASD3044 (6/75) EMI/HMV
S-37063 Angel

FLORILEGIUM SERIES

HUMMEL
Piano Sonatas Op. 81 & Op. 106

MALCOLM BINNS

ENGELBERT HUMPERDINCK
(b. Siegburg 1854; d. Neustrelitz 1921)

An outstandingly talented student in Cologne and Munich, Humperdinck won a state award which entitled him to visit Italy in 1879. There he met Wagner », who invited him to Bayreuth to assist him in the preparations for the first performance of *Parsifal* (to the transition scene in which he is reputed to have contributed a short passage). After winning another prize, Humperdinck returned to Italy and went on to Spain, where he taught for two years in Barcelona, before being appointed a professor in Frankfurt and becoming a music critic there too.

He had written very little before he scored an immediate hit with *Hänsel und Gretel*, produced two days before Christmas 1893: against all probability its combination of folk-like simplicity, with moral overtones, and Wagnerian orchestration was, and remains, a huge success—the forest scenes, indeed, achieve real poetry. Humperdinck retired three years later at the early age of 42, but was lured back to become director of the Master School of Composition in Berlin; he never repeated the impact of his popular fable with any of his other five operas, although *Königskinder* (originally incidental music for a play) had a certain following.

HANSEL UND GRETEL
☐ *(In English)* Neville, Kern, Howard, Hunter, Herincx, Eddy, Robinson/ Sadler's Wells Opera/Bernardi
SXDW3023 (1/76) EMI/HMV Concert Classics

Below: *Humperdinck about the time of his appointment as director in Berlin.*
Right: *The great success of* Hänsel und Gretel *evaded Humperdinck in later operas.*

The Modern Symphony Orchestra
and its Instruments

This book is mainly about composers, rightly placing them above all who merely interpret and organise music, as the source of all musical imagination. However, music is a unique art in that the listener cannot have direct contact with it as a reader can with a book or as one can look at a painting. It is heard through instruments which have to be played by musicians. Music to most people is the sound of the symphony orchestra, and at this point we take a basic look at the symphony orchestra and the components that make up its rich sound.

The Vienna Philharmonic Orchestra, conducted by Eugen Jochum, at the Beethovenhalle in Bonn, West Germany.

The history of the orchestra can be traced back through many centuries, and a great variety of instrumental combinations have been evolved in different periods and different parts of the world. The orchestra as we know it began to take shape in the baroque era mainly as a result of the perfecting of the string instruments in the 17th century. Once these were fully developed the basic string orchestra then became the foundation of the modern symphony orchestra. Between the late baroque times of Bach and Handel and the classical period of Haydn and Mozart, the string section took on the proportions that we expect today, with a gradual addition of woodwind and brass as these instruments also went through their experimental stages. The classical orchestra would only have one or two of each of these instruments, and its flexibility was restrained largely by the still valveless state of the horns and other brass instruments which limited their melodic use and the keys in which they could play. As the valves and crooks were added, composers took advantage of the new opportunities

Although the orchestras gradually increased in size from perhaps thirty players to the hundred or more which is common today in the principal organisations, it was the variety of sounds available that made the most difference. In the baroque and classical orchestras a harpsichord or organ was generally used to pad out the ensemble with a mainly improvised continuo, but this practice died out as the additional instruments became available. By the romantic period of the 19th century the orchestra had become the flexible unit that we know today, and has basically remained the same, though varied with the occasional addition of instruments such as the saxophone family, the piano used as orchestral colour, and endless experiments as modern composers try to extend the range of sounds. A harp or harp section is an expected unit of the modern orchestra. With the modern demand for an ensemble that can play music of all periods the symphony orchestra is likely to remain a fairly stable unit, until electronic devices can completely duplicate its naturally beautiful tones.

Oboe

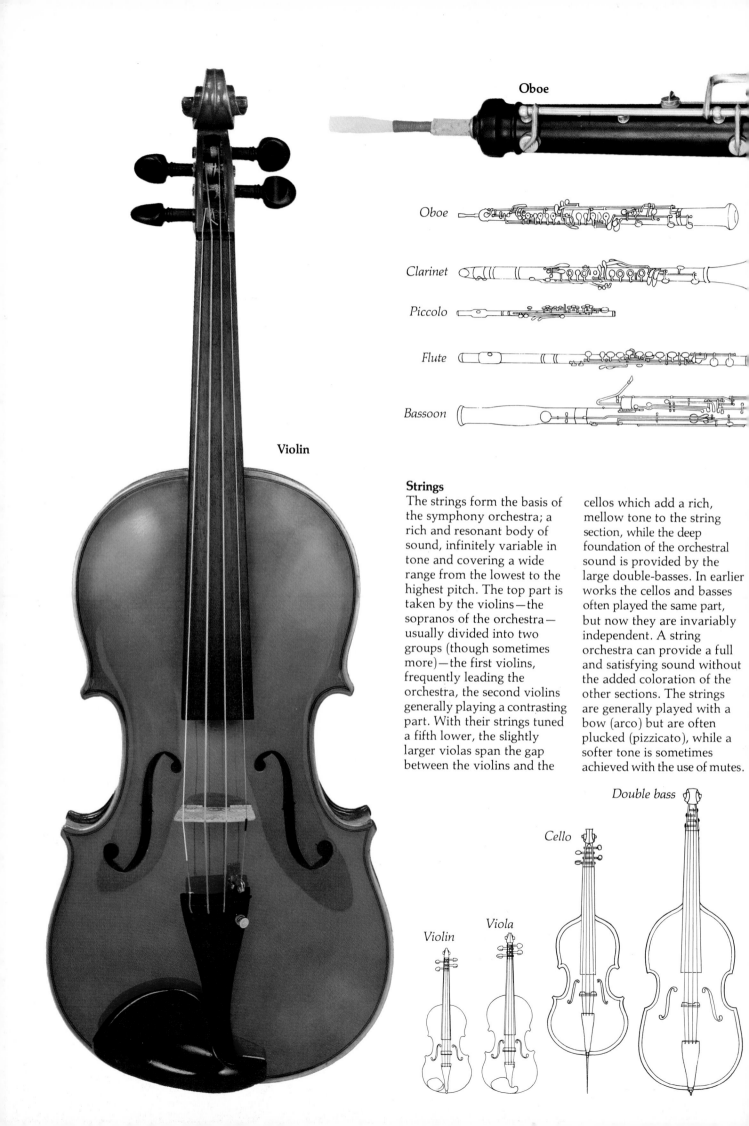

Oboe

Clarinet

Piccolo

Flute

Bassoon

Violin

Strings

The strings form the basis of the symphony orchestra; a rich and resonant body of sound, infinitely variable in tone and covering a wide range from the lowest to the highest pitch. The top part is taken by the violins—the sopranos of the orchestra—usually divided into two groups (though sometimes more)—the first violins, frequently leading the orchestra, the second violins generally playing a contrasting part. With their strings tuned a fifth lower, the slightly larger violas span the gap between the violins and the cellos which add a rich, mellow tone to the string section, while the deep foundation of the orchestral sound is provided by the large double-basses. In earlier works the cellos and basses often played the same part, but now they are invariably independent. A string orchestra can provide a full and satisfying sound without the added coloration of the other sections. The strings are generally played with a bow (arco) but are often plucked (pizzicato), while a softer tone is sometimes achieved with the use of mutes.

Double bass

Cello

Violin   *Viola*

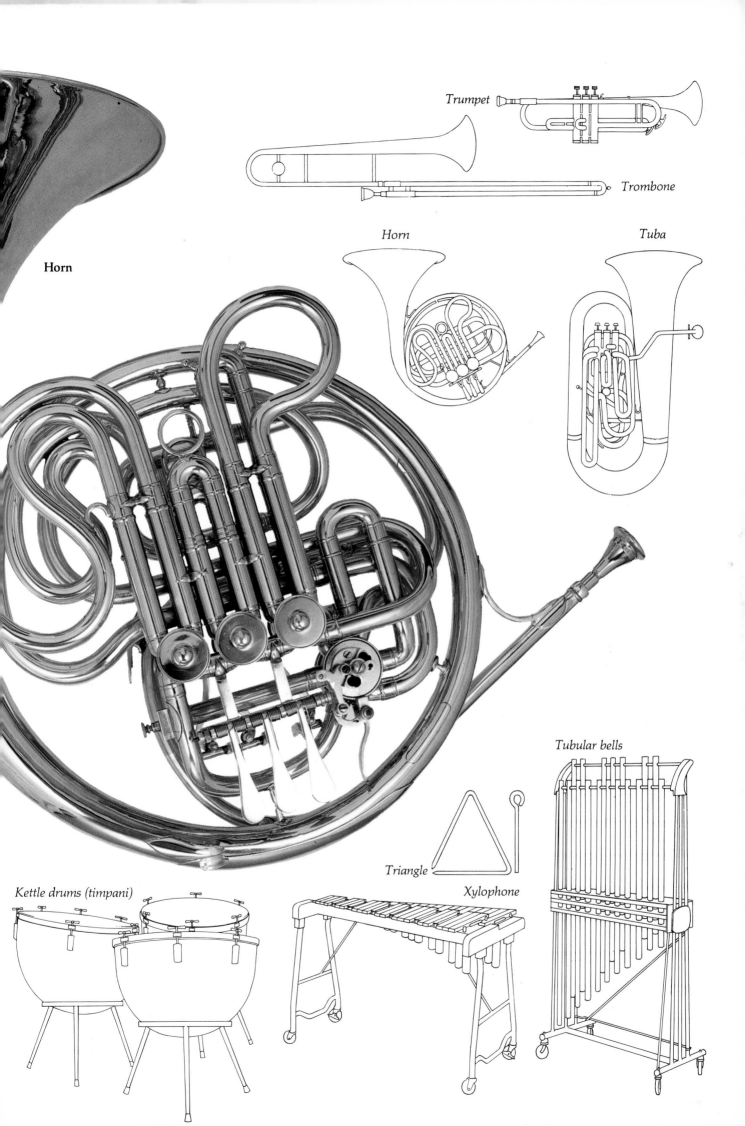

Trumpet

Trombone

Horn

Tuba

Horn

Tubular bells

Triangle

Xylophone

Kettle drums (timpani)

1500

1524 First Lutheran hymn-book published
1536 First book of accompanied songs published in Milan
1549 First book of plainsong published by Crowley

1550

1570 First academy of poetry and music founded in Paris
First festival of St Cecilia held in Normandy
1580 First literary reference to *Greensleeves*
1581 First dramatic ballet, *Ballet Comique de la Royne*, performed
c1586 First sonata published
1587 Monteverdi's first book of madrigals published
1589 Arbeau's *Orchesographie*, an early book of dances, published
1597 First Italian opera, *La Dafne*, performed
Morley's *Plaine and Easie Introduction to Practicall Musick* published

1600

1609 *Three blind mice* published
1627 First German opera produced—*Daphne* Heinrich Schütz
1637 Venice Opera House opens
1642 Monteverdi's *L'Incoronazione di Poppea* performed
1644 Antonio Stradivarius born

A MUSICAL HISTORY

It is not always easy to have a true mental perspective of history. To know where composers and musical works made their mark in time gives us a much clearer idea of how music has progressed and changed; it'is fascinating to realise that Wagner and Verdi were born in the same year, that Puccini was born in the year that Offenbach's *Orpheus in the Underworld* was first produced, that *Carmen* and *Trial by jury* are contemporaries. As all art to some degree depends for its inspiration on what went before, such knowledge helps us to realise how and why masterpieces were created.

This chart gives a basic reference to the musical history of the last 400 years. The diagram on the right shows the names and dates of composers in this book, and the paragraphs above list important events in the musical world. Below are illustrated, in line with their date panels, some of the instruments which have been invented or popularised during the various periods. A glance at the information detailed above and then downwards to the diagram gives an instant view of what was happening and who was alive at the time.

1525

1575

1625

SCHÜTZ 1585-1672

BYRD 1543-1623

TALLIS 1505-1585

BU

JOSQUIN 1445-1521

PALESTRINA 1525-1594

LASSUS 1532-1594

MONTEVERDI 1567-1643

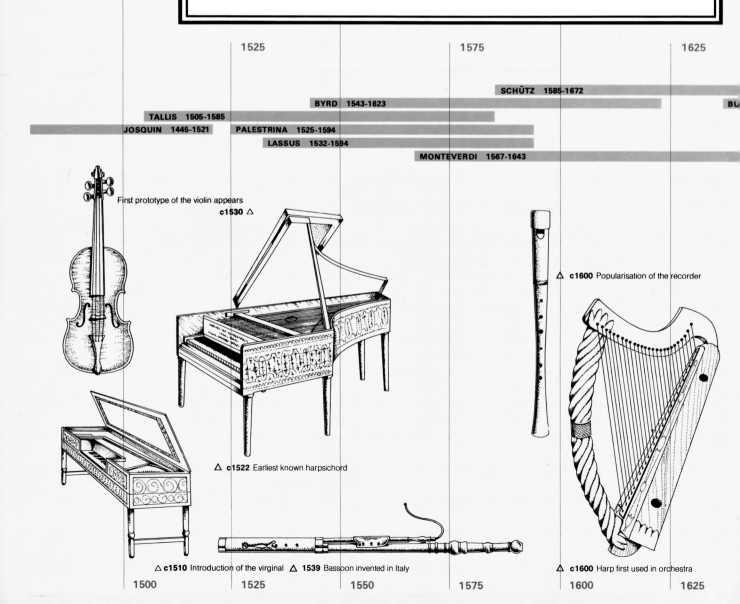

First prototype of the violin appears
c1530 △

△ **c1600** Popularisation of the recorder

△ **c1522** Earliest known harpsichord

△ **c1510** Introduction of the virginal   △ **1539** Bassoon invented in Italy

△ **c1600** Harp first used in orchestra

1500   **1525**   **1550**   **1575**   **1600**   **1625**

1650 | **1700** | **1750** | **1800**

50 12 semitone scale fixed
51 Playford's *English Dancing Master* published
52 Popularisation of the minuet by Lully and others
56 The Italian Opera House opens in London
60 Post of "Master of the King's Musicke" created
63 Drury Lane Theatre opens
66 First signed Stradivarius violins appear
71 Paris Opera founded
73 First French opera performed in Paris—*Cadmus et Hermione* by Lully
74 Matthew Locke writes music for Shakespeare's *The Tempest*
75 Locke composes *Psyche*, earliest surviving English opera
78 First German opera house opens in Hamburg
Purcell writes music for Shakespeare's *Timon of Athens*
79 Purcell becomes organist at Westminster Abbey
86 The tune *Lilliburlero* first mentioned
89 Purcell's *Dido and Aeneas* first produced
92 Purcell's *The Fairy Queen* produced
95 First public concert in Edinburgh

1706 Isaac Watt's *Hymns and Spiritual Songs* published
1710 Establishment of the Academy of Ancient Music in London
1715 Handel's *Water Music* first performed
1720 Clarinet first used in orchestra
1721 Bach's *Brandenburg Concertos* written
1724 Beginning of the Three Choirs Festival
1725 *Gradus ad Parnassum*—early work on counterpoint by Fux
Prague Opera House founded
1728 Gay's *The Beggar's Opera* first produced
1729 Bach's *St Matthew Passion* composed
1731 First concerts in America at Boston and Charleston
1732 Covent Garden Opera House opens
Earliest piano music published (Giustini)
1735 Russian Imperial Ballet founded in St Petersburg
1737 Wesley's *Psalms and Hymns* published
1740 *Rule Britannia* first heard in Arne's masque *Alfred*
1742 First performance of *Messiah* in Dublin
1743 *Messiah* performed in London
1744 Madrigal Society founded in London

1758 First instruction book for the guitar published in England
1762 Arne's ballad opera *Love in a village* produced
1767 Rousseau's *Dictionary of Music* published
First piano heard in England
c1773 Waltz becomes popular in Vienna
1776 First volume of Burney's *General History of Music* published
1781 Mozart's *Idomeneo* performed
1783 Piano pedals patented by Broadwood
1786 Mozart's *The marriage of Figaro* first performed in Vienna
1791 Mozart's *The magic flute* performed, closely followed by his death
The waltz introduced into England
1799 Beethoven's first symphony written

1800 Clementi foun... London
1804 Beethoven's *E...*
1805 Beethoven's *F...*
1808 First opera ho...
1809 Beethoven's *E...*
1811 Prague Conse...
1812 Royal Philharm...
1815 Publishing ho... London
1816 Rossini's *The ...*
1821 Weber's *Der F...*
1822 Royal Academ...
1823 *Home sweet h...*
1824 Beethoven's *C...*
1829 Rossini's *Willia...*
1832 Donizetti's *L'E...*
1835 Donizetti's *Luc...*
Counterpoint ...
1842 First performa... Verdi's *Nabuc...* Vienna Philhar...
1843 Mendelssohn ... *midsummer n...* Wagner's *The ...*
1845 First American... performed
1846 Mendelssohn's...

1725 | **1775**

1675

BOYCE 1710-1779
HANDEL 1685-1759
J. S. BACH 1685-1750
TELEMANN 1681-1767
VIVALDI 1678-1741
...7-1707
GLUCK 1714-1787
PERGOLESI 1710-1736
...ORELLI 1653-1713
PURCELL 1659-1695
COUPERIN 1668-1733
ALBINONI 1671-1751
RAMEAU 1683-1764
D. SCARLATTI 1685-1757
ARNE 1710-1778
J. C. BACH 1735-1782
HAYDN 1732-1809
C. P. E. BACH 1714-1788
BOCCHERINI 1743-1805
MOZART 1756-1791

WAG...
CHOPIN
GLINKA 1804-...
BELLINI 1801-183...
ROSSINI 1792-1868
WEBER 1786-1826
BEETHOVEN 1770-1827
SCHUBERT 1797-1828
DONIZETTI 1797-1848
BERWALD 1796-1868
LISZT
HUMMEL 1778-1837
PAGANINI 1782-1840
SPOHR 1784-1859
BERLIOZ 1803-...
MENDELS...
SCHUMA...
VERD...

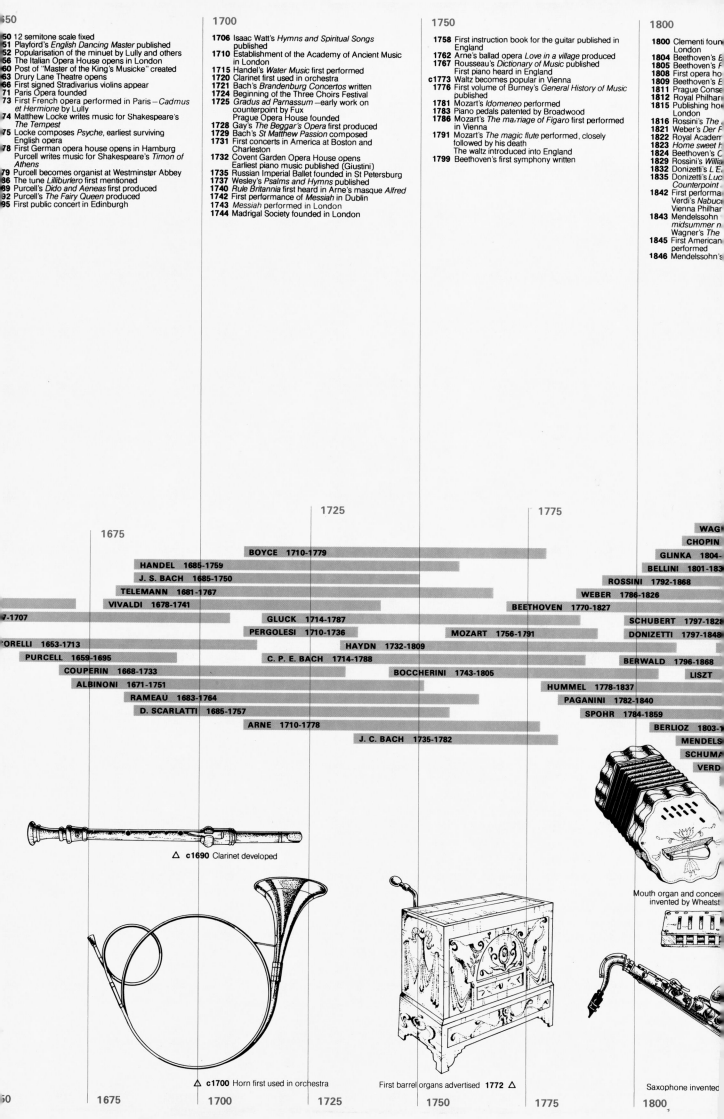

△ **c1690** Clarinet developed

△ **c1700** Horn first used in orchestra

First barrel organs advertised **1772** △

Mouth organ and concer... invented by Wheatst...

Saxophone invented...

1675 | **1700** | **1725** | **1750** | **1775** | **1800**

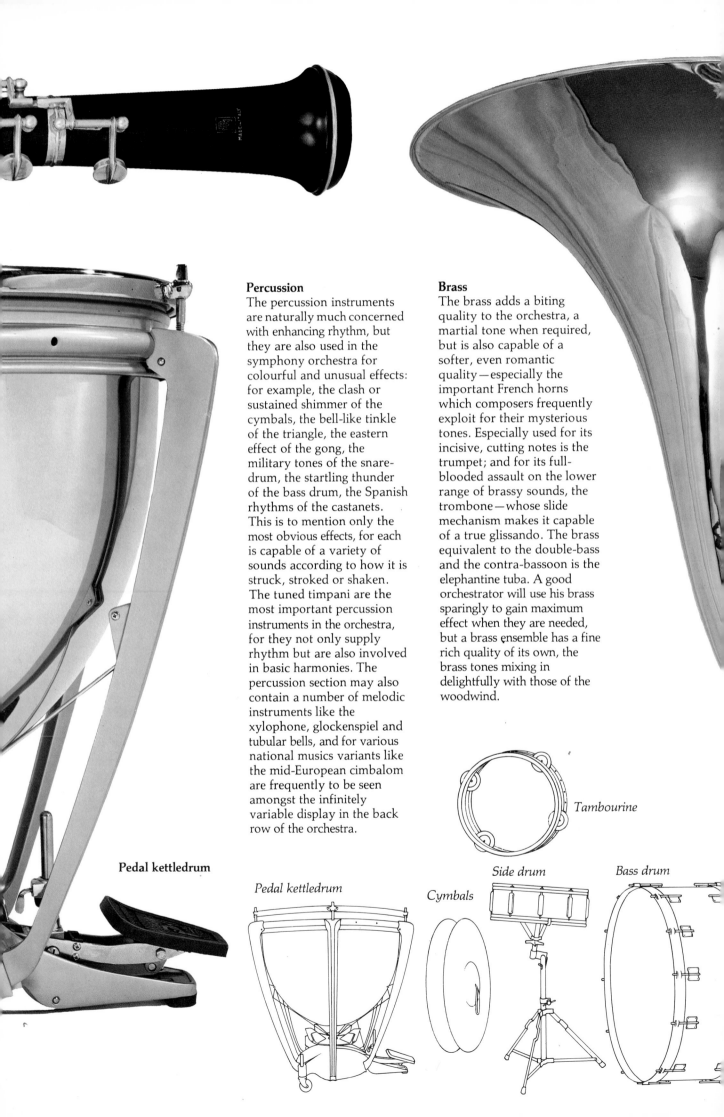

Percussion

The percussion instruments are naturally much concerned with enhancing rhythm, but they are also used in the symphony orchestra for colourful and unusual effects: for example, the clash or sustained shimmer of the cymbals, the bell-like tinkle of the triangle, the eastern effect of the gong, the military tones of the snare-drum, the startling thunder of the bass drum, the Spanish rhythms of the castanets. This is to mention only the most obvious effects, for each is capable of a variety of sounds according to how it is struck, stroked or shaken. The tuned timpani are the most important percussion instruments in the orchestra, for they not only supply rhythm but are also involved in basic harmonies. The percussion section may also contain a number of melodic instruments like the xylophone, glockenspiel and tubular bells, and for various national musics variants like the mid-European cimbalom are frequently to be seen amongst the infinitely variable display in the back row of the orchestra.

Brass

The brass adds a biting quality to the orchestra, a martial tone when required, but is also capable of a softer, even romantic quality—especially the important French horns which composers frequently exploit for their mysterious tones. Especially used for its incisive, cutting notes is the trumpet; and for its full-blooded assault on the lower range of brassy sounds, the trombone—whose slide mechanism makes it capable of a true glissando. The brass equivalent to the double-bass and the contra-bassoon is the elephantine tuba. A good orchestrator will use his brass sparingly to gain maximum effect when they are needed, but a brass ensemble has a fine rich quality of its own, the brass tones mixing in delightfully with those of the woodwind.

Tambourine

Pedal kettledrum

Pedal kettledrum

Cymbals

Side drum

Bass drum

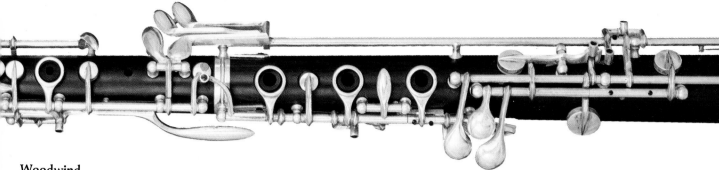

Woodwind

The woodwind add a variety of colours of a reedy or piping nature. The double-reeded oboe has the most distinctive tone, which can either be plaintive or hard, while the single-reeded clarinet is smoother and more agile. A deeper tenor oboe, the cor anglais, is often to be found in the wind section. The deepest

reed tone comes from the bassoon, a natural comic though capable of a beautiful tone, and there is also a deeper-tone double or contra-bassoon. The breathy tones of the flute, its notes produced by blowing over an aperture, and the higher-pitched piccolo are able to stand out clearly above the most massive orchestral sound. Occasionally the mongrel saxophones (brass instruments with reeds) are added to 20th century music.

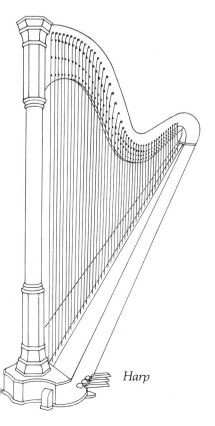

Harp

1850

music-publishing firm in

a composed
io first performed
built in New Orleans
eror concerto written
tory opens
ic Society founded
of Boosey established in

ber of Seville first performed
chütz first performed in Berlin
f Music founded
e written by Sir Henry Bishop
ral symphony written
Tell performed in Paris
d'Amore performed
i Lammermoor and Cherubini's
Fugue published
es of Wagner's Rienzi and

nic Orchestra founded
es incidental music for A
's dream
g Dutchman first performed
era, Leonora by W. H. Fry,

ijah performed

c1850 Growing popularity of the brass band in England
1851 Verdi's *Rigoletto* first performed
1853 Firm of Steinway founded in New York
1855 First Crystal Palace concerts
1856 Firm of Bechstein founded in Berlin
1858 Offenbach's *Orpheus in the Underworld* first
produced
1865 Wagner's *Tristan and Isolde* first performed
1867 New England Conservatory opens in Boston
1871 Royal Albert Hall opens
1873 National Training College of Music founded (later
the Royal College of Music)
1875 Gilbert and Sullivan write *Trial by jury*
Bizet's *Carmen* produced
1877 First production of Tchaikovsky's *Swan Lake*
1881 Boston Symphony Orchestra founded
1882 Berlin Philharmonic Orchestra founded
1883 Royal College of Music established
1891 Carnegie Hall opens in New York
1893 Humperdinck's *Hänsel und Gretel* performed

1900

1900 Philadelphia Orchestra founded
1902 Caruso makes his first recordings
1903 First opera recording—Verdi's *Ernani*
1904 London Symphony Orchestra's first concert
1905 Sir Thomas Beecham makes first conducting
appearance in London
1908 Elgar's *First Symphony* performed
1910 Stravinsky's *The Firebird* performed
1911 Strauss's *Der Rosenkavalier* performed
1916 Holst completes *The Planets*
1924 Gershwin's *Rhapsody in Blue* performed
Juilliard School of Music founded in New York
1927 New York Philharmonic founded
1930 BBC Symphony Orchestra founded
1931 Rachmaninov's music banned in Russia
1932 London Philharmonic Orchestra founded
1934 Glyndebourne Festival Theatre opens
1936 Prokofiev's *Peter and the wolf* performed
1945 Philharmonia Orchestra founded
1946 Royal Philharmonic Orchestra founded

1950

1951 Royal Festival hall opens

1875   **1975**

MOERAN 1894-1950
KODÁLY 1882-1967
SZYMANOWSKI 1882-1937
IRELAND 1879-1962
FALLA 1876-1946
SCHOENBERG 1874-1951
RACHMANINOV 1873-1943
VAUGHAN WILLIAMS 1872-1958
GRANADOS 1867-1916
DUKAS 1865-1935
SIBELIUS 1865-1957
DELIUS 1862-1934
WOLF 1860-1903
ALBÉNIZ 1860-1909

1825

JANÁČEK 1854-1928
RIMSKY-KORSAKOV 1844-1908
GRIEG 1843-1907
MASSENET 1842-1912
DELIBES 1836-1891
SAINT-SAËNS 1835-1921
BRAHMS 1833-1897
J. STRAUSS II 1825-1899
BRUCKNER 1824-1896
FRANCK 1822-1890
ER 1813-1883
1810-1849
857
TCHAIKOVSKY 1840-1893
MUSSORGSKY 1839-1881
BIZET 1838-1875
BRUCH 1838-1920
ELGAR 1857-1934
GOUNOD 1818-1893
DOHNÁNYI 1877-1960
811-1886
CHABRIER 1841-1894
CHAUSSON 1855-1899
SATIE 1866-1925
BLOCH 1880-1959
869
SOHN 1809-1847
NN 1810-1856
1813-1901
PUCCINI 1858-1924
MASCAGNI 1863-1945
OFFENBACH 1819-1880
LALO 1823-1892
SMETANA 1824-1884
BORODIN 1833-1887
WIENIAWSKI 1835-1880
BALAKIREV 1837-1910
DVOŘÁK 1841-1904
SULLIVAN 1842-1900
FAURÉ 1845-1924
BAX 1883-1953

ARNOLD b1921
HINDEMITH 1895-1963
WALTON b1902
BERKELEY b1903
WEILL 1900-1950
ORFF b1895
BLISS 1891-1975
LEONCAVALLO 1858-1919
BUSONI 1866-1924
BOULEZ b1925
GERHARD 1896-1970
RAVEL 1875-1937
VILLA-LOBOS 1887-1959
BARTÓK 1881-1945
HENZE b1926
POULENC 1899-1963
MILHAUD 1892-1974
COPLAND b1900
TIPPETT b1905
MESSIAEN b1908
GERSHWIN 1898-1937
PROKOFIEV 1891-1953
HONEGGER 1892-1955
BERG 1885-1935
BERNSTEIN b1918
BRITTEN 1913-1976
SHOSTAKOVICH 1906-1975

HUMPERDINCK 1854-1921
MAHLER 1860-1911
DEBUSSY 1862-1918
R. STRAUSS 1864-1949
NIELSEN 1865-1931
GLAZUNOV 1865-1936
ROUSSEL 1869-1937
SCRIABIN 1872-1915
IVES 1874-1954
HOLST 1874-1934
WOLF-FERRARI 1876-1948
RESPIGHI 1879-1936
GRAINGER 1882-1961
STRAVINSKY 1882-1971
WARLOCK 1894-1930

na
ne **1829** △

by Adolphe Sax **c1840** △   △ **1843**   Tuba first used in orchestra

1825   **1850**   **1875**   **1900**   **1925**   **1950**   **1975**

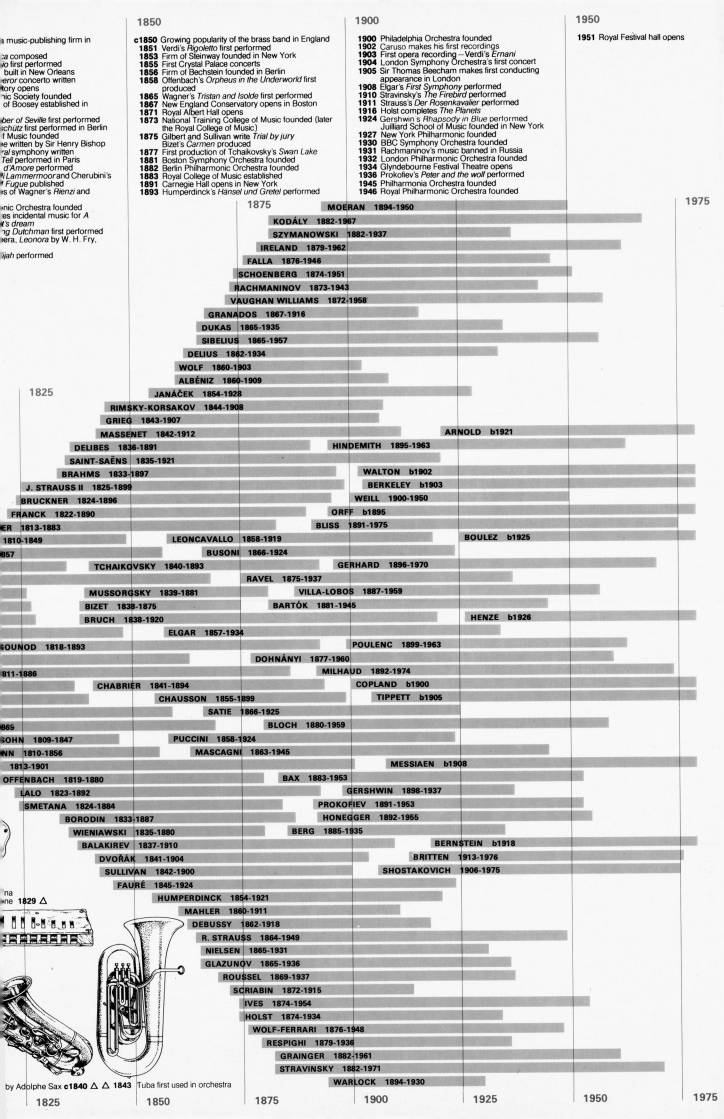

JOHN IRELAND
(b. Bowden, Cheshire, 1879; d. Sussex 1962)

Ireland studied composition under Stanford at the Royal College of Music (where he himself was later to be a professor for many years, several of his pupils becoming famous): from him he derived a Brahmsian tradition, which persisted to some extent even after 1908, when he destroyed all his previous works, and a care for craftsmanship which is apparent in everything he wrote. He never essayed an opera or symphony, but excelled in shorter forms, though his breadth of phrase and powers of construction were by no means merely those of a miniaturist. In particular his numerous songs, which show an informed literary taste, and piano pieces, many of a lyrical character with Nature as their subject, often achieve distinction. His idiom was individual, with richly-textured bitter-sweet harmony and a general atmosphere of poignant meditation: to this was added a vein of pagan mysticism (closely associated with the Channel Islands, where he spent much time) which found expression in, for example, the orchestral *Forgotten rite* and the piano *Island spell* and *Sarnia*.

His first acknowledged compositions were chamber works, but he found general appreciation with the song *Sea fever* (1913), which rapidly became a popular favourite, and the Second Violin Sonata, a romantic work written during the First World War. Besides his nostalgic style, which shows some kinship with that of his near-contemporary Bax », he could command a more vigorous manner, frequently highly concentrated in thought, as in his 1920 piano sonata: the two moods are seen cheek by jowl in the attractive Piano Concerto of 1930, the closest Ireland's style ever came to that of Ravel's ». Another influence he was able successfully to absorb, as in the Sonatina for piano, was that of the neo-classic Stravinsky ». It is perhaps a pity that his more ebullient compositions, like the *London Overture*, should have overshadowed gentler works such as the *Concertino pastorale*.

A LONDON OVERTURE; CONCERTINO PASTORALE; THE HOLY BOY; EPIC MARCH; A DOWNLAND SUITE
☐ Parkin/LPO/Boult/*These Things*
SRCS31 (9/66) Lyrita
ORCHESTRAL WORKS
(Mai-Dun; Legend for piano and orchestra; Satyricon; The Forgotten Rite)
☐ Parkin/LPO/Boult
SRCS32 (9/66) Lyrita
PIANO MUSIC
(Decorations; The undertone; Obsession; The Holy boy; The fire of Spring; Prelude; Rhapsody; The towing path; Merry Andrew; London pieces)
☐ Parkin
SRCS87 (12/75) Lyrita
PIANO MUSIC
(Sonata; Summer evening; Amberley wild brooks; April;Bergomask; For Remembrance; Darkened Valley; Equinox; Soliloquy; On a birthday morning)
☐ Parkin
SRCS88 (4/77) Lyrita
PIANO MUSIC
(Sonatina; Ballade; February's Child; Aubade; Month's mind; Greenways; Sarnia)
☐ Parkin
SRCS89 (6/78) Lyrita
SONGS
(Songs of a wayfarer; When lights go rolling round the sky; Hope the hornblower; Sea fever; 5 poems; Love and friendship; Friendship in misfortune; The one hope; We'll to the woods no more)
☐ Luxon, Rowlands
SRCS65 (5/75) Lyrita
SONGS
Tryst; During music; The Advent; Hymn for a Child; My fair; The Sally Gardens; Soldier's return; The scapegoat; A thanksgiving; All in a garden green; An aside; Report song; The sweet season; Blow out you bugles; If there were dreams to sell; I have twelve oxen; Spring sorrow; The bells of San Marie; The journey; The merry month of May; Vagabond; When I am dead my dearest; Santa Chiara; Great things; If we must part; Tutto e sciolto
☐ Luxon, Rowlands
SRCS66 (7/75)Lyrita
THESE THINGS SHALL BE
☐ Case/LPO/Boult/*Piano Conc.*
SRCS36 (10/68) Lyrita
VIOLIN SONATAS—NO. 1 IN D MINOR: NO. 2 IN A MINOR
☐ Neaman, Parkin
SRCS64 (10/72)Lyrita

Left: *It is by his piano music and songs that John Ireland is chiefly remembered today.*

CHARLES IVES
(b. Danbury, Conn., 1874; d. New York 1954)

After studying with his father—a highly unorthodox and imaginative local band-master—and at Yale, Ives went into insurance and indulged energetically in music as a sideline. Virtually unknown, or at the most derided, until about 1939 when his vast and enormously difficult Second Piano Sonata ("Concord") was at last performed a quarter of a century after it was written—36 years elapsed between the creation of his Third Symphony and its being awarded a Pulitzer Prize—he was belatedly hailed as a founding father of American music and a pioneer of modernism. In his works, all of which date from before 1920, Ives certainly anticipated many internationally famous composers in the experimental techniques with which they are usually associated: harmonies in fourths or whole tones, polytonality, atonality, quarter-tones, serialism, polyrhythms, chord clusters, improvised passages, spatial presentation.

The deliberate chaos of much of his music, plus the vehement scorn he poured on conservatives in his letters and other writings, has often led to his being considered merely a cranky amateur; but diffuse and crude as his work frequently is, it is full of conviction. He himself was a good violinist and organist whose radical outlook was due to his father's insistence that he "stretch his ears" in various ways; and the indiscipline of much of his music arose from his empirical attitude to the organisation of sounds, in which words like "dissonance" or "noise" have no precise significance. Over and above this, he was imbued with the Nature mysticism of the Transcendentalist philosophers: the "Concord" Sonata and *The unanswered question* express these strivings. He made extensive use of the music he knew from his childhood—chapel hymns, traditional American tunes, town band banalities—and delighted in representing the complex jumble of sounds heard simultaneously from different sources, in divergent rhythms and keys, as in *Putnam's camp* (from *Three places in New England*), *Washington's birthday* (in the "Holidays" Symphony) and the Fourth Symphony. The short *Central Park in the dark* and some of the songs, such as *Evening* and *Soliloquy*, reveal the simpler, lyrical, and dare one say the more intrinsically musical, side of Ives.

Above: *Charles Ives, eccentric, iconoclast and innovator.*

ORCHESTRAL SET NO. 2
☐ LSO and Chorus/Stokowski/*Messiaen: L'Ascension*
  PFS4203 (4/72) Decca Phase 4
  21060 London
SONGS
  (At the river; Ann Street; The Housatonic at Stockbridge; From Paracelsus; Thoreau; The Cage; A Christmas carol; In the mornin'; The circus band; A farewell to land; The Indians; The Innate; Like a sick eagle; Majority; Serenity; The things our fathers loved)
☐ DeGaetani/Kalish
  H71325 (11/76) WEA/Nonesuch
  71325 Nonesuch
STRING QUARTET NO. 1
☐ Concord Quartet/*Quartet 2*
  H71306 (8/76) WEA/Nonesuch
  71306 Nonesuch

STRING QUARTET NO. 2
☐ Concord Quartet/*Quartet 1*
  H71306 (8/76) WEA/Nonesuch
  71306 Nonesuch
SYMPHONY NO. 1
☐ Los Angeles PO/Mehta/*Elgar*
  SXL6592 (9/73) Decca
  6816 London
SYMPHONY NO. 1*; SYMPHONIES NOS. 2-3; SYMPHONY NO. 4†; SYMPHONY—NEW ENGLAND HOLIDAYS: ORCHESTRAL SET NO. 1*; THE UNANSWERED QUESTION: CENTRAL PARK: VARIATIONS ON AMERICA*
☐ NYPO/Bernstein/*Philadelphia/Ormandy/†American SO/Stokowski
  77424 (9/74) CBS
  MS-7015 Columbia

LEOŠ JANÁČEK
(b. Hukvaldy, East Moravia, 1854; d. Ostrava 1928)

It would be hard to find a more striking example of a late-maturing artist than Janáček: he was 40 before he wrote his first work of any significance, over 60 before he received more than local recognition, 70 when he started to produce his most characteristic masterpieces. Partly this was due to his unsettled start: he had acquired the basis of a musical education as a choirboy at the Augustinian monastery in Brno, then had managed a year's study in Prague (living in dire poverty, his father having died) before returning to Brno as conductor of its Philharmonic Orchestra; but feeling his knowledge inadequate, at the age of 25 he then spent a year at the Leipzig Conservatory and another in Vienna. On his return he founded his own music school in Brno, where he was to teach for nearly forty years, and only after that did he even begin to write.

Left: Leoš Janáček.

He had always had a deep feeling for the folk music of his native Moravia, which can be heard in his *Lachian dances* and an early opera, *Beginning of a romance*, but of even more influence were the rhythms and intonations of Moravian speech which, together with the sounds of Nature, formed the contours of his extremely individual melodic language. He remained an obscure provincial composer until his opera *Jenufa*, which had been heard in Brno in 1904, was produced in Prague and Vienna in 1916, thanks to pressure from a chance champion; and this changed his life completely.

His intense pantheism and human compassion found expression in the song-cycle *Diary of a young man who disappeared* and, later, the operas *Cunning little vixen* (a tender work of the animal world) and *House of the dead*, based on Dostoyevsky—the subjects and, more especially, the musical idiom of his opera's are entirely unconventional and original. So indeed is all his music, which is instantly recognisable—individual in its harmony (based on an involved theory of his own), mosaic in construction, with short ostinato figures repeated with slight variations, extremely distinctive in its orchestration. In support of this one need look no further than those works of his which appeared in 1926—the strange opera *The Makropoulos affair*, the multi-trumpet Sinfonietta which exudes an aura of exultation, the Capriccio for piano left hand and seven wind instruments, and the brilliantly exciting and utterly unorthodox *Glagolitic Mass*.

Below: *A scene from the English National Opera Production of* The Makropoulos Affair.

(The) CUNNING LITTLE VIXEN
☐ *Cpte.* Kroupa, Prochazkova, Hlavsa, Jedlicka, Heriban, Vonasek, Prague Nat. Theatre/Gregor
MS1181-2 (12/72) Rediffusion/Supraphon

DIARY OF A YOUNG MAN WHO DISAPPEARED
☐ *(in English)* Gale, Bainbridge, Creffield, Biggar, Tear, Ledger
ZRG692 (11/71) Decca Argo⋆

FROM THE HOUSE OF THE DEAD
☐ *Cpte.* Bednar, Tattermuschova, Blachut, Striska, Prague Nat. Theatre/Gregor
SUAST50705-6 (2/73) Supraphon

GLAGOLITIC MASS
☐ Kubiak, Collins, Tear, Schone, Brighton Festival Chorus, RPO/Kempe
SXL6600 (2/74) Decca
26338 London

(The) MAKROPOULOS AFFAIR
☐ *Cpte.* Prylova, Zidek, Vonasek, Tattermuschova, Prague Nat. Theatre/Gregor
SUAST50811-2 (8/72) Supraphon

MALE CHORUSES
(The soldier's lot; Our birch tree; The evening witch; Leave-taking; Czech Legion; The wandering madman; Schoolmaster Halfar; Marycka Magdonova; Seventy thousand)
☐ Moravian Teachers' Chorus/Tucapsky
112 0878 (5/72) Rediffusion/Supraphon

SINFONIETTA
☐ LSO/Abbado/*Hindemith: Symphonic Metamorphoses*
SXL6398 (5/69) Decca
6620 London
☐ Bav. RSO/Kubelik/*Taras Bulba*
2530 075 (9/71) DG⋆

STRING QUARTETS NOS. 1 AND 2
☐ Janacek Quartet
SUAST50556 (7/72) Supraphon

TARAS BULBA
☐ Bav. RSO/Kubelik/*Sinfonietta*
2530 075 (9/71) DG⋆
☐ LPO/Huybrechts/*Lachian Dances*
SXL6507 (10/71) Decca
6718 London

111

ART OF THE NETHERLANDS
Chansons: Allegez moy; El grillo; De tous biens plaine; Guillaume sa va; Adieu mes amours. Instrumental: Fortuna desperata; Vive le roy; La Spagna; La Bernadina. Motets: De profundis; Benedicta es caelorum Regina; Inviolata, integra et casta es, Maria. Mass Movement: Credo super De tous biens.
□ Early Music Consort/Munrow/ *Early Renaissance Music* **SLS5049** (11/76) HMV
CHANSONS AND FROTTOLAS: LA DEPLORATION SUR LA MORT DE J. OKEGHEM
□ Musica Reservata/Morrow **ZRG793** (2/76) Decca Argo∗
CHANSONS AND MOTETS: LA DEPLORATION SUR LA MORT DE J. OKEGHEM
□ Purcell Consort/Burgess/*Dunstable* **ZRG681** (7/71) Decca Argo

JOSQUIN DES PRÉS
(b. Condé, Hainault, c. 1445; d. there 1521)

The pre-eminent position Josquin enjoyed as a central figure in Renaissance music was recognised even in his own generation, when admiration for his great technical skill led to his being described as "princeps musicorum"; but although we today can appreciate his remarkable natural facility for canon and his ability to encompass both old and new traditions, it is his expressive treatment of words—then something novel—and his masterly construction and texture that chiefly impress us.

How keen the competition was for his services may be gathered from the extraordinary list of his appointments: having been a singer in Milan Cathedral, before the age of 30 he was in the employ of the Sforza family in Milan and Rome, then successively a member of the Pope's Sistine Chapel, choirmaster at Cambrai, in the service first of Louis XII of France and then of Duke Hercules I of Ferrara (the vowels of whose title he turned into notes to form the theme of a Mass dedicated to his patron) before ending his days as provost at Condé. During all this time he wrote—at his pleasure, since the evidence is clear that he would not allow himself to be hurried—some twenty

Masses, more than 100 motets and a large number of chansons (many of which became immensely popular) excelling in a wide range of both religious and secular styles. Specially notable is his imitative treatment and equal distribution of voices in his Masses, a form in which the tenor had traditionally been predominant: there are early Masses in complex mensural techniques, Masses on traditional tunes such as *L'homme armé*, and parody works (i.e. quoting themes from other composers, as in his *Mater patris*); but the peaks of his achievement in this field were the *Beata Virgine*, *Pange lingua* and *Da pacem* Masses.

To the motet he brought grandeur and expressive power, as in *Planxit autem David* (David's lament over Saul), *Ave Maria* and *Ave verum*. But not the least of his work was in the sphere of the choral chanson, which he also treated expressively and polyphonically, ranging from the deeply emotional (as in *Cueurs desolez* and the lament on the death of his former teacher Okeghem) to the humorous, often with satirical overtones, as in *El grillo*.

ZOLTÁN KODÁLY
(b. Kecskemét 1882; d. Budapest 1967)

Although the most noteworthy Hungarian composer of the early twentieth century except for his close friend Bartók », Kodály was never as experimental in his work as his great contemporary, and devoted far more of his time to musicology and musical education (in which spheres his importance can scarcely be exaggerated) than to composition. Coming from a family of keen amateur chamber-music players, he learnt the violin in his youth, taught himself the cello, and started writing church music (the result of singing in a provincial cathedral choir) before entering the Budapest Conservatory—where he was later to be a professor from 1907. He produced some early chamber works, but in 1905, deeply interested in authentic Hungarian folk music, as distinct from what passed as such in the outside world, he threw all his energies for the next decade into research, collecting and publishing a vast body of folksong (from 1906 in collaboration with Bartók).

The early influences on his own music of Brahms » and Debussy » were overshadowed by those of folk music, though until the end of the First World War he wrote little but songs and chamber works, which however included the sonata for solo cello, a truly remarkable *tour de force*. What brought him real fame in the music world, outside as well as inside his own country, was the passionately patriotic *Psalmus Hungaricus*, written in 1923 for the fiftieth anniversary of the union of Buda and Pest: it is one of the choral masterpieces of its period. Kodály won even greater general success three years later with the brilliantly colourful comedy *Háry János*, the orchestral suite from

which has become immensely popular thanks to its picturesque meloodiousness and piquant orchestration. In these, as in the later orchestral works of his which continue to be played—dances from different parts of Hungary and the *"Peacock"* Variations—the folk character is all-important. Recognition of the outstanding quality of much of Kodály's abundant choral music has been hampered, apart from his *Te Deum* and wartime *Missa brevis*, by the language problem.

Below: *Kodály, Bartók's partner in his folk-music researches.*

DANCES OF GALANTA
☐ LSO/Kertesz/*Hary Janos (exc.)*
SXL6136 (1/65) Decca
6417 London
☐ Philh. Hungarica/Dorati/*Dances of Marosszek; Concerto for Orchestra; Theatre Ov.*
SXL6712 (12/75) Decca

DANCES OF MAROSSZEK
☐ Philh. Hungarica/Dorati/ *Dances of Galanta; Concerto for Orchestra; Theatre Ov.*
SXL6712 (12/75) Decca
6862 London

HARY JANOS
☐ *Exc.* Ustinov *(narrator)* , Szonyi, Laszlo, Komlassy, Melis, Bende, Polocz Ch./LSO/Kertesz
SXL6631 (11/74) Decca

HARY JANOS—SUITE
☐ Netherlands Radio PO/Dorati/ *Prokofiev*
PFS4355 (5/76) Decca Phase 4
21146 London
☐ Philh. Hungarica/Dorati/ *Symphony in C; Menuetto serio*
SXL6713 (8/76) Decca

MISSA BREVIS
☐ Gale, Le Sage, Francis, Hodgson, Caley, Rippon, Brighton Festival Ch./Heltay/*Pange Lingua*
SXL6803 (12/76) Decca

PEACOCK VARIATIONS
☐ LSO/Kertesz/*Psalmus Hungaricus*
SXL6497 (4/71) Decca
☐ Philh. Hungarica/Dorati/*Concert*
SXL6714 (12/76) Decca

PSALMUS HUNGARICUS
☐ Kozma, Brighton Fest. Chorus/LSO/ Kertesz/*Peacock Vars.*
SXL6497 (4/71) Decca
26186 London

SONATA FOR CELLO AND PIANO
☐ Isaacs, Jones/*Hindemith: Cello Son.*
ZRG762 (4/75) Decca Argo

SONATA FOR SOLO CELLO
☐ Starker/*Duo for violin and cello*
SAGA5386 (10/74) Saga

CELLO CONCERTO
☐ Schiff, New Philh./Mackerras/*Saint-Saens: Cello Conc./Faure: Elegie*
2530 793 (2/77) DG*
☐ P. Tortelier, CBSO/Fremaux/*Sym. Espagnole*
ASD3209 (6/76) EMI/HMV
NAMOUNA—BALLET
☐ *Exc. Suisse/Ansermet/Rapsodie*
SXL6302 (9/67) Decca
STS-15293 London
SYMPHONIE ESPAGNOLE FOR VIOLIN AND ORCHESTRA
☐ Kogan/Philh./Kondrashin/*Tchaikovsky: Serenade melancolique; Meditation*
CFP40040 (4/75) Classics for Pleasure
☐ Y.P. Tortelier/CBSO/Fremaux/*Cello Conc.*
ASD3209 (6/76) EMI/HMV

EDOUARD LALO
(b. Lille 1823; d. Paris 1892)

Lalo had been intended by his father, one of Napoleon's officers, for the army, but when after preliminary studies in Lille he announced that he wanted to make music his career he was forced to break with his family, and left home at 16 to go to Paris. He had great difficulty in making a living, and disappointment at the lack of response to his early songs (which are indeed remarkably fine and quite unjustly neglected today) led him to put aside all thought of serious composition and to become a professional violinist in a string quartet. Not until he was nearly 50 did he return to writing, fired by the unexpected success of some ballet music, under the title *Divertissement*, drawn from an unproduced opera he had entered for a competition. Of Spanish descent himself, for the Spanish virtuoso Sarasate he wrote in rapid succession a violin concerto and then, in 1875, his light-footed *Symphonie espagnole* (a concerto in all but name), which was an instant hit and has been a favourite showpiece for star fiddlers ever since.

In the next few years he began work on the opera *Le Roi d'Ys* (on the same Breton legend as in Debussy's » *Cathédrale engloutie*), probably inspired by the Breton origins of his wife, who had been a harmony pupil of his; he composed a cello concerto and a *Rapsodie norvégienne* for orchestra (originally for solo violin and orchestra, as some of the high violin parts still reveal!); and he saw the production of his ballet *Namouna*, which was coldly received as a whole (except by a few, including Debussy, who was ejected from the hall for his vociferous enthusiasm) but the suites from which quickly found

favour, thanks to Lalo's graceful invention and musicianly orchestral writing. A Symphony in G minor shows that beneath his Gallic lucidity lay a foundation of Brahms ». *Le Roi d'Ys*, of which he had made several revisions, was finally produced in 1888, the freshness of its lyricism and its colourful orchestration making an immediate appeal.

ROLAND DE LASSUS
(b. Mons 1532; d. Munich 1594)

The common Italianised name, Orlando di Lasso, of this cosmopolitan Flemish composer—one of the greatest, and certainly among the most prolific, of the sixteenth century—finds justification in his fundamentally Italianate style, though he spent a good half of his life in Bavaria. So sweet was his voice as a choirboy in his native town of Mons that he was twice carried off before his parents agreed to him entering the service, at the age of 12, of a third attempted abductor, the Viceroy of Sicily, whom he followed to Palermo and Milan. At 21 he was choirmaster at St John Lateran in Rome, but stayed only a year before accompanying a nobleman to England and France, and then settled for two years in Antwerp. It was at this stage that he first showed his extraordinary versatility by publishing one book of Italian madrigals and another of madrigals, French chansons and Latin motets. He then entered the chapel of the Duke of Bavaria, becoming *kapellmeister* some time after 1560; and despite pressing invitations from other aristocratic patrons, including Charles IX of France, he remained in his Munich post until his death.

Among his first important works in Munich was a volume of *Penitential psalms*, which, like the *Lessons from the Book of Job* and the later *Lamentations*, well illustrate his particular strength in meditative and elegiac works in the style known as "musica reservata", i.e. expressive of the emotional content of the text. Yet in various publications of his, deeply religious works of grandeur are found cheek by jowl with humorous secular pieces; and one of the most striking things about Lassus is his enormous range of mastery, embracing every style then current—including Magnificats, Passion settings, German chorale motets, French chansons and Italian *villanelle*. Of his Masses some 40 were "parody" works (i.e. based on a composition by someone else): with the exception of his *Requiem*, however, his works in this field are outshone by (and are more chordal, less polyphonic, than) those of his great contemporary Palestrina ▶. Where Lassus was unrivalled was in his motets, of which he wrote well over 500: although showing great variety and imagination, some of the finest are those with poignant harmonies, such as *Salve regina* and *Tui sunt coeli*.

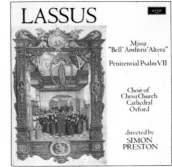

MISSA 'BELL' AMFITRIT 'ALTERA': PENITENTIAL PSALM VIII, NOS. 1-16
☐ Christ Church Cath. Ch./Preston
ZRG735 (8/74) Decca Argo∗
PENITENTIAL PSALM V: MOTETS: OMNES DE SABA VENIENT: SALVE REGINA; ALMA REDEMPTORIS; TUI SUNT COELI
☐ Christ Church Cath. Ch./Preston
ZRG795 (9/76) Decca Argo∗

Left: *Roland de Lassus (or Orlando di Lasso) has been compared for his strength and grandeur to Michelangelo. One of the outstanding figures in 16th-century music, he was much sought after by noble patrons everywhere.*

115

RUGGIERO LEONCAVALLO
(b. Naples 1858; d. Montecatini 1919)

Not even the huge number of performances given of his vastly popular *Pagliacci*—a short but very effective work at the core of the "realistic" school of opera— reconciled Leoncavallo to the all but total failure of another dozen operas and the very moderate success of two more. Despite his limitations, it is impossible not to feel that fate was against him. When he graduated from the Naples Conservatory at the age of 18 his first opera, *Chatterton*, was accepted for production in Bologna, but at the last moment the impresario decamped with the money, and Leoncavallo, left penniless, was reduced to eking out a living as a cafe pianist and singing teacher, wandering for about ten years in England, France, Holland, Germany and Egypt.

Returning to Italy, he vainly waited three years for the publishing house of Ricordi to honour its agreement to produce the first part of his Renaissance trilogy, *I Medici* —for which, as for all his operas, he was his own librettist —and then went over to Ricordi's rival Sonzogno, for whom he wrote *Pagliacci*, which proved an instant triumph in 1892. (For all its obviously stagey passion, it is scored with surprising finesse.) As a result, his two earlier stage pieces were then brought out, but both failed. His *La Bohème* was quite favourably received but was completely swamped by Puccini's » version of the same story, which had appeared the previous year: Puccini had taken the idea from Leoncavallo but had beaten him to production. His *Zaza* had a brief life, but from then on it was downhill all the way. Even *Pagliacci* has suffered from being, seemingly inescapably, paired with Mascagni's » *Cavalleria rusticana*, a much cruder work from the Sonzogno stable brought out two years previously.

I PAGLIACCI *(Cpte.)*
☐ Carlyle, Bergonzi, Taddei, Benelli, Panerai/La Scala/Karajan/*Mascagni*
2709 020 (10/66) DG*
☐ Caballe, Domingo, Milnes, Alldis Ch./ LSO/Santi/*Arias*
SER5635-6 (6/72) RCA
LSC-7090 RCA

Above: *Known only for his* Pagliacci, *Leoncavallo in fact wrote more than a dozen other operas, of which* La Bohème *can bear comparison with Puccini's version.*

Right: *Ruggiero Leoncavallo, who spent ten penniless years in Europe and Egypt before his first success in 1892.*

FERENCZ LISZT
(b. Raiding 1811; d. Bayreuth 1886)

An incomparable virtuoso pianist who dazzled all Europe and held it in thrall; an immensely prolific composer for the instrument who enormously extended its textural possibilities and technical demands, who invented the symphonic poem, and whose harmonically audacious late works foreshadowed elements in the music of Debussy » and Bartók »; an energetic and generous champion of other composers; a Hungarian who could barely speak his native language, preferring French, but whose upbringing was largely Germanic; a one-time Freemason who became an abbé; a man whose father on his deathbed had expressed concern about his weakness for women but whose many amours until the very end of his life became as legendary as his playing—all these, and many more, were facets of the complex personality of Liszt, who has been well described as "among the most striking figures of the whole Romantic epoch".

He had originally been taught the piano by his father, a steward on the Esterházy estate, had given his first concert at the age of nine, and with the support of some rich noblemen had gone to study with Czerny in Vienna, where his playing (and particularly his extemporisation) caused much excitement, and then to Paris, where an operetta of his was produced (he then being 14 years old). The twelve years he spent in France were of the utmost importance in his formation, for there he absorbed the ideas and music of Paganini », Berlioz » and his contemporary Chopin ». At the age of 24 he eloped to Switzerland with the Comtesse d'Agoult (their second daughter Cosima was later to marry Wagner »), and embarked on his sensationally triumphal career as a virtuoso, giving recitals of his own music. The adulation he received often tempted him, in composing, to indulge in shallow and

Left: *Liszt playing, with Paganini and Rossini beside him.*

Below: *Liszt's religious music has been much neglected.*

119

flamboyant pieces, but he also excelled in passionate works of great power, such as the *Dante sonata*, or of imaginative delicacy, like the *Années de pèlerinage*, while the *Studies after Paganini* and *Transcendental studies* bear witness to the lengths to which he was developing keyboard technique. His numerous transcriptions and fantasias on other composers' works, always ingenious, also frequently shed new light on them.

In 1847, while on a concert tour of Russia, he formed a liaison with the Princess Sayn-Wittgenstein, with whom he settled in Weimar, where he held appointments as musical director and conductor to the court. With immense vigour and vision he threw himself into restoring Weimar to its former glories as a pre-eminent centre of the arts, teaching, encouraging "progressive" composers everywhere (among them Wagner, Berlioz and Verdi ») by performing their works, and himself composing a series of orchestral symphonic poems (employing the principle of thematic transformation in accordance with their poetic or dramatic "programme") and of piano

Hungarian rhapsodies, whose themes however were gipsy rather than authentically Hungarian. To this period belong many of his finest works—the large-scale piano sonata, which combines rhetoric and violent intensity with fundamentally classical form; the organ *Prelude and fugue on the name BACH*; the First Piano Concerto, which made history by giving a rhythmic theme to a solo triangle; the *Dante Symphony* and the *Faust Symphony* which, like the Eighth Symphony of Mahler » 45 years later, has a choral finale on the Goethe text. His adventurous artistic policies in Weimar led to disagreements, and he finally resigned, living for some years in Rome, where he took minor orders—which did not however call for celibacy—and composed two oratorios, *St Elizabeth* and the vast-scale *Christus*; but he also spent much time in Budapest, where he was persuaded to head a National Academy of Music, to which flooded a large number of piano pupils, many of whom later became eminent. The effect of his music on many generations to come was incalculable.

Left: *Liszt with admirers.*

Below right: *Liszt's house in Weimar was a magnet for every musician in Europe.*

Right: *Liszt at a fashionable Paris salon. Gounod sits behind him, Saint-Saëns in the centre of the front row.*

LISZT
Sonata in B minor
Dante Sonata
Bagatelle without Tonality
Hungarian Rhapsody No 11
Alfred Brendel, Piano

LISZT
«Années de Pèlerinage» 2
ALFRED BRENDEL

ANNEES DE PELERINAGE
☐ *Cpte.* Berman
2709 076 (12/77) DG*
ANNEES DE PELERINAGE (2ND YEAR)
☐ *Nos. 1-7.* Brendel
6500 420 (11/73) Phonogram
FAUST SYMPHONY
☐ Young, Beecham Choral Society/RPO/
Beecham
SXDW3022 (12/75) EMI/HMV
HUNGARIAN RHAPSODIES
☐ *Cpte.* Kentner
TV34266-8DS (4/71) Decca Turnabout
☐ *2, 5, 9, 10, 15, 19.* Szidon
2530 441 (7/74) DG*
SVBX 5452 Vox

LES PRELUDES
☐ LPO/Haitink/*Orpheus, Tasso*
SAL3750 (12/69) Phonogram
839788 Philips
☐ Berlin PO/Karajan/*Hungarian
Rhapsody 2; Hungarian Fantasia*
139 037 (6/69) DG*
☐ Berlin RSO/Fricsay/*Piano Conc. 1;
Hungarian Rhapsody 2*
2548 235 (11/76) DG Heliodor
MISSA CHORALIS
☐ St. John's College Choir, Cambridge/G.
Guest
ZRG760 (10/73) Decca Argo*
PIANO CONCERTOS NO. 1 IN E
FLAT, NO. 2 IN A
☐ Brendel/LPO/Haitink/*Totentanz*
6500 374 (10/73) Phonogram
☐ Richter, LSO/Kondrashin
6580 071 (2/75) Phonogram
☐ Berman/VSO/Giulini
2530 770 (11/76) DG*
PIANO SONATA IN B MINOR
☐ Brendel/*Annees (2nd Year—exc.);
Bagatelle; Hungarian Rhapsody 11*
TV34232DS (7/70) Decca Turnabout
☐ Arrau/*Harmonies poetiques et
religieuses*
6500 043 (5/72) Phonogram*
☐ Roge/*Liebestraum 3; Annees (1st year—
exc.); Etudes d'execution*
SXL6485 (12/70) Decca
☐ Curzon/*Liebestraum 3; Valse oubliee 1;
Berceuse; Concert Study G.145/2*
SXL6076 (11/63) Decca
PIANO WORKS
Mephisto Waltz No. 1; Harmonies
poetiques et religieuses Nos. 3 and 7;
Liebestraume Nos. 1-31
☐ Ohlsson
HQS1361 (9/76) EMI/HMV
PIANO WORKS
Liebestraum No. 3; Ich liebe dich;
Valse oubliee No. 1; Sonnetto 123 del
Petrarca; Etude de concert No. 3;
Rakoczy March; Isoldens Liebstod;
Danse macabre; Rigoletto paraphrase
☐ Gillespie
ZK9 (4/77) Decca Argo
PIANO WORKS
Harmonies poetiques; 4 pieces G.192;
Valse a capriccio; En reve; Benediction
de Dieu; Hungarian folksongs;
Apparitions No. 1
☐ Louis Kentner
TV34310S (6/71) Decca Turnabout*
PRELUDE AND FUGUE ON THE NAME
BACH
☐ Preston/*Ad nos, ad salutarem undam*
ZRG503 (3/67) Decca Argo*
TRANSCENDENTAL STUDIES
☐ *Cpte.* Lazar Berman
SLS5040 (2/76) HMV
TRANSCRIPTIONS
(Donizetti: Reminiscences de Lucia.
Bellini: Reminiscences de Norma.
Wagner: Tristan and Isolde—Liebestod;
Flying Dutchman—Spinning Chorus,
Senta's Ballad; Lohengrin—Elsa's
bridal procession)
☐ David Wilde
SAGA5437 (5/77) Saga
WEINEN, KLAGEN, SORGEN, ZAGEN
☐ Preston/*Prelude on BACH*
ZRG503 (3/67) Decca Argo
☐ Planyavsky/*Angelus; Kirchliche
Festouverture; Adagio; Trauerode*
ZRG784 (9/76) Decca Argo*

121

GUSTAV MAHLER
(b. Kališt, Bohemia, 1860; d. Vienna 1911)

Mahler's two most quoted sayings, "Tradition is just slovenliness" and "The symphony should be like the world; it must contain everything", furnish clues both to his personal and his artistic credo. Highly strung to the point of neurosis, he hurled himself into his work as a conductor and opera-house director with a perfectionist concern over the smallest detail which brooked no obstacle and frequently left him in a state of nervous

Right: *Gustav Mahler in 1892, the year after his appointment to the Hamburg Opera. At that period he had written little more than the* Lieder eines fahrenden Gesellen *and the First Symphony.*

Below: *Mahler nine years later. By this time he had become the all-powerful artistic director of the Imperial Opera in Vienna (which he ruled with a rod of iron) and had written three more symphonies.*

Bottom: *The first page of Mahler's autograph score of his Sixth Symphony, which he had once thought of calling the 'Tragic'. Unusually for him, it included no vocal parts, and is more classically built.*

collapse. The theatre provided his main livelihood, composition being an obsessive sideline to which he devoted all his spare time and his holidays; but except for some early unpublished attempts at opera he did not write for the stage, and his entire output, apart from some songs and song-cycles, was in the sphere of the symphony—whose form, however, he greatly expanded, particularly in the number of its movements, and whose whole nature he transformed. Taking his cue from Berlioz » and Liszt », he introduced voices into four of his nine symphonies (his unfinished Tenth has been conjecturally completed by a brilliant Mahler scholar); and *Das Lied von der Erde*, a large-scale orchestral song-cycle on texts from the Chinese, was not called a symphony only because of Mahler's superstitious dread that his Ninth (which it would have been) would, as in the case of Beethoven, be his last.

The most potent influence in his formative years had been Bruckner », whose lectures he had attended while a student in Vienna, and for whom he had the highest admiration: from him he derived a love of Wagner » and the conception of vast-scale symphonies (he made the piano reduction of Bruckner's massive Third). To earn a living he worked as a conductor in a succession of opera-houses, including among others Cassel, Prague and Leipzig, before becoming director of the Budapest Opera; but despite his initial enthusiasm he found conditions there irksome, and after only two years went to Hamburg as a staff conductor. In 1897, six years later, he moved to Vienna, largely on the recommendation of Brahms », who had been impressed by him in Budapest. Under his brilliant and uncompromisingly meticulous direction the Vienna Opera attained the highest peak of its artistic fame; but in the pursuit of his ideals his impatiently dictatorial methods caused much friction, and after a decade he had to leave. The death of his elder daughter at this time moved him to write *Das Lied von der Erde*, which, like much of his work, is imbued with the theme of the transitoriness of life. He conducted at the Metropolitan Opera in New York for a brief period, and made annual visits to the USA to work with the New York Philharmonic Society, but by this time his health, never robust, was breaking down.

Mahler's essentially pessimistic nature and the self-pitying emotionalism of his music, which was the expression of an intensely personal philosophy, his use of deliberately banal material (especially quasi-military marches) and of rather sinister distortions, and his penchant for inflated length and for enormous resources—as in the Second "Resurrection" Symphony and, more especially, the so-called "Symphony of a thousand" (No. 8), which requires eight solo voices, a double chorus and a boys' choir in addition to a very large orchestra—have provoked some opposition, but he is now generally accepted as the last of the great Viennese symphonists. Beside his tempestuous works like the Fifth Symphony, however, must be set those which breathe an idyllic atmosphere of the Austrian countryside, like the Fourth or the *Knaben Wunderhorn* songs. Among the peaks of his vocal output are the deeply-felt early (1883) cycle *Lieder eines fahrenden Gesellen* and the moving, if sentimental, 1902 cycle *Kindertotenlieder*.

DAS LIED VON DER ERDE
☐ Minton, Kollo, Chicago SO/Solti
　SET555 (11/72) Decca
　26292 London
☐ Dickie, Fischer-Dieskau, Philh./ Kletzki
　SXLP30165 (8/74) Decca
　S-60260 Seraphim
☐ Ludwig, Kollo/Berlin PO/Karajan/ *Ruckert Lieder*
　2707 082 (12/75) DG*
☐ Baker, King/Concertgebouw/Haitink
　6500 831 (10/76) Phonogram*

DAS KLAGENDE LIED
☐ Reynolds, Zylis-Gara, Kaposy/NPO/ Morris
　SDD-R327 (7/62) Decca Ace of Diamonds

DES KNABEN WUNDERHORN
☐ Norman, Shirley-Quirk, Concertgebouw/Haitink
　9500 316 (11/77) Phonogram
☐ Schwarzkopf, Fischer-Dieskau, LSO/ Szell
　SAN218 (1/69) EMI/HMV Angel
　S-36547 Angel
☐ Baker, Evans, LPO/Morris
　SDD-R326 (6/72) Decca Ace of Diamonds

KINDERTOTENLIEDER
☐ Baker/Israel PO/Bernstein/*Sym. 10—Adagio*
　76475 (4/76) CBS
　M-33532 Columbia

LIEDER EINES FAHRENDEN GESELLEN
☐ Minton/Chicago SO/Solti/*Des Knaben Wunderhorn (exc.)*
　SXL6679 (10/74) Decca
☐ Fischer-Dieskau/Bavarian RSO/ Martin
　2530 630 (9/76) DG

RUCKERT LIEDER
☐ Baker/New Philh./Barbirolli/*Elgar*
　ASD2721 (8/71) EMI/HMV
　S-36796 Angel
☐ Ludwig/Berlin PO/Karajan/*Das Lied von der Erde*
　2707 082 (12/75) DG*

SYMPHONY NO. 1 IN D
☐ Concertgebouw/Haitink
　6500 342 (2/73) Phonogram*
☐ LSO/Solti
　SXL6113 (9/64) Decca
　6401 London
☐ LSO/Levine
　ARL1 0894 (5/75) RCA*
☐ Chicago SO/Giulini
　ASD2722 (8/71) EMI/HMV
　S-36047 Angel*

☐ Boston SO/Ozawa
　2530 993 (5/78) DG

SYMPHONY NO. 2 IN C MINOR
☐ Schwarzkopf, Rossl-Majdan/Philh. & Chorus/Klemperer
　SLS806 (8/71) EMI
　S-3634 Angel
☐ Cotrubas, Ludwig, Vienna State Op. Chorus, VPO/Mehta
　SXL6744-5 (12/75) Decca
　2242 London
☐ Neblett, Horne/Chicago SO & Ch./ Abbado
　2707 094 (6/77) DG*

SYMPHONY NO. 3
☐ Forrester, Netherlands Radio Chorus, Concertgebouw Amsterdam/Haitink
　6700 037 (2/67) Phonogram
　802711 Philips
☐ Lipton, Ware, Ch., NYPO/Bernstein
　77206 (6/74) CBS
　M25-675 Columbia
☐ Horne/Chicago SO & Ch./Levine
　ARL2 1757 (3/77) RCA*

SYMPHONY NO. 4 IN G
☐ Raskin/Cleveland Orch./Szell
　61056 (4/68) CBS Classics
　MS-6833 Columbia
☐ Schwarzkopf, Philh./Klemperer
　ASD2799 (4/73) EMI/HMV
　S-35829 Angel
☐ Price/LPO/Horenstein
　CFP159 (5/71) Classics for Pleasure
　S-2141 Monitor
☐ Blegen/Chicago SO/Levine
　ARL1 0895 RCA*

SYMPHONY NO. 5 IN C SHARP MINOR
☐ Concertgebouw/Haitink/*Sym. 10*
　6700 048 (4/72) Phonogram*
☐ New Philh./Barbirolli/*Ruckert Lieder*
　SLS785 (12/69) HMV

SYMPHONY NO. 6
☐ Chicago SO/Solti/*Lieder eines fahrenden Gesellen*
　SET469-70 (12/70) Decca
　2227 London
☐ NYPO/Bernstein/*Talk*
　77215 (2/68) CBS

SYMPHONY NO. 7 IN B MINOR
☐ Concertgebouw/Haitink
　6700 036 (3/71) Phonogram*
☐ Chicago SO/Solti
　7BB178-22 (8/75) Decca
　2231 London

SYMPHONY NO. 8
☐ Soloists, Vienna State Opera Chorus, Singverein Chorus, Vienna Boys' Chorus, Chicago SO/Solti
　SET534-5 (10/72) Decca
　1295 London

SYMPHONY NO. 9 IN D
☐ Concertgebouw/Haitink
　6700 021 (7/70) Phonogram*
☐ Columbia SO/Walter/*Lieder eines fahrenden Gesellen*
　61369-70 (12/73) CBS Classics
☐ New Philh./Klemperer
　SXDW3021 (1/76) EMI/HMV Concert Classics
　S-3708 Angel
☐ Chicago SO/Giulini
　2707 097 (4/77) DG*

SYMPHONY NO. 10 IN F SHARP *(unfinished draft)*
☐ New Philh./Morris *(realised D. Cooke)*
　6700 067 (3/74) Phonogram*

PIETRO MASCAGNI
(b. Livorno (Leghorn) 1863; d. Rome 1945)

Mascagni's father was opposed to him becoming a musician, but the boy took lessons by stealth and eventually proved himself by composing, at the age of 18, a setting of Schiller's "Ode to joy" which so impressed a local aristocrat that he paid for him to study in Milan. Mascagni repaid this generosity by abandoning his studies and running away to conduct a touring opera company, after which he was reduced to scraping a living as a provincial piano teacher. In 1890 he suddenly found himself famous overnight after the production of the one-act opera *Cavalleria rusticana*, which had won a prize offered by a publishing house; despite crude orchestration and commonplace melodies, the violent passions it depicted, served with a garnish of religiosity, were hailed as marking a new era in the melodramatically effective portrayal of low-class life known as "verismo" or realism. Its triumph was unbounded throughout Europe; and when, two years later, it was paired with Leoncavallo's » *Pagliacci* the two short works became the most frequently played in the whole operatic repertory.

More refinement was shown in the sentimental *L'Amico Fritz* the following year, but out of the fourteen stage works which followed *Cavalleria rusticana* only this and the brutal Japanese opera *Iris* (1898) gained even modest success—the rest were abject failures, *Le Maschere* winning distinction of a kind by being given a simultaneous première in seven Italian cities, of which five received it with hisses and whistles and a sixth would not even allow it to be played to the end. Mascagni's poverty of invention and lack of technique stood no chance once Puccini » appeared on the scene; his appointment as director of the Pesaro Conservatory was terminated because of his protracted absences on conducting tours; and though, in his enthusiasm for Fascism, he hoped to gain Mussolini's favour with his opera *Nerone*, this too failed, and he was ostracised by Toscanini and other prominent musicians. He died, totally discredited, in a hotel just after the end of World War II.

CAVALLERIA RUSTICANA
□ *Cpte.* Cossotto, Martino, Bergonzi, Guelfi, Allegri, La Scala/Karajan/
Leoncavallo: Pagliacci
2709 020 (10/66) DG*

Left: *Mascagni—one big lucky strike, then downhill all the way.*

Below: *Mascagni later in life, gazing at a score—glumly wondering what went wrong?*

JULES MASSENET
(b.Montaud, nr. St Etienne, 1842; d. Paris 1912)

In an earlier generation one might have said that Massenet was the musical equivalent of the popular woman novelist: he poured out a series of 25 operas, limited in range and technical achievement, but mostly of an elegantly sentimental nature. These attained a considerable success with star singers, for whom he wrote graceful melodic lines, and with a bourgeois public of no great musical discernment, which was titillated and gratified by the voluptuous character of many of his subjects, particularly when in religious garb. His younger contemporary d'Indy (who, like Massenet, had been an orchestral drummer) spoke of his "discreet and quasi-religious eroticism". This was a feature of his first real successes, the oratorios *Marie Magdeleine* and *Eve*; and it was one which he later made the most of in the operas *Hérodiade* (on the Salome story) and *Thaïs*, in which a monk is tempted by a courtesan.

Massenet had won the Prix de Rome at the age of 21 after studying at the Paris Conservatoire (where he became a professor fifteen years later), and initially had written a couple of comic operas, some song-cycles (among the earliest in the French repertory) and a good deal of orchestral music. The exotic settings of his first operatic successes, *Le Roi de Lahore* and *Hérodiade*, were however absent from his masterpiece *Manon* (1884), whose delicate score employs a form of leading-motive, after the Wagner » example, and includes dialogue spoken over soft orchestral backgrounds. Massenet was better suited to the quiet sentimentality of *Werther* than to the heroics of *Le Cid* or the attempted realism of *La Navarraise:* of his later operas, *Le Jongleur de Notre-Dame*, based on a mediaeval legend, is the most distinguished.

LE CID
☐ *Cpte.* Ingram, Hodges, Voketaitis, Bumbry, Bergquist, Gardner, Domingo, New York Op. Orch./Queler
79300 (3/77) CBS
M3-34211 Columbia
LE CID—BALLET MUSIC
☐ CBSO/Fremaux/*Scenes pittoresques; La Vierge—Last sleep of the virgin*
ESD7040 (9/77) EMI/HMV
522 Klavier
☐ National PO/Bonynge/*Ariane; Meyerbeer*
SXL6812 (11/76) Decca
7032 London
ESCLARMONDE
☐ *Cpte.* Sutherland, Aragall, Tourangeau, R. Davies, Alldis Ch./Nat. PO/Bonynge
SET612 (11/76) Decca
13118 London
MANON
☐ *Cpte.* de los Angeles, Legay, Dens, Borthayre/Paris Opera-Comique Chorus and Orch./Monteux
SLS5119 (6/78) HMV

I. Massenet

Above: *The young Massenet about the time that he won the Prix de Rome.*

Right: *Though success did not come to Massenet until he was 35, he then made a fortune from his many operas.*

125

FELIX MENDELSSOHN
(b. Hamburg 1809; d. Leipzig 1847)

Those who hold that some measure of adversity is necessary in the making of a great artist are fond of quoting the example of Mendelssohn. Born with the proverbial silver spoon in his mouth to a well-to-do, intellectually distinguished family, he was gifted as an artist, writer and linguist, besides being prodigiously precocious as a musician; he enjoyed success, the friendship of royalty (especially Queen Victoria) and the consistent admiration of the German and English publics; yet as a composer he diminished from "the Mozart of the nineteenth century, the most brilliant among musicians", as Schumann » called him, to a talented, rather academic craftsman. To a large extent this was the result of overwork in non-creative fields brought about by an excessively developed sense of public responsibility, inculcated by his father, a benevolent despot who urged his son to ever greater industry and to "more profound" subjects, and whose cult of domestic virtues in his happy, close-knit family ended by hampering young Mendelssohn's emotional development. Worn out with a multiplicity of administrative and social, as well as professional, obligations, Mendelssohn (like those other geniuses Schubert » and Mozart ») died while still in his thirties.

As a boy he composed voluminously from an early age, receiving every encouragement at home, including private Sunday concerts with his own orchestra. By 12 he had written, among much else, several lively symphonies for strings; at 16 the string Octet, whose astonishing instrumental and contrapuntal skill served an original conception of delightful freshness; and at 17 the magical overture to *A Midsummer night's dream*, which "brought the fairies into the orchestra" and reveals a remarkable ear for limpid and imaginative scoring. His delicate romantic style—he was never to show the darkly passionate face of Romanticism, as did Berlioz » or Liszt »—was nevertheless based on a deep knowledge of Bach », Mozart and other classics which at that time were largely neglected: indeed, at the age of 20 he created a sensation by conducting the first performance since the composer's own time of Bach's *St Matthew Passion*.

He undertook a Grand Tour to broaden his knowledge,

Above: *Highly cultivated in all the arts, Mendelssohn was particularly skilful at water-colours and sketches, many of which survive. This view of Amalfi was painted when he was 22.*

Above: *The flowing lines of Mendelssohn's signature.*

Left: *Mendelssohn's prodigious gifts as a youth rivalled those of Mozart.*

making drawings and musical sketches on his journeys, and writing entertaining letters: an enjoyable visit to the Scottish Highlands resulted in the brilliantly evocative *Hebrides* overture and, later, the "Scottish" Symphony (No.3), while his experiences in Rome and Naples inspired his Fourth Symphony (the "Italian"). Both symphonies show a transparently-coloured lyricism and rhythmic vitality that have ensured their lasting popularity. In 1833, the year of the "Italian" Symphony, Mendelssohn settled in Düsseldorf as general musical director, but two years later, at the age of only 26, was appointed conductor of the famous Gewandhaus Orchestra in Leipzig, which he made the most important musical centre in Germany, energetically introducing new music and works by great historical figures: he was also instrumental in drawing up plans for a new Conservatory there in 1843, and became its virtual director. In that year too he composed the remainder of his *Midsummer night's dream* music for a stage production, matching up the style of his youthful overture of 17 years earlier: its beautiful *Nocturne*, like the *Andante* of the Violin Concerto of the following year, disproves the assertion sometimes heard that his slow movements are less outstanding than his scherzos. The familiarity of this most popular concerto, incidentally, is such that the originality of its form is no longer remarked. Mendelssohn certainly excelled all his life at elfin scherzos, to whose style the finale of the violin concerto and the piano *Rondo capriccioso* are very akin. With the exception of works like the *Variations sérieuses* and the E minor Prelude and Fugue, much of the piano music however, though mellifluous, is very unpretentious: of far greater distinction is his chamber music, still insufficiently known.

In his last years a certain blandness and tameness are evident in Mendelssohn's music—save in the oratorio *Elijah*, written for his "second home", England, and in which his dramatic instincts for once were fully roused: in too many works his ideas and their treatment were lacking in freshness. But what he never lost was the sheer elegance and finish of his workmanship, and in particular his refined ear and unerring instinct for orchestration.

□ Perahia/ASMF/Marriner
76376 (7/75) CBS
M-33207 Columbia
6 PRELUDES AND FUGUES
□ *Cpte.* Adni/*3 Studies*
HQS1394 (8/77) EMI/HMV
SONGS WITHOUT WORDS
□ *Cpte.* Barenboim/*Gondellied; Klavierstucke; Albumblatt*
2740 104 (12/74) DG
STRING QUARTET NO. 4 IN E MINOR
□ Gabrieli Quartet/*4 pieces*
SDD469 (4/75) Decca Ace of Diamonds
STRING SYMPHONIES
□ *Nos.* 9,10, 12: ASMF/Marriner
ZK7 (5/77) Decca Argo
5467 Argo
SYMPHONY NO. 3 IN A MINOR (SCOTTISH)
□ Berlin PO/Karajan/*Hebrides Ov.*
2530 126 (5/72) DG*
□ LSO/Maag/*Hebrides Ov.*
SPA503 (10/77) Decca
STS-15091 London
□ LSO/Abbado/*Sym. 4*
SXL6363 (9/68) Decca
6587 London
□ SNO/Gibson/*Hebrides*
CFP40270 (10/77) Classics for Pleasure
SYMPHONY NO. 4 IN A (ITALIAN)
□ New Philh./Muti/*Schumann: Sym. 4*
ASD3365 (7/77) EMI/HMV
S-37412 Angel
□ LSO/Abbado/*Sym. 3*
SXL6363 (9/68) Decca
6587 London
□ Philh./Klemperer/*Schumann: Sym. 4*
SXLP30178 (2/75) EMI/HMV Concert Classics
S-35629 Angel

□ New Philh./Sawallisch/*Sym. 5*
SAL3727 (9/69) Phonogram
802718 Philips
SYMPHONY NO. 5 IN D MINOR (REFORMATION)
□ NPO/Sawallisch/*Sym 4*
SAL 3727 (9/69) Phonogram
802718 Philips
□ Berlin PO/Karajan/*Sym. 4*
2530 416 (9/74) DG*
□ VPO/Dohnanyi/*Sym. 1*
SXL6818 (2/77) Decca
7038 London
VIOLIN CONCERTO IN D MINOR
□ Accardo/LPO/Dutoit/*E minor Conc.*
9500 154 (3/77) Phonogram*
□ Menuhin, LSO/Fruhbeck de Burgos/*E minor Conc.*
ASD2809 (7/72) EMI/HMV
VIOLIN CONCERTO IN E MINOR
□ Accardo/LPO/Dutoit/*D minor Conc.*
9500 154 (3/77) Phonogram*
□ Suk/Czech PO/Ancerl/*Bruch*
SUAST50546 (8/65) Supraphon
□ Ricci/LSO/Gamba/*Bruch*
SPA88 (10/70) Decca
□ Perlman/LSO/Previn/*Bruch: Vin. Conc. 1*
ASD2926 (1/74) EMI/HMV
S-36963 Angel
□ Menuhin/LSO/Fruhbeck de Burgos/*D minor Conc.*
ASD2809 (7/72) EMI/HMV
S-36850 Angel
□ Campoli/LPO/Boult/*Bruch: Scottish Fantasy*
ECS775 (8/76) Decca Eclipse
STS-15015 London
□ Milstein/Philh./Barzin/*Bruch*
SXLP30245 (10/77) EMI/HMV Concert Classics
S-35730 Angel

CHORAL WORKS
(Hor mein Bitten; 6 Anthems; Beata mortui; Psalm 22; Veni Domine; Ave Maria)
□ Palmer/Schutz Choir/Norrington
ZRG716 (11/72) Decca Argo
ELIJAH
□ *Cpte.* Jones, Baker, Wolff, Gedda, Fischer-Dieskau, NP Choir & Orch./de Burgos
SLS935 (10/68) HMV
S-3738 Angel
HEBRIDES OVERTURE (FINGAL'S CAVE)
□ LSO/Maag/*Sym. 3*
SPA503 (10/77) Decca
STS-15091 London
□ Berlin PO/Karajan/*Sym. 3*
2530 126 (5/72) DG*
□ SNO/Gibson/*Sym. 3*
CFP40270 (10/77) Classics for Pleasure
□ BPO/Karajan/*Nicolai; Wagner; Weber*
SXLP30210 (6/76) EMI/HMV Concert Classics
A MIDSUMMER NIGHT'S DREAM— OVERTURE AND INCIDENTAL MUSIC
□ Harper, Baker, Chorus, Philh./Klemperer
SXLP30196 (2/76) EMI/HMV Concert Classics
S-35881 Angel

□ Vyvyan, Lowe/Cov. Gdn. Female Ch./LSO/Maag
SPA451 (9/76) Decca
STS 15084 London
□ Watson, Wallis/LSO/Previn
ASD3377 (9/77) EMI/HMV
S-37268 Angel
□ Woodland, Watts, Chorus, Concertgebouw/Haitink
SAL3458 (5/66) Phonogram
6570 021 Philips Festivo
OCTET IN E FLAT, OP. 20
□ Vienna Octet/*Rimsky-Korsakov: Quintet*
SDD389 (12/73) Decca Ace of Diamonds
STS-15308 London
□ ASMF/*Boccherini*
ZRG569 (5/68) Decca Argo
6 ORGAN SONATAS
□ W. Dallman
ORYX1813-4 (5/73) Oryx*
OVERTURES
Hebrides; Calm sea and prosperous voyage; Athalia; Son and Stranger; Ruy Blas
□ New Philh./Atzmon
ESD7003 (7/76) EMI/HMV
PIANO CONCERTOS NO. 1 IN G MINOR, NO. 2 IN D MINOR
□ Ogdon/LSO/Ceccato
ASD2546 (7/70) EMI/HMV
Klavier

Felix Mendelssohn Bartholdy
LIEDER OHNE WORTE
SONGS WITHOUT WORDS · ROMANCES SANS PAROLES
Gesamtaufnahme · Complete Recording · Enregistrement intégral
Gondellied op. 102 Nr. 7 · Albumblatt op. 117
2 Klavierstücke · 6 Kinderstücke op. 72
Daniel Barenboim
Piano

OLIVIER MESSIAEN
(b. Avignon 1908)

Accepted as a pupil at the Paris Conservatoire at the age of 11 and subsequently winning numerous prizes there, Messiaen studied composition with Dukas », from whom he derived a certain influence from Franck » which was noted in his earliest works, though that of Satie's » quasi-religious music was closer in time. At the age of 22 he became organist at the Eglise de la Trinité in Paris, a post he held for the greater part of his life. He was a founder-member of the group of avant-garde composers known as Jeune France, and in 1936 was appointed to teaching posts at both the Ecole Normale and the Schola Cantorum in Paris. Called up in the French forces, he was taken prisoner, but was repatriated in 1941 and became a professor at the Conservatoire. As a teacher his own influence has been enormous; his most famous pupil was Boulez ».

Messiaen's entire output is avowedly dedicated to "the service of the dogmas of Catholic theology", and is permeated by a voluptuous mysticism all but hypnotic in effect. This owes much to the highly personal techniques he has evolved, which draw heavily on elements from Oriental music, including obsessional kaleidoscopic near-ostinatos and the suspension of normal Western time-consciousness. Many of his works, such as the ecstatic *Vingt regards sur l'enfant Jésus* for piano, are immensely long. Messiaen has expounded at length the melodic, harmonic and rhythmic principles on which he has built his own musical language: in addition to Indian scales, percussion instruments and rhythms, as in the overtly sensual *Turangalîla* symphony, he has made extensive use of Gregorian chant and, even more, of birdsongs (which are regarded as symbols of divinity)— carefully notated bird-calls form the main substance of the piano *Catalogue d'oiseaux* and the *Oiseaux exotiques* for piano and orchestra. His orchestration is often extremely original as well as complex, with a fondness for sonorities such as the Ondes Martenot, which underline the almost stiflingly luscious character of some of his harmony. Among his major organ works are the early *Le Banquet céleste, La Nativité du Seigneur* (1935), *Les Corps glorieux* and the *Messe de la Pentecôte:* his only important chamber work is the *Quatuor pour la fin du temps* written while he was a prisoner of war.

Right: *Olivier Messiaen as a young man.*

Left: *Messiaen's influence as a teacher has been widespread.*

L'ASCENSION
☐ Preston/*Franck*
  ZRG5339 (3/63) Decca Argo∗
CHRONOCHROMIE
☐ BBC SO/Dorati/*Boulez: Le soleil; Koechlin: Bandar-log*
  ZRG756 (4/76) Decca Argo∗
CATALOGUE D'OISEAUX
☐ Sherlaw Johnson
  2BBA1005-7 (4/73) Decca
LES CORPS GLORIEUX
☐ Preston/*Le banquet celeste*
  ZRG633 (10/70) Decca Argo
NATIVITE DU SEIGNEUR
☐ Simon Preston
  ZRG5447 (3/66) Decca Argo∗
OISEAUX EXOTIQUES
☐ Loriod, Czech PO/Neumann
  SUAST50749 (2/69) Supraphon
  31002 Candide
POEMES POUR MI
☐ Barker/Johnson
  ZRG699 (11/72) Decca Argo
QUATUOR POUR LA FIN DU TEMPS
☐ Stoltzman, Kavafian, Sherry, P. Serkin
  RL11567 (7/77) RCA
TRANSFIGURATION DE NOTRE SEIGNEUR JESUS-CHRIST
☐ Sylvester, Aquino, Chorus, Washington SO/Dorati
  HEAD1-2 (5/74) Decca Headline

VINGT REGARDS SUR L'ENFANT JESUS
☐ Ogdon
  ZRG650-1 (10/69) Decca Argo
☐ P. Serkin/*La rousserelle*
  ARL3 0759 (9/76) RCA
  CRL3-0759 RCA
VISIONS DE L'AMEN
☐ Ogdon/Lucas
  ZRG665 (11/71) Decca Argo

DARIUS MILHAUD
(b. Aix-en-Provence 1892; d. Geneva 1974)

As with all composers of enormous facility, the sheer volume of Milhaud's output, added to its bewildering diversity of style as well as of standard, deters many from making more than the most cursory acquaintance with any of it. Yet among much that is merely flippant, or drily intellectual, or pretentiously overblown, there are works of poetry, of gaiety and of delicacy which it is to be hoped will not be lost as time goes by. Two sources which almost unfailingly drew the best from him were his Jewish faith and his Provençal origins: to the latter we owe such luminous, tangy works as the *Carnaval d'Aix* for piano and orchestra (a re-working of one of his many ballets), the orchestral *Suite Provençale*, the choral *Cantique du Rhône* and the woodwind quintet *Cheminée du Roi René*; to the former the heartfelt emotion of the *Poèmes juifs* and numerous liturgical and Biblical choral works. A quality which Milhaud never lacked however was adventurousness —he was in fact reproached for too great a readiness to follow different styles and to experiment. As early as 1915, when he was barely out of his studies at the Paris Conservatoire (where Dukas » had been one of his teachers), his incidental music for *Oresteia* broke new ground in employing choral groans and cries and solo percussion; his 1923 negro ballet *La Création du monde*, beautifully scored for chamber ensemble, was one of the most successful fusions of the new jazz idiom with "straight" forms such as fugue; he was among the first to feature bitonality in his music; he experimented with symphonies and operas of extreme brevity; his vast-scale opera *Christophe Colomb* called for cinematography, simultaneous dual action and much symbolism; and the 14th and 15th of his eighteen string quartets were playable either separately or together.

At the age of 25 Milhaud spent nearly two years in Rio de Janeiro with the poet Paul Claudel, who had been appointed French Minister there, and this gave him a zest for Brazilian rhythms, which can be heard in many of his works—not only the *Saudades do Brasil*, but the jiggy ballet *Le Boeuf sur le toît* he wrote on returning to Paris,

the *maxixe* of the *Carnaval d'Aix*, the two-piano *Scaramouche*, and much else. In Paris he was drawn into the group of "Les Six", of which he and Honegger » were the most technically accomplished; but quickly tiring of its chic superficiality (exemplified, in his case, by such things as a setting of extracts from an agricultural catalogue), he resumed his collaboration with Claudel in a number of stage and concert works, until the middle 1930s. In 1940 he went to California, where he taught at Mills College and composed the charming *Chansons de Ronsard*, half-a-dozen concertos, four symphonies and other orchestral and chamber works. He returned to Paris in 1947, taking up a teaching post at the Conservatoire and pouring out music in still greater profusion, including two large-scale operas, *Bolivar* and *David*, the latter to celebrate Israel's 3000th anniversary, and another eight concertos, besides more symphonies and choral and chamber music. Delicate in health even as a child, in his last years he was confined to a wheelchair.

BOEUF SUR LE TOIT
☐ French Nat. Orch./Bernstein/
  Creation du Monde; Saudades do Brasil (excs.)
  ASD3444 (2/78) EMI/HMV
  S-37442 Angel
CELLO CONCERTOS NOS. 1 AND 2
☐ Apolin, Brno PO/Waldhans
  SUAST50864 (11/72) Supraphon
CHANSONS DE RONSARD
☐ Seibel, Louisville Orch./Mester/
  Symphony 6
  GL25020 (11/76) RCA Gold Seal
  S-744 Louisville
CREATION DU MONDE—BALLET
☐ French Nat. Orch./Bernstein/*Boeuf sur le toit; Saudades do Brasil (excs.)*
  ASD3444 (2/78) EMI/HMV
  S-37442 Angel
PIANO CONCERTO NO. 2*; SUITE CISALPINE FOR CELLO AND ORCHESTRA†; LA MUSE MENAGERE*
☐ *Johannesen, †Blees/Radio Luxemburg Orch./Kontarsky
  TV34496S (7/75) Decca Turnabout*

SAUDADES DO BRASIL
☐ William Bolcom/*Rag caprices/Spring*
  H71316 (1/76) WEA Nonesuch*
VIOLIN CONCERTO NO. 2
☐ Gertler, Prague SO/Smetacek/
  Malipiero: Vln. Conc.
  110 1120 (11/73) Rediffusion/
  Supraphon

Below: *Milhaud, the most prolific and experimental composer of the French group called 'Les Six'.*

ERNEST JOHN MOERAN
(b. Heston, Middlesex, 1894; d. Kenmare, Co. Kerry, 1950)

Moeran, a late starter in his musical career, was the son of a Norfolk clergyman, with a background of little more than hymns, violin playing and school music when he entered the Royal College in London. After only 18 months, however, the First World War broke out and Moeran at once volunteered, serving in the army throughout the four years and being badly wounded. On demobilisation he decided to devote himself to composition, and for three years studied with Ireland », the influence of whose harmonic style can be seen in his song-cycle *Ludlow town*; but Ireland was careful not to inhibit the folksong-like lyricism (as in his String Quartet) which came naturally to his pupil from his regional upbringing. (Moeran had indeed himself collected a number of Norfolk folksongs.)

After performances of his two orchestral Rhapsodies in 1924 Moeran widened his horizons, making friends with Warlock », through whom he fell under the spell of Delius », whose pantheistic ideas accorded well with his own intense love of Nature: this new stylistic departure marks his setting of poems by Joyce (to whom he was drawn by being Irish on his mother's side). The year 1931 saw the production of a vivacious string trio and the poignant *Lonely waters* for small orchestra, which ends with an unaccompanied voice singing the folksong on which it is based. With increasing sureness of technique he wrote a choral suite on Elizabethan verses, *Songs of Springtime*, and a choral *Nocturne* on Delius's death, before tackling for the first time a large-scale form: his G minor Symphony of 1937, which owes something to the example of Sibelius », represents him at the peak of his powers, and was overtly inspired by the scenery of Co. Kerry and of East Norfolk. An altogether jollier Irish flavour permeates the Violin Concerto of five years later; his *Sinfonietta* is knit together by a theme common to all three of its movements; and Moeran's late marriage to a cellist led to a poetically lyrical concerto and a sonata for cello. Save to those who affect to scorn what has been called the "English pastoral school", Moeran's music appeals to all by its fresh, open-air charm.

CELLO SONATA IN A MINOR*:
PRELUDE FOR CELLO AND PIANO*:
PIANO WORKS
   (Bank holiday; 2 Legends; Stalham River; Prelude and berceuse; Toccata; White mountain.)
   □ *Coetmore/Parkin
   SRCS42 (10/72) Lyrita
LONELY WATERS
   □ English Sinf./Dilkes/*Leigh; Ireland; Butterworth; Warlock*
   CSD3705 (4/72) EMI/HMV
LUDLOW TOWN—SONG CYCLE
   □ Shirley-Quirk/Isepp/*Purcell; Humfrey; Butterworth*
   SAGA5260 (10/66) Saga
SINFONIETTA
   □ LPO/Boult/*Bax; November Woods; Holst: Fugal Ov.*
   SRCS37 (10/68) Lyrita
   4038 HNH
SYMPHONY IN G MINOR
   □ English Sinfonia/Dilkes
   ASD2913 (8/73) EMI/HMV
   □ New Philh./Boult
   SRCS70 (7/75) Lyrita
   4014 HNH

CLAUDIO MONTEVERDI
(b. Cremona 1567; d. Venice 1643)

In the course of his 60-year career Monteverdi played a decisive part in the change from the older style of unaccompanied vocal polyphony to the new harmonic style supporting a solo voice; and he has gone down in history as the first great writer of operas and as a technical innovator. The staging of his works in recent years has made abundantly clear his gift for expressive dramatic composition.

His first publications (collections of motets, sacred madrigals and canzonets written at the ages of 15, 16 and 17 respectively!) were, as might be expected, in the orthodox style he had inherited from his teacher in Cremona. But at about the age of 23 he entered the service of the Duke of Mantua as a viol player and singer, and learnt something of musical currents elsewhere when he accompanied his master on a military campaign in Hungary, a political journey in Flanders and, most significantly of all, a visit to Florence for the wedding of Maria de'Medici to Henri IV of France in 1600: there Peri's *Euridice* (almost the very first opera) was performed for the first time. Not to be outdone, at the Duke's urging Monteverdi, now made musical director, wrote his own *Favola d'Orfeo* on the same subject, and this was produced in 1607 with all the considerable instrumental resources the court could muster: it is now the earliest opera in the repertory. It was a work of genius, in which the basic expressive declamation of the text, to which Monteverdi accorded supremacy, was expanded at times into melodic *arioso* or, at particularly emotional moments, even further elaborated instrumentally.

This was followed up a year later with *Arianna*, the music of which has unfortunately been lost except for Ariadne's lament, which enjoyed an immense success and was sung throughout Italy; and also from 1608 dates the satirical *Ballo dell'ingrate*. The magnificent *Vespers* of 1610 combine the orthodox polyphonic style with Monteverdi's new passionate declamation and rich orchestral coloration. By this time he had published five books of madrigals which show his increasing harmonic daring and his use of dissonance as a means of expressive verbal treatment. In the fifth book, additionally, some of the madrigals have a continuo part; and this unusual feature was to be further developed in successive publications, so that by the seventh book madrigals give way to solos, duets and trios with accompaniment.

In 1612 the new Duke of Mantua dismissed Monteverdi, who however was appointed *maestro di cappella* at St Mark's, Venice, the next year, and there produced a great quantity of religious music. Even after taking holy orders in 1632 he was irresistibly drawn to theatrical styles: his eighth book of madrigals ("Warlike and amorous") contains the dramatic narrative with orchestra *Il Combattimento di Tancredi e Clorinda*, which produced the novel string effects of *tremolo* and *pizzicato*. Monteverdi was already over 70; but astonishingly enough he went on to write five more operas for Venetian commercial theatres. Of these only two survive—*Il Ritorno d'Ulisse* and his masterpiece *L'Incoronazione de Poppea*, the first opera on a historical, as opposed to a mythical, subject.

Right: *Portrait of Monteverdi, after a woodcut on the title-page of a collection published in 1644, the year after his death in Venice, where he had been active for so long.*

IL COMBATTIMENTO DI TANCREDI E CLORINDA
IL BALLO DELLE INGRATE
☐ Harper, Watson, Howells, Alva, Wakefield, Dean, Ambrosian Singers, ECO/Leppard
6500 457 (7/73) Phonogram
(La) FAVOLA D'ORFEO
☐ *Cpte.* Rogers, Petrescu, Reynolds, Bowman, Partridge, Dean, Hamburg Monteverdi Ch./Camerata Accademica/Jurgens
2723 018 (11/74) DG
L'INCORONAZIONE DI POPPEA
☐ Cpte. Donath, Soderstrom, Berberian, Esswood, Luccardi, Hannsmann, MCA/ VCM/Harnoncourt
6-35247 (3/75) Telefunken∗
MADRIGALS
(*Book IV:* Si, ch'io vorrei morire; Ah, dolente partita; La piaga; Sfogava con le stelle. *Book VII:* Chiome d'oro; Amor che deggio far; Non vedro mai le stelle; O come sei gentile; Eccomi pronta ai baci; Al lume delle stelle. *Book VIII:* Lamento dell ninfa. *Scherzi musicali:* Dolce miei sospiri; Damigella.)
☐ Purcell Consort/Burgess
ZRG668 (4/71) Decca Argo
MADRIGALS
(*Book V:* Questi vaghi concenti. *Book VI:* Presso un fiume tranquillo; A Dio, Florida bella; Qui rise, O Tirse. *Book VII:* Amor che deggio far. *Book VIII:* Altri canti d'amor.)
☐ Hamburg Monteverdi Ch./Leonhardt Consort/Jurgens
AW6 41182 (5/67) Selecta Telefunken
MADRIGALI GUERRIERI (BOOK VIII)
(Sinfonia; Altri d'amor; Hor che'l ciel; Gira il nemico; Se vittorie si belle; Armato il cor; Ogni amante e guerrier; Ardo avvampo; Il ballo.)
☐ Glyndebourne Ch./Leppard
6500 663 (1/75) Phonogram
VESPERS (VESPRO DELLA BEATA VIRGINE)
☐ Soloists, Salisbury Cathedral Boys' Choir, Monteverdi Choir and Orch./ Eliot Gardiner
SET593-4 (4/74) Decca
☐ Soloists, Regensburger Domspatzen and instrumental ens./Schneidt
2723 043 (11/75) DG

131

wolfgang Amade Mozart

WOLFGANG AMADEUS MOZART
(b. Salzburg 1756; d. Vienna 1791)

The composer most universally loved and revered by musicians, who as a child prodigy was shown off throughout Europe by his father (a violinist in the Archbishop of Salzburg's service) and fêted everywhere, and who later achieved many resounding successes (such as the sensational triumph of his opera *The Marriage of Figaro* in both Vienna and Prague), was buried in an unmarked pauper's grave at the age of 35. This melancholy state of affairs, which reflects on the world's ability to accommodate a genius in its midst, arose because Mozart's natural brilliance made him outspoken and impatient of compromise with the slower-witted and those of more superficial tastes, and because of his feckless way of life at a time when free-lance composing without the support of

ARIAS
Nozze di Figaro—Deh vieni, non tardar; Voi che sapete; Non so piu. Don Giovanni—Batti, batti; Vedrai carino. Cosi fan tutte—Come scoglio. Chi sa, chi sa, K582. Misera, dove son, K369. Vado ma dove, K583. Ch'io me scordi di te, K505.)
☐ Ameling, ECO/Waart
6500 544 (10/74) Phonogram*

ARIAS
(Non piu, tutto ascoltai, K490; Al desio, K577; Vorrei spiegarvi, K418; Bella mia fiamma, K528; Ch'io mi scordi di te, K505; Nehmt meinen Dank, K383; Vado ma dove, K583.)
☐ M. Price, LPO/Lockhart
LRL1 5077 (10/75) RCA

BASSOON CONCERTO IN B FLAT, K191
☐ Chapman, ASMF/Marriner/*Clarinet Conc. Andante for Flute, K315*
6500 378 (8/74) Phonogram*
☐ Brooke, RPO/Beecham/*Clarinet Conc.*
SXLP30246 (9/77) EMI/HMV Concert Classics
S-60193 Seraphim

CASSATIONS: NO. 1 IN G, K63; NO. 2 IN B FLAT, K100
☐ Vienna Mozart Ens./Boskovsky
SXL6500 (7/71) Decca
STS-15302 London

CHAMBER WORKS FOR WIND
(Serenades Nos. 10-12; Divertimenti Nos. 3, 4, 8, 9, 12-14, 16, K. Anh227; Adagios K410 and K411.)
☐ London Wind Soloists/Brymer
SDDL405-9 (9/73) Decca Ace of Diamonds

CLARINET CONCERTO IN A, K622
☐ McCaw/New Philh./Leppard/*Nielsen*
UNS239 (11/71) Transatlantic/Unicorn
☐ De Peyer/LSO/Maag/*Sym. 38*
SDD331 (12/72) Decca Ace of Diamonds
☐ Brymer, ASMF/Marriner/*Bassoon Conc.; Andante for Flute, K315*
6500 378 (8/74) Phonogram
S-60193 Seraphim
☐ Prinz/VPO/Munchinger/*Flute & Harp Conc.*
SPA495 (7/77) Decca
STS-15071 London

CLARINET QUINTET IN A, K581
☐ Brymer/Allegri Quartet/*Trio K498*
6500 073 (2/71) Phonogram*
☐ de Peyer/Amadeus Quartet/*Oboe Qt*
2530 720 DG*
☐ de Peyer/Melos Ensemble/*Weber*

HQS1395 (9/77) EMI/HMV

CLARINET TRIO IN E FLAT MAJOR, K498
☐ Brymer/Ireland/Bishop/*Clarinet Quintet, K581*
6500 073 (2/71) Phonogram*

CONCERTO IN E FLAT FOR TWO PIANOS, K365
☐ Brendel, Klien, VSO/Angerer/*Sonata for two pianos, K449*
TV34064S (1/67) Decca Turnabout
34064 Turnabout
☐ Emil and Elena Gilels/VPO/Bohm/*Conc. 27*
2530 456 (11/74) DG*

COSI FAN TUTTE
☐ Cpte. Schwarzkopf, Ludwig, Steffek, Kraus, Taddei, Berry, Chorus/Philh./Bohm
SLS5028 (10/75) HMV
S-3631 Angel
☐ Cpte. Lorengar, Berganza, Berbie, Davies, Krause, Bacquier, Cov. Gdn Ch./LPO/Solti
D56D4 (8/77) Decca
1442 London
☐ Cpte. Caballe, Baker, Cotrubas, Gedda, Ganzarolli, Van Allen, Cov. Gdn./C. Davis
6707 025 (2/75) Phonogram*

DANCES
(Contredanses Nos. 1, 27, 28, 61, 72, 73, 84-9, 92-9. German dances Nos. 12-17, 43-60, 62-71. Landler Nos. 77-82.)
☐ Vienna Mozart Ens./Boskovsky
SDDH347-51 (10/72) Decca Ace of Diamonds

DIVERTIMENTO IN E FLAT, K563
☐ Grumiaux, Janzer, Czako
SAL3664 (8/68) Phonogram
☐ Stern, Zukerman, Rose
76381 (8/75) CBS
M-33266 Columbia

DIVERTIMENTI FOR STRING ORCHESTRA, K136-8
☐ ASMF/Marriner/*Serenade 6*
ZRG554 (2/68) Decca Argo*
☐ I Musici/*Serenade 6*
6500 536 (8/74) Phonogram*

DIVERTIMENTO NO. 10 IN F FOR 2 HORNS AND STRING QUARTET, K247

DIVERTIMENTO NO. 11 IN D, K251
☐ ECO/C. Davis
SOL60029 (4/61) L'Oiseau Lyre

DIVERTIMENTO NO. 17 IN D FOR 2 HORNS AND STRING QUARTET, K334
☐ Vienna Octet/*Divertimento K136*
SDD251 (12/70) Decca Ace of Diamonds
STS-15304 London

DON GIOVANNI
☐ Cpte. Sutherland, Schwarzkopf, Sciutti, Waechter, Alva, Frick, Taddei, Cappuccilli/Philh./Giulini
SLS5083 (7/77) HMV
S-3605 Angel
☐ Cpte. Wixell, Arroyo, Burrows, Kanawa, Ganzarolli, Roni, Van Allen, Freni, Cov. Gdn./Davis
6707 022 (11/73) Phonogram*

Far left: *Mozart as seen by a Salzburg sculptor in 1789.*

Left: *The monument to Mozart in the Burggarten, Vienna.*

Top: *Six quartets were dedicated to Haydn by 'his friend Mozart'.*

a patron was unknown.

His dazzling early life—made much of by royalty, nobility and musical connoisseurs, decorated by the Pope, and with a large number of successful performances of his compositions to his credit (including his fourth and sixth operas, written at the age of 14 and 16)—did not make it easy for him to settle down in provincial Salzburg, least of all under an overbearing Archbishop unsympathetic to music. Nor, despite continued efforts, was he able to secure a permanent appointment in any of the centres which had hailed him as a visiting keyboard player, violinist and composer. His travels of course broadened his experience by bringing him into contact with other composers (including Haydn », his admiration for whom

was warmly reciprocated) and with leading players such as those in Mannheim, which was famous for its orchestra; but his triumphs outside Salzburg (like that of the opera *Idomeneo* at Munich, two days after his 25th birthday) irked his master, who in 1781 literally kicked him out.

Mozart spent his remaining ten years in Vienna, teaching, giving concerts, for which he wrote some of his finest piano concertos, and continuing to pour out works of every kind—symphonies, string quartets, wind serenades, miscellaneous chamber music (including violin sonatas, string quintets, piano trios and quartets and the superlative Clarinet Quintet), all his great operas, and dance music, to provide which he held the only court appointment that came his way. He became interested in

(Die) ENTFUHRUNG AUS DEM SERAIL
☐ *Cpte.* Auger, Grist, Schreier, Neukirch, Moll, Dresden Staatskapelle/ Bohm/*Impresario*
2740 102 (10/74) DG
FLUTE CONCERTOS NO. 1 IN D, K313; NO. 2 IN D, K314
☐ Adeney, ECO/Leppard/*Andante, K315*
CFP40072 (7/74) Classics for Pleasure
FLUTE QUARTETS: NO. 1 IN D, K285; NO. 2 IN G, K285a; NO. 3 IN C, K285b; NO. 4 IN A, K295
☐ Bennett, Grumiaux Trio
6500 034 (6/71) Phonogram★
FLUTE AND HARP CONCERTO IN C, K299
☐ Monteux, Ellis/ASMF/Marriner/ *Sinfonia Concertante, K297*
6500 380 (12/74) Phonogram★
☐ Tripp, Jellinek/VPO/Munchinger/ *Clarinet Conc.*
SPA495 (7/77) Decca
HORN CONCERTOS NOS. 1-4, K412, 417, 447 AND 495
☐ Tuckwell/LSO/Maag
SDD364 (4/73) Decca Ace of Diamonds
6403 London
☐ Tuckwell/ASMF/Marriner/*Rondo K371; Fragment*
ASD2780 (4/72) EMI/HMV
S-36840 Angel
☐ Civil, ASMF/Marriner/*Rondo, K371*
6500 325 (5/74) Phonogram★
☐ D. Brain/Philharmonia/Karajan
ASD1140 (9/73) EMI/HMV
☐ Civil/Philh./Klemperer
SXLP30207 (2/76) EMI/HMV Concert Classics
S-35689 Angel
LIEDER
(Die ihr des unermesslichen Weltalls; Gesellenreise; Die Zufriedenheit; Die betrogene Welt; Das Veilchen; Lied der Freiheit; Das Lied der Trennung; Abendempfindung; Geheime Liebe; Die Zufriedenheit im niedrigen Stande; Wie unglucklich bin ich; An die Freundschaft; Die grossmutige Gelassenheit; Das Traumbild; Ich wurd auf meinem Pfad; An Chloe.)
☐ Fischer-Dieskau/Barenboim
ASD2824 (2/73) EMI/HMV
LIEDER
(Als Luise die Briefe; Die Zufriedenheit; An die Hoffnung; An die Einsamkeit; Sehnsucht nach dem Fruhlinge; Die grossmutige Gelassenheit; Die kleine Spinnerin; Ridente la calma; Das Lied der Trennung; Der Zauberer; Dans un bois solitaire; Oiseaux, si tous les ans; Abendempfindung; Gesellenreise; An die Freundschaft; Eine kleine deutsche Kantata.)
☐ J. Gomez/Constable
SAGA5441 (6/77) Saga
MASONIC MUSIC
(O heiliges Band, K148; Dir, Seele des Weltalls, K429; Die ihr einem neuen Grade, K468; Sehen wie den starren Forscherauge, K471; Maurerische Trauermusik, K477; Zerfliesset heut, K483; Ihr unsre neuen Leiter, K484;

Die ihr des unermesslichen Weltalls, K619; Laut verkunde unsre Freude, K623; Lasst uns mit geschlungnen Handen, K623a.)
☐ Krenn, Krause, Edinburgh Fest. Ch./ LSO/Kertesz
SXL6409 (10/69) Decca
26111 London
MASS IN C MAJOR, K317 (CORONATION)
LITANIAE LAURETANAE, K195
☐ Cotrubas, Watts, Tear, Shirley-Quirk, Oxford Schola Cantorum, ASMF/ Marriner
ZRG677 (9/72) Decca Argo★
MASS IN C MINOR, K427
☐ Cotrubas, Kiri Te Kanawa, Krenn, Sotin, Alldis Ch., NPO/Leppard
ASD2959 (6/74) EMI/HMV
S-60257 Seraphim

MOZART: REQUIEM

Sheila Armstrong · Janet Baker · Nicolai Gedda · Dietrich Fischer-Dieskau

John Alldis Choir & English Chamber Orchestra conducted by Daniel Barenboim

REQUIEM MASS IN D MINOR, K626
☐ Armstrong, Baker, Gedda, Fischer-Dieskau, Alldis Choir, ECO/Barenboim
ASD2788 (7/72) EMI/HMV
S-36842 Angel
☐ Donath, Minton, Davies, Nienstedt, Alldis Choir, BBC SO/Davis
SAL3649 (3/68) Phonogram
802862 Philips
☐ Tomova-Sintov, Baltsa, Krenn, van Dam/Vienna Singverein/Berlin PO/ Karajan
2530 705 (12/76) DG★
MUSICAL JOKE, K522
☐ Vienna Mozart Ens./Boskovsky/ *Serenade 1*
SXL6499 (2/71) Decca
STS-15301 London
LE NOZZE DI FIGARO
☐ *Cpte:* della Casa, Gueden, Danco,

Siepi, Corena, Poell/Vienna State Op. Ch./VPO/E. Kleiber
GOS585-7 (4/70) Decca Ace of Diamonds
1402 London
☐ *Cpte.* Norman, Freni, Minton, Ganzarolli, Wixell, BBC Chorus, BBC SO/Davis
6707 014 (11/71) Phonogram★
☐ Harper, Blegen, Berganza, Fischer-Dieskau, Evans, McCue, Alldis Choir/ECO/Barenboim
SLS995 (7/77) HMV
OBOE CONCERTO IN C, K314
☐ Holliger/New Philh./Waart/*R. Strauss*
6500 174 (1/72) Phonogram
OVERTURES
Idomeneo; Die Entfuhrung aus dem Serail; La finta giardinera; Impresario; Le nozze di Figaro; Die Zauberflote;

Freemasonry and wrote several Masonic works as well as the opera *The magic flute*, which is imbued with its symbolism: it was largely due to financial help from a fellow-Mason that in his last years he managed to survive at all. His last work, left incomplete when he died, was a Requiem (commissioned by a mysterious stranger) which Mozart, whose thoughts frequently dwelt on death, became convinced was intended for himself.

His ability to think out a work, complete in every detail, in his head in advance explains such feats as his writing in a mere fortnight his last three great symphonies (the finale of the so-called "Jupiter" in C being a most astonishing piece of contrapuntal virtuosity); but one of his most awesome characteristics was the sheer perfection of his

technique in whatever he touched. With his gifts for beauty of sound, for warm and profound, sometimes passionately subjective, feelings under an elegant exterior, for melodic distinction, harmonic subtlety and an unerring ear for instrumentation, for commensurate mastery in the then still new field of the solo concerto and in symphonic construction, for a dramatic sense encompassing the whole range of styles from *opera seria* and *buffa* to German comic or solemn *Singspiel* (incidentally developing to a new high level both characterisation and the art of the operatic finale), it is little wonder that he ranks among the supreme musical geniuses of all time.

Above: *Mozart's birthplace in Salzburg attracts thousands of pilgrims to the town that never appreciated him.*

Top right: *Mozart the infant prodigy being shown off by his father before the Empress Maria Theresa.*

Cosi fan tutte; La Clemenza
Don Giovanni
☐ RPO/Davis
 CFP40033 (3/73) Classics for Pleasure
 S-60037 Seraphim
PIANO CONCERTOS 1-9, 11-27
☐ Barenboim/ECO
 SLS5031 (1/76) HMV
PIANO CONCERTO NO. 6 IN B FLAT, K238
☐ Ashkenazy/LSO/Schmidt-Isserstedt/
 Conc. 20
 SXL6353 (10/68) Decca
 6579 London

PIANO CONCERTO NO. 8 IN C, K246
☐ Barenboim/ECO/*Conc. 25*
 ASD3033 (1/75) EMI/HMV
PIANO CONCERTO NO. 9 IN E FLAT, K271
☐ Ashkenazy/LSO/Kertesz
 SXL6259 (1/67) Decca
☐ Brendel, Solisti di Zagreb/Janigro/
 Conc. 14
 HM30SD (6/73) Pye/Vanguard*
PIANO CONCERTO NO. 11 IN F, K413
☐ Barenboim/ECO/*Conc. 16*
 ASD2999 (9/74) EMI/HMV
PIANO CONCERTO NO. 12 IN A, K414

☐ Brendel, ASMF/Marriner/*Conc. 17*
 6500 140 (2/74) Phonogram
 6599054 Philips
☐ Lupu/ECO/Segal/*Conc. 21*
 SXL6698 (3/75) Decca
 6894 London
PIANO CONCERTO NO. 13 IN C, K415
☐ Barenboim/ECO/*Conc. 17*
 ASD2357 (4/68) EMI/HMV
PIANO CONCERTO NO. 14 IN E FLAT, K449
☐ Barenboim/ECO/*Conc. 15*
 ASD2434 (10/68) EMI/HMV
☐ Brendel, Solisti di Zagreb/Janigro/
 Conc. 9
 HM30SD (6/73) Pye/Vanguard
PIANO CONCERTO NO. 15 IN B FLAT, K450
☐ Barenboim/ECO/*Conc. 14*
 ASD2434 (10/68) EMI/HMV
☐ R. Casadesus, Cleveland/Szell/
 Conc. 17
 61348 (3/73) CBS Classics
 MS-7245 Columbia
PIANO CONCERTO NO. 16 IN D, K451
☐ Barenboim/ECO/*Conc. 11*
 ASD2999 (9/74) EMI/HMV
PIANO CONCERTO NO. 17 IN G, K453
☐ Brendel/Volksoper Orch./Angerer/
 Conc. 19
 TV34080S (8/67) Decca Turnabout*
☐ Anda/Salzburg Mozarteum/*Conc. 21*
 138783 (9/62) DG
☐ R. Casadesus, Cleveland/Szell/
 Conc. 15
 61348 (3/73) CBS Classics
 MS-7245 Columbia
☐ Brendel/ASMF/Marriner/*Conc. 14*
 6500 140 (2/74) Phonogram
PIANO CONCERTO NO. 18 IN B FLAT, K456
☐ Barenboim/ECO/*Conc. 24*
 ASD2887 (7/73) EMI/HMV
PIANO CONCERTO NO. 19 IN F, K459
☐ Serkin, Columbia SO/Szell/*Conc. 20*
 61136 (7/70) CBS Classics
 MS-6534 Columbia
☐ Brendel/ASMF/Marriner/*Conc. 23*
 6500 283 (11/72) Phonogram*
☐ Pollini/VPO/Bohm/*Conc. 23*
 2530 716 (1/77) DG*
PIANO CONCERTO NO. 20 IN D MINOR, K466
☐ Barenboim/ECO/*Conc. 23*
 ASD2318 (7/67) EMI/HMV

☐ Ashkenazy/LSO/Schmidt-Isserstedt/
 Conc. 6
 SXL6353 (10/68) Decca
 6579 London
☐ Serkin, Columbia SO/Szell/*Conc. 19*
 66136 (7/70) Phonogram
 MS-6534 Columbia
☐ Annie Fischer/Philh./Boult/*Conc. 23*
 SXLP30148 (9/72) EMI/HMV
 Concert Classics
☐ Gulda/VPO/Abbado/*Conc. 21*
 2530 548 (11/75) DG*
☐ Richter/Warsaw National PSO/
 Wislocki/*Beethoven*
 2548 106 (10/75) DG Heliodor
PIANO CONCERTO NO. 21 IN C, K467
☐ Anda/Salzburg Mozarteum/*Conc. 17*
 138783 (9/62) DG
☐ Barenboim/ECO/*K595*
 ASD2465 (2/69) EMI/HMV
☐ Annie Fischer/Philh./Sawallisch/
 Conc. 22
 SXLP30124 (10/71) EMI/HMV
 Concert Classics
☐ Lupu/ECO/Segal/*Conc. 12*
 SXL6698 (3/75) Decca
☐ Vered/LPO/Segal/*Conc. 23*
 PFS4340 (12/75) Decca Phase 4
 21138 London
PIANO CONCERTO NO. 22 IN E FLAT, K482
☐ Annie Fischer/Philh./Sawallisch/
 Conc. 21
 SXLP30124 (10/71) EMI/HMV
 Concert Classics
☐ Brendel/ASMF/Marriner/*Rondos K382 & K386*
 9500 145 (10/77) Phonogram*
PIANO CONCERTO NO. 23 IN A, K488
☐ Curzon/LSO/Kertesz/*Conc. 24*
 SXL6354 (11/68) Decca
 6580 London
☐ Barenboim/ECO/*Conc. 20*
 ASD2318 (7/67) EMI/HMV
☐ Brendel/ASMF/Marriner/*Conc. 19*
 6500 283 (11/72) Phonogram*
☐ Vered/LPO/Segal/*Conc. 21*
 PFS4340 (12/75) Decca Phase 4
 21138 London
☐ Kempff/Bamberg SO/Leitner/*Conc. 24*
 2535 204 (12/76) DG
☐ Pollini/VPO/Bohm/*Conc. 19*
 2530 716 (1/77) DG*

PIANO CONCERTO NO. 24 IN C MINOR, K491
☐ Curzon/LSO/Kertesz/*Conc. 23*
   SXL6354 (11/68) Decca
   6580 London
☐ Barenboim/ECO/*Conc. 18*
   ASD2887 (7/73) EMI/HMV
☐ Haebler/LSO/Davis/*Conc. 11*
   6580 069 (12/73) Phonogram
☐ Kempff/Bamberg SO/Leitner/*Conc. 23*
   2535 204 (12/76) DG Privilege∗
PIANO CONCERTO NO. 25 IN C, K503
☐ Barenboim/ECO/*Conc. 8*
   ASD3033 (1/75) EMI/HMV
☐ Brendel/VPM/Angerer/*Conc. 27*
   TV34129S (3/68) Decca Turnabout∗
☐ Bishop-Kovacevich/LSO/Davis/
   Conc. 21
   6500 431 (4/74) Phonogram∗
☐ Moravec/Czech PO/Vlach/*Fantasia,*
   K475
   110 1559 (4/76) Rediffusion/Supraphon
PIANO CONCERTO NO. 26 IN D, K537, "CORONATION"
☐ R. Casadesus/Columbia SO/Szell/
   Conc. 27
   61597 (2/75) CBS Classics
   MS-6403 Columbia
PIANO CONCERTO NO. 27 IN B FLAT, K595
☐ Brendel/VPM/Angerer/*Conc. 25*
   TV34129S (3/68) Decca Turnabout∗
☐ Gilels/VPO/Bohm/*Conc. for 2 pianos,*
   K365
   2530 456 (11/74) DG∗
☐ Brendel/ASMF/Marriner/*Conc. 18*
   6500 948 (4/75) Phonogram∗
☐ R. Casadesus/Columbia SO/Szell/
   Conc. 26
   61597 (2/75) CBS Classics
   MS-6403 Columbia
PIANO QUARTET NO. 1 IN G MINOR, K478
PIANO QUARTET NO. 2 IN E FLAT, K493
☐ Pro Arte Piano Quartet
   SOL285 (1/66) L'Oiseau-Lyre
PIANO SONATAS NOS. 1-17; SONATA, K533/494
☐ Balsam
   OLS177-181 (6-7/63) L'Oiseau-Lyre
PIANO SONATAS: NO. 11 IN A, K331; NO. 13 IN B FLAT, K333
☐ Brendel/*Adagio, K540*
   9500 025 (6/76) Phonogram∗
QUINTET IN E FLAT FOR PIANO AND WIND, K452
☐ Ashkenazy/London Wind Soloists/
   Beethoven: Piano and Wind Quintet
   SXL6252 (11/66) Decca
   6494 London
SERENADE NO. 6 IN D (SERENATA NOTTURNA)
☐ Philh./C. Davis/*Concert*
   SXLP20019 (1/62) EMI/HMV Concert
   Classics
☐ I Musici/*Divertimenti, K136-8*
   6500 536 (8/74) Phonogram∗
☐ ASMF/Marriner/*Divertimenti, K136-8*
   ZRG554 (2/68) Decca Argo∗
☐ ECO/Britten/*Sym. 40*
   SXL6372 (10/68) Decca
   6598 London
☐ LSO/Maag/*Concert*
   ECS740 (3/75) Decca Eclipse

SERENADE NO. 7 IN D, K250 (HAFFNER)
☐ Vienna Mozart Ens/Boskovsky
   SXL6614 (3/74) Decca
☐ Bavarian RSO/Kubelik
   2535 139 (4/76) DG Privilege
☐ Dresden Staatskapelle/de Waart/
   March, K249
   6500 966 (6/76) Phonogram∗
SERENADE NO. 9 IN D, K320, "POSTHORN"
☐ Dresden Staatskapelle/De Waart/
   Marches 10, 11
   6500 627 (4/75) Phonogram∗
SERENADE NO. 10 IN B FLAT FOR 13 WIND INSTRUMENTS, K361
☐ London Wind Soloists
   SXL6409 (11/63) Decca
☐ Netherlands Wind Ens./de Waart
   839 734 (12/72) Philips∗
SERENADE NO. 11 IN E FLAT, K375
☐ Netherlands Wind Ens./de Waart/
   Ser. 12
   802 907LY (5/72) Phonogram∗
☐ New London Wind Ens./*Ser. 12*
   CFP40211 (11/75) Classics for Pleasure
SERENADE NO. 12 IN C MINOR, K388
☐ Netherlands Wind Ens./de Waart/
   Ser. 11
   802 907LY (5/72) Phonogram∗
☐ New London Wind Ens./*Ser. 11*
   CFP40211 (11/75) Classics for Pleasure
SERENADE NO. 13 IN G FOR STRINGS (EINE KLEINE NACHTMUSIK)
☐ Philh./C. Davis/*Concert*
   SXLP20019 (1/62) EMI/HMV
   Concert Classics
   S-60057 Angel
☐ I Musici/*Violin Conc. 5; Adagio and*
   Fugue in C minor, K546
   6500 537 (8/73) Phonogram∗
☐ ASMF/Marriner/*Sinfonia Concertante,*
   K364; Sym. 32
   ZRG679 (1/71) Decca Argo∗
☐ VPO/Bohm/*Saint-Saens*
   2530 731 (12/76) DG
SINFONIA CONCERTANTE IN E FLAT, K364
☐ Grumiaux, Pelliccia/LSO/Davis/*Vln.*
   Conc. 2
   SAL3492 (4/65) Phonogram
   835256 Philips
☐ I. Oistrakh, D. Oistrakh/Moscow PO/
   Kondrashin/*Haydn*
   SDD445 (4/75) Decca Ace of Diamonds
STRING QUARTETS
☐ *Cpte.* Quartetto Italiano
   6747 097 (9/74) Phonogram
STRING QUARTET IN E FLAT, K428
☐ Melos Quartet/*Qt. 17*
   2530 800 (5/77) DG∗
STRING QUARTET IN B FLAT, K458 (HUNT)
☐ Amadeus Quartet/*Haydn: Quartet 77*
   138886 (4/64) DG
☐ Melos Quartet/*Qt. 16*
   2530 800 (5/77) DG∗
STRING QUARTET IN D, K499
☐ Vienna Philharmonic Quartet/
   Quartet 22
   SDD291 (7/72) Decca Ace of
   Diamonds
   STS-15116 London
☐ Quartetto Italiano/*Quartet 21*
   6500 241 (7/72) Phonogram
☐ Alban Berg Quartet/*Quartet 21*
   AW6 41999 (9/76) Selecta/Telefunken∗

STRING QUARTET IN D, K575
☐ Weller Quartet/*Quartet 23*
   SDD325 (7/72) Decca Ace of Diamonds
☐ Quartetto Italiano/*Quartet 20*
   6500 241 (7/72) Phonogram
☐ Alban Berg Quartet/*Quartet 20*
   AW6 41999 (9/76) Selecta/Telefunken
☐ Kuchl Quartet/*Quartet 23*
   SDD509 (22/76) Decca Ace of Diamonds
STRING QUARTET IN B FLAT, K589
☐ Vienna Philharmonic Quartet
   SDD291 (7/71) Decca Ace of Diamonds
   STS-15116 London
STRING QUARTET IN F, K590
☐ Weller Quartet
   SDD330 (7/72) Decca Ace of Diamonds
   STS-15291 London
☐ Kuchl Quartet/*Quartet 21*
   SDD509 (11/76) Decca Ace of Diamonds
STRING QUINTETS 1-6
☐ Amadeus Quartet, Aronowitz
   2740 122 (12/75) DG
SYMPHONY NO. 25 IN G MINOR
☐ ASMF/Marriner/*Sym. 29*
   ZRG706 (4/72) Decca Argo∗
SYMPHONY NO. 29 IN A
☐ LSO/Davis/*Syms. 25, 32*
   SAL3502 (5/65) Phonogram
   835262 Philips
☐ ASMF/Marriner/*Sym. 25*
   ZRG706 (4/72) Decca Argo∗
☐ ECO/Barenboim/*Syms. 30 & 34*
   ASD2806 (7/72) EMI/HMV
☐ Vienna CO/Entremont/*Sym. 28*
   76581 (6/77) CBS
SYMPHONY NO. 31 IN D (PARIS)
☐ ECO/Barenboim/*Sym. 41*
   ASD2379 (9/69) EMI/HMV
SYMPHONY NO. 34 IN C
☐ ECO/Barenboim/*Syms 29 & 30*
   ASD2806 (7/72) EMI/HMV
SYMPHONIES NOS. 35, 36, 38-41
☐ Columbia SO/Walter
   77308 (12/74) CBS
   MS-6493 Columbia
SYMPHONY NO. 35 IN D (HAFFNER)
☐ ECO/Barenboim/*Sym. 32, Sym. 38*
   ASD2327 (9/67) EMI/HMV
   S-36512 Angel
SYMPHONY NO. 36 IN C (LINZ)
☐ LPO/Mackerras/*Sym. 38*
   CFP40079 (9/74)
☐ Concertgebouw/Jochum/*Sym. 38*
   6580 023 (2/72) Phonogram
SYMPHONY NO. 38 IN D (PRAGUE)
☐ ECO/Barenboim/*Sym. 32, Sym. 35*
   ASD2327 (9/67) EMI/HMV
   S-36512 Angel
☐ LSO/Maag/*Clarinet Conc.*
   SDD331(12/72) Decca Ace of
   Diamonds
☐ LPO/Mackerras/*Sym. 36*
   CFP40079 (9/74)
☐ ECO/Britten/*Schubert: Sym. 8*
   SXL6539 (6/72) Decca
   6741 London
SYMPHONY NO. 39 IN E FLAT
☐ ECO/Barenboim/*Sym. 40*
   ASD2424 (8/68) EMI/HMV
☐ VPO/Kertesz/*Sym. 33*
   SXL6056 (9/63) Decca
   STS-15274 London
☐ LSO/Davis/*Sym. 40*
   6580 029 (11/71) Phonogram
   6500 559 Philips
SYMPHONY NO. 40 IN G MINOR
☐ ECO/Barenboim/*Sym. 39*
   ASD2424 (8/68) EMI/HMV

☐ ECO/Britten/*Serenata notturna*
   SXL6372 (10/68) Decca
   6598 London
☐ Sinfonia of London/Collins/*Sym. 41*
   CFP127 (1/72) Classics for Pleasure
☐ LSO/Davis/*Sym. 39*
   6580 029 (1171) Phonogram
   6500 559 Philips
☐ LSO/Davis/*Beethoven: Sym. 5*
   6833 102 (12/73) Phonogram
SYMPHONY NO. 41 IN C (JUPITER)
☐ Boston SO/Jochum/*Schubert: Sym. 8*
   2530 357 (4/74) DG∗
☐ ECO/Barenboim/*Sym. 31*
   ASD2379 (9/69) EMI/HMV
☐ Sinfonia of London/Collins/*Sym. 40*
   CFP127 (1/72) Classics for Pleasure
VESPERAE SOLENNES DE CONFESSORE IN C, K339
☐ Kanawa, Bainbridge, Davies, Howell,
   LSO and Ch./Davis
   6500 271 (4/73) Phonogram∗
VIOLIN CONCERTO NO. 2 IN D, K211
☐ Krebbers/Netherlands Chbr. Orch./
   Zinman/*Conc. 4*
   6580 120 (6/76) Phonogram
VIOLIN CONCERTO NO. 3 IN G. K216
☐ Szeryng/New Philh./Gibson/*Conc. 4*
   6500 036 (1/72) Phonogram
☐ D. Oistrakh/Philh./*Beethoven Pno.*
   Conc. 4
   SXLP30086 (10/67) EMI/HMV
   Concert Classics
☐ Loveday, ASMF/Marriner/
   Concertone
   ZRG729 (1/73) Decca Argo∗
VIOLIN CONCERTO NO. 4 IN D, K218
☐ Szeryng/New Philh./Gibson/*Conc. 3*
   6500 036 (1/72) Phonogram
☐ Grumiaux, LSO/Davis/*Conc. 1*
   6580 009 (10/72) Phonogram
☐ Krebbers/Netherlands Chbr. Orch./
   Zinman/*Conc. 2*
   6580 120 (6/76) Phonogram
VIOLIN SONATAS NOS. 17-28, 32-34, F MAJOR
☐ Goldberg, Lupu
   13BB207-12 (11/75) Decca
DIE ZAUBERFLOTE
☐ *Cpte.* Frick, Gedda, Crass, Unger, Popp,
   Janowitz, Schwarzkopf, Ludwig, Berry,
   Putz, Chorus, Philharmonia/Klemperer
   SLS912 (11/64) HMV
☐ *Cpte.* Lipp, Gueden, Loose, Simoneau,
   Jaresch, Bohme, Berry, Schoeffler/
   Vienna State Op. Ch./VPO/Böhm
   GOS501-3 (2/67) Decca Ace of
   Diamonds

MODEST MUSSORGSKY
(b. Karevo, Govt. of Pskov, 1839; d. St Petersburg 1881)

In one respect Mussorgsky is almost unique—that until quite recently practically none of his music was heard as he wrote it, without touching-up by other hands. Any indignation or censure, however, would be misplaced, since he left everything in such a state of chaos that without their well-meant intervention it would probably never have been heard at all; and though today we would prefer to have the music, warts and all, as this most original and individual composer conceived it, to his contemporaries his bare harmonies, elliptical modulations and unorthodox orchestration seemed intolerably crude.

The son of landed gentry, he went into the Guards' cadet school at 12 and joined the regiment when he was 17: the hard-drinking habits he acquired there were to have a disastrous effect on his future. He was at that time merely a piano-playing dilettante, according to a contemporary; but meetings with Dargomizhky and Balakirev » turned his mind to music, and in 1858 he resigned his commission to study with the latter (though he was an unsystematic worker). The emancipation of the serfs in 1861, with which he was heartily in sympathy, left him in unaccustomed poverty, and he was obliged to take minor clerical posts in the civil service, being constantly in trouble because of his heavy drinking and mental instability; for a couple of years he lived as a kind of "drop-out" in a commune. He finally drank himself to death.

His profound human sympathy with the peasants was shown in his one completed opera, *Boris Godunov*, in which the Russian people are as much a focal point as is the powerfully-drawn figure of the Tsar. The work suffered many vicissitudes and revisions, the most generally encountered version being by his friend Rimsky-Korsakov », who, in addition to "correcting" the harmony and orchestration, also changed the sequence of the final scenes. Two other operas, the historical drama *The Khovansky plot* and the rustic comedy *Sorochintsy Fair*, had to be completed by others: the Prelude to the former, depicting dawn over the Kremlin, is sometimes played on

its own; the latter contains a version, heavily revised by Rimsky-Korsakov, of *Night on the bare mountain*, which had previously been included in the ballet-opera *Mlada* jointly planned with Borodin » and others of the "kuchka", and had before that been a separate orchestral piece. Mussorgsky's one major instrumental work, the *Pictures from an exhibition*, whose finale stretches piano sonorities to their limits, is more usually heard in the brilliantly imaginative orchestration by Ravel ». His three song-cycles—*The Nursery*, *Sunless* and the fantastic and dramatic *Songs and dances of Death*—are remarkable examples of his utterly original style, following in naturalistic declamation the inflections of Russian speech.

BORIS GODUNOV
☐ *(Rimsky-Korsakov version)* Ghiaurov, Talvela, Vishnevskaya, Spiess, Keleman, Vienna State Op. Chorus/VPO/ Karajan
SET514-7 (11/71) Decca
1439 London
☐ *Cpte. (original version)* Talvela, Gedda, Mroz, Kinasz, Haugland, Lukomska, Polish Radio Chorus and Orch./ Semkow
SLS1000 (9/77) HMV
SX-3844 Angel

KHOVANSCHINA—PRELUDE (DAWN OVER THE MOSCOW RIVER)
☐ New Philh./Mackerras/*Pictures*
VSD71188 (12/74) Pye/Vanguard
☐ LSO/Solti/*Borodin; Glinka*
SXL6263 (2/67) Decca
6785 London
☐ Berlin PO/Solti/*Borodin; Glinka*
SPA257 (7/73) Decca
6944 London

NIGHT ON THE BARE MOUNTAIN
(arr. Rimsky-Korsakov unless stated)
☐ *(Orig. version)* LPO/Lloyd-Jones/ *Borodin; Rimsky*
6580 053 (6/72) Phonogram
☐ LPO/Mackerras/*Glinka: Ruslan and Ludmila Ov.; Tchaikovsky: 1812 Ov.; Wagner: Lohengrin:—Prelude to Act 3*
CFP101 (4/71) Classics for Pleasure
☐ LSO/Solti/*Borodin; Glinka*
SXL6263 (2/67) Decca
6785 London

Left: *Ilya Repin's portrait of the battered Mussorgsky.*

☐ Berlin PO/Solti/*Borodin; Glinka*
SPA257 (7/73) Decca
6944 London
☐ Orch. de Paris/Rozhdestvensky/ *Borodin; Rimsky Korsakov*
ESD7006 (9/76) EMI/HMV
S-36889 Angel
☐ Berlin PO/Maazel/*Respighi; Rimsky Korsakov*
2548 267 (7/77) DG Heliodor
138033 DG

THE NURSERY; SONGS AND DANCES OF DEATH; SUNLESS
☐ Slobodskaya, Newton
5357 (5/74) Saga

PICTURES FROM AN EXHIBITION
(piano)
☐ Ashkenazy/*Orch. version*
SXL6328 (12/67) Decca

PICTURES FROM AN EXHIBITION
(orch. Ravel)
☐ Chicago SO/Reiner/*Night on the bare mountain*
CCV5038 (10/58) Camden Classics
☐ Berlin PO/Karajan/*Ravel*
139010 (11/66) DG*
☐ New Philh./Mackerras/*Khovanschina —Prelude*
VSD71188 (12/74) Pye/Vanguard
☐ Los Angeles PO/Mehta/*Piano version*
SXL6328 (12/67) Decca
☐ Chicago SO/Giulini/*Prokofiev*
2530 783 (4/77) DG*

SONGS AND DANCES OF DEATH
☐ Arkhipova/Wustman/*Tchaikovsky; Rachmaninov*
ASD3103 (9/76) EMI/HMV

carl nielsen
HYMNUS AMORIS
SLEEP

Kirsten Schultz · Bodil Gobel · Tonny Landy · Bent Norup
Mogens Schmidt Johansen · Hans Christian Andersen
DANISH RADIO CHORUS
COPENHAGEN BOYS CHOIR
Danish Radio Symphony Orchestra
MOGENS WOLDIKE

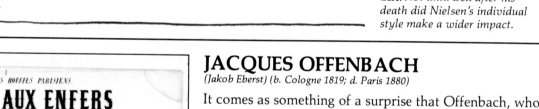

Left: *Not until well after his death did Nielsen's individual style make a wider impact.*

Above: *The impudent wit of Offenbach's Orpheus in the Under- world in 1858 became the rage of Paris.*

JACQUES OFFENBACH
(Jakob Eberst) (b. Cologne 1819; d. Paris 1880)

It comes as something of a surprise that Offenbach, who put *opéra-bouffe* on the map and whose music is the very embodiment of the frivolity of the French Second Empire, should have been German by birth (he was the son of the cantor in the Cologne synagogue); but he went to Paris at the age of 14 and there spent the rest of his life, except for visits to England and, later, the USA. He studied the cello for a year, played in the orchestra of the Opéra-Comique, and became conductor at the Comédie Française. With the composition of operettas for the Bouffes-Parisiens, of which he became manager in 1855, he found his true vocation: he stayed in management only six years (with another two-year spell at the Théâtre de la Gaieté twelve years later), but in 25 years he turned out 90 high-spirited theatre pieces (plus occasional extras such as the ballet *Le Papillon* for the Opéra), and their verve, wit and sparkling tunes and orchestration became the rage of Paris.

Audiences were delighted by the flippant social and political satire of these pieces; and though, inevitably, some of their topical point is lost today, many of them are still extremely amusing, while their music has become a happy-hunting-ground for arrangers making up other works (e.g. the ballet *Gaieté Parisienne*). Some of Offenbach's greatest successes were *Orpheus in the Underworld* (1858) and *La Belle Hélène*, both skits on classical legends; *La Vie Parisienne*, dealing satirically with visitors to the Exposition Universelle and the ways of servants and masters; *La Grande Duchesse de Gérolstein*,

CARL NIELSEN
(b. Nörre Lyndelse, Odense, 1865; d. Copenhagen 1931)

Great as were the dissimilarities in temperament and musical style between the two men, Nielsen's stature in the music of his native Denmark is akin to that of his exact counterpart Sibelius » in Finland's; but where the latter seemed primarily concerned with reflecting the bleak face of Nature in his homeland, Nielsen's interest lay rather in human beings—it was typical that his delightful Wind Quintet should depict the divergent personalities of the players for whom he wrote it. A further difference was that his works did not begin to impinge on the world outside Denmark until twenty years after his death.

The son of a humble artisan, Nielsen was enabled by the help of friends to study at the Copenhagen Conservatory under Mendelssohn's » friend Gade; and from his mid-twenties he was for fifteen years a second violin in the Royal Orchestra, which introduced his First Symphony in 1892. This was to some extent influenced by Brahms » but was nevertheless already a very personal work, embodying a tug-of-war between two keys which was to become

habitual with him. He began to conduct his own works—his now popular Second Symphony ("The Four Temperaments") in 1901, his opera *Saul and David* the following year. (All Nielsen's six symphonies except the First and Fifth carry sub-titles, but he was insistent that, save in the Second, they should not be regarded as in any sense programmatic.) He wrote incidental music for various theatre plays, and the comedy opera *Maskarade* (still popular in Denmark); and in 1908 he was appointed conductor of the Royal Orchestra—a post to which he was not altogether suited but which he held until 1914.

It was only after this that he was able to give himself more fully to composition (although he conducted the Copenhagen Music Society's yearly half-dozen concerts from 1915, and taught at the Conservatory). "Music, like life, is inextinguishable", he declared, and this characteristically vigorous and positive attitude, besides giving the Fourth Symphony its title, imbues most of his work, in which a quirky sense of the grotesque is often to be found. In the Flute Concerto, for example, the soloist is teased by vulgar intrusions by the bass trombone; the sterner Clarinet Concerto is all but disrupted by a freely aggressive side-drum. This gratuitous introduction of an element of struggle is seen at its most violent in the Fourth Symphony, in whose finale two sets of timpani fight out a duel, and the two-movement Fifth, whose very existence at one point seems threatened by a militant side-drum; but another aspect of it is the "progressive tonality" (an initial key being overcome by another) which Nielsen favoured. One of his very last works, the *Commotio* for organ (on the plan of a Bach Toccata), is also one of his greatest.

SERENATA IN VANO
☐ Tivoli Concert Ens./*Sym. 2/Little Suite*
  TV34049S (4/68) Decca Turnabout
SLEEP, OP. 18
☐ Danish RO and Ch./Woldike/*Hymnus*
  ASD3358 (9/77) EMI/HMV
STRING QUARTET NO. 2 IN F MINOR, OP. 5
STRING QUARTET NO. 3 IN E FLAT, OP. 14
☐ Copenhagen Quartet
  TV34187S (6/68) Decca Turnabout
SYMPHONIES NOS. 1-6; FLUTE CONCERTO; CLARINET CONCERTO; VIOLIN CONCERTO; ORCHESTRAL WORKS

☐ Soloists/Danish RSO/Blomstedt
  SLS5027 (10/75) HMV
  S-6097 Seraphim
SYMPHONY NO. 4, OP. 29 (INEXTINGUISHABLE)
☐ Royal Danish Orch./Markevich/*Sagadrom*
  2548 240 (11/76) DG Heliodor
  34050 Turnabout
SYMPHONY NO. 5, OP. 50
☐ Bournemouth SO/Berglund
  ASD3063 (6/75) EMI/HMV
SYMPHONY NO. 6 (SINFONIA SEMPLICE)
☐ LSO/Schmidt/*Humoresques*
  RHS329 (1/75) Unicorn

---

which mocked the complacent incompetence of the army's upper crust; and *La Fille du Tambour-major*, his last operetta to be produced in his lifetime.

In his final years he stepped outside his usual sphere to write the more ambitious *Tales of Hoffmann*, which had to be put in shape and its orchestration completed after his death by Guiraud (who had added the recitatives to Bizet's » *Carmen*). The overplayed *Barcarolle* from this opera gives no idea of its striking atmosphere of fantasy.

LA GRANDE DUCHESSE DE GEROLSTEIN
☐ *Cpte*. Crespin, Vanzo, Burles, Meloni, Massard, Toulouse Capitol Ch. and Orch./Plasson
  79207 (4/77) CBS
  M2-34576 Columbia

ORPHEUS IN THE UNDERWORLD
☐ *Exc. in English*. Sadler's Wells/Faris
  CSD1316 (9/60) EMI/HMV
OVERTURES
  Orpheus in the Underworld; La grande duchesse de Gerolstein; La belle Helene; Barbe-bleu; La vie Parisienne
☐ CBSO/Fremaux
  ESD7034 (4/77) EMI/HMV
  517 Klavier
LE PAPILLON—BALLET
☐ LSO/Bonynge
  SXL6588 (5/73) Decca
  6812 London
TALES OF HOFFMANN
☐ *Cpte*. Sutherland, Domingo, Bacquier, Ambrosian Singers/LSO/Bonynge
  SET454-7 (11/72) Decca
(La) VIE PARISIENNE
☐ *Cpte*. Crespin, Mesple, Lublin, Chateau, Masson, Senechal, Toulouse Capitol Ch. and Orch./Plasson
  SLS5073 (5/77) HMV
  SX-3829 Angel

CARL ORFF
(b. Munich 1895; d. there 1982)

Orff represented the extreme of reaction against the operatic ideals and techniques of Wagner » and Strauss », and was a pioneer in Minimal Art long before the term was invented. Whether in his folk-tale operas *Der Mond* and the musically slightly more interesting *Die Kluge*, in his scenic cantatas, of which the 1937 *Carmina Burana* (based on songs in low Latin and low German from the Bavarian monastery of Benediktbeuren) is far and away the most successful, or in his Greek tragedies, he adopted a limited style which was deliberately simplistic, relying on plain rhythmic declamation, usually against a percussive rhythmic background, with an irreducible minimum of harmonic thought and no counterpoint at all. This new anti-intellectual primitivism, which in his weaker works attained a vacuous repetitiousness and lack of invention that produced only exasperation in the listener, nevertheless made an evident "gut-appeal" to a pop-orientated world, judging by the existence of a dozen current recorded versions of *Carmina Burana*, the work which first made his name. Orff gained considerable fame as a music educationist, using a system of his own that called for specially designed instruments.

CARMINA BURANA
☐ Popp, Unger, Wolansky, Noble, Chorus, NPO/Fruhbeck de Burgos
SAN162 (6/66) EMI/HMV Angel
☐ Mandac, Kolk, Milnes, Chorus, Boston SO/Ozawa
LSB4006 (11/70) RCA
LSC-3161 RCA
☐ Armstrong, English, Allen, Choruses/ LSO/Previn
ASD3117 (10/75) EMI/HMV
S-37117 Angel
☐ Janowitz, Stolze, Fischer-Dieskau, Berlin Op./Jochum
139362 (7/68) DG*
CATULLI CARMINA
☐ Auger, Ochman/Berlin Op.Ch./Jochum
2530 074 (10/71) DG*
☐ Mai, Buchner/Leipzig Radio Ch. and Orch./Kegel
6500 815 (1/76) Phonogram*
DER MOND
☐ *Cpte.* Teschler, Lunow, Klotz, Terzibaschian, Schall, Suss, Leipzig Radio Ch. and Orch./Kegel
6700 083 (11/75) Phonogram*

NICCOLÒ PAGANINI
(b. Genoa 1782; d. Nice 1840)

Apart from Liszt », no virtuoso ever caught the imagination both of the general public and of musicians to the same extent as Paganini, whose wizardry on the violin created the utmost sensation wherever he went and led the superstitious to believe that he must be in league with the devil. The effect he created was intensified by his tall, thin, cadaverous appearance, waxen features and long black hair; and he played little but his own music, which was conceived only in terms of maximum showmanship and hence was frequently very shallow in character. He was also very careful to safeguard the secrets of his pyrotechnics, not publishing in his lifetime more than his 24 *Caprices*—which inspired other composers such as Schumann », Brahms », Liszt and Rachmaninov »—and some of his guitar works.

As a child he had been made to work hard at the violin by his father and had studied in Genoa and Parma, making his first concert tour at the age of 13 and beginning to compose at about the same time. When he threw off parental discipline he plunged into a life of gambling and dissipation, and at the age of 19 virtually withdrew from the world for three years to live with a

titled Tuscan lady: during this time he took up the guitar, for which he was also to write quite copiously. From 1805 he was musical director to Napoleon's sister the Princess of Lucca for eight years, though granted frequent leave of absence to give concerts. His appearance in Milan in 1813 created a furore which could be appeased only by his giving 37 concerts there in the one season. He continued to lead an irregular life, which played havoc with his health; but an extensive tour in 1828 had audiences in Vienna, Germany, Paris and Britain in frenzies of enthusiasm and excitement. He commissioned from Berlioz » a concerto for viola (an instrument he also played), but in fact never performed his *Harold in Italy*, either because it was not showy enough or because by this time (1834) his declining health forced him to limit his appearances to a minimum.

Paganini's technical innovations of every kind brought about a revolution in violin playing and offer a perpetual challenge to present-day virtuosos. More of his concertos seem constantly to be coming to light, but the favourite is No. 2, whose finale is *La Campanella*, which Liszt made even more famous in his piano transcription.

CAPRICES, OP. 1
☐ Ricci
  ECS803 (7/77) Decca Eclipse
  6163 London
☐ Perlman
  ASD3384 (10/77) EMI/HMV
  S-36860 Angel
6 SONATAS FOR VIOLIN AND GUITAR, OP. 2
☐ Terebesi, Prunnbauer
  AS6 41936 (3/77) Selecta/Telefunken*
6 SONATAS FOR VIOLIN AND GUITAR, OP. 3
☐ Terebesi, Prunnbauer
  AS6 41995 (2/77) Selecta/Telefunken*
TRIO FOR VIOLIN, CELLO AND GUITAR, OP. 68
☐ Williams, Loveday, Fleming
  72678 (8/68) CBS
  MS-7163 Columbia
VIOLIN CONCERTOS NOS. 1-6
☐ Accardo/LPO/Dutoit
  2740 121 (11/75) DG*
VIOLIN CONCERTO NO. 1 IN E FLAT, OP. 6
  (usually transcribed in D)
☐ Perlman/RPO/Foster/*Sarasate: Carmen Fantasy*
  ASD2782 (5/73) EMI/HMV
  S-36836 Angel
☐ Szeryng/LSO/Gibson/*Concerto 4*
  9500 069 (10/76) Phonogram*
☐ Accardo/LPO/Dutoit/*Le streghe*
  2530 714 (11/76) DG*
☐ Ashkenasi/VSO/Esser/*Conc. 2*
  2535 207 (12/76) DG Privilege
  139424 DG
☐ Belkin/Israel PO/Mehta
  SXL6798 (2/77) Decca
  7019 London
VIOLIN CONCERTO NO. 2 IN B MINOR, OP. 7 (LA CAMPANELLA)
☐ Ashkenasi/VSO/Esser/*Conc. 1*
  2535 207 (12/76) DG Privilege
  139424 DG
☐ Accardo/LPO/Dutoit/*Primavera; Cenerentola Vars.*
  2530 900 (10/77) DG
VIOLIN CONCERTO NO. 3 IN E
☐ Accardo/LPO/Dutoit/*Viola Son.*
  2530 629 (5/76) DG*
VIOLIN CONCERTO NO. 4 IN D MINOR
☐ Ricci/RPO/Bellugi/*Le streghe; Bottesini*
  RHS304 (4/71) Unicorn
  M-30574 Columbia
☐ Szeryng/LSO/Gibson/*Concerto 1*
  9500 069 (10/76) Phonogram*

Right: *Paganini's playing enthralled musicians and the general public alike*
Left: *Paganini's contemporary Ingres saw him in a more romantic light in 1819.*

GIOVANNI PIERLUIGI DA PALESTRINA
(b. Palestrina, nr. Rome, 1525; d. Rome 1594)

Palestrina's huge body of vocal music—including over 100 Masses, over 250 motets, eight Magnificats, 60 sacred and 100 secular madrigals—has for long been held up to music students as the model of classical polyphony at its most polished and disciplined. Holding a balance between contrapuntal and harmonic thinking, it avoided the very elaborate contrapuntal type of setting which obscured the liturgical texts (to which the Council of Trent took exception); but the legend that his *Papae Marcelli* Mass influenced the Council's decree is without foundation, and some of his Masses in fact did not accord with that decree, including words extraneous to the sanctioned text and taking secular songs (such as the famous *L'homme armé*) for their basis. Palestrina was not an innovator, nor did he have the versatility of his contem-porary Lassus »; he was less interested in the expressive setting of words than in smooth, consonant vocal lines; but for sheer nobility and purity of sound he had few equals.

His career was distinctly unsettled. After singing as a boy chorister in Santa Maria Maggiore in Rome, to which his local bishop had been transferred, he became organist and choirmaster of Palestrina Cathedral at the age of 19. Seven years later Pope Julius III, another ex-bishop of Palestrina, appointed him choirmaster to the Cappella Giulia; he became a member of the Pontifical Choir, only to be dismissed along with other married singers by a later Pope. Undeterred, he succeeded Lassus at St John Lateran (where he composed his *Lamentations*), but resigned after a few years and returned to Santa Maria Maggiore as choirmaster. It was while there that

IOANNES PETRUS ALOISIUS PRÆNESTINUS

Palestrina

MUSICÆ PRINCEPS

PALESTRINA

VENI SPONSA CHRISTI

CHOIR OF ST. JOHN'S COLLEGE, CAMBRIDGE
GEORGE GUEST

PALESTRINA
Missa Aeterna Christi munera
Oratio Jeremiae Prophetae
Motetti

PRO CANTIONE ANTIQUA LONDON

he published his first book of motets. In 1567 he entered the service of Cardinal Ippolito d'Este, but four years later went back to the Cappella Giulia as musical director.

A wave of epidemics in the 1570s carried off two of his sons and two brothers, and although he himself recovered from a serious illness his wife died. At this he decided to become a priest, but surprisingly, after taking minor orders, suddenly married a wealthy widow and showed himself a good business man in the management of her affairs. (His interest in money is also clear from the prohibitive salary he demanded from two would-be employers, the Emperor Maximilian and the Duke of Mantua). He was held in the very highest esteem by his contemporaries, and during the last twelve years of his life produced many of his finest works, including the *Assumpta est Maria* Mass and the *Song of Songs*.

AVE REGINA
☐ Carmelite Priory/McCarthy/
  Palestrina/Victoria
  SOL283 (1/66) L'Oiseau-Lyre
ECCE EGO JOANNES—MASS
☐ Thomas, Allister, Fleet, Keyte, London
  Carmelite Priory/McCarthy/*Sine
  nomine*
  SOL269 (7/64) L'Oiseau-Lyre
EXULTATE DEO—MOTET
☐ St. John's College Choir/G. Guest/
  *Magnificat VI toni; Veni sponsa
  Christe—Mass; Motets*
  ZRG578 (9/68) Decca Argo
LITANIAE DE BEATA VIRGINE MARIA
☐ King's College Choir/Willcocks/*Stabat
  Mater; Hodie beata virgo; Magnificat
  a 8*
  ZK4 (12/76) Decca Argo
MISSA—ASSUMPTA EST MARIA
☐ St. John's College Choir/G. Guest/
  Missa brevis/Antiphon—Assumpta est
  ZRG690 (1/72) Decca Argo★

Left: *Both these portraits of
Palestrina describe him
as 'Musicae princeps'.*

MISSA PAPAE MARCELLI
☐ King's College Choir/Willcocks/*Missa
  brevis*
  HQS1237 (6/71)EMI/HMV
  S-60187 Seraphim
ORATORIO JEREMIAE PROPHETAE
☐ Pro Cantione Antiqua, Turner/*Sicut
  cervus; O bone Jesu; Super flumine;
  Missa aeterna Christi*
  2533 322 (12/76) DG Archiv
  Produktion
SINE NOMINE—MASS
☐ Thomas, Allister, Fleet, Keyte,
  Carmelite Priory/*Ecce ego
  Joannes*
  SOL269 (7/64) L'Oiseau-Lyre
SONG OF SONGS—MOTETS
☐ Cantores in Ecclesia
  SOL338-9 (10/74) L'Oiseau-Lyre
**SUPER FLUMINE BABYLONIS—
MOTET**
☐ Pro Cantione Antiqua, Turner/*Sicut
  cervus; O bone Jesu; Oratio Jeremiae;
  Missa aeterna Christi*
  2533 322 (12/76) DG Archiv
  Produktion★

PALESTRINA

argo

ASSUMPTA EST MARIA

MISSA BREVIS

CHOIR OF ST. JOHN'S COLLEGE, CAMBRIDGE
director
GEORGE GUEST

GIOVANNI BATTISTA PERGOLESI
(*b. Jesi, nr. Ancona, 1710; d. Pozzuoli 1736*)

The mere ten years between his entering the Naples Conservatory and dying from tuberculosis did not allow Pergolesi time to achieve very much, but it is open to doubt whether his slender talent would have developed more fully or shown greater originality had he lived longer.

On leaving the Conservatory, where he had shown himself a gifted violinist, he became *maestro di cappella* to the Prince of Stigliano, equerry to the Viceroy of Naples; and for him he composed most of his instrumental music—though the melodious Concertinos with which he is credited are of arguable authenticity. Four serious operas aroused little enthusiasm (*L'Olimpiade* in fact was pelted off the stage in Rome, much to the composer's chagrin), but he had greater success with an *opera buffa* in Neapolitan dialect, *Lo frate 'nnammorato*, and with the comic intermezzi in his serious operas. Of these by far the most celebrated is the lively *La Serva padrona*, though its fame derives less from its initial performances than from those after the composer's death and, particularly, from the work being made a rallying-point for the heated squabbles which took place in Paris in 1752 between supporters of Italian and French styles of opera. As a result, a *Serva padrona* fever swept Europe, and it had a profound effect on French *opéra-comique*. Pergolesi's last work, his *Stabat Mater*, has also enjoyed a certain popularity despite very conspicuous weaknesses. His extraordinary posthumous success led to many works by others being attributed to him; and despite strenuous efforts by scholars, doubts still exist about the authenticity of much of his music.

Right: *Opera buffa may be said
to owe its existence to
Pergolesi, though many works
bearing his name prove
not to be by him at all.*

CONCERTI ARMONICI NOS. 5 AND 6
(*Dubious*)
☐ Stuttgart CO/Munchinger/*Flute
  concerti*
  SDD319 (3/72) Decca Ace of
  Diamonds
  6395 London
**CONCERTI FOR FLUTE AND STRINGS
NOS. 1 AND 2**
(*Dubious*)
☐ Rampal, Stuttgart CO/Munchinger/
  Concerti armonici
  SDD319 (3/72) Decca Ace of
  Diamonds
  6395 London
MAGNIFICAT
☐ Vaughan, Baker, Partridge, Keyte,
  King's College Choir, ASMF/
  Willcocks/*Vivaldi: Gloria*
  ZRG505 (1/67) Decca Argo★

STABAT MATER
☐ Raskin, Lehane, Naples Rossini Orch./
  Caracciolo
  SDD385 (7/74) Decca Ace of
  Diamonds

argo
VIVALDI
GLORIA
Pergolesi
Magnificat

Elizabeth Vaughan
Janet Baker
Ian Partridge
Christopher Keyte

The Academy of
St. Martin-in-the-Fields
Leader Neville Marriner

directed by
DAVID WILLCOCKS

The Choir of King's College Cambridge

FRANCIS POULENC
(b. Paris 1899; d. there 1963)

Of the young French composers who, at the end of the First World War, turned their backs on the traditional "good taste" and refinement of French art and, in accord with the spirit of the time, revelled in impudent wit and flippancy, Poulenc was undoubtedly the most *gamin*. Some of his popularity was due to his ebullient piano-playing, which matched the unquenchable zest of his personality. Though he had studied the piano, he had had little formal training in composition when he became the youngest member of the group of "Les Six"; and despite his rhythmic vivacity and melodic charm, a basic technical weakness is apparent throughout his output in his short-breathed phrases and inability to develop material. He combined Satie's » jokiness with an almost classical lucidity (a reaction against impressionism) and a delicate vein of sentimentality, plus a tinge of Stravinskian harmony.

His ballet *Les Biches* of 1923 was one of his first big successes, but he wrote with facility a number of short piano pieces, several concertos for keyboard instruments (including one originally intended for choreography, *Aubade*), chamber music, and particularly songs—an area in which he excelled (often himself playing the piano parts for his friend, the baritone Pierre Barnac) and in which he revealed highly sophisticated literary tastes. Some of his best song collections are the early *Le Bestiaire* and, twenty years later, *Tel jour, telle nuit*, the *Fiançailles pour rire* and *Banalités*.

An increased seriousness of purpose became evident from the mid-thirties with the writing of the Organ Concerto and a number of religious works, including the *Litanies à la Vierge noire*, the Mass, the Easter motets and the *Stabat Mater;* and after the 1939-45 war, during which he produced the unaccompanied choral cantata *La Figure humaine*, Poulenc felt ready to tackle opera. *Les Mamelles de Tirésias*, a surrealist comedy to a libretto by Apollinaire (one of his favourite poets for song-settings), was in his familiar frivolous vein; but in 1957 he astonished everyone with his most considerable work, the deeply-felt and expressive drama *Les Dialogues des Carmélites* (a story of religious persecution during the French Revolution), and two years later came the tense monodrama *La Voix humaine*.

Above: *Francis Poulenc, photographed during the early '30s.*

Left: *Poulenc (right) with Lennox Berkeley.*

LES BICHES
☐ CBSO/Fremaux/*Honegger, Ibert, Satie*
　ASD2989 (5/74) EMI/HMV
CHAMBER WORKS
　(Violin Sonata; Cello Sonata; Flute Sonata; Clarinet Sonata; Oboe Sonata; Elegie for horn and piano; Sonata for 2 clarinets; Sonata for clarinet and bassoon; Sonata for horn, trumpet and trombone.)
☐ Menuhin, Fournier, Debost, Portal, Civil, Wilbraham/Fevrier
　EMSP553 (3/76)
CONCERTO IN D MINOR FOR 2 PIANOS AND ORCHESTRA
☐ Poulenc, Fevrier, Paris Cons./Pretre/ *Conc. champetre*
　ASD517 (4/63) EMI/HMV
GLORIA
☐ Burrowes, CBSO and Ch./Fremaux/ *Piano Conc.*
　ASD3299 (12/76) EMI/HMV
　S-37246 Angel
**4 MOTETS POUR LE TEMPS DE NOEL
4 MOTETS POUR UN TEMPS DE PENITENCE**
☐ Christ Church Choir, Oxford/Preston *Stravinsky: Mass*
　ZRG720 (1/74) Decca Argo∗
ORGAN CONCERTO
☐ Duruflé, ORTF/Pretre/*Gloria*
　ASD2835 (2/73) EMI/HMV
　S-35953 Angel
PIANO CONCERTO IN C SHARP MINOR
☐ Ortiz, CBSO/Fremaux/*Gloria*
　ASD3299 (12/76) EMI/HMV
3 PIECES; MELANCOLIE; SUITE FRANCAISE
☐ Andre Previn/*Roussel: 3 pieces; Sonatine*
　61782 (7/77) CBS Classics
SONGS
　(5 Poemes de Max Jacob; 3 Chansons de F. Garcia-Lorca; La courte paille; Metamorphoses; 3 Poemes de Louise de Vilmorin; Fiancailles pour rire)
☐ F. Palmer/Constable
　ZRG804 (8/75) Decca Argo
TRIO FOR OBOE, BASSOON AND PIANO
☐ Melos Ensemble/*Son. for clar. and bsn./ Ravel/Francaix*
　ASD2506 (4/70) EMI/HMV
　S-36586 Angel

SERGEI PROKOFIEV
(b. Sontsovka, Ekaterinoslav Govt, 1891; d. Moscow 1953)

Many *enfants terribles* seem to end their days as respectable members of the Establishment, their erstwhile iconoclasm overtaken by the march of time. If Prokofiev at least escaped that fate—for crass Soviet officialdom was hostile to his musical style—his later works do lack the angular acerbity of those which first made his name and reveal a hitherto unaccustomed lyricism and warmth.

He was musically very precocious, writing a three-act opera in short score at the age of nine and a fully-scored one at 12; but a disparaging remark about the "elementary harmony" of a symphony produced at the same tender age stung him into vowing that such a reproach would never need to be made again. While at the St Petersburg Conservatory, where Rimsky-Korsakov » was among his teachers, he became an outstanding pianist, and won a prize with his first piano concerto, which upset even some of his supporters by its percussive astringency. A strong vein of dry, grotesque humour (exemplified, even by the

title, in his piano suite *Sarcasms*) informed his music, whose tendency to stridency is most evident in the *Scythian suite* of 1914, which owed much to the example of Stravinsky's » *Sacre du printemps*. His most appealing works of this period are the exhilarating Third Piano Concerto and the delicately parodistic First ("Classical") Symphony, both of which reveal a penchant for wry side-slips of tonality. In 1918, after the Revolution, he went via Japan to the USA, where his first great operatic success, the fantastic comedy *Love of three oranges*, was given in 1921. From the following year he made his home in Paris, where Diaghilev mounted his ballets *Chout* (*The Buffoon*, actually composed in 1915), *Le Pas d'acier* and *L'Enfant prodigue*, and his orchestral works were championed by the conductor-publisher Koussevitzky. A horrific opera *The Fiery angel*, composed in the mid-twenties, was not produced in Prokofiev's lifetime, but material from it was used again (a common practice with him) in his Third Symphony.

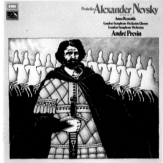

ALEXANDER NEVSKY, OP. 78
☐ Reynolds, LSO Chorus, LSO/Previn
ASD2800 (7/72) EMI/HMV
S-36843 Angel
CHOUT—BALLET SUITE, OP. 21b
☐ LSO/Abbado/*Romeo*
SXL6286 (5/67) Decca
CINDERELLA—BALLET SUITES NOS. 1 & 2
☐ Cov. Gdn. Orch./Rignold
ECS597 (7/71) Decca Eclipse
STS-15193 London
CLASSICAL SYMPHONY, OP. 25
☐ LSO/Sargent/*Peter and the Wolf*
SPA90 (9/70) Decca
STS-15114 London
☐ ASMF/Marriner/*Bizet*
ZRG719 (12/73) Decca Argo★
☐ LSO/Weller/*Sym. 7*
SXL6702 (5/75) Decca
6897 London
☐ Chicago SO/Giulini/*Mussorgsky*
2530 783 (4/77) DG★
LIEUTENANT KIJE, OP. 60
☐ Cleveland/Szell/*Kodaly: Hary Janos*
61193 (2/71) CBS Classics
MS-7408 Columbia
☐ LSO/Previn/*Shostakovich: Sym. 6*
ASD3029 (12/74) EMI/HMV
S-37026 Angel
☐ Netherlands Radio PO/Dorati/*Kodaly*
PFS4355 (5/76) Decca Phase 4
21146 London
THE LOVE OF THREE ORANGES
☐ *Suite*. LSO/Dorati/*Scythian Suite; Bartok*
6582 011 (2/76) Phonogram
75030 Mercury
PETER AND THE WOLF, OP. 67
☐ Flanders (narrator)/Philharmonia/ Kurtz/*Saint-Saens: Carnaval*
ASD299 (12/59) EMI/HMV
S-60172 Angel
☐ Baker (narrator)/New Philh./Leppard/ *Britten*
CFP185 (1/72) Classics for Pleasure

Left: *Sergei Prokofiev, just after his return to the Soviet Union in 1934.*

He continued to tour as a pianist and conductor, but after his permanent return to the USSR in 1934 this ceased, and whereas in the score for the film *Lieutenant Kije* of that year he could indulge in his old satiric manner, a radical change of style was soon apparent in the ballet *Romeo and Juliet* and the Second Violin Concerto. The extremely popular children's tale *Peter and the wolf* had the didactic overtones dear to the Soviet mind, and nationalist fervour was powerfully expressed in the epic film *Alexander Nevsky*, the music for which was re-cast as a cantata. Some concession to current tastes during the war period, though without his sacrificing artistic integrity, can be observed in the ballet *Cinderella*, the Second String Quartet (based on Caucasian folk tunes), the Fifth Symphony and the unusually gentle Flute Sonata (most often heard in the version as the Second Violin Sonata). Perhaps the peaks of his later achievements were the opera *War and peace* and the Sixth Symphony; after that he was constrained by pressures and by ill-health into writing several chauvinistic works of little value.

Above: *Prokofiev's challenging gaze, caught in this portrait by Shukhayev, epitomised his whole personality.*

☐ Farrow (narrator)/LSO/Previn/ *Britten*
  ASD2935 (12/73) EMI/HMV
  S-36962 Angel
☐ Richardson (narrator)/LSO/Sargent/ *Sym. 1*
  SPA90 (9/70) Decca
  STS-15114 London
PIANO CONCERTOS NOS. 1-5
☐ Beroff, Leipzig Gewandhaus/Masur/ *Ov. on Hebrew Themes*
  SLS882 (10/74) HMV

PIANO CONCERTOS: NO. 1 IN D FLAT: NO. 2 IN G MINOR
☐ Ashkenazy/LSO/Previn/*Ov. on Hebrew Themes*
  SXL6767 (6/76) Decca
  7062 London
PIANO CONCERTO NO. 3 IN C, OP.26
☐ Katchen, LSO/Kertesz/*Ravel, Gershwin*
  SXL6411 (5/70) Decca
☐ Argerich, BPO/Abbado/*Ravel*
  139349 (2/68) DG*

☐ Janis, Moscow PO/Kondrashin/ *Rachmaninov*
  6580 (12/73) Phonogram
  75019 Mercury
☐ Ashkenazy/LSO/Previn/*Sym. 1; Autumnal*
  SXL6768 (11/76) Decca
PIANO CONCERTO NO. 5
☐ Richter/Warsaw Nat. PSO/Rowicki/ *Ravel*
  2548 104 (11/75) DG Heliodor
☐ Ashkenazy/LSO/Previn/*Conc. 4*
  SXL6769 (5/77) Decca
PIANO SONATAS NOS. 7 AND 8
☐ Ashkenazy
  SXL6346 (10/68) Decca
  6573 London
ROMEO AND JULIET—BALLET
☐ *Cpte.* Cleveland Orch/Maazel
  SXL6620-2 Decca
  2312 London

☐ *Cpte.* LSO/Previn
  SLS864 (12/73) HMV
  S-3802 Angel
☐ *Exc.* Cleveland/Maazel
  SXL 6668 (1/75) Decca
  6865 London
SCYTHIAN SUITE
☐ LSO/Dorati/*Love of Three Oranges —Suite; Bartok*
  6582 011 (2/76) Phonogram
  75030 Mercury
☐ Moscow PO/Kondrashin/*Seven, they are seven; Shostakovich: Sym. 2*
  ASD3060 (5/75) EMI/HMV
SEVEN, THEY ARE SEVEN— CANTATA, OP. 30
☐ Elbikov, Moscow RO and Ch./ Rozhdestvensky/*Scythian Suite; Shostakovich: Sym. 2*
  ASD3060 (5/75) EMI/HMV
STRING QUARTET NO. 2
☐ Prague Quartet/*Tchaikovsky: Quartet 1*
  111 0698 (1/71) Rediffusion/ Supraphon
SYMPHONY NO. 5 IN B FLAT, OP. 100
☐ Berlin PO/Karajan
  139040 (6/69) DG*
☐ Boston SO/Koussevitsky (recorded in 1945)
  VL12021 (7/77) RCA
SYMPHONY NO. 6 IN E FLAT MINOR, OP. 111
☐ LPO/Weller
  SXL6777 (9/76) Decca
SYMPHONY NO. 7 IN C MINOR, OP. 131
☐ LSO/Weller/*Sym. 1*
  SXL6702 (5/75) Decca
  6897 London
VIOLIN CONCERTO NO. 1 IN D MAJOR, OP. 19
☐ Chung/LSO/Previn/*Conc. 2*
  SXL6773 (3/77) Decca
  6997 London
☐ Milstein/Philh./Giulini/*Conc. 2*
  SXLP 30235 (3/77) EMI/HMV
  Concert Classics
  S-36009 Angel
VIOLIN CONCERTO NO. 2 IN G MINOR, OP. 63
☐ Heifetz, Boston SO/Munch/*Sibelius*
  LSB4048 4/72) RCA
  LSC-4010 RCA
☐ Szeryng/LSO/Rozhdestvensky/ *Sibelius*
  SAL3571 (9/66) Phonogram
☐ D. Oistrakh, Philh./Galliera/ *Miakovsky*
  SXLP 30155 (9/73) EMI/HMV
  Concert Classics
  S-60223 Seraphim
☐ Chung/LSO/Previn/*Conc. 1*
  SXL6773 (3/77) Decca
  6997 London
☐ Milstein/New Philh./ Fruhbeck/*Conc. 2*
  SXLP30235 (3/77) EMI/HMV
  Concert Classics
  S-36009 Angel
WAR AND PEACE
☐ *Cpte.* Kibkalo, Vishnevskaya, Klepatskaya, Vlassov, Verbitskaya, Kossittayna, Arkhipova, Bolshoi Theatre/Melik-Pashaev
  SLS837 (2/73) HMV
  M4-33111 Columbia/Melodiya

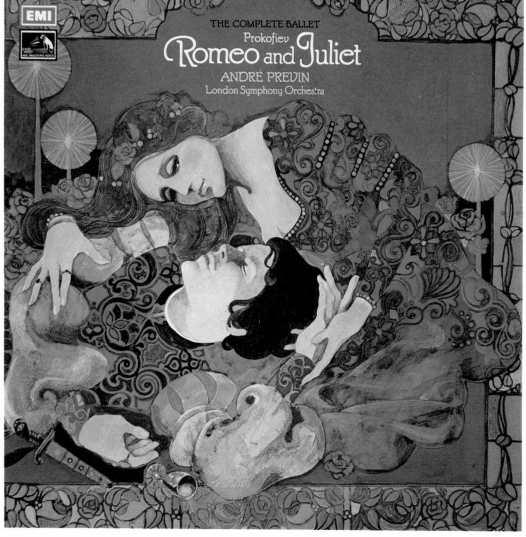

GIACOMO PUCCINI
(b. Lucca 1858; d. Brussels 1924)

Puccini's apparently unassailable position in the operatic world as a sure box-office winner principally rests on two qualities—a gift for writing melodic lines grateful to singers and audiences, and a superb sense of theatre. If those melodies were never very subtle or expanded into longer paragraphs as Verdi's » were, and if they were often rammed home very obviously on unison strings, at least that made them easier to remember; and if his dramatic field was limited in depth and his taste often conspicuously questionable, he knew exactly how to screw up maximum emotional tension and extract the utmost from every sentimental or melodramatic situation.

The fifth generation of a family of composers, he studied in Milan and was encouraged by his teacher Ponchielli to enter for an operatic competition in which he was completely unsuccessful, but thanks to lobbying by friends (including the writer and musician Boito) his piece, *Le Villi*, was produced in 1884 with modest success. (The oft-repeated story that the said competition was won by Mascagni's » *Cavalleria rusticana* is nonsense, as a glance at the respective dates shows.) He attracted the support of the influential publisher Ricordi, but his *Edgar* was a failure, partly because of its poor libretto; and Ricordi's faith was first justified only in 1893, with the production of *Manon Lescaut*, which began a fashion with Puccini for heroines who suffer for love (usually frail little creatures).

It also marked the start of his habit of taking established stage successes, or subjects already appealing to other composers, as the basis for his operas. He had embarked on *Manon Lescaut* with the knowledge of Massenet's » exquisite setting behind him; now be began *La Bohème* only after learning that Leoncavallo » was already at work on the subject. His opera was produced in 1896, a year before Leoncavallo's, which it overwhelmed by its enormous popular success—despite initial disapprobation by the critics. It was Verdi's expressed admiration for Sardou's play *Tosca* that fired Puccini to set it, but he ignored the political background which gave the story significance, and saw it only as a sensational melodrama. His next two operas, in which he introduced more local colour, were based on sentimental and superficial stage hits by David Belasco: *Madama Butterfly* was originally a disaster, though the pathetic figure of the deserted Japanese child-bride soon won sympathy, and *The Girl of the Golden West* (more subtle in its harmony) has never caught on with the general public.

There was an extension of style in the three one-acters produced in New York in 1918. *Il Tabarro*, a grim little story, shows that Puccini had absorbed ideas from Debussy »; but the gem of the *trittico* is the sparkling *Gianni Schicchi*, his only comedy, vivid in characterisation and brilliant in craftsmanship. His last opera, *Turandot*, which he did not live to complete, reveals a notable advance in harmony and orchestration, with much gorgeous exotic colour to heighten its atmosphere of sadism.

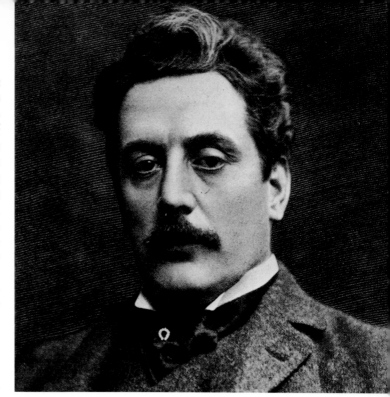

Above: *Puccini's operas are a mainstay of the repertory.*

LA BOHEME
☐ *Cpte.* Freni, Harwood, Pavarotti, Panerai, Maffeo, Ghiaurov, German Opera Chorus, Berlin PO/Karajan
SET565-6 (8/73) Decca
1299 London
☐ *Cpte.* de los Angeles, Amara, Bjorling, Nahr, Merrill, Reardon, Tozzi, Corena, Columbus Boy Choir, RCA Victor Chorus and Orch./Beecham
SLS896 (11/74) HMV

S-6099 Seraphim
☐ *Cpte.* Tebaldi, Bergonzi, Bastianini, Cesari, Siepi, Corena/Accademia di Santa Cecilia Ch. and Orch./Serafin
D5D2 (8/76) Decca
1208 London
(The) GIRL OF THE GOLDEN WEST
☐ *Cpte.* Tebaldi, MacNeil, Del Monaco, Tozzi, De Palma, Santa Cecilia/Capuana
GOS594-6 (7/70) Decca Ace of Diamonds
1306 London
GIANNI SCHICCHI
☐ Gobbi, Domingo, Cotrubas/LSO/Maazel
76563 (5/77) CBS
M-34534 Columbia
MADAMA BUTTERFLY
☐ *Cpte.* Scotto, Stasio, Bergonzi, Panerai, Rome Opera Chorus and Orch., Barbirolli
SLS927 (9/67) HMV
S-3702 Angel
☐ *Cpte.* Freni, Ludwig, Pavarotti, Kerns, Vienna State Opera Chorus, VPO/Karajan
SET584-6 Decca
13110 London
MANON LESCAUT
☐ *Cpte.* Caballe, Domingo, Tear, Ambrosian Opera Chorus, New Philh./Bartoletti
SLS962 (9/72) HMV
S-3782 Angel
MESSA DI GLORIA
☐ Lovaas, Hollweg, McDaniel, West German Radio Ch./Frankfurt RO/Inbal
9500 009 (2/77) Phonogram*
TOSCA
☐ *Cpte.* Callas, di Stefano, Gobbi, La Scala/da Sabata
SLS825 (3/73) HMV
☐ *Cpte.* Price, Domingo, Milnes, Alldis Ch./New Philh./Mehta
ARL2 0105 (3/74) RCA*
☐ *Cpte.* Caballe, Carreras, Wixell/Cov. Gdn. Orch. & Ch./C. Davis
6700 108 (5/77) Phonogram*
TURANDOT
☐ *Cpte.* Sutherland, Caballe, Pavarotti, Ghiaurov, Alldis Choir, LPO/Mehta
SET561-3 (9/73) Decca
13108 London
☐ *Cpte.* Nilsson, Mercuriali, Corelli, Scotto/Rome Opera/Molinari-Pradelli
SLS921 (5/66) HMV
S-3671 Angel

HENRY PURCELL
(b. London c. 1659; d. there 1695)

A reference to Purcell by James II's Attorney-General, Roger North, succinctly sums up his stature: "the Orpheus Britannicus . . . a greater musical genius England never had". He indeed excelled in every branch of music to which he turned his hand, and it is only regrettable that so much of his invention should have gone into forms for which it is difficult to find a place in today's world—the copious incidental music for unrevivable plays, the masque-like quasi-operas without dramatic continuity that lead a fringe existence to a play (such as *The Fairy Queen*, which sets not a word of Shakespeare though written for a Restoration production of *A Midsummer night's dream*), the verse anthems with string orchestra favoured by Charles II, not least the Welcome Songs (often to texts of sheer doggerel) written for some formal occasion or other. Concert performances, which present these out of context, are rare, and the gramophone is now the chief medium for keeping this splendid music alive.

Purcell's father and uncle were both Gentlemen of the Chapel Royal, where he himself, as a boy chorister, imbibed the Lully-derived French style which had just been brought in at the Restoration. He then studied with John Blow, who seems to have stepped down in 1679 to allow his brilliant pupil to take over as organist in Westminster Abbey. At the age of 21 Purcell wrote his first Welcome Song and his first theatre music, two fields in which he was to be in increasing demand; and from shortly afterwards dates the series of full anthems, verse anthems and other church music. In 1682 he was appointed organist of the Chapel Royal, and the following year composed the first of his odes on St Cecilia's Day and brought out his first publication, twelve trio-sonatas which (unlike the slightly earlier string Fantasias, which were in the old polyphonic style) "faithfully endeavoured a just imitation of the most famous Italian masters". *Dido and Aeneas*, his only "real" opera (i.e. with uninterrupted music) and a masterpiece of concentrated drama, was written in 1689 for a fashionable girls' school: it is the earliest English opera to be still regularly staged. Subsequent theatre pieces—*Dioclesian*, *King Arthur*, *The Fairy Queen*, *The Indian Queen*—though substantial and containing much fine music, are unfortunately not self-contained.

Purcell showed exceptional skill in the flexible setting of the English language, and some of his solo song-scenas (like *Mad Bess* and *The Blessed Virgin's expostulation*) are remarkable examples of dramatised declamation. He was particularly adept, in songs and other works also, at using a ground bass, ingeniously spinning phrases of uneven length over the rigid pattern (as in the *Evening hymn* and Dido's final lament, *When I am laid in earth*).

Above & right: *Henry Purcell, perhaps the greatest of all English composers.*

Below: *The opening of the so-called 'Golden Sonata' in F, in Purcell's autograph.*

ANTHEMS
Rejoice in the Lord alway; Blow up the trumpet in Sion; O God, .Thou art my God; O God, Thou hast cast us out; My heart is inditing; Remember not, Lord, our offences
☐ Bowman, Rogers, Van Egmond, King's College Choir, Leonhardt Ens./Willcocks/*Chacony*
AS6 41123 (9/70) Selecta/Telefunken

ANTHEMS
They that go down to the sea in ships; Jehova, quam multi sunt hostes mei; My beloved spake; O sing unto the Lord a new song; Lord, how long wilt Thou be angry; Who hath believed our report
☐ Parker, Brett, Tear, Brown, Keyte, St John's College Ch., ASMF/Guest
ZRG5444 (12/64) Decca Argo

CHACONY IN G MINOR *(ed. Britten)*
☐ ECO/Britten/*Frank Bridge; Britten; Delius; Elgar*
SXL6405 (7/69) Decca
☐ Leonhardt Ens./Willcocks/*Anthems*
AS6 41123 (9/70) Selecta/Telefunken

COME YE SONS OF ART—ODE FOR THE BIRTHDAY OF QUEEN MARY
☐ N. Burrowes, Bowman, Brett, Lloyd, Early Music Consort/Munrow/*Love's Goddess*
ASD3166 (4/76) EMI/HMV
S-37251 Angel

DIDO AND AENEAS
☐ *Cpte.* Clark, Baker, Sinclair, Herincx, St. Anthony Singers, English Chamber Orch./Lewis
SOL60047 (11/57) L'Oiseau-Lyre*

(The) FAIRY QUEEN
☐ Sheppard, Bevan, Platt, Knibbs, Clarke, Deller, Buttrey, Jenkins, Stour Music Fest./Deller
HMD 218 (2/78) Pye/Vanguard
S-311/2 Vanguard

FUNERAL MUSIC FOR QUEEN MARY
☐ King's College Ch., Philip Jones Ens./Ledger/*Anthems*
ASD3316 (3/77) EMI/HMV
S-37282 Angel

KING ARTHUR *(abridged)*
☐ Anthony, Harper, Cameron, Whitworth, Alan, Morison, St. Anthony Singers, Philomusica/Dart
SOL60008-9 (10/59) L'Oiseau-Lyre

ODE ON ST CECILIA'S DAY
☐ Woolf, Esswood, Tatnell, Young, Rippon, Shirley-Quirk, Tiffin School Choir, Ambrosian Singers, ECO/Mackerras
2533 042 (3/71) DG Archiv Produktion*

ORCHESTRAL AND INSTRUMENTAL WORKS
Overture in D minor; Pavan in B; Ground in D minor; Overture and Suite (Crown the Altar); Pavan in A minor; Fantasia in 3 parts in D; Overture in G minor; Suite in D; Pavan in G; Sefauchi's farewell; A new ground; Sonata in A minor
☐ Leonhardt Consort
AW6 41222 (1/68) Selecta/Telefunken

THEATRE MUSIC
Abdelazer; Distressed Innocence; The Married Beau; The Gordian Knot Untied
☐ J. Roberts, The Academy of Ancient Music/Hogwood
DSLO504 (6/76) L'Oiseau-Lyre

SERGEI RACHMANINOV
(b. Oneg, Novgorod Govt, 1873; d. Beverly Hills, 1943)

That Rachmaninov should have felt a conflict between his various gifts as a composer, a conductor and a pianist (one of the greatest of our time) is understandable: harder to explain is the striking contrast between his taciturn, aloofly aristocratic personality and the heart-on-sleeve emotionalism and yearning melancholy of his music, which has made as widespread an appeal to mass audiences as that of his idolised Tchaikovsky ».

He was in fact an aristocrat by birth, who left his native country at the Revolution, never to return. Though he had begun his musical studies in St Petersburg, at 12 he was sent to the Moscow Conservatoire, whose traditions were very different, and where he met and was profoundly influenced by Tchaikovsky. As his graduate exercise he wrote, in a fortnight, a one-act opera, *Aleko*, as a result of which the publisher Gutheil accepted several of his works. The wildfire popularity of his Prelude in C sharp minor (the incessant demands for which became a well-nigh intolerable cross for him as a recitalist) immediately brought him international notice; but for a while he remained in Moscow and directed a private opera company. Despite a highly successful appearance in London in 1898 playing and conducting his own music, he was much cast down by the disastrous reception at home of his First Symphony, and fell into a depression from which he was finally roused only by hypnosis; in gratitude he dedicated his ensuing Second Piano Concerto (now enormously popular) to the doctor.

He made a deep impression as conductor of the Imperial Grand Theatre (where Chaliapin was one of his singers), but two operas of his own failed through their poor librettos; in order to gain more time to compose he retreated to Dresden, where he wrote his Second Symphony and the tone-poem *The Isle of the dead*. In 1909 Rachmaninov made his first concert tour in the USA, for which he composed his Third Piano Concerto: while there he declined an invitation, repeated later, to become conductor of the Boston Symphony Orchestra. After setting Poe's *The Bells* (which he rated one of his best compositions) he became conductor of the Moscow Philharmonic concerts, but the death of his erstwhile fellow-student Scriabin » turned his thoughts once more to the piano. His last major work before leaving Russia was his Vesper Mass. In the last third of his life, when he alternated between the USA and his villa on Lake Lucerne, he unwillingly devoted much of his time to his career as a pianist; but the final decade saw the production of some of his best works—the *Rhapsody on a theme by Paganini* for piano and orchestra (which, like a number of his compositions, quotes the *Dies Irae*), the Third Symphony and the *Symphonic dances*.

Though Rachmaninov's long surging melodic lines and warmly romantic orchestration constitute his greatest attractions to the ordinary listener, some of his most rewarding and personal art is to be found in his songs, many of which are of a quality which makes one deplore their comparative neglect.

Left: *Rachmaninov, one of the great pianists and a composer of abiding popularity.*
Left (inset): *He reluctantly continued his pianistic career throughout his life.*

(The) ISLE OF THE DEAD
☐ LSO/Previn/*Sym. Dances*
  ASD3259 (9/76) EMI/HMV
  S-37158 Angel
PIANO CONCERTOS NOS. 1-4;
RHAPSODY ON A THEME OF
PAGANINI
☐ Ashkenazy/LSO/Previn
  SXL6565-7 (9/72) EMI/HMV
  Concert Classics
  2311 London
PIANO CONCERTO NO. 1 IN F# MINOR
☐ Janis/Moscow PO/Kondrashin/
  Prokofiev
  6582 008 (12/73) Phonogram
  75019 Mercury
☐ Ashkenazy/LSO/Previn/*Conc. 2*
  SXL6554 (9/72) Decca
  6774 London
PIANO CONCERTO NO. 2 IN C MINOR
☐ Ashkenazy/Moscow PO/Kondrashin/
  Etudes tableaux
  SXL6099 (4/64) Decca
  6390 London
☐ Katchen/LSO/Solti/*Balakirev*
  SDD181 (10/68) Decca Ace of Diamonds
  STS-15086 London
☐ Richter/Warsaw PO/Wislocki/
  Preludes
  138 076 (1/64) DG*
☐ Ashkenazy/LSO/Previn/*Conc. 1*
  SXL6554 (9/72) Decca
  6774 London
☐ Anievas/New Philh./Atzmon/
  Paganini Rhapsody
  ASD2361 (4/68) EMI/HMV
  S-60091 Seraphim
☐ Varsi/Rotterdam PO/Gardelli/
  Tchaikovsky
  6580 141 (11/76) Phonogram
PIANO CONCERTO NO. 3 IN D MINOR
☐ Ashkenazy/LSO/Fistoulari
  SXL6057 (6/63) Decca
  6359 London
☐ Ashkenazy/Philadelphia/Ormandy
  ARL1 1324 (5/76) RCA*
☐ Gavrilov/USSR SO/Lazarev
  ESD7032 (4/77) EMI/HMV
☐ Berman/LSO/Abbado
  76597 (6/77) CBS
  XM-34540 Columbia
PIANO CONCERTO NO.4 IN G MINOR
☐ Michelangeli/Philh./*Gracis/Ravel*
  SXLP30196 (9/74) EMI/HMV
  Concert Classics
  S-35567 Angel
PIANO SONATA NO. 2 OP. 36
☐ Horowitz
  72940 (11/71) CBS
24 PRELUDES
☐ *Cpte.* Ashkenazy
  5BB221-2 (2/76)
  Rediffusion/Supraphon
☐ Nos. 3, 5, 6, 8, 12, 13 *only*/Richter/
  Conc. 2
  138076 (1/60) DG*
RHAPSODY ON A THEME OF
PAGANINI
☐ Ashkenazy/LSO/Previn/*Conc. 4*
  SXL6556 (9/72) Decca
  6776 London
☐ Anievas/New Philh./Atzmon/*Conc. 2*
  ASD2361 (4/68) EMI/HMV
  S-60091 Seraphim
☐ Katchen/LPO/Boult/*Dohnanyi*
  SDD428 (10/74) Decca Ace of
  Diamonds
☐ Ortiz/New Philh./Koizuini/*Dohnanyi*
  ASD3197 (6/76) EMI/HMV
  S-37178 Angel

(The) BELLS—CHORAL SYMPHONY,
OP. 35
☐ Armstrong, Tear, Shirley-Quirk, LSO
  and Ch./Previn
  ASD3284 (12/76) EMI/HMV
  S-37169 Angel

SUITE NO. 1 FOR TWO PIANOS, OP. 5
☐ Ashkenazy/Previn/*Suite 2*
  SXL6697 (6/76) Decca
  6893 London
SUITE NO. 2 FOR TWO PIANOS, OP. 17
☐ Ashkenazy/Previn/*Suite 1*
  SXL6697 (6/75) Decca
  6893 London
SONGS
  (Oh, never sing to me again; The harvest
  of sorrow; How fair this spot; In my
  garden at night; To her; Daisies; the
  pied piper; Dreams; A-oo-; The Quest;
  The Muse; The storm; The poet; The
  morn of life; What wealth of rapture;
  Dissonance; Vocalise)
☐ Soderstrom/Ashkenazy
  SXL6718 (7/75) Decca
SONGS
  (In the silent night; So many hours,
  so many fancies; The soldier's wife; A
  dream; I wait for thee; The little
  island; Midsummer nights; The world
  would see thee smile; Believe it not;
  Spring waters; Fate; Day to night
  comparing we the Wind her way;
  Arion; The Raising of Lazarus; So
  dread a fate I'll ne'er believe; Music)
☐ Soderstrom/Ashkenazy
  SXL6772 (12/76) Decca
SONGS
  (By the grave; Twilight; The answer;
  The Lilacs; Loneliness; On the death
  of a linnet; Melody; Before the image;
  No prophet; Sorrow in springtime;
  To the children; Before my window;
  The fountains; Night is mournful;
  The ring; Powder'd paint)
☐ Soderstrom/Ashkenazy
  SXL6832 (12/77) Decca
SYMPHONIC DANCES
☐ Philadelphia/Ormandy/*Hindemith*
  61347 (3/73) CBS Classics
SYMPHONIES NOS. 1-3; THE ROCK,
OP. 7
☐ Suisse Romande/LPO/Weller
  D9D3 (9/76) Decca
SYMPHONY NO. 1
☐ SRO/Weller
  SXL6583 (4/73) Decca
  6803 London
SYMPHONY NO. 2 IN E MINOR
(uncut versions)
☐ LSO/Previn
  ASD2889 (4/73) EMI/HMV
  S-36954 Angel
☐ Halle/Loughran
  CFP40065 (9/74) Classics for Pleasure
☐ LPO/Weller
  SXL6623 (11/73) Decca
SYMPHONY NO. 3 IN A MINOR
☐ LSO/Previn/*The Rock*
  LSB4090 (5/73) RCA
  AGL1-1527 RCA
☐ LPO/Weller
  SXL6720 (10/75) Decca
☐ LSO/Previn/*Aleko (exc)*
  ASD3369 (8/77) EMI/HMV
  S-37260 Angel
VARIATIONS ON A THEME OF
CORELLI
ETUDES TABLEAUX
☐ Ashkenazy
  SXL6604 (5/73) Decca
  6822 London
VESPER MASS, OP. 371
☐ USSR Academy Choir/Sveshnikov
  ASD2973 (6/74) EMI/HMV
  S-4124 Melodiya/Angel

JEAN-PHILIPPE RAMEAU
(b. Dijon, 1683; d. Paris, 1764)

Rameau's career was a curious one: until the age of 40 he was, to the outside world, no more than a talented provincial organist of intellectual pretensions; from 50 he was the most famous French opera composer of his time, held in the highest esteem at the court of Louis XV (who ennobled him) and enthusiastically acclaimed by the general public—though constantly a source of controversy in the musical profession.

He followed in his father's footsteps as a church organist, first in Avignon, then successively in Clermont-Ferrand, Paris (where he published his first volume of harpsichord pieces), Dijon, Lyons and then Clermont again (the post he had left ten years previously in search of wider responsibilities). For seven years he lived there quietly, devoting himself to writing a treatise on harmony: this he managed to get published when he returned to Paris in 1722, but it was bitterly attacked by other theoreticians, against whom he defended himself vigorously. The appearance of a second book of harpsichord pieces brought him some recognition, and he built up a reputation as a performer and teacher. The theatre, however, had captured his interest, but he got nowhere until the financier La Poupelinière became his patron, around 1730, and introduced him to various librettists, including Voltaire.

Rameau's first opera in 1733, *Hippolyte et Aricie*, based on Racine's "Phèdre" but given a happy ending, adopted Italian fashions, grafting them on to the Lully tradition, and marked a break with the fashionable light-hearted *opéras-ballets* of Campra. It was to be followed in the next thirty years by another 17 full-scale, and a dozen shorter, stage works, in which Rameau's solidly based style, expressive harmony and modulations and human characterisation brought opera to a new level of development (paving the way, as we can see with hindsight, for Gluck »). His orchestration, in particular, marked a great step forward from Lully's practice, and several of his works contained set-pieces (such as the earthquake in the enormously successful *Les Indes galantes* of 1735) which were the astonishment of the time, although, inevitably, conservative musicians considered his writing "noisy and violent". The great wealth of sparkling dances in his operas holds much attraction for listeners today. Among his chief works produced at the Opéra were *Castor et Pollux*, *Les Fêtes d'Hébé*, *Dardanus* and *Zoroastre*: ironically, since Rameau was initially accused of being too Italian, his comedy *Platée* (first performed at Versailles) was thrust into prominence as the French counterblast to the Italian comic style exemplified by Pergolesi's » *Serva padrona*.

MAURICE RAVEL
(b. Ciboure, nr. St-Jean-de-Luz, 1875; d. Paris 1937)

The traditional French ideals of formal precision, fastidious taste, consummate craftsmanship and lucidity have never been better exemplified than in the music of Ravel, the son of a Swiss father and Basque mother. From the one he may have inherited the love of minutiae which found expression in the jewelled subtlety of his orchestral scoring and, for example, in the complex ticking and tinkling sounds of the watchmaker's shop in which his brilliantly witty and risqué opera *L'Heure espagnole* is set; to the other is certainly due the delight in Spanish colours and rhythms which pervades many of his works.

A pupil, at the Paris Conservatoire, of Fauré », to whom he dedicated his early string quartet, he was much influenced by Chabrier », Liszt », whose virtuoso piano writing he was to surpass in such imaginative works as *Gaspard de la nuit* (although he himself was not remarkable as a pianist), and Rimsky-Korsakov »; and initially he was regarded with considerable suspicion as a musical revolutionary. His first piano pieces and songs, and particularly the overture to an unwritten opera, in fact aroused such hostility that not only were three attempts at the Prix de Rome unsuccessful, but in 1905 he was not even admitted to the preliminary round—despite the recognition he had already won with the *Pavane pour une Infante défunte*, the piano *Jeux d'eau* and the String Quartet. This provoked a huge scandal in the musical world, and affected Ravel to the extent of his refusing the Légion d'Honneur when he was offered it in 1920.

The period up to the first World War saw the production of a large number of the works, very characteristic in their colourful harmony, by which Ravel is best known—the exquisitely fashioned *Introduction and Allegro* for an instrumental septet in which the harp

ALBORADA DEL GRACIOSO
☐ NPO/Burgos/Falla/Granados/Ravel/ Pavane
SXL6287 (11/67) Decca
☐ Orch. de Paris/Karajan/*La Valse*; *Rapsodie Espagnole Tombeau*
ASD2766 (3/72) EMI/HMV
S-36839 Angel

STRASBOURG PHILHARMONIC ORCHESTRA
DIRECTOR
ALAIN LOMBARD
RAVEL
THE TWO
PIANO CONCERTOS
ANNE QUEFFÉLEC

Left: *For all the voluptuous brilliance of his orchestration, Ravel's original conceptions were almost always in terms of the piano.*

has a prominent part; the *Rapsodie espagnole*, one of the very few orchestral works of his which did not first appear in a piano version; the one-act opera *L'Heure espagnole* and his masterpiece, the voluptuously beautiful *Daphnis et Chloë* written for the Diaghilev Ballet; the impressionistic *Miroirs* (which influenced Debussy ») and dazzling *Gaspard de la nuit* for piano and the charming *Ma mère l'oye* suite for piano duet; and the song-cycles *Shéhérazade* and the drily ironic *Histoires naturelles*.

Left: *Rameau was no more than a provincial organist and theoretician until he turned to the operatic stage.*

CASTOR ET POLLUX
- ☐ Vandersteene, Souzay, Scovotti, Schele, Stockholm Chbr. Ch./VCM/ Harnoncourt
  HF6 35048 (12/72) Selecta/Telefunken★

(Les) FETES D'HEBE—BALLET
- ☐ Connors, Ambrosian Singers, ECO/ Leppard
  ASD3084 (6/76) EMI/HMV

HARPSICHORD WORKS
Vol. 1: 1-10; Vol. 2: 11-34 (*11 included in error—not intended for performance*); Vol. 3: 35-50; 51-56
Nos. 1-10 and 51-56
- ☐ Trevor Pinnock
  CRD1020 (6/76) CRD
Nos. 12-22, 35-41
- ☐ Trevor Pinnock
  CRD1010 (2/75) CRD
Nos. 23-24, 42-50
- ☐ Trevor Pinnock
  CRD1030 (5/77) CRD

HIPPOLYTE ET ARICIE
- ☐ Tear, Hickey, Baker, Woodland, Shirley-Quirk, Stalman, St Anthony Singers, ECO/Lewis
  SOL286-8 (4/66) L'Oiseau-Lyre

5 PIECES DE CLAVECIN EN CONCERT
- ☐ Brüggen, S. Kuijken, W. Kuijken, Leonhardt
  AS6 41133 (1/72) Selecta/Telefunken★

(La) TEMPLE DE LA GLOIRE
Suite No. 1
- ☐ ECO/Leppard/*Gretry: Suite*
  SOL297 (2/67) L'Oiseau-Lyre
Suite No. 2
- ☐ ECO/Leppard/*Campra: L'Europe galante*
  SOL302 (2/68) L'Oiseau-Lyre

ZOROASTRE
7 Dances
- ☐ Melkus Ensemble/*C.P.E. Bach; Starzer*
  2533 303 (8/76) DG Archiv Produktion

- ☐ Philh./Giulini/*Daphnis; Rapsodie; Pavane*
  SXLP30198 (4/76) EMI/HMV Concert Classics

BOLERO
- ☐ SRO/Ansermet/*Dukas/Honegger*
  SXL6065 (2/64) Decca
  6367 London
- ☐ LSO/Monteux/*Ma Mere/La valse*
  6580 106 (6/75) Phonogram
  6570 092 Philips Festivo
- ☐ Concertgebouw/Haitink/*La Valse; Le tombeau; Pavane*
  9500 314 (11/77) Phonogram★

CONCERTO FOR THE LEFT HAND
- ☐ W. Haas/Monte Carlo Op./Galliera/ Pno. Conc. in G
  SAL3766 (1/70) Phonogram
- ☐ Katchen/LSO/Kertesz/*Prokofiev; Gershwin*
  SXL6411 (5/70) Decca
- ☐ François/Paris Conservatoire/ Cluytens/*Pno. Conc. in G*
  CFP40071 (8/74) Classics for Pleasure
- ☐ Katchen/LSO/Kertesz/*Pno. Conc. in G*
  SDD486 (1/76) Decca Ace of Diamonds
- ☐ Queffelec/Strasbourg PO/Lombard/ *G major Concerto*
  STU70928 (9/76) RCA/Erato

CONCERTO IN G FOR PIANO AND ORCHESTRA
- ☐ Michelangeli, Philh./Gracis/ *Rachmaninov*
  SXLP30169 (9/74) EMI/HMV Concert Classics
  S-35567 Angel

- ☐ Bernstein/Columbia SO/ *Shostakovich Conc. 2*
  72170 (7/64) CBS
  MS-6043 Columbia
- ☐ Katchen/LSO/Kertesz/*Bartok: Pno. Conc. 3*
  SXL6209 (9/66) Decca
- ☐ Argerich, Berlin PO/Abbado/*Prokofiev*
  139 349 (2/68) DG★
- ☐ M. Haas, Monte Carlo Op./ Galliera/*Pno. Conc. for the left hand*
  SAL3766 (1/70) Phonogram
- ☐ M. Haas/Paris Nat./Paray/*Prokofiev*
  2548 104 (11/75) DG Heliodor
- ☐ Katchen/LSO/Kertesz/*Pno. Conc. For the left hand*
  SDD486 (1/76) Decca Ace of Diamonds

DAPHNIS ET CHLOE—BALLET
- ☐ Cpte. Cov. Gdn. Ch./LSO/Monteux
  SDD170 (3/68) Decca Ace of Diamonds
  STS-15090 London
- ☐ Cpte. Chorus/Boston SO/Ozawa
  2530 563 (4/76) DG★
- ☐ Suite No. 2 only: Berlin PO/Karajan/ *Debussy: La Mer: L'apres-midi*
  138923 (3/65) DG★
- ☐ Suite No. 2, Philh./Giulini/*Rapsodie; Pavane; Alborada*
  SXLP30198 (4/76) EMI/HMV Concert Classics

GASPARD DE LA NUIT
- ☐ Ashkenazy/*Chopin, Debussy*
  SXL6215 (1/66) Decca
- ☐ Abbey Simon/*Valses nobles*
  TV34397S (4/73) Decca Turnabout★

(L')HEURE ESPAGNOLE

- ☐ Danco, Derenne, Suisse/Ansermet
  ECS786 (11/76) Decca Eclipse

INTRODUCTION AND ALLEGRO
- ☐ Melos Ensemble/*Roussel; Debussy; Guy-Ropartz*
  SOL60048 (9/62) L'Oiseau-Lyre★

MA MERE L'OYE
- ☐ LSO/Monteux/*Bolero; La valse*
  6580 106 (/75) Phonogram
- ☐ NYPO/Boulez/*La valse; Menuet antique*
  76306 (5/75) CBS
- ☐ Scottish National/Gibson/*Bizet: Jeux d'enfants; Saint-Saens; Carnival*
  CFP40086 (6/75) Classics for Pleasure

MIROIRS: JEUX D'EAU
- ☐ Pascal Roge/*Ma mere l'oye*
  SXL6715 (11/75) Decca

PAVANE POUR UNE INFANTE DEFUNTE
- ☐ Boston SO/Abbado/*Daphnis & Chloe—Suite 2; Debussy Nocturnes*
  2530 038 (6/71) DG★
- ☐ LSO/Monteux/*Rapsodie Espagnole; Debussy: Prelude a l'Apres-midi; Nocturnes (exc.)*
  SDD425 (9/74) Decca Ace of Diamonds
  STS-15356 London
- ☐ New Philh./Giulini/*Daphnis; Rapsodie; Alborada*
  SXLP30198 (4/76) EMI/HMV Concert Classics

LA VALSE CHOREOGRAPHIC POEM
- ☐ SRO/Ansermet/*Bolero; Dukas; Honegger*
  SXL6065 (2/64) Decca
  6367 London

- ☐ Orch. de Paris/Karajan/*Rapsodie Espagnole; Alborada; Tombeau*
  ASD2766 (3/72) EMI/HMV
  S-36839 Angel
- ☐ Paris Conservatoire/Cluytens/ *Bolero; Pavane; Alborada*
  CFP40036 (6/73) Classics for Pleasure
- ☐ LSO/Monteux/*Bolero; Ma Mere*
  6580 106 (6/75) Phonogram
  6570 092 Philips Festivo
- ☐ NYPO/Boulez/*Menuet antique; Ma Mere*
  76306 (5/75) CBS
  M-32838 Columbia

VALSES NOBLES ET SENTIMENTALES
- ☐ NYPO/Boulez/*Une barque sur l'ocean; Le Tombeau de Couperin*
  73212 (5/74) CBS
  M-32159 Columbia
- ☐ Paris Conservatoire/Cluytens/ *Tombeau de Couperin; Menuet antique; Une barque*
  CFP40095 (11/75) Classics for Pleasure
- ☐ Concertgebouw/Haitink/*Rapsodie; Menuet*
  9500 347 (10/77) Phonogram★

VIOLIN SONATA
- ☐ Wallez/Rigutto/*Debussy/Faure*
  7174 (8/76)

VOCAL WORKS
Trois poemes de Stephane Mallarme; Chansons madecasses; Histoires naturelles; Cinq melodies populaires grecques
- ☐ F. Palmer, Constable, Nash Ens./ Rattle
  ZRG834 (3/76) Decca Argo

The war, in which Ravel served as an ambulance driver, seems to have turned his thoughts towards still greater simplification and classical clarity, which are to be observed in the Piano Trio and the *Tombeau de Couperin* (a significant title); but shortly after the war the first signs of mental ill-health began to appear, and he wrote but little, amusing himself with mechanical toys.

His music of the period, apart from the whimsical short opera *L'Enfant et les sortilèges*, was unusually severe, and he found pleasure in even more meticulous orchestral detail, writing the superbly scored though musically empty *Bolero* and orchestrating Mussorgsky's » *Pictures from an exhibition*. Two piano concertos (one for left hand only) composed in 1931 show an incisive and piquant style, including jazzy elements, but not without a certain reserved sensuousness; but a car accident the following year put a premature end to his creativity.

OTTORINO RESPIGHI
(b. Bologna 1879; d. Rome 1936)

Although he enjoyed a considerable reputation in his lifetime as one of Italy's leading composers, Respighi's great technical facility far outstripped his creative capacity, so that much of his later work reveals a conspicuous falling-off in quality of invention (the one-act *Maria Egiziaca*, the seventh of his nine operas, is an exception) and also includes a large number of transcriptions of music by other composers: he was an extremely cultured musician and edited many early works.

After studying in his native Bologna, he went to St Petersburg as first viola in the opera orchestra, and while there took lessons in composition and orchestration from Rimsky-Korsakov ≫, who was one of his greatest formative influences: a year later he travelled to Berlin for further study with Bruch ≫. He then played the violin and viola in a chamber ensemble for five years, became pianist in a singing academy, and following the success of two operas in his home town, in 1913 was appointed a professor of composition at the Santa Cecilia Conservatory in Rome, and began a career as conductor of his own music.

Apart from his popular ballet after Rossini ≫, *La Boutique fantasque*, and the attractive and delicate suites of *Ancient airs and dances* and *The Birds* (again transcriptions of old masters), almost his only works now heard are his picturesque and sumptuously-scored symphonic suites *The Fountains of Rome* and *The Pines of Rome* (which made history of a kind by being the first orchestral work to include a gramophone record—of a nightingale): in the later *Roman festivals* the tendency to grandiosity unfortunately erupted into empty noisiness.

ANCIENT AIRS AND DANCES—
SUITES 1-31
☐ Philh. Hungarica/Dorati
  6582 010 (4/76) Phonogram
  75009 Mercury
☐ Los Angeles Chbr. Orch./Marriner
  ASD3188 (6/76) EMI/HMV
  S-37301 Angel
(The) BIRDS
☐ ASMF/Marriner/*Trittico*
  ASD3327 (3/77) EMI/HMV
(La) BOUTIQUE FANTASQUE
(Rossini arr. Respighi)
☐ RPO/Dorati/*Suite Rossiniana*
  PFS4407 (12/77) Decca
THE PINES OF ROME: THE FOUNTAINS OF ROME
☐ LSO/Kertesz/*The Birds*
  SXL6401 (7/69) Decca
☐ New Philh./Munch
  SDD494 (8/76) Decca Ace of Diamonds
  21024 London
☐ Philadelphia/Ormandy/*Feste Romane*
  30077 (9/76) CBS Harmony
  MS-6587 Columbia
☐ Berlin PO/Maazel/*Mussorgsky; Rimsky*
  2548 267 (7/77) DG Heliodor
  138033 DG

Left: *Ottorino Respighi*

NIKOLAI RIMSKY-KORSAKOV
(b. Tikhvin, Govt. of Novgorod, 1844; d. Lyubensk, Govt. of St Petersburg, 1908)

A cynic seeking an illustration for the text "Altruism does not pay" need look no further than Rimsky-Korsakov: having devoted much of his time and energy to orchestrating, putting in order and completing works by his less systematic, less thorough, less professional friends, he has met with obloquy from later generations for having modified their character. Yet without him Dargomizhky's *Stone guest*, Borodin's ≫ *Prince Igor* and Mussorgsky's ≫ *Boris Godunov* and *The Khovansky plot* would never have seen the light at all.

His professionalism however had been hard won. As a member of a naval family he had become a cadet; at the age of 17, already "dazzled" by the music of Glinka ≫, he had met Balakirev ≫, who had fostered his musical tastes and, seeing his feeling for orchestral colour, encouraged him to write a symphony, despite his lack of grounding even in elementary harmony. He managed to write some

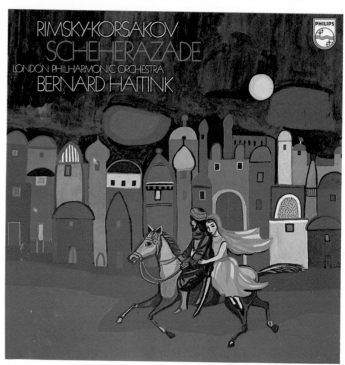

of this during a long overseas naval tour, and with Balakirev's help it was finished and performed in 1865 — the first Russian symphony of any consequence. In the Balakirev circle he continued to compose, though most of the works then created were extensively revised later (as was his common practice), and their success led to his being appointed professor of composition at the St Petersburg Conservatory in 1871. Very conscious of his own ignorance, he so steeped himself in the study of harmony and counterpoint to keep ahead of his pupils that the "kuchka" composers began to regard him as a reactionary academic. He quitted the navy in 1873, and the next year started to acquire a thorough practical knowledge of instruments as Inspector of Naval Bands, and succeeded Balakirev as director of the Free School of Music, where he gathered a new circle of composers around him, including Liadov, Arensky and Glazunov ».

His deep involvement in academic studies, which is manifest in some rather dry chamber works, was tempered by an interest in folk music which resulted in his compiling and publishing an important collection of folksongs, and by his work as editor of Glinka's operas. He had already written his own first opera, *The Maid of Pskov*, but now turned to gentler national subjects on folk myths — *May night* and *The Snow-maiden*. His absorption in vivid instrumental writing (which was to culminate in a textbook on the art of orchestration) resulted in three brilliant concert pieces — the *Spanish caprice* (in which, he declared, "colour is the essence, not the dressing"), *Scheherazade* and the *Russian Easter Festival*, all written within two years — before he decided (perhaps as the outcome of hearing Wagner's » *Ring*) to concentrate on opera composition, in which indeed he found his true métier.

The succession of stage works which followed fall roughly into two categories, the epic and the fantastic, both often with a flavour of the supernatural. To the former belong *Sadko* and *The invisible city of Kitezh*, to the latter the sparkling *Tale of Tsar Saltan* and his very last opera, the remarkable *Golden cockerel*, whose biting satire on rulers' ineptitude (Rimsky-Korsakov had already been in trouble with the authorities for his sympathies with the 1905 revolutionaries) caused it to be banned, and it was not produced until after his death. Though his operas are rarely given on the stage in this country, some have been recorded, and isolated excerpts such as the *Flight of the bumble-bee* (from *Tsar Saltan*), the *Song of the Indian guest* (from *Sadko*) and the *Hymn to the sun* (from *Golden cockerel*) have become extremely well known.

CAPRICCIO ESPAGNOL
□ LPO/Pritchard/*Chabrier: Espana;
   Ravel: Rapsodie espagnole*
   CFP169 (8/71) Classics for Pleasure
□ Orch. de Paris/Rozhdestvensky/*Russ.
   Easter Fest. Ov.; Borodin; Mussorgsky*
   ESD7006 (9/76) EMI/HMV
   S-36889 Angel
□ LSO/Argenta/*Granados: Chabrier;
   Moszkowski*
   ECS797 (6/77) Decca Eclipse
   6006 London
□ BPO/Maazel/*Mussorgsky,
   Respighi*
   2548 267 (7/77)
□ BPO/Maazel/*Respighi: Pines,
   Mussorgsky: Night*
   2548 267 (7/77) DG Heliodor
   138033 DG
**FLIGHT OF THE BUMBLEBEE:
DUBINUSHKA: SADKO—MUSICAL
PICTURE: CHRISTMAS EVE—SUITE:
RUSSIAN EASTER FESTIVAL OV.;
MAY NIGHT—OV.**
□ SRO/Ansermet
   SDD281 (5/71) Decca Ace of
   Diamonds
(The) GOLDEN COCKEREL—SUITE
□ Bournemouth SO/Berglund/
   Prokofiev: Summer Night
   ASD3141 (12/75) EMI/HMV
MAY NIGHT
□ *Cpte.* Krivchenja, Lisoksky, Matjusthina,
   Sapegina, Troitsky, Yelnikov, Budrin,
   Moscow RO and Ch./Fedoseyev
   2709 063 (11/76) DG*

**RUSSIAN EASTER FESTIVAL
OVERTURE, OP. 36**
□ Orch. de Paris/Rozhdestvensky/
   Capriccio; Borodin; Mussorgsky
   ESD7006 (9/76) EMI/HMV
   S-36889 Angel
SCHEHERAZADE
□ Phil./Kletzki
   SXLP20026 (1/62) EMI/HMV
   Concert Classics
□ BPO/Karajan
   139022 (3/68) DG*
□ LSO/Monteux
   SPA89 (9/70) Decca
   STS-15158 London
□ LPO/Haitink
   6500 410 (1/74) Phonogram*
□ Chicago SO/Reiner
   CCV5010 (6/75) Camden Classics
   LSC-2446 RCA
□ RPO/Stokowski
   ARL1 1182 (4/77) RCA*
□ RPO/Beecham
   SXLP30253 (10/77) EMI/HMV
   Concert Classics
   S-35505 Angel
SNOW MAIDEN
□ *Cpte.* Arkhipova, Vedernikov,
   Sokolik, Arkhipov, Budrin, Moscow
   Radio SO and Ch./Fedoseyev
   SLS5102 (11/77) HMV
SYMPHONY NO. 2 (ANTAR)
□ Utah SO/Abravanel/*Ippolito-Ivanov;
   Gliere*
   VCS10060 (11/71) Pye/Vanguard

Left: *Rimsky-Korsakov, by far
the most professional of the
Russian nationalist composers,
whose works he was often left to
put in order.*

GIOACCHINO ROSSINI
(b. Pesaro 1792; d. Passy, nr. Paris, 1868)

Perhaps no other composer, not even Handel », ever enjoyed such prodigious and widespread popular acclaim and left so lively and ebullient a musical heritage as Rossini, who had the curious distinction of having been born on a leap-year February 29: certainly no other became the rage of Europe shortly after the age of 21 and, after a crowded career, retired exactly halfway through his lifespan, at 38. Many stories are told of his laziness, but someone who could write over 30 operas in 20 years can scarcely be culpable of that particular failing.

He had started life with no natural advantages beyond his musical genius and his high-spirited, fun-loving nature: his parents were a small-time singer and a theatre horn-player, and he himself had a rather irregular, though fortunately sound, education as a singer, accompanist, horn-player and cellist. Through the influence of a kindly nobleman, his one-act farce *La Cambiale di matrimonio* ("The marriage contract") was produced in Venice when he was 18, and its reception led to four more at the same theatre, including *La Scala di seta* and *Signor Bruschino*: meantime *La Pietra del paragone* ("The Touchstone")—in which for the first time Rossini employed the device of building up excitement by a long crescendo on a repeated phrase, which was to become his trademark—was so great a success in Milan that he was exempted from military service. In 1813 he scored a triumph in Venice in both comic opera (with which his name is nowadays primarily associated) and serious opera with, respectively, *L'Italiana in Algeri* and *Tancredi*, the latter causing a furore: a cavatina from it, "Di tanti palpiti", quickly became the rage of Italy.

Rossini was engaged to provide two operas annually in Naples, and the next eight years saw the composition of several of his masterpieces, including the scintillating comedy *The Barber of Seville* (1816)—which, like many now favourite operas, suffered a disastrous first night: its overture, lifted from the romantic *Elisabetta, Regina d'Inghilterra* of the year before (the first work in which he abandoned unaccompanied recitative and wrote out the singers' embellishments in full instead of leaving it to their fancy), had actually already done service in yet another previous work! Two more very successful comedies were *Cenerentola* ("Cinderella" with the magic element eliminated) and *La Gazza ladra* ("The thieving magpie"); but Rossini also developed the romantic vein with *La Donna del lago* ("The Lady of the lake") and serious opera with *Otello* (which held the stage until supplanted by Verdi's » setting 70 years later), *Moses in Egypt* and *Semiramide*, though he was taken to task for the "noisiness" of his vivid orchestration.

At this point he was to have written an opera for London, but although he enjoyed a brilliant social (and financial) season in England the theatre manager went bankrupt. Through the good offices of the French ambassador, Rossini was instead appointed musical director of the Théâtre des Italiens in Paris: there he presented a star cast in his cantata *Il Viaggio a Reims* during the coronation celebrations for Charles X, who showered him with favours. Two impressive French adaptations of former works, *Le Siège de Corinthe* and *Moïse*, made him the idol of Paris too, and these were followed up with his first opera in the French language, the riotously comic *Comte Ory*, and, in 1829, the large-scale

Above: *Rossini in his old age, the year before he died.*
Above right: *Rossini at the height of his fame.*

Guillaume Tell. This was to have been the first of five operas for the French stage, but the king's abdication and the 1830 revolution put an abrupt end to the plan.

The vexatious litigation to obtain his money seriously affected Rossini's nerves, and his health suffered further in succeeding years from domestic and political troubles in Bologna and Florence, to which he withdrew: almost his only composition of this period was a *Stabat Mater* he had begun long previously. In 1855 he decided to spend the rest of his life in Paris. There he was able to hold brilliant salons frequented by artists and intelligentsia, and to bask in his reputation as a wit and epicure. He no longer gave much attention to writing, but his invariably elegant and vivacious art found expression in the *Petite Messe solennelle* (an ironic title, in view of the work's length) and in the whimsical and humorous small pieces entitled *Péchés de ma vieillesse* (from which Respighi » drew the material for his *Boutique fantasque* ballet).

Right: *A highly ornate 18th-century oboe belonging to Rossini, made in Milan.*

BARBER OF SEVILLE
☐ *Cpte.* Callas, Alva, Gobbi, Philh./
Galliera
SLS853 (12/74) HMV
S-3559 Angel
☐ *Cpte.* Berganza, Alva, Montarsolo,
Malagu, Dara, Prey, Cesare, Roni,
Ambrosian Singers, LSO/Abbado
2720 053 (10/72) DG
2709 041 DG
(La) CENERENTOLA
☐ *Cpte.* Berganza, Montarsolo, Alva,
Capecchi, Guglielmi, Zannini, Trama,
LSO and Ch./Abbado
2709 039 (6/72) DG*
**ELISABETTA REGINA
D'INGHILTERRA**
☐ *Cpte.* Caballe, Carreras, Masterson,
Creffield, Benelli, Jenkins, Ambrosian
Singers, LSO/Masini
6703 067 (9/76) Phonogram*
(L') ITALIANA IN ALGERI
☐ *Cpte.* Berganza, Alva, Corena, Panerai,
Tavolaccini, Truccato-Pace, Montarsolo,
Maggio Musicale Fiorentino/Varviso
SET262-4 (5/64) Decca
1375 London
OVERTURES
Barber of Seville; Semiramide;
Thieving Magpie; William Tell;
Silken Ladder
☐ LSO/Gamba
SXL2266 Decca
6204 London
Barber of Seville; William Tell;
Thieving Magpie; Signor Bruschino;
Siege of Corinth; Silken Ladder
☐ New Philh./Gardelli
SDD392 (10/73) Decca Ace of
Diamonds
STS-15307 London
William Tell; Thieving Magpie;
Semiramide; Signor Bruschino;
Italian Girl in Algiers
☐ RPO/Davis
CFP40077 (6/74) Classics for Pleasure
William Tell; Silken Ladder; Signor
Bruschino; Barber of Seville; Thieving
Magpie; Cinderella
☐ Chicago SO/Reiner
CCV5020 (6/75) Camden Classics
LSC-2318 RCA
Barber of Seville; Italian Girl in
Algiers; Marriage contract; Silken
Ladder; Tancredi; Signor Bruschino;
Turk in Italy; Inganno felice
☐ ASMF/Marriner
6500 878 (10/75) Phonogram*
PETITE MESSE SOLENNELLE
☐ Lovaas, Fassbaender, Schreier,
Fischer-Dieskau, Hirsch, Sawallisch,
Munich Vocal Ens./Sawallisch
SER5693-4 RCA
ARL2-2626 RCA

SEMIRAMIDE
☐ *Cpte.* Sutherland, Horne, Rouleau,
Serge, Malas, Ambrosian Singers,
LSO/Bonynge
SET317-9 (10/66) Decca
1383 London
STABAT MATER
☐ Lorengar, Minton, Pavarotti, Sotin,
LSO and Ch./Kertesz
SXL6534 (2/72) Decca
26250 London
STRING SONATAS NOS. 1-6
☐ 1-6 I Musici/*Bottesini*
6747 038 (5/73) Phonogram
6500 245 Philips
☐ 1-6 ASMF/Marriner/Donizetti
ZK26-7 (12/77) Decca Argo
ZRG 603 Argo

Above: *Autograph of an ensemble from Rossini's* William Tell.

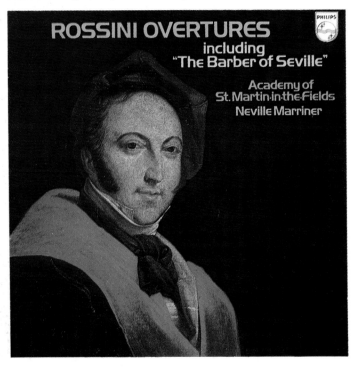

BACCHUS ET ARIANE—BALLET
☐ Brno PO/Neumann/*Sym. 3*
   SUAST50482 (9/66) Supraphon
3 PIECES; SONATINA FOR PIANO
☐ Andre Previn/*Poulenc*
   61782 (7/77) CBS Classics
SERENADE FOR FLUTE, VIOLIN,
VIOLA, CELLO AND HARP, OP. 30
☐ Melos Ensemble
   SOL60048 (9/62) L'Oiseau-Lyre
   60048 Oiseau
(The) SPIDER'S BANQUET
☐ Suisse/Ansermet/*Petite Suite;*
   Honegger: Sym. Mov. 1
   ECS756 (7/75) Decca Eclipse
STRING QUARTET IN D, OP. 45
☐ Novak Quartet/*Martinu: Quartet 6*
   SUAST50950 (10/72) Supraphon
SYMPHONY NO. 3 IN G MINOR,
OP. 42
☐ NYPO/Boulez/*Dukas: La peri*
   76519 CBS
   M-34201 Columbia

Above: *Like Rimsky-Korsakov, Roussel had been a naval officer.*

ALBERT ROUSSEL
(b. Tourcoing 1869; d. Royan 1937)

Roussel was a late starter in music, giving up his career as a naval officer (which had taken him several times to the Orient) at the age of 25 in order to study composition: he became one of Vincent d'Indy's first pupils at the newly founded Schola Cantorum in Paris, where he himself became a professor in 1902. Apart from a symphony subtitled *Poème de la forêt*, he published little of consequence until a journey to Cochin-China and India in 1909, which eventually prompted him to write two exotically-coloured works, *Evocations* for chorus and orchestra and the opera-ballet *Padmâvati*: the completion of this latter was delayed by the 1914-18 war, in which his work as a Red Cross driver at the battle of the Somme completely undermined his health.

He had previously written a ballet, *The Spider's banquet*, successfully produced in 1913, whose idiom, as in most of his early works, derived from Debussy » with a strong admixture of d'Indy's classical reserve and his own individual sense of colour; but all traces of impressionism

disappeared in his post-war compositions, which are more boldly dissonant (owing something to Stravinsky ») and have the dryness of a good champagne. The symphonic poem *Pour une fête de printemps* was a transitional work leading to the period of his fullest maturity, to which belong the delightful *Serenade* and, in the orchestral field, the *Suite in F* and the energetic and closely-reasoned Third and Fourth Symphonies (the former written for the fiftieth anniversary of the Boston Symphony Orchestra): all of these are noticeably more complex in texture than before. The ballets *Bacchus et Ariane* and *Aeneas*, containing some of his finest music, are rarely heard—though this would not have worried Roussel, who made no effort to seek popular favour and regarded music as "the most hermetic and least accessible of the arts".

He is a connoisseurs' composer, but the logic and intellectual integrity of his music appeal to the discerning; and his songs rank among the subtlest in the French repertoire.

CAMILLE SAINT-SAËNS
(b. Paris 1835; d. Algiers 1921)

An age which tends to look down on craftsmanship is unlikely to raise much admiration for Saint-Saëns, who could be termed the complete professional. A musician of wide culture and a first-rate pianist, he rated emotional involvement lower than elegance, lucidity and technical fluency, and composed prolifically "as an apple-tree produces apples", in his own words. The sheer polish, and often the wit, of his music nevertheless continues to attract those to whom refinement, brilliant effect and skill compensate for some lack of originality (preoccupation with which he deplored). He had been precociously gifted, writing music and studying the score of Mozart's » *Don Giovanni* at the age of six; by the time he entered the Paris Conservatoire at 13 he was already a public performer, and at 18 he wrote his first symphony. Four years later he was appointed organist at the church of the Madeleine, and for the next twenty years held this key post, also touring extensively as a virtuoso. Though he taught but seldom (Fauré » was one of his few pupils), he did much to encourage French composers of instrumental music, rather than opera, who received scant support from the Paris public.

A meeting in 1852 with Liszt », who was to become a close friend, had important consequences on his style: four programmatic symphonic poems—the best known being *Danse macabre*, in which the xylophone suggests the rattle of dry bones and the skeleton's fiddle has the E string de-tuned by a semitone—are on the Liszt model; and cyclic form (in which a single theme recurs throughout a work, perhaps in transformation) is often employed, as in the fourth of his five piano concertos and his most played large-scale composition, the Third Symphony (for orchestra and organ), which was dedicated to Liszt's memory. Of his concertos, the most frequently heard are the G minor (No. 2) for piano and the A minor for cello; besides three violin concertos there are some brilliant showpieces for that instrument.

He wrote 13 operas, of which only *Samson et Dalila* is generally known: ironically, though several of his lesser stage pieces were produced in Paris, this work (which contains much sensual music but is very static) was rejected by the Opéra and first presented, through Liszt's influence, in Weimar. Like many musicians who set out as progressives, Saint-Saëns became increasingly conservative in the latter part of his life. Again ironically, his best-loved composition was intended only for private performance—the witty and beautifully written *Carnival of the animals*, which is far better in its original chamber version and without well-meant spoken interpolations by comic writers.

CARNIVAL OF THE ANIMALS
☐ H. Menuhin, Simon, Clark/Philh./ Kurtz/*Prokofiev*
ASD299 (12/59) EMI/HMV
☐ Katin, Fowke, Scottish National/ Gibson/*Bizet: Jeux d'enfants; Ravel: Ma Mere*
CFP40086 (6/75) Classics for Pleasure
☐ Collard, Beroff/Inst. Ens.
ASD3348 EMI/HMV
☐ Bron, Vesuvius Ens./*Poulenc: Babar*
BRNA502 (9/77)
CELLO CONCERTO IN A MINOR, OP. 33
☐ Du Pre/New Philh./Barenboim/ *Schumann*
ASD2498 (11/69) EMI/HMV
S-36642 Angel
☐ Tortelier/CBSO/Fremaux/*Cello works*
ASD3053 (7/75) EMI/HMV
☐ Fournier/Lamoureux Orch./Martinon/ *Bruch; Lalo*
2536 157 (4/76) DG
DANSE MACABRE
☐ Scottish National/Gibson/*Dukas, Rossini*
MFP57012 (11/73) Music for Pleasure
☐ Paris Cons./Martinon/*Rouet d'Omphale/Bizet; Ibert*
ECS782 (8/76) Decca Eclipse
INTRODUCTION AND RONDO CAPRICCIOSO, OP. 28
☐ Perlman, Orch. de Paris/Martinon/ *Havanaise/Chausson; Ravel*
ASD3125 (1/76) EMI/HMV
S-37118 Angel
PIANO CONCERTO NO. 2 IN G MINOR
☐ Rubinstein/Philadelphia/Ormandy/ *Falla: Nights*
SB6841 (12/70) RCA
LSC-3165
☐ Ciccolini, Orch. de Paris/Baudo/ *Conc. 4*
CSD3750 (6/74) EMI/HMV
☐ Adni/Royal Liverpool PO/Groves/ *Mendelssohn*
ASD3208 (8/76) EMI/HMV
PIANO CONCERTO NO. 5 IN F
☐ Ciccolini, Orch. de Paris/Baudo/ *Concs. 1-4, Etude; Septet*
SLS802 (6/71) HMV
SYMPHONY NO. 3 IN C MINOR
☐ CBSO/Fremaux
ESD7038 (10/77) EMI/HMV
☐ Los Angeles PO/Mehta
SXL6482 (1/71) Decca
☐ Chicago SO/Barenboim
2530 619 (4/76) DG*

Above: *Saint-Saëns, a respected figure in French music.*

VIOLIN CONCERTO NO. 3
☐ Campoli, LSO/Gamba/*Sarasate etc.*
ECS663 (2/73) Decca Eclipse
☐ Milstein/Philh./Fistoulari/*Intro. and rondo; Chausson: Poeme*
SXLP30159 (5/74) EMI/HMV
Concert Classics
S-36005 Angel
☐ Chung/LSO/Foster/*Vieuxtemps*
SXL6759 (9/76) Decca
6992 London
☐ Stern/Orch. de Paris/Barenboim/ *Chausson; Faure*
76530 (4/77) CBS
M-34550 Columbia
VIOLIN CONCERTI 1-3: LA MUSE ET LE POÈTE; HAVANAISE; MORCEAU DE CONCERT; INTRODUCTION AND RONDO CAPRICCIOSO; CAPRICE ANDALOU; LE DELUGE— PRELUDE; ROMANCES IN C AND D FLAT/(Ysaye: Caprice)
☐ Hoelscher, Kirschbaum, New Philh./ Dervaux
SLS5103 (12/77) HMV

ERIK SATIE
(b. Honfleur 1866; d. Paris 1925)

An eccentric of fitful musical education who lived most of his life in poverty and whose music has always been of specialist appeal, Satie nevertheless was a significant influence in French music. Early studies at the Paris Conservatoire had been uncongenial and unfruitful, but his use of sequences of unresolved chords of the ninth in his *Sarabandes*, and his piano pieces of static, Greek-frieze-like quality (under such titles as *Gymnopédies* and *Gnossiennes*), strongly influenced Debussy » and Ravel »; and his interest in Gregorian chant was fanned by his involvement with the mystical Rosicrucian sect, even though he did not share its views. He wrote various trifles while working as a café pianist, but at the age of 40 decided to study at the Schola Cantorum under d'Indy and Roussel ». During and after his contrapuntal training there he produced many piano miniatures of extraordinary economy and simplicity (already reacting against Debussy's impressionism), frequently without key-signatures or bar-lines, and with jokey titles and facetious verbal commentaries.

He became a well-known "character" in Parisian artistic circles (though living in an industrial suburb and remaining very much an individualist), and was friendly with Cocteau, Picasso and Diaghilev, with all of whom he collaborated in the Cubist ballet *Parade* (1917), a work of studied anti-emotional objectivity. Its technique of juxtaposing apparently trivial melodic fragments and basic harmonies in an unexpectedly effective mosaic was further developed in another ballet with Picasso, *Mercure*; but undoubtedly Satie's most important work was the "symphonic drama" *Socrate* (1918), whose austerity and formalised simplicity influenced Stravinsky » and has a quiet beauty. His last ballet, *Relâche*, a surrealist affair with a cinema interlude directed by René Clair, had a *succès de scandale*, especially with the Bright Young Things and the group of "Les Six", who looked to him as a mentor and guide.

Right: *Erik Satie, whose most important work,* Socrate, *was written in 1918.*

Above: *A witty drawing of Erik Satie by Alfred Frueh.*

GYMNOPEDIES 1 & 3 (ORCH. DEBUSSY)
☐ LSO/Previn/*Ibert; Francaix*
LSB4094 (9/73) RCA
☐ CBSO/Fremaux/*Honegger; Ibert; Poulenc*
ASD2989 (5/74) EMI/HMV

PARADE—BALLET
☐ Luxemburg RO/De Froment/Die Reihe Ens./*Relache; La belle excentrique; Les pantines; Piege de Meduse; Petites pieces montees; Embryons desseches.*
STGBY646 (12/71) Decca Vox
31018 Candide

PIANO WORKS
Trois Gymnopedies; Sonatine bureaucratique; Prelude en tapisserie; Passacaille; Croquis et agaceries; Embryons desseches; Trois Gnossiennes; Vieux sequins; Reverie; Avant-dernieres pensees; Premier menuet; Les trois Valses; Véritables preludes flasques.
☐ F. Glazer
STGBY633 (2/70) Decca/Vox

PIANO WORKS
Trois Gymnopedies; Trois morceaux en forme de poire; Passacaille; Trois Gnossiennes; La belle excentrique; Preludes flasques; Veritables preludes flasques; Le piege de Meduse; Descriptions automatiques; Embryons desseches; Avant-dernieres pensees.
☐ A. Ciccolini
ASD2389 (9/68) EMI/HMV

SOCRATE
☐ Cuenod, Parsons
Nimbus 2104 (1/78) Nimbus

SONGS
La Diva de l'empire; Les anges; Les fleurs; Sylvie; Elegie; Hymne: Salut drapeau; Chanson; Tendrement; Chanson medievale; Air de Genevieve; Petit air; Je te veux; Gnossienne No. 2; Le Piccadilly; Pieces froides—Airs a faire fuir No. 2; Poudre d'or; Gymnopedie No. 1; Vexations.
☐ M. Dickinson, P. Dickinson
RHS338 (11/76) Unicorn

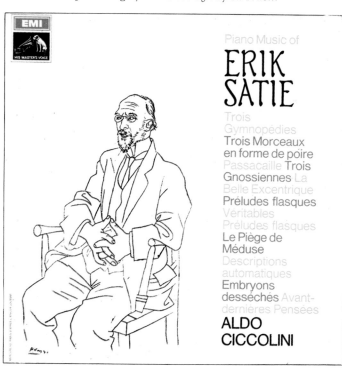

DOMENICO SCARLATTI
(b. Naples 1685; d. Madrid 1757)

By one of the ironies of time, the music of Domenico Scarlatti is now considerably more often performed than that of his father Alessandro; yet the latter was the most celebrated opera composer in Europe, while the former, after spending the first half of his life overshadowed by his illustrious father, worked in virtual isolation at the royal court of Spain for some 27 years. Contemporary accounts however make it clear that he was known from an early age as a brilliant harpsichordist, even surpassing Handel », whose admiration he reciprocated. At first he followed in his father's footsteps by writing operas in Naples and, for the exiled Queen of Poland, in Rome; then he became *maestro di cappella* in the Vatican service for five years before being appointed to a similar post in the royal chapel at Lisbon. A number of religious works (some still to be discovered) were composed during this period, including an impressive *Stabat Mater*.

Among his duties at Lisbon was to teach the harpsichord to the Infanta Maria Barbara, and when she married the heir to the Spanish throne in 1729 he followed her to Madrid: he was then nearly 44 years old, but Spain acted as an enormous stimulus to his genius, and the music by

Below: Scarlatti at about the time of his move to Madrid.

which he is mainly known to posterity springs from after this catalytic move. It consists of more than 550 keyboard sonatas of unparalleled exuberance and virtuosity—even so, possibly only a proportion of the pieces he played to regale the solitary-minded and music-mad royal couple. A mere thirty were published in his lifetime, in London; the rest exist only in copies by royal scribes, and no autographs survive. These sonatas, for which, confusingly, two numbering systems are in use, an arbitrary one by Longo (L.) and another, more chronological, by Kirkpatrick (Kk.), are nearly all single-movement pieces in binary form, though treated with the greatest freedom. They are of an incredible variety and richness of invention, ranging from ebullient movements exulting in extravagant virtuoso effects to deeply expressive and sensual pieces: a large number are characterised by a vivacious wit and by harmonic punning (described by the composer as "an ingenious jesting with art"), and are influenced to a remarkable degree by the forms, rhythms, harmonies and instrumental colour of Spanish folk music. Scarlatti was one of the greatest innovators in the development of keyboard music, but his works lose something of their incisive quality if not played on the harpsichord.

KEYBOARD SONATAS
Kirkpatrick Nos. 9, 24, 29, 33, 87, 132, 146, 169, 202, 245, 322, 380, 505, 519, 544.
☐ George Malcolm (harpsichord)
ECS542 (4/70) Decca Eclipse
KEYBOARD SONATAS
Kirkpatrick Nos. 206, 259, 260, 308, 309, 394, 395, 402, 403, 429, 430, 446, 460, 461.
☐ Blandine Verlet (harpsichord)
6581 028 (4/77) Phonogram
KEYBOARD SONATAS
Kirkpatrick Nos. 120, 165, 192, 502/ *Böhm; Handel; Rameau*
☐ Gustav Leonhardt (harpsichord)
AS6 41045 (7/67) Selecta/Telefunken
KEYBOARD SONATAS
Kirkpatrick Nos. 2-20, 24, 29, 33, 44, 46, 52, 96, 113-116, 119, 120, 140, 141, 175, 208, 209, 215, 216, 238, 239, 242, 243, 252, 253, 259-264, 358, 359, 402, 403, 420-423, 426-429, 434-436, 441, 442, 460, 461, 470, 471, 479, 481, 490, 491, 492, 513, 518, 519, 524, 525, 544, 545, 552, 553.
☐ Huguette Dreyfus (harpsichord)
EK6 35086 (4/75) Selecta/Telefunken
KEYBOARD SONATAS
Kirkpatrick Nos. 42, 153, 168, 178, 185, 192, 212, 214, 255, 278, 325, 380, 399, 407, 444, 531.
☐ Joseph Payne (harpsichord)
TV34434S (7/73) Decca Turnabout
STABAT MATER
☐ Freni, Berganza, Isoir, Kuentz Chbr./ Mackerras
2533 324 DG Archiv Produktion

ARNOLD SCHOENBERG
(b. Vienna 1874; d. Los Angeles, 1951)

Paradoxically, the man who brought about the most fundamental musical revolution for three centuries (the abandonment of the orthodox key system), and became either a father-figure or a bogeyman, according to the point of view held, whose influence almost no composer since the 1920s has escaped, was a notable pedagogue who in his teaching adopted the strictest traditional disciplines —but, to add a further twist, himself was largely self-taught. His earliest compositions, like *Verklärte Nacht*, a programmatic work for string sextet, and the cantata *Gurrelieder* (which demands gargantuan choral and orchestral forces, but also contains scoring of the utmost delicacy) were couched in a freely tonal post-romantic idiom ultimately deriving from Wagner's » *Tristan*. Working in parallel with the expressionist painters, his friends, he followed a path of unfettered subjectivity and introversion which led him from the lavishly scored symphonic poem *Pelleas und Melisande* through the *First Chamber Symphony*, which employed chords built of fourths rather than thirds, to a batch of more experimental works in 1909—the Op. 11 *Three piano pieces*, the Op. 15 songs, the *Five orchestral pieces* and the monodrama *Erwartung*, which are not "atonal" (a term Schoenberg rejected as meaningless) but "pantonal". The peak of this early period of expressionist intensity was reached in the nightmare visions of *Pierrot lunaire*, a melodrama of great technical complexity for soprano and five instrumentalists in which Schoenberg introduced a novel kind of "speech-song". Performances of all these works aroused vociferous opposition, but upheld by an earnest and pugnacious belief in himself he developed his ideas with uncompromising logic while teaching in Berlin and Vienna (where his

two most famous pupils were Berg » and Webern).

There was a gap of almost a decade, due largely to the war and to his intellectual self-searchings, before Schoenberg's next compositions; but by 1921, in his 47th year, he had evolved his world-shaking theory of "composition with twelve notes related only to each other"—in which a predetermined series of all the twelve different notes, with certain possible inversions, retrogressions and transpositions, provides all the material for a composition. This serial method (which creates such bewilderment in listeners accustomed to traditional tonal procedures) was first employed in the piano *Suite* and Op. 23 *Five pieces* and in the *Serenade* for baritone and seven instruments; but it can be seen at its most skilfully deployed in the Op. 31 *Variations* for orchestra. In 1933 the Nazis dismissed Schoenberg from his post and he moved to the USA, where he resumed his teaching; but the dissimilar musical climate of California was responsible for some softening of the asperities of his music—not just the appearance of a couple of quasi-educational works with key signatures (the *Suite for strings* and the *Theme and variations* for band), but a more basic reconciliation with the romantic tradition. Outstanding works of this final period are the violin and piano concertos, the *Ode to Napoleon* and *A survivor of Warsaw* (both calling for a reciter), and the unfinished opera *Moses und Aron* which, like several of his later works, is testimony to his religious and ethical philosophies.

Right: *Schoenberg's ideas revolutionised 20th-century music.*

Below: *The opening of Schoenberg's* Klavierstück, *Op.33A.*

CHAMBER SYMPHONY, OP. 9
☐ London Sinfonietta/Atherton/ *Verklarte Nacht*
SDD519 (5/77) Decca Ace of Diamonds
5 PIECES FOR ORCHESTRA
☐ LSO/Dorati/*Berg: 3 pieces; Webern: 5 pieces*
SAL3539 (1/66) Phonogram
GURRELIEDER
☐ Thomas, Napier, Minton, Bowen, Nimsgern, Reich, BBC SO and Ch./Boulez
78264 (4/75) CBS
M2-33303 Columbia
MOSES UND ARON
☐ *Cpte.* Cassily, Palmer, Knight, Winfield, Noble, Angas, BBC SO and Ch./Boulez
79201 (12/75) CBS
M2-33594 Columbia
PELLEAS UND MELISANDE, OP. 5
☐ BPO/Karajan
2530 485 (10/76) DG*
PIANO WORKS
3 pieces, Op. 11; 6 pieces, Op. 19; 5 pieces, Op. 23; Suite; Pieces, Op. 33
☐ Pollini
2530 531 (5/75) DG*
PIERROT LUNAIRE—SONG CYCLE, OP. 21
☐ De Gaetani, Contemporary Chbr. Ens./Weisberg
H71251 (5/73) WEA/Nonesuch*
STRING QUARTET IN D: STRING QUARTETS 1-4
☐ M. Price, La Salle Quartet/*Webern; Berg*
2720 029 (11/71) DG
☐ Valente, Juilliard Quartet
79304 (1/78) CBS
M3-34581 Columbia

SUITE FOR 7 INSTRUMENTS, OP. 29
☐ Melos Ensemble/*Berg: 4 pieces*
SOL282 (10/65) L'Oiseau-Lyre
SUITE FOR STRINGS IN G
☐ RPO/Del Mar/*Britten; Lutyens*
ZRG754 (10/74) Decca Argo
3 PIECES FOR CHAMBER ORCHESTRA
☐ London Sinfonietta/Atherton/*Pierrot Lunaire; Ein Stelldichein; Nachtwandler; Herzgewachse*
SDD520 (5/77) Decca Ace of Diamonds
VERKLARTE NACHT
☐ ASMF/Marriner/*Hindemith: Funf Stucke; Webern; Satze*
ZRG763 (1/75) Decca Argo
☐ BPO/Karajan
2530 627 (5/76) DG
☐ *Sextet version:* London Sinfonietta/ Atherton/*Chamber Symphony No. 1*
SSD519 (5/77) Decca Ace of Diamonds

FRANZ SCHUBERT
(b. Vienna 1797; d. there 1828)

Romantic legends about Schubert, fortified by a musical comedy loosely based on his life, have tended to obscure the harsher realities. For this great genius (the first native Viennese master), the undersized and short-sighted son of a suburban schoolmaster, was familiar with privation, was unable to obtain a steady post, hated teaching (to which he was driven for a time), had to be supported by devoted friends, and was prone to melancholia and ill-health; he died of typhoid at the age of 31, having produced in only 16 years nearly a thousand works, including a treasury of over 600 songs—more wonderful music, as has been sadly remarked, than the world has time to get to know. Melodic invention, in particular, poured out of him in an astonishing flow. Yet he was by no means merely an untutored "natural": at eleven he had, like Haydn », become a chorister in the Imperial Chapel, and had been well schooled musically by the *kapellmeister*, Haydn's friend Salieri (who also taught Beethoven »); and though almost any poetry of sufficient imagery, good or bad, immediately awoke a response in him, the discovery of various preliminary drafts reveals that not all his works were dashed off in a white-hot burst of inspiration.

Lyrical writing was his natural instinct: he had composed an extended scena-like song when only 14, and though two years later he had written his first symphony and three string quartets, these clearly derived from the Haydn tradition and showed none of the individuality and amazing technical and dramatic mastery of the songs *Gretchen at the spinning-wheel* (written when he was 17) or *The Erl-king* (a few months later). At the same time songs like *Heidenröslein* illustrate a vein of folk-like melody frequently to be encountered in his music; another example is *Die Forelle* (The Trout), which he took as a theme for variations in a piano quintet of sunny mood. Other instances of works incorporating previous compositions of his are the A minor String Quartet, which takes up an entr'acte from his *Rosamunde*, the deeply intense D minor String Quartet, which includes variations on the song *Death and the maiden*, and the epic piano Fantasy based on the song *Der Wanderer*. Schubert's particular contribution to the development of the *lied*, apart from the sheer quantity and quality of his output, lay in making the piano an equal partner with the voice, frequently evoking a mood in a few notes or by some small detail: the peaks of his achievement were the two cycles *Die schöne Müllerin* (The maid of the mill) and *Winterreise* (Winter journey), the latter expressing in music new depths of bleakness and despair.

It was not until his early twenties that Schubert achieved in instrumental music anything like the easy maturity of his vocal writing. His graceful and charming Fifth Symphony had been clearly indebted to Mozart »; but his Eighth was an eloquently personal and poetic creation, in turn elegiac and gently resigned (whether it was in fact unfinished, or whether the recipient lost the last two movements, which had certainly been started, has not been unequivocally established), and the "Great" C major was a work of such scope and originality that it

Below: *Autograph of Schubert's setting (1815) of Goethe's poem 'Der Fischer'.*

Right: *The most prolific and best loved song-writer of all time—Franz Schubert.*

FRANZ SCHUBERT.
SEINEM ANDENKEN

FRANZ SCHUBERT

baffled the orchestra which first essayed it. Problems of large-scale construction were not easily solved by Schubert (and, in the case of his dozen or more theatre pieces, never were), and some of his works, like the late and unusually profound piano sonatas, tend to length; but it is in his chamber music that he showed the perfect balance between lyrical invention and sureness of design. The "Death and the maiden" Quartet, the mellifluous Trio in B flat and the sublime String Quintet in C are outstanding here: an earlier serenade-like Octet is of a more relaxed nature. Some of his finest music is to be found in his works for piano duet—a medium rarely heard in the concert-hall but somewhat better served on disc.

Left: At his request Schubert was buried close to Beethoven.

CELLO SONATA IN A MINOR, D.821 (ARPEGGIONE)
☐ Rostropovich/Britten/*Bridge: Cello Sonata*
SXL6426 (10/70) Decca
6649 London
☐ Harrell/Levine/*Mendelssohn: Sonata 2*
ARL1 1568 (9/76) RCA*
DIE SCHONE MULLERIN: WINTERREISE: SCHWANENGESANG
☐ Fischer-Dieskau, Moore
SLS840 (2/76) HMV
DIE SCHONE MULLERIN (*Cpte.*)
☐ Pears/Britten
SXL2200 (6/60) Decca
☐ Fischer-Dieskau, Moore
2530 544 (8/75) DG*
FANTASY IN C, D.760 (WANDERER)
☐ Kars/*Impromptus Nos. 9 and 10*
SXL6502 (5/71) Decca
☐ Pollini/*Piano Sonata No. 16*
2530 473 (1/75) DG
☐ Brendel/*Son. 21, D.960*
6500 285 (11/72) Phonogram
GRAND DUO: FANTASIA IN F MINOR
☐ Brendel/*Crochet*
TV34144S (9/69) Decca Turnabout
IMPROMPTUS, D.899 (1-4); D.935 (5-8); D.946 (9-11)
☐ 1-8. Kempff
139 149 (1/67) DG*
☐ 1-8. Brendel
TV34141S (3/69) Decca Turnabout
☐ 1-8. Eschenbach
2530 633 (4/76) DG
☐ 5-11. Brendel
6500 928 (9/75) Phonogram
☐ 1-4. Brendel/*Sonata, D.958*
6500 415 (3/73) Phonogram*
☐ 9-11. Brendel/*Moments musicaux*
TV34142S (2/70) Decca Turnabout
☐ 9-11. Kempff/*Klavierstuck in A; Allegretto in C minor; 13 Variations*
2530 090 (9/71) DG
LIEDER DUETS
☐ Baker, Fischer-Dieskau, Moore
2530 328 (6/73) DG
MOMENTS MUSICAUX
☐ Curzon/*Beethoven*
SXL6523 (1/72) Decca
6727 London
☐ Brendel/*Piano Sonata No. 14*
6500 418 (10/73) Phonogram*

☐ Brendel/*Three Pieces, op. posth.*
TV34142S (2/70) Decca Turnabout
OCTET IN F
☐ Melos Ens.
ASD2417 EMI/HMV
S-36529 Angel
☐ Vienna Octet
SDD230 (7/70) Decca Ace of Diamonds
OVERTURE IN C (IN THE ITALIAN STYLE)
OVERTURE, FIERRABRAS
OVERTURE, ROSAMUNDE
☐ VPO/Kertesz/*Sym. 8*
SXL6090 (7/64) Decca
PIANO QUINTET IN A (THE TROUT)
☐ Curzon, Vienna Octet
SDD185 (12/68)
6090 London
☐ Haebler, Grumiaux, Janzer, Czako, Cazawan
SAL3621 (10/67) Phonogram
☐ Gilels, Zepperitz, Amadeus Quartet/*Quartettsatz*
2530 646 (8/76) DG*
☐ Rhodes, Hortnagel, Beaux Arts Trio
9500 071 (8/76) Phonogram
PIANO SONATA NO. 14 IN A MINOR, D.784
☐ Ashkenazy/*Son. 13; Hungarian Melody; 12 Waltzes*
SXL6260 (3/67) Decca
☐ Lupu/*Brahms: Intermezzi and Rhapsody*
SXL6504 (5/71) Decca
6716 London
☐ Brendel/*Moments musicaux*
6500 418 (10/73) Phonogram*
PIANO SONATA NO. 16 IN B MINOR, D.845
☐ Pollini/*Fantasy*
2530 473 (1/75) DG
☐ Brendel/*Misc. Piano Works*
6500 929 (9/75) Phonogram*
PIANO SONATA NO. 17 IN D, D.850
☐ Curzon/*Impromptus*
SXL6135 (11/64) Decca
☐ Brendel/*Deutsche Tanze 1-16*
6500 763 (7/75) Phonogram*
☐ Ashkenazy/*4 German Dances*
SXL6739 (4/77) Decca
6961 London
PIANO SONATA NO. 18 IN G, D.894
☐ Brendel/*Piano Sonata No. 15*
6500 416 Phonogram*

☐ Lupu/*2 Scherzi D.593*
SXL6741 (5/76) Decca
6966 London
PIANO SONATA NO. 19 IN C MINOR, D.958
☐ Brendel/*Four Impromptus, D.899*
6500 415 (3/73) Phonogram*
PIANO SONATA NO. 20 IN A, D.959
☐ Brendel
6500 284 (4/73) Phonogram*
☐ Serkin
61645 (12/76) CBS Classics
MS-6849 Columbia
PIANO SONATA NO. 21 IN B FLAT, D.960
☐ Brendel/*Fantasy in C*
6500 285 (11/72) Phonogram
☐ Curzon
SXL6580 (12/73) Decca
PIANO TRIO NO. 1 IN B FLAT
☐ Trio di Trieste
2538 213 (7/73) DG Privilege
☐ D. Oistrakh, Knushevitzky, Oborin
CFP40037 (5/74) Classics for Pleasure
ROSAMUNDE—BALLET
☐ Concertgebouw/Haitink
SAL3535 (12/65) Phonogram
SONATA FOR VIOLIN AND PIANO IN A MAJOR, D.574; SONATINAS FOR VIOLIN AND PIANO NOS. 1-3
☐ H. Szeryng, I. Haebler
6500 885 (3/76) Phonogram
SONG RECITALS
Geheimnis; Die Forelle; Der Konig in Thule; Gretchen am Spinnrade; Der Hirt auf dem Felsen; Auf der Riesenkopfe; Du bist die Ruh'; La Pastorella; Heidenroslein; Schwanengesang; Wehmut; Der Blinde Knabe
☐ Price/Lockhart
CFP166 (8/71) Classics for Pleasure
Gretchen am Spinnrade; Was bedeutet die Bewegung; Ach, um deine feuchten Schwingen; Schwestergruss; Schlummerlied; An die untergehende Sonne; Mignon I-III; Kennst du das Land; Berthas Lied in der Nacht; Epistle an Herrn Josef Spaun; Ellens Gesang I-III; Claudine von Villa Bella; An die Nachtigall; Des Madchens Klage; Delphine; Wiegenlied; Schlafe, schlafe; Die Manner sind mechant; Iphigenia; Das Madchen; Die junge Nonne
☐ Baker/Moore
SLS812 (9/71) HMV
Fischerweise; Lachen und Weinen; Heidenroslein; Lob der Tranen; Der Musensohn; Die Winterreise (exc.); Horch, horch die Lerch; Fruhlingsglaube; Die Forelle; Standchen; An die Laute; An Silvia; Nacht und Traume; Litanei auf das Fest Aller Seelen
☐ Hill/Walker
SAGA5404 (11/75) Saga
STRING QUARTETS NOS. 9, 12-15
☐ Amadeus Quartet
2733 008 (2/73) DG Privilege
STRING QUARTET NO. 14 IN D MINOR (DEATH AND THE MAIDEN)
☐ Hungarian Quartet
TV34472S (7/74) Decca Turnabout*
☐ Melos Quartet
2530 533 (5/75) DG
STRING QUARTET NO. 12 IN C MINOR (QUARTETTSATZ) STRING QUARTET NO.15 IN G MAJOR
☐ Gabrieli Quartet
SDD512 (5/77) Decca Ace of Diamonds

STRING QUINTET IN C
☐ Melos Quartet, Rostropovich
2530 980 (6/78) DG
☐ Aeolian Qt./Schrecker
SAGA5266 (10/66) Saga
☐ Alberni Quartet, Igloi
CRD1018 (11/75) CRD
SYMPHONIES 1-6, 8-9; ROSAMUNDE —INCIDENTAL MUSIC
☐ BPO/Bohm
2740 127 (1/76) DG
SYMPHONY NO. 1 IN D
☐ BPO/Bohm/*Sym. 2*
2530 216 (4/72) DG*
SYMPHONY NO. 2 IN B FLAT
☐ BPO/Maazel/*Sym. 3*
2538 166 (7/73) DG Privilege
☐ BPO/Bohm/*Sym. 1*
2530 216 (4/72) DG*
SYMPHONY NO. 3 IN D
☐ BPO/Bohm/*Sym. 4*
2530 526 (5/73) DG*
☐ BPO/Maazel/*Sym. 2*
2538 166 (7/73) DG Privilege
☐ RPO/Beecham/*Sym. 5*
SXLP30204 (2/76) EMI/HMV Concert Classics
SYMPHONY NO. 4 IN C MINOR ('TRAGIC')
☐ BPO/Bohm/*Sym. 3*
2530 526 (5/73) DG*
SYMPHONY NO. 5 IN B FLAT
☐ BPO/Bohm/*Sym. 8*
139162 (5/67) DG*
☐ Dresden Staatskapelle/Sawallisch/*Sym. 8*
6580 010 (12/71) Phonogram
☐ RPO/Beecham/*Sym. 3*
SXLP30204 (2/76) EMI/HMV Concert Classics
SYMPHONY NO. 6 IN C
☐ BPO/Bohm/*Rosamunde*
2530 422 (12/74) DG*
SYMPHONY NO. 8 IN B MINOR (UNFINISHED)
☐ BPO/Karajan/*Beethoven: Overtures*
139001 (4/66) DG*
☐ VPO/Kertesz/*Schubert Overtures*
SXL6090 (7/64) Decca
☐ ECO/Britten/*Mozart: Sym. 38*
SXL6539 (6/72) Decca
6741 London
☐ Boston SO/Jochum/*Mozart: Sym. 41*
2530 357 (4/74) DG*
☐ VPO/Krips/*Beethoven: Sym. 8*
SXL6549 (1/73) Decca
☐ BPO/Bohm/*Sym. 5*
139162 (5/67) DG*
☐ Dresden Staatskapelle/Sawallisch/*Sym. 5*
6580 010 (12/71) Phonogram
SYMPHONY NO. 9 (GREAT C MAJOR)
☐ LPO/Boult
ASD2856 (12/72) EMI/HMV
☐ BPO/Bohm
138877 (11/64) DG*
☐ Boston SO/Munch
CCV5054 (2/69) Camden Classics
☐ LPO/Pritchard
CFP40233 (8/76) Classics for Pleasure
☐ Concertgebouw/Haitink
9500 097 (2/77) Phonogram*
☐ LSO/Krips
SPA467 (4/77) Decca
STS-15140 London
WINTERREISE (*Cpte.*)
☐ Pears/Britten/*Schumann: Dichterliebe*
SET270-1 (7/65) Decca
1261 London
☐ Hotter, Werba
2726 030 (2/75) DG

ROBERT SCHUMANN
(b. Zwickau 1810; d. Endenich, nr. Bonn, 1856)

From his father, a bookseller who had made translations of Byron, Schumann inherited literary tastes which dominated his thoughts equally with the piano, at which he loved to improvise: in one particular sense they moulded his personality, for the romantic novelist Jean-Paul Richter, with whom he was obsessed, "was constantly portraying himself in his works, always in the form of two persons", as Schumann noted, and this influenced him to do the same as a split personality, named Florestan in extrovert moods and Eusebius in introvert. Sent as an unwilling student of law to Leipzig and Heidelberg, he instead studied the music of Bach » and Beethoven », and took piano lessons from Friedrich Wieck, the father of a child prodigy, Clara: Wieck declared that he could make him an outstanding player if he would only apply himself systematically. This ambition had to be abandoned when he permanently injured his right hand by the use of a mechanical device for strengthening the fingers. But he had begun to compose for the piano: the "Abegg" Variations (the name was derived from that of a girl he had met—all his life Schumann indulged a love of cryptograms and secret references), *Papillons* and the Op. 7 *Toccata*.

From his father Schumann had also inherited mental instability; in his teens a sister had drowned herself; and in 1833, in a fit of despair, he attempted suicide, recording in his diary his fear of insanity. Recovering, he undertook the editorship of the newly-founded *Neue Zeitschrift für Musik*, and for the following decade generously championed the cause of younger composers such as Chopin », Mendelssohn » and, later, Brahms »: he invented the "Members of League of David" pledged to combat the "Philistines" (older-generation pedants and purveyors of salon trivialities), both of which were personified in the piano pieces which occupied him in the 1830s. These were mostly small in scale, imaginative and fanciful in mood, calling into play the expressive sonorities beginning to be possible on the instrument (including the sustaining pedal) and revelling in syncopations and rhythmic complexities: *Carnaval*, *Fantasiestücke*, *Kinderscenen*, *Etudes symphoniques*, *Kreisleriana*, etc. Meantime he had fallen in love with Clara Wieck, now making a reputation as a concert pianist.

Until 1840 he had written virtually nothing except for the piano; but in that year, after a long struggle (ending in legal proceedings) with her father, who violently opposed the match because of Schumann's instability, drunkenness and lack of money, he married Clara, who was to become the most famous interpreter of his music. In his new-found domestic bliss he turned to song-writing, and in a single year poured out over 130 of his finest *lieder*, which are notable for their romantic sensibility, literary finesse and the important role allotted to the piano, which is frequently given lengthy poetic postludes. The following year Schumann concentrated on writing for the orchestra, with which he was less at ease, completing two symphonies (the latter of which, later revised and called No. 4, is remarkable for its use of thematic transformation) and beginning a piano concerto which was eventually to become his most popular large-scale work. Extended structure, never his strong point, was most successfully achieved in this and in the chamber works—the string quartets, piano quintet and piano quartet—of 1842.

Above: *Robert Schumann as a young man.*
Far left: *Robert and Clara Schumann just after the Piano Concerto's première.*

ANDANTE AND VARIATIONS IN B FLAT (1843)
☐ Ashkenazy, Frager, Tuckwell, Fleming, Weill/*Etude Op. 56, No. 4; Mozart: Son. in D, K448*
SXL6130 (11/64) Decca
6411 London
ARABESKE IN C, OP. 18
☐ Claudio Arrau/*Faschingsschwank; Humoreske*
SAL3690 (4/69) Phonogram
839709 Philips
CARNAVAL, OP. 9
☐ Kempff/*Fantasia*
2530 185 (3/72) DG
CELLO CONCERTO IN A MINOR
☐ Du Pre/New Philh./Barenboim/ *Saint-Saens: Cello Conc. 1*
ASD2498 (11/69) EMI/HMV
☐ Rostropovich/Leningrad PO/ Rozhdestvensky/*Piano Conc.*
2538 025 (12/71) DG Privilege
☐ Gendron/VSO/Dohnanyi/ *Tchaikovsky*
6580 131 (8/76) Phonogram

After this his health began to deteriorate and his music started to lose its freshness, often tending to sprawl ineffectually or to over-use rhythmic patterns. He had bad bouts of lethargy, melancholia and singing in the ears (not improved by being caught in revolutionary riots in Dresden, to which he had moved, or subsequently by strong criticism of his inadequacy as conductor of the Düsseldorf orchestra): however, he continued to compose —the *Scenes from "Faust"* and the Cello Concerto date from this period. In 1854 be began to suffer from delusions, and after attempting to drown himself in the Rhine was confined to an asylum.

169

SCHUMANN
THE FOUR SYMPHONIES
Overture, Scherzo and Finale
Manfred Overture
The Dresden State Orchestra
Wolfgang Sawallisch

DAVIDSBUNDLERTANZE, OP. 6
☐ Arrau/*Nachtstucke*
  6500 178 (7/73) Phonogram∗
☐ Parahia/*Fantasiestucke*
  73202 (10/73) CBS
  M-32299 Columbia
DICHTERLIEBE, OP. 48
☐ Pears/Britten/*Schubert: Winterreise*
  SET270-1 (7/65) Decca
  1261 London
☐ Schreier, Shetler/*Liederkreis, Op. 24*
  2530 353 (3/74) DG
☐ Ian Partridge, Jennifer Partridge/
  Liederkreis, Op. 39
  CFP40099 (2/75) Classics for Pleasure
ETUDES SYMPHONIQUES, OP.13
☐ Murray, Perahia/*Papillons*
  76635 CBS
☐ Ashkenazy/*Fantasia*
  SXL6214 (4/66) Decca
  6471 London
☐ Brendel/*Fantasia*
  VCS10020 (4/72) Pye/Vanguard
FANTASIA IN C, OP. 17
☐ Ashkenazy/*Sym. Studies*
  SXL6214 (3/66) Decca
  6471 London
☐ Brendel/*Sym. Studies*
  VCS10020 (4/72) Pye/Vanguard
☐ Kempff/*Carnaval*
  2530 185 (3/72) DG
☐ Pollini/*Piano Sonata No. 1*
  2530 379 (5/74) DG∗
FANTASIESTUCK, OP. 12
☐ Perahia/*Davidsbundlertanze*
  73202 (10/73) CBS
  32299 Columbia
FRAUENLIEBE UND LEBEN
☐ Baker, Isepp/*Brahms, Schumann
  Lieder*
  SAGA5277 (4/66) Saga
☐ M. Price, Lockhart/*Recital*
  CFP40078 (9/74) Classics for Pleasure
☐ Baker/Barenboim/*Liederkreis, Op. 39*
  ASD3217 (7/76) EMI/HMV
  S-37222 Angel
5 STUCKE IM VOLKSTON, OP. 102
☐ M. Rostropovich, B. Britten/*Cello
  Son; Debussy: Cello Son.*
  SXL2298 (1/62) Decca
  6237 London
KREISLERIANA
☐ Ashkenazy/*Humoreske*
  SXL6642 (10/74) Decca
  6859 London
☐ Arrau/*Sonata 2*
  6500 394 (6/75) Phonogram∗
LIEDERKREIS, OP. 39
☐ Reynolds, Parsons/*Mahler*
  SOL-R327 (7/72) L'Oiseau-Lyre
☐ Ian Partridge, Jennifer Partridge/
  Dichterliebe
  CFP40099 (2/75) Classics for Pleasure
☐ Baker/Barenboim/*Frauenliebe und
  Leben*
  ASD3217 (7/76) EMI/HMV
  S-37222 Angel

PAPILLONS, OP. 2
☐ Murray, Perahia/*Etudes symphoniques*
  76635 CBS
  M-34539 Columbia
PIANO CONCERTO IN A MINOR
☐ Richter/Warsaw PO/Rowicki/*Cello
  Conc.*
  2538 025 (12/71) DG Privilege
☐ Barenboim/LPO/Fischer-Dieskau/
  Introduction and Allegro
  ASD3053 (3/75) EMI/HMV
☐ Anda/Berlin PO/Kubelik/*Grieg: Conc.*
  138888 (3/64) DG∗
☐ Lupu/LSO/Previn/*Grieg*
  SXL6624 (2/74) Decca
  6840 London
☐ Bishop/BBC SO/Davis/*Grieg*
  6500 166 (3/72) Phonogram∗
☐ Solomon/Philh. Menges/*Grieg*
  CFP40255 (12/76) Classic for Pleasure
**PIANO QUARTET IN E FLAT
MAJOR, OP. 47; PIANO QUINTET IN
E FLAT MAJOR, OP.44**
☐ Rhodes, Bettelherm, Beaux Arts Trio
  9500 065 (5/76) Phonogram∗
**PIANO SONATA NO. 1 IN F SHARP
MINOR, OP. 11**
☐ Pollini/*Fantasia*
  2530 379 (5/74) DG∗
**PIANO SONATA NO. 2 IN G
MINOR, OP. 22**
☐ Arrau/*Kreisleriana*
  6500 394 (6/75) Phonogram∗
**SYMPHONIES 1-4: MANFRED
OVERTURE: OVERTURE, SCHERZO
AND FINALE**
☐ Dresden Staatskapelle/Sawallisch
  SLS867 (2/74) HMV
SYMPHONY NO. 1 IN Bb, 'SPRING'
☐ BPO/Karajan/*Sym. 4*
  2530 169 (11/74) DG
☐ LSO/Krips/*Sym. 4*
  ECS758 (3/75) Decca Eclipse
  STS-15019 London
☐ Cleveland/Szell/*Sym. 3*
  61595 (3/75) CBS Classics
☐ BPO/Kubelik/*Sym. 4*
  2535 116 (9/75) DG Privilege
SYMPHONY NO. 2 IN C, OP. 61
☐ BPO/Karajan/*Overture, Scherzo
  and Finale*
  2530 170 (10/75) DG
☐ BPO/Kubelik/*Genoveva Ov.*
  2535 117 (9/75) DG Privilege
**SYMPHONY NO. 3 IN E FLAT,
'RHENISH'**
☐ BPO/Karajan
  2530 447 (9/74) DG
☐ VPO/Solti/*Sym. 4*
  SXL6356 (1/68) Decca
  6582 London
☐ Cleveland/Szell/*Sym. 1*
  61595 (3/75) CBS Classics
☐ BPO/Kubelik/*Manfred Ov.*
  2535 118 (9/75) DG Privilege
SYMPHONY NO. 4 IN D MINOR
☐ BPO/Karajan/*Sym. 1*
  2530 169 (11/74) DG
☐ Philh./Klemperer/*Mendelssohn: Sym. 4*
  SXLP30167 (2/75) EMI/HMV
  Concert Classics
  S-35629 Angel
☐ VPO/Solti/*Sym. 3*
  SXL6356 (1/68) Decca
  6582 London
☐ LSO/Krips/*Sym. 1*
  ECS758 (3/75) Decca Eclipse
  STS-15019 London
☐ BPO/Kubelik/*Sym. 1*
  2535 116 (9/75) DG Privilege
**VIOLIN SONATA NO. 1 IN A
MINOR, OP. 15**
☐ Wallez/Rigutto/*Sonata 2*
  7292 (8/76) Selecta/French Decca
WALDSCENEN
☐ Arrau/*Fantasiestucke*
  6500 423 (7/75) Phonogram∗

HEINRICH SCHÜTZ
(b. Köstritz, Saxony, 1585; d. Dresden 1672)

Composers may be of importance in the development of their art without necessarily producing works which make an immediate impact on later generations as being of genius; but in the case of Schütz, even those knowing nothing of his special significance cannot fail to recognise the grandeur and dramatic force of his music. Yet he was also an important historical figure, enriching German culture with the new techniques that had made northern Italy pre-eminent in the musical world.

Coming from a good family, he became a chorister in the Landgrave's chapel at Cassel, studied law (in which he showed some brilliance) and was then sent by the benevolent Landgrave to Venice, where he studied for three years under Gabrieli and eagerly imbibed the polychoral techniques for which St Mark's had become famous: while there he published a book of five-part Italian madrigals. On his teacher's death in 1612 he

THE CHRISTMAS STORY
☐ Partridge, Heinrich Schutz Choir/
  Norrington
  ZRG671 (10/71) Decca Argo∗
DEUTSCHES MAGNIFICAT
☐ Schutz Choir and Ens./Norrington/
  Motets
  ZRG666 (5/71) Decca Argo∗
MOTETS
  Herr unser Herrscher; Ach Herr, straf
  mich nicht; Unser Herr Jesus; Cantate
  Domino; Ich freu mich des; Wie
  lieblich.
☐ Schutz Choir and Ens./Norrington/
  Deutsches Magnificat
  ZRG666 (5/71) Decca Argo
MUSIKALISCHE EXEQUIEN
☐ Dresden Keruzchor/Mauersberger
  6580 039 (5/73) Phonogram
PSALMS OF DAVID
  Nos. 1, 2, 6, 8, 23, 84, 100, 110, 111,
  115, 121, 122, 128, 130, 136, 137, 150
☐ Regensburg Cathedral Choir/*Choral
  Works*
  2722 007 (10/72) DG
**THE RESURRECTION (HISTORIA
DER AUFERSTEHUNG JESU CHRISTI)
(EASTER ORATORIO)**
☐ Soli, Heinrich Schutz Choir, Ens./
  Norrington
  ZRG639 (10/70) Decca Argo

Right: *Heinrich Schütz, the most important figure in German church music of the 17th century.*

SCHÜTZ
ST. MATTHEW PASSION
PETER PEARS   JOHN SHIRLEY-QUIRK
HEINRICH SCHÜTZ CHOIR
director
ROGER NORRINGTON

ST MATTHEW PASSION
☐ Pears, Shirley-Quirk, McCulloch,
  Langridge, Luxon, Dickinson,
  Thomas, Heinrich Schutz Choir/
  Norrington
  ZRG689 (3/72) Decca Argo

CANTATE DOMINO

Schütz Double Choir Motets

HEINRICH SCHÜTZ CHOIR
director
ROGER NORRINGTON

returned to Cassel as *kapellmeister*, but a lengthy tug-of-war between the Landgrave and the Elector of Saxony resulted in his taking up a similar appointment in Dresden in 1617. The disruption caused by the Thirty Years' War spurred him to make protracted visits to the royal court in Copenhagen and to plead, in vain, for his release at home, but after 1655 matters in Dresden improved.

Schütz's earlier works imported to Germany the ideals he had absorbed in Italy, including those of operatic monody. His *Psalms of David* (1619) reflect the splendours of the Venetian tradition, with opulent texture and a virtuoso use of brass coloration: *Zion spricht*, for example, employs two four-part choirs and two six-part vocal and instrumental ensembles. *The Resurrection*, on the other hand, is characterised by restrained use of colour, the Evangelist being accompanied by four gambas, the other characters only by organ. After some Latin motets (*Cantiones sacrae*) Schütz wrote the first German opera, *Dafne*, on the text which had been used in Florence in 1600; but unfortunately the music of this was destroyed in a fire. Later came the *Musicalische Exequien* (a German funeral Mass), German motets, and three collections of *Symphoniae sacrae* which contain several masterpieces of the highest order, such as that on the subject of Saul on the road to Damascus. In his later years Schütz curbed his love of elaboration. The *Christmas Oratorio* of 1664 struck a balance between Italianate style and the solid contrapuntal Lutheran tradition: the various groups of characters are differentiated by their accompanying instrumental colour. The Evangelist is accompanied only by the continuo: in the Passion settings of the next two years (the most important precursors of Bach's ») further simplification takes place, his words now being delivered in unaccompanied chant.

PIANO CONCERTO IN F SHARP
MINOR, OP. 20
☐ Ashkenazy/LPO/Mehta/*Prometheus*
SXL6527 (1/72) Decca
PIANO SONATAS NOS. 1 AND 3
☐ Lazar Berman
ASD3396 (12/77) EMI/HMV
M-34565 Columbia
PIANO SONATAS NOS. 3-5
☐ Ashkenazy
SXL6705 (11/75) Decca
6920 London
POEM OF ECSTASY
☐ Boston SO/Abbado/*Tchaikovsky:*
Romeo and Juliet Ov.
2530 137 (4/72) DG
☐ Los Angeles PO/Mehta/*Schoenberg:*
Verklärte Nacht
SXL6325 (1/68) Decca
PROMETHEUS—POEM OF FIRE,
OP. 60
☐ LPO/Maazel/*Piano Conc.*
SXL6527 (1/72) Decca

Left: *Mystic visionary or
hysterical decadent? Attitudes to
Scriabin have veered from one
extreme to the other.*

DMITRI SHOSTAKOVICH
(b. St. Petersburg 1906; d. Moscow 1975)

Shostakovich was the first composer of recognised international stature to emerge under the Soviet regime in Russia; but though many of his compositions were overtly inscribed to political events and achievements, the dark pessimism of his late works runs completely counter to the Soviet ideal of optimistic art for the stimulation of the common man. His First Symphony, written at the age of 19 as a graduation exercise from the Leningrad Conservatoire, was hailed with enthusiasm and widely publicised as a brilliant product of the new system: brilliant it certainly was, but fundamentally orthodox and distinctly eclectic (by no means a rare quality in a young composer). Its main aspects, a brash energy and a grotesque wit, were developed in, respectively, two rather disappointing further symphonies, and various film and stage works, notably the satiric opera *The Nose* (which offered much scope for orchestral effect) and the ballet *The Age of gold* (a parody of the League of Nations): of more lasting appeal were an engaging concerto for piano and trumpet (Shostakovich was himself an excellent pianist, who wrote well for his instrument) and a cello sonata.

The honeymoon period with the authorities came to an end in 1936 when his opera *Lady Macbeth of Mtsensk*, initially successful, was denounced as degrading and musically brutal: it was not rehabilitated until 1962, when it was re-titled *Katerina Ismailova*. The composer withdrew his new Fourth Symphony, whose size and emotionalism owed much to the example of Mahler », and his Fifth the following year (one of his most tranquil) was penitently subtitled "An artist's reply to just criticism". It was at this time that he entered the more private world of the string quartet: his fifteen works in this genre form the most important addition to that repertory since

Bartók », though his expansiveness is at the other extreme from that master's terse compression. There was, however, progressively a move towards greater thematic economy, and the Eighth Quartet of 1962, like several works from then on, was partly autobiographical, quoting his own music and exploiting the "musical letters" of his name.

An ardently patriotic note, often almost crudely bombastic, informs the works written during the Second World War, chief of which was the Seventh ("Leningrad") Symphony, whose repetition of a banal tune typifying the Nazi invaders was mocked in Bartók's *Concerto for orchestra;* but even so the composer was under pressure to bring his style closer to folk art, and the Ninth was decidedly, and delightfully, lightweight. The peak of his symphonic achievement was the Tenth (1953), a non-programmatic work of eloquence, free from the erratic standards of hitherto; and from that decade also date two fine concertos, the First for violin and the First for cello. The sombrely impassioned intensity of his last symphonies, as of his last songs, gives them a special place in his output: the choral cantata-like Symphony No. 13 is based on poems on the Nazi massacre of Jews and Russians, No. 14 (which follows the song-cycle-symphony tradition of Mahler and Britten », to whom it is dedicated) is an anthology of poems on death. Despite conspicuous unevenness, Shostakovich's music is one of the last great outcrops of the classical heritage.

Above right: *Shostakovich, the
USSR's most considerable
composer, whose symphonies and
quartets are already recognised as
modern classics.*

ALEXANDER SCRIABIN
(b. Moscow 1872; d. there 1915)

It is significant that interest in Scriabin's music, having dwindled to practically nothing after an enormous vogue around the time of the First World War, should be reviving at the present day, when pseudo-religions, artistic nihilism and drug-induced "trips" are rampant. For Scriabin, at least in the last decade of his life, gave himself up whole-heartedly to a self-centred mysticism (loosely based on Theosophist philosophies), indulging himself in a decadent, exotically convoluted style (a kind of aural equivalent of Art Nouveau), and making extensive use, in music of overwrought emotionalism bordering on ecstasy, of a personal "mystic chord" which he built up of superimposed fourths.

He had begun his career, however, as an exceptionally brilliant pianist who, after studying at the Moscow Conservatoire, made a number of highly successful European tours playing his own music. This was deeply indebted to Chopin », whose influence is manifest in such miniatures as his early Preludes, in the idyllic Piano Concerto and in his first three piano sonatas, to Liszt », from whom he derived the "diabolism" which was to erupt in later works, and to Wagner », whose chromatic harmony led him to far-reaching experiments. The change in his style dates from about 1903, when he gave up a teaching post in Moscow to devote himself entirely

to composing, mostly in Brussels, and performing. The atmosphere of his *Divine poem* for orchestra, the last of his three symphonies, was to be greatly intensified in the trance-like *Poem of ecstasy* (1908), and seven further piano sonatas showed an increase in hysteria, in violence and (after the apocalyptic No. 7, the "White Mass") in compression of thought. His numerous shorter piano pieces reached a peak of delirious excitement in *Vers la flamme*, and his last completed composition, *Prometheus, the poem of fire* (which contained a part for "colour organ"), was meant to lead to a final *Mystery* which would be a synthesis of all the arts and include the use of perfume.

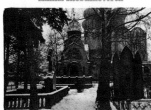

CELLO CONCERTO NO. 1
□ Rostropovich/Philadelphia/Ormandy/
Sym. 1
72081 (9/60) CBS
MS-6124 Columbia
CELLO CONCERTO NO. 2, OP. 126
□ Rostropovich/Boston SO/Ozawa/
Glazunov
2530 653 (11/76) DG*
KATERINA ISMAILOVA, OP. 114
□ *Cpte.* Andreyeva, Bulavin, Radzievsky,
Yefimov, Stanislavsky Musical Drama
Theatre Ch. and Orch./Provatorov
SLS5050 (8/76) HMV

(The) NOSE, OP. 15
□ *Cpte.* Akhimova, Lomonossov,
Soloists, Ch. and Ens. of Moscow
Musical Theatre/Rozhdestvensky
SLS5088 (9/77) HMV
PIANO CONCERTO NO. 1
□ Ogdon, Wilbraham/ASMF/
Marriner/*Stravinsky*
ZRG674 (2/72) Decca Argo*
□ Ortiz, Senior/Bournemouth SO/
Berglund/*Conc. 2; 3 Fantastic Dances*
ASD3081 (6/75) EMI/HMV
S-37109 Angel
SYMPHONY NO. 4, OP. 43
□ Philadelphia/Ormandy
61696 (8/76) CBS Classics
MS-6459 Columbia

PIANO CONCERTO NO. 2, OP. 101
□ Bernstein/NYPO/*Ravel*
72170 (7/64) CBS
MS-6043 Columbia
□ Ortiz/Bournemouth SO/Berglund/
Conc. 1; 3 Fantastic Dances
ASD3081 (6/75) EMI/HMV
S-37109 Angel
PIANO QUINTET, OP. 57
□ Melos Ensemble/*Prokofiev: Wind
Quartet*
SOL267 (6/64) L'Oiseau-Lyre
24 PRELUDES AND FUGUES, OP. 87
□ *Nos. 4, 12, 14, 15, 17, 23.* A. Richter
6580 084 (12/74) Phonogram
**6 ROMANCES ON VERSES OF
ENGLISH POETS FOR BASS AND
CHAMBER ORCHESTRA, OP.140
SUITE OF 6 SONGS TO POEMS OF
MARINA TSVETAEVA FOR
MEZZO-SOPRANO AND CHAMBER
ORCHESTRA, OP. 143a
SUITE ON VERSES BY
MICHELANGELO FOR BASS AND
ORCHESTRA, OP. 145a**
□ Nesterenko, Bogacheva, Moscow RSO
and CO/Shostakovich/Barshai
SLS5078 (5/77) HMV
STRING QUARTETS 1-13
□ Borodin Quartet
SLS879 (6/74) HMV
STRING QUARTETS 7, 13, 14
□ Fitzwilliam Quartet
DSL09 (12/77) L'Oiseau-Lyre*
STRING QUARTETS NOS. 4 AND 12
□ Fitzwilliam Quartet
DSL023 (10/77) L'Oiseau-Lyre
STRING QUARTETS NOS. 8 AND 15
□ Fitzwilliam Quartet
DSL011 (4/76) L'Oiseau-Lyre*
SYMPHONY NO. 1 IN F MINOR
□ Philadelphia/Ormandy/*Cello Conc.*
72081 (9/60) CBS
MS-6124 Columbia
□ LSO/Martinon/*Age of Gold—ballet*
ECS580 (2/71) Decca Eclipse
STS-15180 London

SYMPHONY NO. 5, OP. 47
□ USSR SO/M. Shostakovich
ASD2668 (5/71) EMI/HMV
S-40163 Melodiya/Angel
□ Chicago SO/Previn
ASD3440 (6/78) EMI/HMV
S-37285 Angel
□ Bournemouth SO/Berglund
ESD7029 (2/77) EMI/HMV
S-37279 Angel
SYMPHONY NO. 6, OP. 53
□ LSO/Previn/*Prokofiev: Lt. Kije*
ASD3029 (12/74) EMI/HMV
S-37026 Angel
□ Berlin Radio SO/Kleinert/*Stravinsky*
6580 042 (12/71) Phonogram
**SYMPHONY NO. 7 IN C, OP. 60
(LENINGRAD)**
□ Bournemouth SO/Berglund
SLS897 (10/74) HMV
□ Moscow PO/Kondrashin
SLS5109 (2/78) HMV
SYMPHONY NO. 8
□ LSO/Previn
ASD2917 (10/73) EMI/HMV
S-36980 Angel
SYMPHONY NO. 10, OP. 93
□ BPO/Karajan
139020 (1/69) DG*
□ LPO/A. Davis
CFP40216 (5/75) Classics for Pleasure
S-60255 Seraphim
□ LPO/Haitink
SXL6838 (10/77) Decca
7061 London
SYMPHONY NO. 14, OP. 135
□ Vishnevskaya, Reshetin/Moscow
PO/Rostropovich
ASD3090 (12/75) EMI/HMV
M-34507 Columbia/Melodiya
SYMPHONY NO. 15 IN A, OP. 141
□ Moscow Radio SO/Maxim
Shostakovich/*Quartet No. 11*
ASD2857 (11/72) EMI/HMV
M-34507 Melodiya/Angel
VIOLIN CONCERTO NO. 1
□ D. Oistrakh, New Philh./M.
Shostakovich
ASD2936 (1/74) EMI/HMV
S-36964 Angel

JEAN SIBELIUS
(b. Tavastehus 1865; d. Järvenpää 1957)

Unlike the many cases where composers vainly sought support or had to struggle to make a livelihood, Sibelius was fortunate enough to receive an annual grant from the Finnish government which left him free to compose—and this only four years after he had completed his musical education (which he had taken up after reading for the law) in Helsingfors, Berlin and Vienna. This enlightened patronage made possible the appearance on the international scene of not only the greatest composer Finland has ever produced, but one whose work is totally imbued with an instantly recognisable national atmosphere, powerfully evoking the bleak Nordic landscape, mostly at the mercy of elemental natural forces.

Episodes and characters from the Finnish national epic, the *Kalevala*, play a significant part in his orchestral tone-poems (though the first, in 1892, was entitled simply *A Saga*)—from the four early *Legends*, which include the sombre-coloured *Swan of Tuonela* with its haunting cor anglais solo, and *Pohjola's daughter*, to *Tapiola* (named after the mythological god of the forest), which contains a storm sequence as terrifying as that in his incidental music to *The Tempest*. The blatantly patriotic *Finlandia* and the hackneyed *Valse triste* were early pieces, but other orchestral works of infinitely finer quality are *Nightride and sunrise*, *The Bard* and *The Oceanides*. A technically demanding but popular violin concerto, and a suite-like string quartet ("Voces intimae"), both date from the first decade of this century; but apart from these, some fine songs and a number of rather trivial piano pieces, the remainder of his output, on which his reputation securely rests, consists of seven symphonies.

Very diverse in character, these share a highly individual treatment of the orchestra, and their methods of construction—favouring the enunciation of a mosaic of short motifs which are not fully synthesised until later—have been the subject of much discussion. No. 1 and the very popular No. 2 conspicuously derive from the Russian tradition; No. 3 is sparer and more classical, No. 5 heroic and optimistic; but critical opinion is agreed in considering the remaining three the summit of his achievement. No. 4 is a work of stark introspection, No. 6 offers, in the composer's own phrase, a draught of "pure cold spring water", and No. 7 is a stern, closely-reasoned symphony in one fluid, tremendous movement. During the final thirty years of his life Sibelius wrote nothing, a keenly-awaited eighth symphony never materialising.

Left: *This head of Finland's greatest composer stands in the capital, Helsinki.*

174

Above: *Sibelius's granite-like appearance was in keeping with his powerful, austere music.*

(The) BARD
☐ Bournemouth SO/Berglund/*Sym. 4*
  ASD3340 (6/77) (SQ) EMI/HMV
FINLANDIA
☐ Bournemouth SO/Berglund/*Valse triste; King Christian II Suite; Swan of Tuonela; Lemminkainen's return*
  TWO380 (9/72) EMI/Studio 2
☐ BPO/Karajan/*Valse triste; Swan of Tuonela; Tapiola*
  139 016 (3/68) DG*
☐ Halle/Barbirolli/*Pohjola's Daughter; Valse triste; Karelia Suite; Lemminkainen's return*
  ASD2272 (7/66) EMI/HMV
  S-60208 Seraphim
☐ SRO/Stein/*Pohjola's Daughter; En Saga; Night-Ride and Sunrise*
  SXL6542 (6/72) Decca
  6745 London
☐ BPO/Karajan/*En Saga; Tapiola; Swan*
  ASD3374 (12/77)
  S-37408 Angel
FOUR LEGENDS FROM THE KALEVALA
☐ Royal Liverpool PO/Groves
  ASD3092 (9/75) EMI/HMV
  S-37106 Angel
☐ Helsinki RSO/Kamu/*Karelia*
  2530 656 (10/76) DG*
KARELIA—SUITE
☐ Halle/Barbirolli/*Finlandia; Pohjola's Daughter; Valse triste; Lemminkainen's return*
  ASD2272 (7/66) EMI/HMV
  S-60208 Seraphim
☐ LSO/Gibson/*Sym. 5*
  SPA122 (5/71) Decca
  STS-15189 London

☐ Helsinki RSO/Kamu/*Four Legends*
  2530 656 (10/76) DG*
KING CHRISTIAN II—SUITE
☐ Bournemouth SO/Berglund/*Finlandia; Valse triste; Swan of Tuonela; Lemminkainen's return*
  TWO380 (9/72) EMI/Studio 2
KULLERVO SYMPHONY
☐ Kostia, Vitanen, Helsinki University Male Voice Choir, Bournemouth SO/Berglund
  SLS807 (7/71) HMV
  S-3778 Angel
(The) OCEANIDES
☐ RPO/Beecham/*Pelleas; Tapiola*
  SXLP30197 (2/76) EMI/HMV
  Concert Classics
  S-35458 Angel
PELLEAS AND MELISANDE— INCIDENTAL MUSIC
☐ RPO/Beecham/*Tapiola; Oceanides*
  SXLP30197 (2/76) EMI/HMV
  Concert Classics
  S-35458 Angel
POHJOLA'S DAUGHTER
☐ Halle/Barbirolli/*Finlandia; Valse triste; Karelia Suite; Lemminkainen's return*
  ASD2272 (7/66) EMI/HMV
  S-60208 Seraphim
☐ SRO/Stein/*En Saga; Finlandia; Night-Ride and Sunrise*
  SXL6542 (6/72) Decca
  6745 London
EN SAGA
☐ BPO/Karajan/*Finlandia; Tapiola; Swan*
  ASD3374 (12/77)
  S-37408 Angel
☐ Bournemouth SO/Berglund/*Sym. 5*
  ASD3038 (1/75) EMI/HMV
  S-37104 Angel

☐ SRO/Stein/*Pohjola's Daughter; Finlandia; Night-Ride and Sunrise*
  SXL6542 (6/72) Decca
  6745 London
SONGS
  In the evening; Was it a dream; Autumn evening; The diamond on the March snow; The Tryst; Arioso; Spring flies fast; Since then I have asked no further; But there's still no bird for me; On a balcony by the sea; The first kiss; Black roses; Sigh, rushes, sigh; Come away, Death.
☐ Flagstad, LSO/Fjelstad
  ECS794 (4/77) Decca Eclipse
  33216 London
SWAN OF TUONELA
☐ Bournemouth SO/Berglund/*Finlandia; King Christian Suite II Suite; Valse triste; Lemminkainen's return*
  TWO380 (9/72) EMI/Studio 2
☐ Hallé/Barbirolli/*Sym. 2*
  ASD2308 (4/67) EMI/HMV
  S-36425 Angel
☐ BPO/Karajan/*Tapiola Finlandia; Valse triste*
  139 016 (3/68) DG*
SYMPHONIES 1-7; TAPIOLA, FINLANDIA
☐ Boston SO/Davis
  6709 011 (9/77) Phonogram*
SYMPHONY NO. 1 IN E MINOR
☐ VPO/Maazel/*Karelia Suite*
  JB42 (9/78) Decca Jubilee
☐ Helsinki RSO/Kamu/*The Bard*
  2530 455 (9/74) DG*
☐ Bournemouth SO/Berglund/*Scenes historiques*
  ASD3216 (12/76) EMI/HMV
  S-60289 Seraphim

SYMPHONY NO. 2 IN D MAJOR
☐ Concertgebouw Orch./Szell
  6580 051 (11/72) Phonogram
  6570 084 Philips
☐ Stockholm PO/Dorati
  CCV5029 (11/68) Camden Classics
☐ BPO/Kamu
  2530 021 (4/71) DG*
☐ LSO/Monteux
  ECS789 (10/76) Decca Eclipse
  STS-15098 London
☐ RPO/Barbirolli
  GL25011 (10/76) RCA Gold Seal
  7008 Quintessence
SYMPHONY NO. 3 IN C
☐ VPO/Maazel/*Sym. No. 6*
  JB44 (9/78) Decca Jubilee
☐ Helsinki PO/Kamu/*The Bard*
  2530 422 (12/74) DG
☐ Boston SO/C. Davis/*Sym. 6*
  9500 142 (8/77) Phonogram
SYMPHONY NO. 4 IN A MINOR
☐ VPO/Maazel/*Tapiola*
  JB45 (9/78) Decca Jubilee
☐ BPO/Karajan/*Swan*
  138974 (6/66) DG*
☐ Boston SO/C. Davis/*Tapiola*
  9500 143 (8/77) Phonogram
SYMPHONY NO. 5 IN E FLAT
☐ SNO/Gibson
  CFP40218 (9/75) Classics for Pleasure
☐ Bournemouth SO/Berglund/*En Saga*
  ASD3038 (1/75) EMI/HMV
  S-37104 Angel
☐ LSO/Gibson/*Karelia Suite*
  SPA122 (5/71) Decca
  STS-15189 London
☐ BPO/Karajan/*Tapiola*
  138973 (9/65) DG*
☐ NYPO/Bernstein/*Pohjola's Daughter*
  61808 (8/77) CBS Classics
  MS-6749 Columbia
SYMPHONY NO. 6 IN D MINOR
☐ BPO/Karajan/*Sym. 7*
  139032 DG*
☐ Boston SO/C. Davis/*Sym. 3*
  9500 142 (8/77) Phonogram
☐ NYPO/Bernstein/*Sym. 7*
  61806 (8/77) CBS Classics
SYMPHONY NO. 7 IN C MAJOR
☐ Bournemouth SO/Berglund/*Tapiola; Oceanides*
  ASD2874 (7/73) EMI/HMV
☐ VPO/Maazel/*Sym. No. 5*
  JB46 (9/78) Decca Jubilee
☐ NYPO/Bernstein/*Sym. 6*
  61806 (8/77) CBS Classics
TAPIOLA
☐ VPO/Maazel/*Sym. No. 4*
  JB45 (9/78) Decca Jubilee
  6592 London
☐ BPO/Karajan/*Sym. 5*
  138973 (9/65) DG*
☐ BPO/Karajan/*En Saga;· Finlandia; Swan*
  ASD3374 (12/77) EMI/HMV
  S-37408 Angel
☐ RPO/Beecham/*Pelleas; Oceanides*
  SXLP30197 (2/76) EMI/HMV
  Concert Classics
(The) TEMPEST—INCIDENTAL MUSIC
☐ R. Liv.PO/Groves/*In memoriam*
  ASD2961 (2/74) EMI/HMV
VALSE TRISTE
☐ Halle/Barbirolli/*Finlandia; Pohjola's Daughter; Lemminkainen's return Karelia Suite*
  ASD2272 (7/66) EMI/HMV
  S-60208 Seraphim
☐ BPO/Karajan/*Finlandia; Swan of Tuonela; Tapiola*
  139 016 (3/68) DG*
☐ Bournemouth SO/Berglund/*Finlandia; King Christian II Suite; Swan of Tuonela; Lemminkainen's return*
  TWO380 (9/72) EMI/HMV Studio 2
VIOLIN CONCERTO
☐ Chung/LSO/Previn/*Tchaikovsky*
  SXL6493 (11/70) Decca
  6710 London
☐ Heifetz, Chicago SO/Hendl/*Prokofiev*
  LSB4048 (4/72) RCA
  LSC-4010 RCA
☐ Oistrakh, Moscow Radio SO/ Rozhdestvensky
  ASD2407 (10/68) EMI/HMV

BEDŘICH SMETANA
(b. Litomyšl 1824; d. Prague 1884)

Asked to name the composer who first distilled the essence of the Bohemian countryside in his music, most people would think of Dvořák ». In fact he only continued the pioneer work of the man in whose orchestra he had been a viola player, and whom the Czechs themselves revere as the father of their national music—Smetana.

Though he was precociously gifted, circumstances for some time delayed his taking up the study of music, and finally, in order to make ends meet while having lessons in Prague he himself acted as music tutor to the family of Count Thun. During this time he wrote a number of polkas for the young pianist who was shortly to become his first wife. Following the revolution of 1848, in which he took part, he opened a music school, with the encouragement of Liszt », who also introduced him to a publisher. But conditions proved not to be favourable, and after the death of his little daughter (which impelled him to write his elegiac Piano Trio in G minor) he moved to Sweden, where he spent five successful years, first as a teacher and then conductor of the Philharmonic Society on Göteborg. While there he wrote three programmatic symphonic poems in the Lisztian mould—*Richard III*, *Wallenstein's camp* and *Hakon Jarl.*

Military defeats causing Austria to relax its grip on Bohemia, there was a big upsurge of nationalist feeling; and Smetana, a fervent patriot, returned to Prague in 1863, opening another music school and becoming conductor of a choral society. The following year a new theatre was opened for works in Czech, and for it Smetana (who soon afterwards became conductor there) wrote eight operas, beginning with the historical *Brandenburgers in Bohemia* and then creating his comic masterpiece *The bartered bride*, whose vitality and sparkling melodic invention have won it a firm place in international affection. After this came the heroic tragedy *Dalibor* and the national festival opera *Libuše*, followed by light comedies of Bohemian rural life. Though the dance rhythms and melodic cast of his music are typically

Bohemian, it was virtually only in the *Czech dances* for piano that Smetana quoted actual folk tunes.

In 1874 Smetana suddenly became completely deaf, and was obliged to resign from his theatre post. His first string quartet, as its sub-title "From my life" indicates, was autobiographical, and a persistent high violin E in the last movement represents the fatal whistling in his ears. Nevertheless from this period of deafness also date his last rustic operas and the imposing cycle of six symphonic poems on nationalist subjects called *Má Vlast* (My country). The second of these, *Vltava*, is Smetana's most popular composition and describes in music the course of the river on which Prague stands; No. 4, *From Bohemia's woods and fields*, is also often heard. A deeply melancholic second string quartet, again autobiographical, was written in 1882: the following year Smetana's mind gave way, and he ended his days in an asylum.

Right: *Smetana, the father of Czech musical nationalism.*

THE BARTERED BRIDE
☐ *Cpte.* Soloists, Prague Nat. Theatre Ch. & Orch./Chalabala
SUAST50397-9 (12/72) Supraphon
☐ *Overture, Polka, Furiant* Israel PO/ Kertesz/*Vltava; Dvorak*
SPA202 (8/72) Decca
DALIBOR
☐ *Cpte.* Jindrak, Priybl, Svork, Horacek, Svehla, Kniplova, Svobodova, Janku, Prague Nat. Theatre/Krombholc
SUAST509713 (10/72) Supraphon
1040/2 Genesis
MA VLAST
☐ Czech PO/Ancerl
SUAST50521-3 (7/73) Supraphon
☐ Boston SO/Kubelik
2707 054 (12/71) DG*

☐ VPO/Kubelik
DPA575-6 (3/77) Decca
STS-15096 London
☐ *Vltava only* Israel PO/Kertesz/ *Bartered Bride; Dvorak*
SPA202 (8/72) Decca
☐ *Vltava only* BPO/Karajan/*Dvorak*
ASD3407 (10/77) EMI/HMV
PIANO TRIO IN G MINOR
☐ Beaux Arts Trio/*Chopin: Pno. Trio*
6500 133 (12/71) Phonogram*
STRING QUARTET NO. 1 IN E MINOR
☐ Smetana Quartet/*String Qt. 2*
SUAST50448 Supraphon
SYMPHONIC POEMS
Carnival in Prague; Hakon Jarl; Richard III; Wallensteins Lager
☐ Bav. RO/Kubelik
2530 248 (11/72) DG

LOUIS SPOHR
(b. Brunswick 1784; d. Cassel 1859)

Like Spohr's widespread fame as a violinist, his great success as a composer, enjoying a reputation equal to Beethoven's » throughout the nineteenth century, has now faded to a fact in the history books. Though occasional performances are still given of the eighth of his fifteen violin concertos (cast "in the form of a song *scena*"), of his two clarinet concertos, and of a few of his chamber works—notably the delightful Octet and the witty Nonet—next to nothing is heard of his ten operas (of which *Zemire and Azor* and *Jessonda* were particularly popular), his nine symphonies (several with programmatic titles), his oratorios (some of which were written for England), his 34 string quartets (including some very fine examples) or his songs. Yet his melodic fluency, which sometimes tempted him into excessive length, and the unerring skill of his instrumentation were universally recognised—as was the unexpected nature of his modulations, which were responsible for the much-quoted charge of over-chromaticism. His music is a curious mixture of the conventionally classical and the romantic; and though he was baffled by Beethoven's later style and by Weber's » *Der Freischütz* (whose introduction of the supernatural into opera he had anticipated in his own *Faust*), he was an ardent admirer of Wagner », whose *Flying Dutchman* and *Tannhäuser* he conducted—the latter in the face of considerable opposition. Incidentally, his *Faust*, which was *not* based on Goethe, shows the use of leading-motives before Wagner, as well as scenes constructed as continuous wholes.

All his life, in addition to his activities as a composer, Spohr was busy as an eminent concert violinist. Following his first tour at the age of 14, he had been enabled by the Duke of Brunswick to continue his studies with a famous teacher, who took him to Russia: on his return he entered the ducal orchestra, and two years later became leader of the Duke of Gotha's orchestra. Touring as a soloist the while, he wrote three operas for Hamburg, became leader of the new Theater an der Wien in Vienna, produced his *Faust* in Prague, and became conductor of the Frankfurt Opera. (His claim to have been the first to conduct with a baton in London the following year may have been an exaggeration.) When Weber declined the appointment as musical director to the Elector of Cassel he recommended Spohr for the post, which he filled with distinction for more than a quarter of a century, but increasingly at loggerheads with his employer on account of his liberal politics and musical sympathies.

CLARINET CONCERTO NO. 1 IN C MINOR, OP. 26
☐ De Peyer, LSO/Davis/*Weber: Clar. Conc.*
SOL60035 (11/61) L'Oiseau-Lyre∗
CLARINET CONCERTO NO. 2 IN E FLAT, OP. 57
☐ Denman, Sadler's Wells Orch./Vivienne/*Stamitz: Clar. Conc. 3*
ORYX1828 (12/73) Peerless/Oryx∗
CONCERTANTE NO. 1 FOR VIOLIN, HARP AND ORCHESTRA
☐ H. Schneeberger, U. Holliger, ECO/Graf/*Fl. and Harp Son.*
CRD30-407 (8/76) CRD

NONET IN F, OP. 31
☐ Vienna Octet/*Dble. Qt.*
SDD416 (7/74) Decca Ace of Diamonds
STS-15074 London
OCTET IN E, OP. 32
☐ Vienna Octet/*Beethoven: Pno. Quint.*
SDD256 (10/70) Decca Ace of Diamonds
VIOLIN CONCERTO NO. 8 IN A MINOR, OP. 47 (GESANGSZENE)
☐ H. Bress, SO/Beck/*Vln. Conc. 9*
SOL278 (4/66) L'Oiseau-Lyre

Above: *Spohr, who enjoyed a huge reputation in his day, but whose star is momentarily in eclipse.*

JOHANN STRAUSS II
(b. Vienna 1825; d. there 1899)

It was his father (also Johann, 1804-1849) who, with Lanner, had started the waltz on its course as the dance that was to become the craze of Vienna, but it was the younger Johann, the most brilliant of his three sons, who was to become the "waltz king", pouring out a profusion of elegantly melodious dances which presented to the world a roseate picture of the Imperial capital. His father had attempted to head him off from following in his footsteps, but he studied the violin and composition in secret and at the age of 19 appeared with his own orchestra, playing music by his father and himself. Five years later, on his father's death, he amalgamated the two orchestras and began a career which was to take him to Germany, Poland, St Petersburg (for summer concerts during a whole decade), London, Paris and the USA, and to bring him lasting fame. A statue of him playing his violin is one of Vienna's best-known landmarks.

His nearly 200 waltzes—which are *chains* of lilting tunes, of great diversity and often with extensive and atmospheric introductions and codas—and his numerous polkas and other dances, many of whose titles contain topical allusions, are also remarkable for their subtle and brilliant scoring (the zither in *Tales from the Vienna woods*, for example, is of haunting effect), and have been admired by serious composers as dissimilar as Brahms » and Wagner » and by innumerable musicians since. *The blue Danube*, however, was originally for chorus and was not a success, though it has become the very epitome of Viennese charm: other famous waltzes are *Artists' life*, *Wine, women and song*, *Voices of Spring* and the *Emperor*. Following Offenbach's »visit to Vienna to supervise the production of some of his stage works, Strauss turned his attention to operetta and produced sixteen pieces in this genre. Some of these were fatally flawed by their librettos, but *Die Fledermaus* (The Bat) in 1874 was a masterpiece and is universally loved: of the other operettas the most completely satisfactory was *The gipsy baron (Der Zigeunerbaron)*.

DIE FLEDERMAUS
☐ *Cpte.* Rothenberger, Gedda, Holm, Berry, Fischer-Dieskau, Fassbaender/ Vienna Op./VSO/Boskovsky
SLS964 (2/73) HMV
S-3790 Angel
☐ *Cpte.* Varady, Popp, Kollo, Weikl, Prey, Rebroff/Bavarian State Op. Orch. & Ch./C. Kleiber
2707 088 (10/76) DG*

MUSIC OF THE STRAUSS FAMILY
J. Strauss II: Champagne Polka, Vienna Blood, New Pizzicato Polka, Explosions, Vienna Bonbons, Persian March, The Hunt, Voices of Spring, Pizzicato Polka, Blue Danube, Perpetuum mobile, Eljen a Magyar, Bandit Galop, Artist's Life, Thunder and Lightning, Morning Papers, Emperor Waltz, Wo die Zitronen bluhn, Napoleon March, Roses from the South, Tales from the Vienna Woods; *Josef Strauss:* Spharenklange, Plappermaulchen, Lieb' und Lust, Feuerfest, Jockey, Eingesendet; *E. Strauss:* Bahn frei; *J. Strauss I:* Radetzky March.
☐ VPO/Boskovsky
SDDC298-300 (10/71) Decca Ace of Diamonds
Josef Strauss: Eingesendet. *E. Strauss:* Bahn frei. *J. Strauss II:* In a Viennese Park; Tales from the Vienna Woods; Egyptian March; Gypsy Baron March; Roses from the South; Pizzicato Polka (with Josef Strauss); Morning Papers; Bandits
☐ Halle/Loughran
CFP40256 (11/76) Classics for Pleasure

WALTZES
Blue Danube; Wine Women and Song; Tales from the Vienna Woods; Vienna Blood; Emperor Waltz
☐ VSO/Horenstein
GL25019 (10/76) RCA Gold Seal
7051 Quintessence
Blue Danube; Vienna Blood; Roses from the South; Wine, Women and Song; Tales from the Vienna Woods; Emperor Waltz
☐ J. Strauss Orch. of Vienna/Boskovsky
ESD7025 (12/76) EMI/HMV

THE WORLD OF JOHANN STRAUSS —VOL. 1
On the beautiful blue Danube Waltz; Pizzicato Polka; Roses from the South Waltz; The Hunt Polka; Thousand and one nights—Intermezzo; Tales from the Vienna Woods Waltz; Egyptian March; Vienna Blood Waltz; Perpetuum mobile; Voices of Spring Waltz
☐ VPO/Boskovsky
SPA10 (4/69) Decca

THE WORLD OF JOHANN STRAUSS —VOL. 2
Gipsy Baron Overture; Accelerations Waltz; Annen Polka; Radetsky March; Leichtes Blut Polka; Tritsch-Tratsch Polka*; Artists' Life Waltz*; New Pizzicato Polka*; Emperor Waltz*
☐ VPO/Boskovsky*, Knappertsbusch
SPA73 (8/70) Decca

THE WORLD OF JOHANN STRAUSS —VOL. 3
Die Fledermaus Overture; Thunder and Lightning Polka; Wine, Women and Song Waltz; Explosions Polka; Fledermaus Waltz; Morning Papers; Persian March; Liebeslieder Waltz; Eljen a Magyar Polka; Vienna Bonbons
☐ VPO/Boskovsky
SPA312 (11/73) Decca

Right: *A drawing made in 1896 of the 'waltz king' Johann Strauss the younger, who had taken not only Vienna but the whole of Europe by storm with his lilting dances.*

Above: *The melody of the most famous waltz of all time, The Blue Danube (as untruthful a description as could be imagined), written out by Johann Strauss and signed, as he so often had to do, for someone's autograph album.*

Top: *Strauss was a practical musician whose innumerable dances were written for his own orchestra, with which he toured throughout Europe and in the USA, being greeted everywhere with rapturous enthusiasm.*

Right: *As a conductor and a composer of operas and concert works of dazzlingly virtuosic orchestration, Richard Strauss had a golden touch.*

RICHARD STRAUSS
(b. Munich 1864; d. Garmisch-Partenkirchen 1949)

One of the few twentieth-century composers to have several operas firmly in the international repertoire; the most successful writer of symphonic poems, eclipsing Sibelius » in popularity and sheer brilliance; along with Ravel » and Respighi » one of the greatest of all virtuoso orchestrators: such—together with his distinction as a conductor—are Strauss's chief passports to the Pantheon of fame.

The son of a horn-player in the Munich Opera, he acquired an extraordinary mastery in writing for orchestra at a very early age—his first publication was an orchestral march composed when only twelve—and at 21 (already with his wind Serenade and Violin Concerto, a quartet and two symphonies to his credit) he first assisted, then succeeded, von Bülow as conductor of the Meiningen orchestra before joining the Munich Opera. During this time he had transferred his musical allegiances from Brahms » to Liszt » and Wagner »: in 1894 he conducted at Bayreuth, had his first, very Wagnerian, opera *Guntram* produced, married the leading soprano, and began a regular association with the Berlin Philharmonic, taking over the Berlin Court Opera four years later. Meanwhile he had created a sensation with a succession of vividly scored and harmonically audacious tone-poems which raised programmatic writing to a new level of virtuosity— these included the passionate *Don Juan*, the rollicking *Till Eulenspiegel's merry pranks* and the witty but humane *Don Quixote* (with a solo cello representing the hero).

Mahler » described Strauss as a "great opportunist", and besides the unmistakable whiff of bombast and vulgarity in *Thus spake Zarathustra*, the questionable taste of his self-aggrandisement and self-satisfaction (reviling his opponents the while) in the autobiographical *A hero's life* and *Sinfonia domestica* aroused considerable criticism. But even this paled besides the outrage caused by his one-act operas *Salome*, at first branded as obscene, and *Elektra*, considered brutal and anti-vocal, in both of which Strauss revelled in elaborate orchestral detail and exotic colouring. *Der Rosenkavalier* (1911) was also charged with being immoral, but its humour, its luscious vocal writing (Strauss had a love-affair with the soprano voice all his life) and particularly its beguiling waltzes soon carried all before them, and the opera quickly became a universal favourite. Its supremacy was not

Above: *In Strauss's last years his genius flowered anew.*

challenged by any of his ten subsequent operas, of which the most distinguished were the small-scale *Ariadne auf Naxos* (originally the two-in-one entertainment at the end of *Le bourgeois gentilhomme*), the lyrical *Arabella*, and *Capriccio*, a conversation-piece with some of the elegance of his revered Mozart ». His comedy *Intermezzo* had again depicted his relationship with his temperamental wife: his *Silent woman* caused an upheaval (because his librettist was Jewish) with the Nazis, as a result of which Strauss resigned the presidency of the *Reichsmusik-kammer*.

After the exhaustion of his first creative fires, it is undeniable that Strauss came to rely on his extraordinary technical facility and his skill at spinning complex textures; but in his eighties he enjoyed an Indian summer, in which he produced works suffused with a golden mellow glow— the Second Horn Concerto and the Oboe Concerto, the elegiac *Metamorphosen* (a lament for his defeated country), and (after a number of fine *lieder* in his youth) the final beautiful *Four last songs* for soprano and orchestra.

Left: *The controversial young Richard Strauss, whose series of vivid tone-poems had caused a sensation.*

ORCHESTRAL WORKS
Don Juan; Till Eulenspiegel; Salome— Dance of the Seven Veils; Also sprach Zarathustra; Don Quixote; Ein Heldenleben; Tod und Verklarung; Metamorphosen
☐ BPO/Karajan
2740 111 (10/74) DG*
AN ALPINE SYMPHONY, OP. 64
☐ Dresden Staatskapelle/Kempe
ASD3137 (4/76) EMI/HMV
ALSO SPRACH ZARATHUSTRA
☐ Chicago SO/Reiner
CCV5040 (6/68) Camden Classics
☐ VPO/Karajan
SDD175 (7/68) Decca Ace of Diamonds
STS-15083 London
☐ BPO/Karajan
2530 402 (6/74) DG*
☐ RPO/Lewis/*Till*
SPA397 (7/75) Decca
☐ Chicago SO/Solti/*Don Juan; Till*
SXL6749 (12/75) Decca
6978 London

RICHARD STRAUSS

□ Dresden Staatskapelle/Kempe/*Till;
Salome—Dance
ESD7026 (4/77) EMI/HMV
ARABELLA
□ *Cpte.* Della Casa, London, Edelmann,
Gueden, Dermota, VPO/Solti
GOS571-3 (8/72) Decca Ace of
Diamonds
S-63522 Richmond
AUS ITALIEN—SYMPHONIC POEM,
OP. 16
□ Dresden Staatskapelle/Kempe
ASD3319 (2/77) EMI/HMV
CAPRICCIO
□ *Cpte.* Janowitz, Fischer-Dieskau,
Schreier, Prey, Ridderbusch,
Troyanos, Bav. RO/Bohm
2709 038 (8/72) DG*
DON JUAN—SYMPHONIC POEM,
OP. 20
□ Chicago SO/Reiner/*Rosenkavalier
Waltzes; Burleske*
CCV5051 (6/68) Camden Classics
□ BPO/karajan/*Till Eulenspiegel;
Salome—Dance*
2530 349 (6/74) DG*
□ Concertgebouw/Haitink/*Elgar:
Enigma Vars.*
6500 481 (3/75) Phonogram*
□ VPO/Karajan/*Tchaikovsky: Romeo
and Juliet*
SPA119 (10/71) Decca
6209 London
□ Chicago SO/Solti/*Also sprach; Till
Eulenspiegel*
SXL6749 (12/75) Decca
6978 London
□ BPO/Bohm/*Till, etc.*
2535 208 (12/76) DG Privilege
138866 DG
DON QUIXOTE—FANTASTIC
VARIATIONS, OP. 35
□ Tortelier/Dresden Staatskapelle/
Kempe/*Rosenkavalier Waltzes*
ASD3074 (7/75) EMI/HMV
□ Rostropovich/BPO/Karajan
ASD3118 (6/76) EMI/HMV
S-37057 Angel
□ Fournier/BPO/Karajan
2535 195 (8/76) DG Privilege
ELEKTRA
□ *Cpte.* Nilsson, Resnik, Collier, Krause,
Stolze, Vienna Op. Ch. and PO/Solti
SET354-5 (11/67) Decca
1269 London
FOUR LAST SONGS
□ Schwarzkopf/Berlin RSO/Szell/*Songs*
ASD2888 (9/73) EMI/HMV
S-36347 Angel
□ Janowitz/BPO/Karajan/*Tod*
2530 368 (12/74) DG*
EIN HELDENLEBEN—SYMPHONIC
POEM, OP. 40
□ BPO/Karajan
ASD3126 (10/75) EMI/HMV
S-37060 Angel
□ Dresden Staatskapelle/Kempe/*Concert*
SLS880 (6/74) HMV
□ Los Angeles PO/Mehta
SXL6382 (6/69) Decca
6608 London
□ Concertgebouw/Haitink
6500 048 (1/71) Phonogram*
□ BPO/Karajan
2535 194 (8/76) DG Privilege
138025 DG
HORN CONCERTOS NOS. 1 AND 2
□ Brain/Philh./Sawallisch/*Hindemith*
HLS7001 (3/72) EMI/HMV
METAMORPHOSEN FOR 23 SOLO
STRINGS
□ BPO/Karajan/*Mozart: Adagio
and Fugue in C minor, K546;
Beethoven: Grosse Fuge*
2530 066 (6/73) DG*
□ Dresden Staatskapelle/Kempe/
Concert
SLS861 (10/73) HMV
OBOE CONCERTO
□ Holliger/New Philh./De Waart/
Mozart
6500 174 (1/72) Phonogram*

DER ROSENKAVALIER
□ *Cpte.* Crespin, Jungwirth, Minton,
Donath, Vienna Opera Chorus,
VPO/Solti
SET418-21 (9/69) Decca
□ *Cpte.* Schwarzkopf, Edelmann,
Ludwig, Waechter, Stich-Randall,
Welitsch, Chorus, Philh./Karajan
SLS810 (10/71) HMV
ROSENKAVALIER—WALTZES
FROM THE OPERA
□ Chicago SO/Reiner/*Don Juan;
Burleske*
CCV5051 (6/68) Camden Classics
□ Dresden Staatskapelle/Kempe/
Don Juan
ASD3074 (7/75) EMI/HMV
SALOME
□ *Cpte.* Nilsson, Waechter, Stolze,
Hoffman, Kmentt, VPO/Solti
SET228-9 (3/62) Decca
1218 London
SERENADE FOR 13 WIND
INSTRUMENTS IN E FLAT, OP. 7
□ Netherlands Wind Ens./De Waart/
Sym. for Wind
6500 097 (12/71) Phonogram*
SONATINA FOR 16 WIND
INSTRUMENTS, NO. 1 IN F
□ Netherlands Wind Ens./De Waart/
Suite
6500 297 (10/72) Phonogram*
SINFONIA DOMESTICA
□ BPO/Karajan
ASD2955 (4/74) EMI/HMV
S-36973 Angel
TILL EULENSPIEGEL—SYMPHONIC
POEM, OP. 28
□ VPO/Karajan/*Tod; Salome—Dance*
SDD211 (12/69) Decca Ace of
Diamonds
6211 London
□ BPO/Karajan/*Don Juan;
Salome—Dance*
2530 349 (6/74) DG*
□ RPO/Lewis/*Also sprach*
SPA397 (7/75) Decca
□ Chicago SO/Solti/*Don Juan; Also
sprach*
SXL6749 (12/75) Decca
6978 London
□ BPO/Bohm/*Don Juan, etc.*
2535 208 (12/76) DG Privilege
138866 DG
□ Dresden Staatskapelle/Kempe/*Also;
Salome—Dance*
SLS894 HMV
TOD UND VERKLARUNG
□ VPO/Karajan/*Till; Salome—Dance*
SDD211 (12/69) Decca Ace of Diamonds
6211 London
□ BPO/Karajan/*Four Last Songs*
2530 368 (12/74) DG
□ VPO/Reiner/*Till*
ECS674 (5/73) Decca Eclipse
□ LSO/Horenstein/*Hindemith*
RHS312 (8/73) Unicorn
71307 Nonesuch
VOCAL RECITALS
□ Janet Baker, Moore/*Schubert, Wolf*
ASD2431 (1/69) EMI/HMV
□ Schwarzkopf, LSO/Szell/*Mozart*
ASD2493 (3/70) EMI/HMV

IGOR STRAVINSKY
(b. Oranienbaum, nr. St Petersburg, 1882; d. New York 1971)

Stravinsky's bewildering changes of style in the course of his career (which have been likened to those of his contemporary Picasso) often prompted accusations of "reaction at all costs" and publicity-seeking: it would be truer to say that they sprang from an exceptionally keen and original mind which, having explored to the full any one set of possibilities, was not content to repeat his effects. As a centre of artistic polemics and as an influence on others he was one of the great key figures of this century; and we are fortunate in having a number of recordings of him conducting his own works.

As was the case with so many composers, his father, a famous operatic bass, was against him becoming a musician and sent him to study law; but a fellow-student was a son of Rimsky-Korsakov », who encouraged and taught Stravinsky, and whose influence is apparent in a youthful symphony and (along with that of the French impressionists) in *The Firebird*, his first ballet for the great impresario Diaghilev. In this scintillating fairy-tale score, which brought him fame overnight in 1910, the most significant pointer to the future was the *Infernal dance*. The following year Diaghilev produced his *Petrushka*,

Above: *Stravinsky's meteoric career began with* The Firebird.

whose vivid colours, rhythmic and harmonic novelty and subtle characterisation all contributed to its overwhelming effect, and in 1913 the elemental *Rite of Spring*. Its orgiastic violence and iconoclastic concepts of rhythm, harmony and instrumentation initially created a scandal, but it has long since been recognised as a major landmark in twentieth-century music.

Stravinsky had by this time left Russia for good. Finding himself in Switzerland at the outbreak of World War I, without any hope of the large forces he had hitherto demanded, he made a virtue of necessity and wrote theatre works—*Renard*, the narrated mime *The Soldier's tale* and the choreographic cantata *The Wedding* —which employed only chamber instrumental groups, though of unusual constitution (*The Wedding* was written for four pianos and percussion). This economy of means turned his thoughts towards a "neo-classical" style which was to exert a profound influence throughout Europe: reacting against romantic warmth, it deliberately adopted a non-expressive stance, favouring the use of wind instruments as being more "objective" than strings. The *Symphonies of wind instruments* and the drily witty Octet exemplify this trend. This neo-classical phase also involved both highly individualised regenerations of the past, as in *Pulcinella* (based on Pergolesi ») and pastiche, as in *The Fairy's kiss* (where the model was Tchaikovsky ») and, in structure at least, the opera *The Rake's progress*. Another aspect of this objectivity was his cultivation of a grave, austere "Apollonian" (as opposed to "Dionysian") style, as in his ballets on classical Greek legends *Apollo Musagetes* and *Orpheus* and the melodrama *Persephone*, and in works set in Latin in order to lend them distance and a hieratic, monumental quality, such as the opera-oratorio *Oedipus Rex* and the masterly *Symphony of psalms*.

After the death of Schoenberg », to whose musical theories he had been strongly opposed, he suddenly capitulated and from 1952 onwards (by which time he had long been settled in the USA) embraced dodecaphony, at first slightly tempered, as in the *Cantata* and the ballet *Agon*, later in its strictest form. These final works, from *Threni* onwards, are all tautly compressed, and breathe asceticism or aridity, according to the listener's viewpoint.

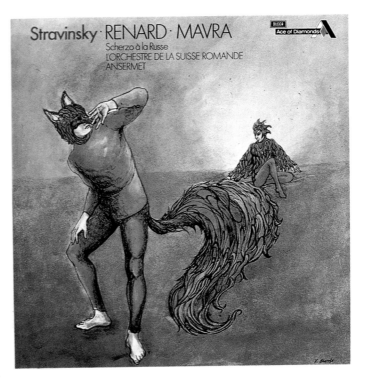

Stravinsky · RENARD · MAVRA
Scherzo à la Russe
L'ORCHESTRE DE LA SUISSE ROMANDE
ANSERMET
DECCA Ace of Diamonds

APOLLO
☐ ASMF/Marriner/*Pulcinella*
ZRG575 (10/68) Decca Argo∗
BALLETS—FIREBIRD: PETRUSHKA; RITE OF SPRING
☐ LPO/Haitink
6747 094 (10/74) Phonogram
☐ Columbia SO/Stravinsky/*Talk by composer*
78307 (11/76) CBS
CANTATA ON ANONYMOUS 15th AND 16th CENTURY ENGLISH LYRICS
☐ Kern, Young, St Anthony Sgrs., ECO/Davis/*Mass*
SOL265 (11/63) L'Oiseau-Lyre
CAPRICCIO FOR PIANO AND ORCHESTRA
☐ Magaloff/Suisse/Ansermet/*Piano & Wind Conc.*
SDD242 (4/71) Decca Ace of Diamonds
STS-15048 London
☐ Ogdon/ASMF/Marriner/ Shostakovich
ZRG674 (2/71) Decca Argo∗
CONCERTO FOR PIANO AND WIND INSTRUMENTS
☐ Magaloff/Suisse/Ansermet/*Capriccio*
SDD242 (3/71) Decca Ace of Diamonds
STS-15048 London

CONCERTO FOR 16 INSTRUMENTS IN E FLAT (DUMBARTON OAKS)
☐ Los Angeles CO/Marriner/*Conc. in D; Danses concertantes*
ASD3077 (7/75) EMI/HMV
S-37081 London
CONCERTO FOR STRINGS IN D
☐ Los Angeles CO/Marriner/*Conc. in E flat; Danses concertantes*
ASD3077 (7/75) EMI/HMV
S-37081 London
FAIRY'S KISS
☐ *Divertimento only:* Suisse/Ansermet/ *Soldier's Tale*
SDD247 (2/71) Decca Ace of Diamonds
THE FIREBIRD—BALLET
☐ *Cpte.* Haitink
6500 483 (11/75) Phonogram∗
☐ *Cpte.* RPO/Dorati
VAR1022 (4/77) CRD/Enigma Classics
☐ *Suites only:* PCO/Monteux/*Petrushka*
SPA152 (1/72) Decca
STS-15197 London
☐ *Suite only:* Berlin Radio SO/Maazel/ *Song of the Nightingale*
2548 145 (4/74) DG Heliodor
☐ *Suite only:* NYPO/Bernstein/*Petrushka*
61122 (9/70) CBS Classics

FIREBIRD, PETRUSHKA; THE RITE OF SPRING
☐ LPO/Haitink
6747 094 (10/74) Phonogram
JEU DE CARTES—BALLET
☐ LSO/Abbado/*Firebird*
2530 537 (8/75) DG∗
MASS FOR VOICES AND WOODWINDS
☐ Murray, Allister, Fleet, Keyte, St Anthony Sgrs., ECO/Davis/*Cantata*
SOL265 (11/63) L'Oiseau-Lyre
MAVRA
☐ Carlisle, Watts, Sinclair, MacDonald, Suisse/Ansermet/*Renard; Scherzo*
SDD241 (11/70) Decca Ace of Diamonds
STS-15102 London
OCTET FOR WIND
☐ Boston Symphony Chbr. Players/ *Pastorale; Ragtime; Concertino*
2530 551 (1/76) DG∗
OEDIPUS REX
☐ Pears, Meyer, McIntyre, Dean, R. Davies, Luxon, McCowen, Alldis Ch., LPO/Solti
SET616 (2/78) Decca
PETRUSHKA—BALLET
☐ *Cpte.* NYPO/Boulez
73056 (9/74) CBS
M-31076 Columbia
☐ *Cpte.* LPO/Haitink
6500 483 (11/75) Phonogram
6500 458 Philips
☐ *Cpte.* LSO/Dutoit
2530 711 (5/77) DG∗
☐ *Cpte.* Paris Cons./Monteux/*Firebird*
SPA152 (1/72) Decca
STS-15197 London
☐ *Suite only:* NYPO/Bernstein/*Firebird*
61122 (9/70) CBS Classics
PULCINELLA—BALLET
☐ Tyler, Franzini, Garmei, Suisse/ Ansermet
SDD245 (4/71) Decca Ace of Diamonds
PULCINELLA—BALLET SUITE
☐ ASMF/Marriner/*Apollo*
ZRG575 (10/68) Decca Argo∗
☐ Suisse Romande/Ansermet/*Song of the Nightingale*
ECS776 (10/76) Decca Eclipse
STS-15011 London
(The) RAKE'S PROGRESS
☐ *Cpte.* Young, Raskin, Sarfaty, Reardon, Garrard, Manning, Sadler's Wells, RPO/Stravinsky
77304 (3/65) CBS
M35-710 Columbia

RENARD—A BURLESQUE
☐ English, Mitchinson, Glossop, Rouleau, Suisse Romande/Ansermet/ *Mavra; Scherzo*
SDD241 (11/70) Decca Ace of Diamonds
STS-15102 London
RITE OF SPRING—BALLET
☐ Columbia SO/Stravinsky/*talk by composer*
72054 (4/61) CBS
☐ LSO/Davis
6580 013 (10/72) Phonogram
☐ Chicago SO/Solti
SXL6691 (11/74) Decca
6885 London
☐ LPO/Haitink
6500 482 (11/75) Phonogram∗
☐ LSO/Abbado
2530 635 (5/76) DG∗
☐ Minneapolis SO/Dorati/*Petrushka*
6582 021 (8/77) Phonogram
☐ Concertgebouw/Davis
9500 323 (3/78) Phonogram
(The) SOLDIER'S TALE
☐ Nash Ensemble/Howarth/*Dumbarton Oaks Concerto; Octet*
CFP40098 (2/75) Classics for Pleasure
SONG OF THE NIGHTINGALE
☐ Berlin RSO/Maazel/*Firebird*
2548 145 (4/74) DG Heliodor
☐ Suisse Romande/Ansermet/ *Pulcinella*
ECS776 (10/76) Decca Eclipse
STS-15011 London
SYMPHONY IN C
☐ Columbia SO/Stravinsky/*Sym. of Psalms*
72181 (8/64) CBS
MS-6548 Columbia
☐ SRO/Ansermet/*Sym. of Wind, 4 Etudes, Suites 1 & 2*
ECS820 (8/78) Decca Eclipse
6190 London
SYMPHONY IN THREE MOVEMENTS
☐ SRO/Ansermet/*Sym. of Psalms*
ECS820 (8/78) Decca Eclipse
6190 London
SYMPHONY OF PSALMS
☐ Columbia SO/Stravinsky/*Sym. in C*
72181 (8/64) CBS
☐ SRO/Ansermet/*Sym. in 3 Movts.*
ECS820 (8/78) Decca Eclipse
6190 London
VIOLIN CONCERTO
☐ Kyung Wha-Chung, LSO/Previn/ *Walton*
SXL6601 (5/73) Decca

ARTHUR SULLIVAN
(b. London 1842; d. there 1900)

The century-old cult of the Gilbert-and-Sullivan operettas (which only the expiry of the copyright saved from total mummification) has resulted in many people being practically unaware of Sullivan as an individual at all. It is one of history's ironies that throughout his life he was constantly being urged not to waste his time on such frivolities as light opera but to concentrate on serious composition, particularly sacred music, and conducting—which brought him a knighthood at the age of 41.

As the son of a leading bandmaster and as a chorister in the Chapel Royal, he received a good musical background, and subsequently at the Royal Academy of Music was the first recipient of the Mendelssohn scholarship, which enabled him to study in Leipzig and absorb the German

tradition. On his return he took posts as an organist and made his name in 1862 with his incidental music to *The Tempest*: this led to a commission for a festival cantata and to his "Irish" Symphony, which charmed by its vitality and melodic freshness. The death of his father prompted his *In Memoriam* overture; the following year Sullivan was instrumental in re-discovering Schubert's » *Rosamunde* music, wrote a *Marmion* overture and produced, within a fortnight, his first stage comedy *Cox and Box*. He was still mainly occupied with oratorios and cantatas, with editing and writing hymns, and with conducting (he maintained regular associations during his life with London, Glasgow and Leeds), when he was introduced to W. S. Gilbert, an ingenious librettist with a taste for topsy-turvy comedy situations and topical satire *à la* Offenbach ». Their first collaboration, for Christmas 1871, was unremarkable, but it led to an 18-year partnership which produced more than a dozen runaway successes.

The first, their only piece to be continuously composed, without dialogue, was *Trial by jury*. While shouldering extra responsibilities as director, for three years, of a new conservatoire, later to become the Royal College of Music, Sullivan composed *The Sorcerer* and *HMS Pinafore*, which broke all records by running for 700 consecutive nights and was extensively pirated in the USA. The further triumphs of *The Pirates of Penzance* and *Patience* enabled their impresario to open a new theatre for the "Savoy operas", as they were grandiloquently called; and later in the decade came *Iolanthe, The Mikado, The Yeomen of the guard* (an attempt at a more serious manner) and *The Gondoliers*. At this point a rupture between librettist and composer turned Sullivan's thoughts, encouraged by the enthusiastic reception of his cantata *The golden legend*, again to serious music, and a new theatre was built for his one "grand" opera, *Ivanhoe*, but this proved a disappointment. Much as he would have deplored the fact, his reputation rests on the melodic charm, polished craftsmanship, lucid instrumentation and gift for parody in his operettas.

Above: *Did an insatiable public restrict Sullivan's scope?*

Left: *Sullivan's intrinsic seriousness can be perceived in this well-known portrait of him by Sir John Millais.*

OVERTURE DI BALLO
☐ RLPO/Groves/*Symphony*
   ASD2435 (2/69) EMI/HMV
THE GONDOLIERS; COX AND BOX
☐ D'Oyly Carte Opera Co./Godfrey
   SKL4138-40 (11/61) Decca
HMS PINAFORE; TRIAL BY JURY
☐ Morison, Sinclair, Lewis, G. Baker,
   Cameron, Brannigan, Glyndebourne
   Fest. Chorus, PAO/Sargent
   SXLP30088-9 (10/67) EMI/HMV
   Concert Classics
IOLANTHE
☐ Cpte. Baker, Wallace, Young, Brannigan/
   Glyndebourne Ch./Pro Arte/Sargent
   SXLP30112-3 (11/68) EMI/HMV
   Concert Classics
THE MIKADO
☐ Studholme, D. Nash, Kern, Allister,
   Revill, Wakefield, Holmes, J. Heddle
   Nash, Dowling, Sadler's Wells Opera
   Chorus and Orch./Faris
   SOC244-5 (9/71) World Records
☐ D'Oyly Carte Opera Co./R. Nash
   SKL5158-9 (1/74) Decca
OVERTURES
   HMS Pinafore; Pirates of Penzance;
   Iolanthe; Mikado; Yeomen of the
   Guard; Gondoliers; Overture di Ballo
☐ RPO/Walker/Sargent; New SO/
   Godfrey
   SPA259 (11/72) Decca
☐ RLPO/Groves
   TWO403 (3/73) EMI/Studio 2

PATIENCE
☐ Morison, M. Thomas, Sinclair,
   Young, Baker, Cameron, Shaw,
   Glyndebourne/Pro Arte/Sargent
   SXDW3031 (8/77) EMI/HMV
   Concert Classics
PINEAPPLE POLL—BALLET
(arr. Mackerras)
☐ RPO/Mackerras
   ESD7028 (2/77) EMI/HMV
PIRATES OF PENZANCE
☐ D'Oyly Carte Op. Co./Godfrey
   SKL4925-6 (9/68) Decca
☐ Morison, Harper, Thomas, Sinclair,
   Lewis, Baker, Cameron, Milligan,
   Brannigan, Glyndebourne Fest.
   Chorus, PAO/Sargent
   SXLP30131-2 (12/71) EMI/HMV
   Concert Classics
   S-6102 Seraphim
RUDDIGORE
☐ Baker, Lewis, Brannigan, Morison,
   Sinclair, Glyndebourne Fest. Ch./Pro
   Arte Orch./Sargent
   SXDW3029 (4/77) EMI/HMV
   Concert Classics
SYMPHONY IN E FLAT ('IRISH')
☐ RLPO/Groves/*Overture di Ballo*
   ASD2435 (2/69) EMI/HMV
YEOMEN OF THE GUARD
☐ D'Oyly Carte Opera Co./Sargent
   SKL4624-5 (11/64) Decca

George Baker, John Cameron
Richard Lewis, Owen Brannigan
James Milligan, Elsie Morison
Marjorie Thomas, Monica Sinclair

Above: *Appreciation of Szymanowski is beginning to grow.*
Right: *A page from Szymanowski's score of his 3rd Symphony.*

THOMAS TALLIS
(b. ?, Leicestershire c. 1505; d. Greenwich 1585)

The title "father of English cathedral music" sometimes bestowed on Tallis makes sense only in that he was one of the first to write for the Anglican service ("Tallis in the Dorian mode" is still in the repertory); but the particular interest of his historical position is that he bridged the transition from the Roman rite. He had been organist or choirmaster at Waltham Abbey before its dissolution in 1540; shortly afterwards he is known to have been a Gentleman of the Chapel Royal, of which, in the mid-1570s, he became joint organist with Byrd », his junior by some forty years. In 1575 Queen Elizabeth granted them her sole patent to print music, which they subsequently pleaded to exchange for an annual grant, and their first publication, each contributing half, was a volume of *Cantiones sacrae.*

Tallis's works cannot be definitely dated, but the Latin church music almost certainly preceded the English—some Latin motets indeed were later adapted as English anthems. His remarkable motet in forty parts (eight five-part choirs), *Spem in alium*, contrasts with the simplicity of, for example, *O nata lux*: other fine Latin motets are *O sacrum convivium* and *Audivi media nocte*. Another of his masterpieces is the gravely beautiful *Lamentations of Jeremiah.* Two of his tunes for a 1567 psalter have become famous out of context—one adapted as "Tallis's canon", the other taken by Vaughan Williams » as the theme of his string Fantasia.

CANTIONES SACRAE
(jointly with Byrd)
☐ Cantores in Ecclesia/Howard
   SOL311-3 (12/69) L'Oiseau-Lyre
LAMENTATIONS OF JEREMIAH
☐ Pro Cantione Antiqua/Turner/*Byrd: Mass*
   2533 113 (10/72) DG Archiv/ Produktion*
SPEM IN ALIUM (40-part motet)

☐ Clerkes of Oxenford/Wulstan/*Tallis recital*
   CFP40069 (7/74) Classics for Pleasure
☐ King's College Choir/Willcocks/ *Motets*
   ZK30-1 (1/78) Decca Argo

Right: *An Italian engraving of Thomas Tallis.*

KAROL SZYMANOWSKI
(b. Timoshovka, Ukraine, 1882; d. Lausanne 1937)

In so far as Szymanowski's music is known— which is unfortunately not very far, though its subtlety and refinement of thought make a strong appeal to connoisseurs—it is only that of his middle period. It is an overworked convention to divide a composer's output into three periods, but in the present case this is valid because of the marked changes in his style. Polish musicians however consider his last works to represent him at his best.

A leg injury in boyhood made it necessary for him to be educated at home, amid his cultured and intensely musical aristocratic family, and it was not until he was about 20 (having written various piano pieces strongly influenced by Chopin », including a B flat minor Etude whose later popularity hung around his neck like Rachmaninov's » C sharp minor Prelude round his) that he was able to go and study in Warsaw. But lured by the spell of Strauss's » orchestral music, he went for three years to Berlin, where he became the centre of a small colony of Polish musicians. His opera *Hagith* clearly shows its descent from Strauss's *Salome*, and much of his music of this period is turgid, febrile and tortuously chromatic.

A taste for mysticism, fed by his admiration for Scriabin », and a growing interest in Oriental philosophy coincided with his discovery of Debussy » and of Stravinsky's » *Petrushka*, which both acted as antidotes to the Germanic style which had possessed him. It was now that he produced the sensual, ecstatic, elaborately textured works by which he is chiefly remembered: the piano *Métopes* (on classical Greek legends), the Third Symphony (which contains a vocal setting of a Persian "Song of the night"), the voluptuous, iridescent First Violin Concerto, the violin *Mythes*, the virtuoso piano *Masques*, and the *Songs of a love-crazed muezzin*.

In the 1917 Revolution his family's estates were plundered and destroyed, and only with some difficulty did he make his way to Warsaw two years later. His interest was caught by the folk music of the Tatra mountains, which he visited for his health, and its influence is to be perceived in the simpler, more nationalist character of the *Slopiewnie* songs (to surrealist texts), and more especially in the crisp, polytonal Mazurkas for piano. Meanwhile, however, Szymanowski's operatic masterpiece *King Roger*, which is imbued with a luminous pantheism, had received its first performance. For three years he headed the Warsaw State Conservatory, composing during this time his magnificent *Stabat Mater*, a work of almost Byzantine austerity: then came the colourful folk ballet *Harnasie*, about the bandits of the Tatras, and the *Symphonie concertante* for himself to play. By this time, however, his health was breaking down, and he died of tuberculosis in a sanatorium.

PYOTR ILYICH TCHAIKOVSKY
(b. Kamsko-Votinsk 1840; d. St Petersburg 1893)

If concert promoters were ever to choose a patron saint it should by rights by Tchaikovsky, for whose music the public, certainly in Britain, seems to have an insatiable appetite and any concert of whose works is assured of a good response. Yet strangely enough most of his music initially met with scant success, and he himself was a solitary, introspective, hyper-sensitive figure perpetually worried about his inability to create large-scale works without the seams showing. The secret of his popularity lies in his profusion of deeply expressive melody, his full-blooded "writing from the heart" and his warm, often highly original orchestration; yet side by side with an emotionalism which at times approaches hysteria goes an intimate, almost aristocratic lyricism which certainly owes something to his lifelong love of Mozart ».

As a youth he had been sent to a school of jurisprudence and became a clerk in the Ministry of Justice; but on reaching the age of 21 his musical instincts could not be thwarted, and he studied composition seriously at the new conservatoire in St Petersburg—to such effect that at the end of his course he was engaged by Nicolas Rubinstein as a professor at the Moscow Conservatoire. A meeting with Balakirev » and his circle revealed that his aims differed from theirs (their approach being both more nationalistic and less professional), though he dedicated to Balakirev his romantic fantasy-overture *Romeo and Juliet* and, very much later, his splendidly dramatic *Manfred* symphony. He had already composed his first symphony, sub-titled "Winter daydreams", and the first of his ten operas: his first piano concerto (now enormously popular) followed a few years later.

A wealthy widow became his "fairy godmother", for a dozen years making him an allowance: they never met, but corresponded regularly, and to her Tchaikovsky dedicated his Fourth Symphony, which is haunted throughout by the intervention of its initial "Fate" motif. From this period also date the orchestral fantasy *Francesca da Rimini* and his graceful *Swan lake*, the first of his three ballets, the level of music for which art he raised to a then unknown height of distinction. While working on his operatic masterpiece *Eugene Onegin* he was so overcome by the emotional situation of its heroine that he was misled, despite his homosexual nature, into marrying an ardent admirer. The result was catastrophic: after two months he fled, attempted suicide, and was sent to recover from his breakdown on Lake Geneva and in Italy—this was shortly afterwards to figure in the unusually sunny *Italian caprice*.

Resigning from his teaching post, he threw himself entirely into composition: one of his finest works, the

Left: Tchaikovsky in later life, from a painting by Serov.

and music by Glinka, Liadov and Rimsky-Korsakov

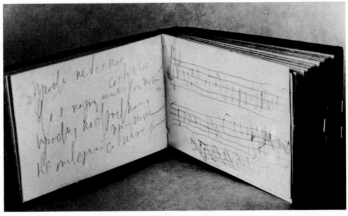

Left: A preliminary sketch in Tchaikovsky's notebook for his opera The Queen of Spades.

CAPRICCIO ITALIEN
☐ BPO/Karajan/*Liszt; J. Strauss II*
2545 010 DG/Heliodor
☐ LSO/Alwyn/*1812; Marche slave*
SPA108 (3/72) Decca
STS-15221 London
☐ Philh./Kletzki/*Violin Conc.*
CFP40083 (12/74) Classics for Pleasure

EUGENE ONEGIN
☐ Cpte. Kubiak, Burrows, Weikl, Ghiaurov, Alldis Choir/Royal Opera Orch., Covent Garden/Solti
SET596-8 (6/75) Decca
13112 London

FRANCESCA DA RIMINI
☐ Washington NSO/Dorati/*Hamlet; Voyevode*
SXL6627 (2/74) Decca
6841 London
☐ Leningrad PO/Rozhdestvensky/*Khachaturian*
2538 345 (11/74) DG Privilege
☐ LPO/Handley/*Hamlet*
CFP40223 (1/76) Classics for Pleasure

HAMLET
☐ Washington National SO/Dorati/*Francesca da Rimini; Voyevode*
SXL6627 (2/74) Decca
6841 London
☐ LPO/Handley/*Francesca*
CFP40223 (1/76) Classics for Pleasure

MANFRED SYMPHONY
☐ USSR SO/Svetlanov
ASD2558 (3/70) EMI/HMV
Y-34609 Odyssey/Melodiya

MARCHE SLAVE
☐ LSO/Previn/*1812; Romeo and Juliet*
ASD2894 (7/73) EMI/HMV
S-36890 Angel
☐ LSO/Alwyn/*1812; Capriccio Italien*
SPA108 (3/72) Decca
STS-15221 London
☐ New Philh./Del Mar/*1812; Romeo and Juliet*
CN2021 (9/76) Pickwick/Contour

THE NUTCRACKER
☐ Cpte. LSO/Previn
SLS834 (1/73) HMV
S-3788 Angel
☐ Cpte. LSO/Dorati
6780 250 (11/75) Phonogram

Piano Trio, was written in memory of Nicolas Rubinstein, who had been a staunch champion of his music and laid the foundations for its wide acceptance. Tchaikovsky's reputation was spreading outside Russia, and by about 1885 he had recovered to such an extent that he now appeared with increasing frequency as a conductor, though typically racked with home-sickness on every journey yet longing to get away again. The last five years of his life saw a remarkable sequence of some of his greatest compositions: the *Sleeping Beauty* and *Nutcracker* ballets, the melodramatic opera *The Queen of Spades* (based, like *Eugene Onegin*, on Pushkin), the Fifth Symphony, which absorbs folk material, and the gloom-ridden Sixth ("Pathétique"). A week after the première of this last, he died (as had his mother when he was fifteen) of cholera.

Above: *Tchaikovsky stood apart from the nationalists.*

□ *Cpte.* Concertgebouw/Dorati
6747 364 (1/77) Phonogram
6747257 Philips
□ *Cpte.* Bolshoi Theatre Orch./
Rozhdestvensky
SXDW3028 (11/76) EMI/HMV
Concert Classics
M2-33116 Columbia
□ *Suite only.* BPO/Karajan/*Serenade*
139 030 (6/69) DG
□ *Suite only.* Boston Pops/Fiedler/
Grieg: Peer Gynt
PFS4352 (5/76) Decca Phase 4
21142 London
□ *Suite only.* Philh./Markevich/
Mendelssohn
SIT66034 (9/60)
PIANO CONCERTOS 1-3
□ Gilels, NPO/Maazel
SLS865 (2/74) HMV
S-3798 Angel
PIANO CONCERTO NO. 1
□ Ashkenazy/LSO/Maazel
SXL6058 (6/63) Decca
6360 London
□ Argerich/RPO/Dutoit
2530 112 (10/71) DG*
□ Katin/LSO/Cundell/*Concert Fantasia*
SPA168 (11/71) Decca
STS-15227 London
□ Gilels, New Philh./Maazel/*Conc. 3*
ASD3067 (4/75) EMI/HMV
□ Gilels/Chicago SO/Reiner
CCV5016 (6/75) Camden Classics
VICS 1039 RCA

□ Berman/BPO/Karajan
2530 677 (3/76) DG*
□ Wild/RPO/Fistoulari
GL25013 (10/76) RCA Gold Seal
PIANO CONCERTO NO. 3
□ Gilels/New Philh./Maazel/*Conc. 1*
ASD3067 (4/75) EMI/HMV
ROMEO AND JULIET
□ BPO/Karajan/*1812 Ov.*
139 029 (6/69) DG*
□ VPO/Karajan/*R. Strauss*
SPA119 (10/71) Decca
6209 London
□ LSO/Previn/*1812 Ov.; Marche Slave*
ASD2894 (7/73) EMI/HMV
S-36890 Angel
□ Boston SO/Abbado/*Scriabin: Poem of Ecstasy*
2530 137 (4/72) DG*
□ Washington National PO/Dorati/
Fatum; The Tempest
SXL6694 (2/75) Decca
6891 London
□ Dresden Staatskapelle/Sanderling/
Borodin Sym. No. 2
2548 226 (4/76) DG/Heliodor
□ New Philh./Del Mar/*1812; Marche slave*
CN2021 (9/76) Pickwick/Contour

SERENADE IN C FOR STRINGS
□ Dresden Staatskapelle/Suitner/
Dvorak: Serenade in E
2584 121 (4/75) DG Privilege
□ ASMF/Marriner/*Sextet 'Souvenir de Florence'*
ZRG584 (4/69) Decca Argo*
□ ASMF/Marriner/*Dvorak: Serenade in E*
ZRG848 (7/76) Decca Argo*
□ ECO/Leppard/*Dvorak*
9500 105 (3/77) Phonogram*
□ LSO/Barbirolli/*Arensky*
SXLP30239 (5/77) EMI/HMV
Concert Classics
S-36269 Angel
SLEEPING BEAUTY
□ *Cpte.* LSO, Previn
SLS5001 (12/74) HMV
SX-3812 Angel
□ *Exc.* New. Philh./Stokowski/*Swan Lake*
PFS4083 (10/66) Decca Phase 4
21008 London
□ *Exc.* VPO/Karajan/*Swan Lake*
JB35 (9/78) Decca Jubilee
□ *Exc.* Philh./Karajan/*Swan Lake*
SXLP30200 (2/76) EMI/HMV
Concert Classics
S-35740 Angel
□ *Exc.* LSO/Previn
ASD3370 (8/77) EMI/HMV
S-37261 Angel
SOUVENIR DE FLORENCE, OP.80
□ *Orch. version.* Netherlands CO/
Zinman/*Verdi*
9500 104 (6/77) Phonogram*
STRING QUARTET NO. 1 IN D MAJOR, OP. 11
□ Prague Quartet/*Prokofiev*
111 0698 (1/71) Rediffusion/
Supraphon
SUITE NO. 3
□ LPO/Boult
ASD3135 (11/75) EMI/HMV
SWAN LAKE
□ *Cpte.* Netherlands RPO/Fistoulari
10BB168-70 (10/74) Decca
21101 London
□ Nat. PO/Bonynge
D37D3 (9/77) Decca
2315 London
□ *Cpte.* LSO/Previn
SLS5070 (12/76) HMV
SX-3834 Angel
□ *Exc.* VPO/Karajan/*Sleeping Beauty*
JB35 (9/78) Decca Jubilee
□ *Exc.* New Philh./Stokowski/*Sleeping Beauty*
PFS4083 (10/66) Decca Phase 4
21008 London
□ *Exc.* LSO/Monteux
6580 020 (2/72) Phonogram
□ *Exc.* Philh./Karajan/*Sleeping Beauty*
SXLP30200 (2/76) Concert Classics
S-35740 Angel
SYMPHONIES 1-6; MANFRED
□ USSR SO/Svetlanov
SLS881 (9/74) HMV
□ LPO/Rostropovich
SLS5090 (10/77) HMV
SYMPHONY NO. 1 IN G MINOR (WINTER DAYDREAMS)
□ VPO/Maazel
SXL6159 (7/65) Decca
□ New Philh./Muti
ASD3213 (7/76) EMI/HMV
S-37114 Angel
SYMPHONY NO. 2 IN C MINOR (LITTLE RUSSIAN)
□ NPO/Abbado
139381 (2/70) DG
□ Dresden PO/Masur/*Romeo and Juliet*
2538 233 (6/73) DG Privilege
SYMPHONY NO. 4 IN F MINOR
□ LSO/Szell
SPA206 (3/72) Decca
6987 London
□ BPO/Karajan
139017 (4/68) DG*
□ Concertgebouw/Haitink
6500 012 (11/70) Phonogram
7300016 Philips

□ Leningrad PO/Mravinksy
2538 178 (12/74) DG Privilege
2535 235 DG
□ BPO/Karajan
ASD2814 (6/75) EMI/HMV
□ VPO/Abbado
2530 651 (11/76) DG*
SYMPHONY NO. 5 IN E MINOR
□ BPO/Karajan
2530 699 (8/76) DG*
□ Leningrad PO/Mravinsky
2538 179 (3/75) DG Privilege
2535 236 DG
□ Concertgebouw/Haitink
6500 922 (2/76) Phonogram*
□ BPO/Karajan
2530 699 (8/76) DG*
□ LSO/Dorati
6582 013 (10/76) Phonogram
□ New Philh./Horenstein
GL25007 (10/76) RCA Gold Seal
SYMPHONY NO. 6 IN B MINOR (PATHETIQUE)
□ Concertgebouw/Haitink
6500 081 (3/71) Phonogram*
□ VPO/Abbado
2530 350 (7/74) DG*
□ Leningrad PO/Mravinsky
2538 180 (12/74) DG Privilege
2535 237 DG
□ Philh./Giulini
SXLP30208 (6/76) EMI/HMV
Concert Classics
S-60031 Seraphim
□ LSO/Tjeknavorian
LRL1 5129 (11/76)
□ BPO/Karajan
2530 774 (6/77) DG*
VARIATIONS ON A ROCOCO THEME
□ P. Tortelier, Northern Sinfonia/
Y. P. Tortelier/*Grieg*
ASD2954 (2/74) EMI/HMV
□ Rostropovich/BPO/Karajan/
Dvorak: Cello Conc.
139 044 (10/69) DG*
□ Gendron/VSO/Dohnanyi/*Pezzo cappriccioso; Schumann*
6580 131 (8/76) Phonogram
VIOLIN CONCERTO IN D
□ Chung/LSO/Previn/*Sibelius*
SXL6493 (11/70) Decca
6710 London
□ Zukerman/LSO/Dorati/*Mendelssohn*
72768 (11/69) CBS
MS-7313 Columbia
□ Grumiaux/New Philh./Krenz/
Serenade melancolique
9500 086 (6/76) Phonogram*
□ Milstein/Pittsburgh SO/Steinberg/
Concert
SXLP30225 (1/77) EMI/HMV
Concert Classics
□ Belkin/New Philh.Ashkenazy/*Valse-Scherzo*
SXL6854 (10/77) Decca
1812 OVERTURE
□ LSO/Previn/*Marche Slave; Romeo and Juliet*
ASD2894 (7/73) EMI/HMV
S-36890 Angel
□ Minneapolis SO/Dorati/*Beethoven: Wellington's Victory*
SAL3461 (5/64) Phonogram
□ LSO/Alwyn/*Capriccio Italien; Marche slave*
SPA108 (3/72) Decca
STS-15221 London
□ New Philh./Del Mar/*Marche slave; Romeo and Juliet*
CN2021 (9/76) Pickwick/Contour
□ Philadelphia/Ormandy/*Beethoven: Wellingtons Sieg*
LSB4031 (7/71) RCA
LSC-3204 RCA

GEORG PHILIPP TELEMANN
(b. Magdeburg 1681; d. Hamburg 1767)

In the cases of Bach » and Handel » the sheer size of their output leaves one wondering how, with their other responsibilities, they found time to create it all. What then is one to say of their contemporary Telemann, a friend of them both (and godfather to Bach's son Carl Philipp Emanuel »), who composed about as much as the two of them together? (Handel remarked that Telemann could write an eight-part motet as quickly as anyone else could write a letter). As happens with all exceptionally prolific composers, commentators who have not troubled to look at more than a fraction of his music have tended to dismiss him as merely facile and superficial—most unjustly, as the increasing availability of his works makes clear; and though contemporary evaluations are often fallible, it is worth remembering that in his day Telemann ranked higher than Bach, who was appointed Cantor in Leipzig only after Telemann had declined the post.

His extraordinary energy and vitality made themselves evident very early, since although he was virtually self-taught musically he mastered a number of instruments, and taught himself composition by poring over scores of older masters; and while studying languages in Leipzig he founded a Collegium Musicum and wrote operas for the theatre there. He accepted a succession of posts as organist and *kapellmeister*—in Sorau (where his lively mind absorbed the Polish and Moravian folk music he heard), in Eisenach, in Frankfurt (where he was musical director to the city, whose concerts he made famous), and to the Prince of Bayreuth; finally, in 1721, he became Cantor of the Johanneum and city musical director in Hamburg, where he spent the rest of his life.

There, as well as writing the remainder of his forty or so operas (including *The Patience of Socrates*, his first in Hamburg, and *Pimpinone*, on the same plot as Pergolesi's » later *Serva padrona*), he poured out an incredible amount of music in which, alert as he was to all new ideas, he created a synthesis of the solid German contrapuntal tradition with Italianate melody, the French suite form (particularly after a visit to Paris in 1737, though he had always been an admirer of Lully) and Polish dance elements. In all he composed some 45 Passion settings, twelve sets of cantatas for the church year, numerous services and oratorios, of which *The Day of judgment* is the best known, 600 French overtures or orchestral suites, many with programmatic titles such as *Don Quixote* or *The Hamburg ebb and flow*, some 200 concertos (some of which, like that in G for viola—perhaps the earliest for that instrument—have become popular) and a mass of instrumental music of all kinds, including five sets of *Musique de table*; in 1728 he published a collection entitled *The constant music-master* in 25 fortnightly parts in which some of the pieces were ingeniously written so as to be read in different clefs for different instruments.

CONCERTO IN F FOR RECORDER, BASSOON AND STRINGS: CONCERTO IN G FOR 4 VIOLINS: CONCERTO IN F FOR 2 HORNS, 2 VIOLINS AND CONTINUO: CONCERTO IN B FLAT FOR 3 OBOES, 3 VIOLINS AND CONTINUO
☐ VCM/Harnoncourt
　AW6 41204 (7/67)
　Selecta/Telefunken
CONCERTO IN D FOR TRUMPET AND STRINGS*
CONCERTO IN G FOR VIOLA AND STRINGS†
☐ *Wilbraham, †Shingles, ASMF, Marriner/*Concerti by Vivaldi, Handel, Arne, Bach, Corelli, Fasch*
　D69D3 (9/77) Decca
CONCERTO IN B FLAT FOR 3 OBOES, 3 VIOLINS AND CONTINUO: CONCERTO IN C MINOR FOR OBOE AND STRINGS: CONCERTO IN D FOR TRUMPET, STRINGS AND CONTINUO: CONCERTO IN F FOR 3 VIOLINS AND STRINGS
☐ Scherbaum, Koch, Melkus, various Ens./Wenzinger
　135 080 (11/68) DG Privilege
CONCERTO FOR G FOR VIOLA AND STRINGS
☐ Streatfield, ASMF/Marriner/*Gabrieli; Handel, Vivaldi*
　SOL276 (3/65) L'Oiseau-Lyre
☐ Doktor, Concerto Amsterdam/Bruggen/ *Suite for Solo Violin; Suite—La Lyra*
　AS6 41105 (4/70) Selecta/Telefunken

DON QUIXOTE—SUITE
☐ ASMF/Marriner/*Overture in D; Vla. Conc. in G*
　ZRG836 (2/76) Decca Argo*
OVERTURES
　Overture in C; Overture des Nations anciens et modernes; Overture in C (Hamburger Ebb and Fluth)
☐ ASMF/Marriner
　ZRG837 (4/77) Decca Argo*
PIMPINONE—OPERA
☐ Cianella, Wenk, Stuttgart Bach Soc./ Rilling
　TV34124S (6/68) Decca Turnabout
QUARTETS FOR FLUTE, VIOLIN, CELLO AND HARPSICHORD
(Parisian)
☐ Cpte. Amsterdam Quartet
　TK11565 (1/70)
　641183 Telefunken
SUITE IN A MINOR FOR FLUTE AND STRINGS
☐ Munrow, ASMF/Marriner/ *Sammartini: Recorder Concs. in F and B flat*
　ASD3028 (11/74) EMI/HMV
　S-37019 Angel
SUITE IN F FOR 4 HORNS, 2 OBOES AND STRINGS
☐ Spach, Roth, Mainz CO/Kehr/*Vivaldi: Conc. P320; Rosetti: Horn Conc.*
　TV34078S Decca Turnabout*
DER TAG DES GERICHTS
☐ Landwehr, Herrmann, Canne-Meijer, Equiluz, Egmond, Ch. and VCM/ Harnoncourt
　FA6-35044 (3/67) Selecta/Telefunken

Above: *The enormously productive Telemann, director of music for Hamburg, whose lively intelligence, enterprise and tireless vitality caused him to be much more highly esteemed by his contemporaries than Bach.*

MICHAEL TIPPETT
(b. London 1905)

Unlike those composers whose music is a self-sufficient independent creation, Tippett is a mystic whose abstruse philosophies, worked out with knotty intellectual effort, form an integral element in his work. Deeply concerned with social problems, spiritual values and humane ideals— during the Depression he conducted an orchestra of unemployed professionals, his first great breakthrough was with the oratorio *A child of our time*, on an individual wartime tragedy, and he elected to go to prison as a conscientious objector—he has pursued his own musical path, which has taken some disconcerting changes of direction, regardless of fashion or of difficulties of comprehension; he is now the most thought-provoking of Britain's senior composers.

He was a late developer, taking up further study at the age of 25 after having already been active as a musician, and at 30 withdrawing all he had composed till then. Under the influence of the ebullient sprung rhythms of the Elizabethan madrigalists he wrote his Second String Quartet and the Concerto for double string orchestra (which, like *A child of our time*, includes the "blues" harmony of negro spirituals which has been a strand in his make-up right through to his Third Symphony more than thirty years later). The elaborate vocal line of his cantata *Boyhood's end*, and its richly-written piano accompaniment, revealed a new personality on the English scene. Its

complexity of texture was further developed in the *Fantasia concertante on a theme of Corelli*: and there is a wealth of expressive polyphony in the visionary *Midsummer marriage*, his first opera, whose Jungian libretto (his own, as in all his operas) was at first considered impenetrable. Tippett described his piano concerto as an extension of this opera.

But then came a reaction, and he exchanged his luxurious lyricism for a sparse and abrasive style (owing something to Stravinsky ») in which disjunct contrasting blocks of material are juxtaposed as in a mosaic. The chief works in this new style were the largely declamatory opera *King Priam*, the Second Piano Sonata, the Second Symphony, and the *Concerto for orchestra*. The "complex yet luminous" (his words) metaphysical cantata *The vision of St Augustine* of 1966, the year in which Tippett was knighted, prepared the way for a further stage in his output, in which, especially after the clearer-textured, lighter-coloured opera *The knot garden* of 1970 (of which *Songs for Dov* was a spin-off), he seemed to be drawing together diverse threads from his past, now coupled with an intense homage to Beethoven ». This was discernible in the Third Piano Sonata and made explicit by a quotation from the Choral Symphony in his Third Symphony—in which a solo soprano sings in a mainly "blues" idiom.

Above: *Tippett's MS of the slow movement of his 2nd Symphony.*

Right: *Tippett in 1955, the year of* The Midsummer Marriage.

192

Above: *Sir Michael Tippett just before the première of his opera* The Ice Break.

BOYHOOD'S END—CANTATA FOR TENOR AND PIANO
☐ P. Langridge, J. Constable/*Heart's Assurance: Songs for Ariel; Songs for Achilles*
DSLO14 (11/76) L'Oiseau-Lyre

(A) CHILD OF OUR TIME—ORATORIO
☐ Norman, Baker, Cassilly, Shirley-Quirk, BBC Sgrs., BBC Choral Soc. and SO/Davis
6500 985 (11/75) Phonogram⋆
☐ Morison, Bowden, Lewis, Standen, Liv. Phil. Choir, RLPO/Pritchard/*Ritual Dances*
DPA571-2 (3/77) Decca

CONCERTO FOR DOUBLE STRING ORCHESTRA
☐ Moscow CO and Bath Fest. CO/Barshai/*Britten*
SXLP30157 (10/73) EMI/HMV Concert Classics

CONCERTO FOR ORCHESTRA
☐ LSO/Davis/*4 Ritual dances*
6580 093 (1/75) Phonogram⋆

FANTASIA CONCERTANTE ON A THEME OF CORELLI
☐ ASMF/Marriner/*Conc. for Dble. String Orch; Little music*
ZRG680 (1/72) Decca Argo

(The) HEART'S ASSURANCE— SONG CYCLE
☐ P. Langridge, J. Constable/*Songs for Ariel; Songs for Achilles*
DSLO14 (11/76) L'Oiseau-Lyre

(The) KNOT GARDEN
☐ Cpte. Herincx, Minton, Gomez, Barstow, Carey, Tear, Hemsley, Cov. Gdn. Orch./Davis
6700 063 (4/74) Phonogram⋆

(The) MIDSUMMER MARRIAGE
☐ Cpte. Remedios, Carlyle, Herincx, Harwood, Burrows, Watts, Dean, Bainbridge, Cov. Gdn. Orch./Davis
6703 027 (5/71) Phonogram⋆

4 RITUAL DANCES
☐ Cov. Gdn. Orch./Pritchard/*Child of our Time*
DPA571-2 (3/77) Decca
☐ Cov. Gdn. Orch./Davis/*Orch. Conc.*

6580 093 (1/75) Phonogram⋆

PIANO SONATAS NOS. 1-3
☐ Paul Crossley
6500 534 (11/74) Phonogram⋆

SONG FOR DOV
☐ Tear, London Sinfonietta/Atherton/*Messiaen: Poèmes*
ZRG703 (5/73) Decca Argo⋆

STRING QUARTETS NOS. 1-3
☐ Lindsay Quartet
DSLO10 (12/75) L'Oiseau-Lyre⋆

SYMPHONY NO. 1
☐ LSO/Davis/*Suite in D*
9500 107 (10/76) Phonogram⋆

SYMPHONY NO. 2
☐ LSO/Davis/*Weeping babe; Hrn. quartet; Hrn. Son.*
ZRG535 (1/68) Decca Argo⋆

SYMPHONY NO. 3
☐ Harper, LSO, Davis
6500 662 (1/75) Phonogram⋆

(The) VISION OF ST AUGUSTINE
☐ Shirley-Quirk, LSO and Ch./Tippett/*Fantasy*
SER5620 (4/72) RCA

193

RALPH VAUGHAN WILLIAMS
(b. Down Ampney, Gloucestershire, 1872; d. London 1958)

Vaughan Williams's personal appearance—like a somewhat abstracted, unassuming, blunt-spoken farmer—so exactly accorded with the "homespun" image of a proportion of his works (which exerted an almost overwhelming influence on so many composers of what has been pejoratively called the "English pastoral" school) that his true range of utterance is sometimes underestimated. He was certainly chiefly responsible for the final emergence of a national style that had shaken itself free from German traditions; yet his own leisurely musical education had been conservative—Cambridge, under Parry and Stanford at the RCM and under Bruch ≫ in Berlin— though at the age of 36 he unexpectedly took some lessons with Ravel ≫. He had by then been active for a few years with the English Folk Song Society, collecting (especially from Norfolk, which provided the background for some early orchestral pieces) and absorbing their often modal idiom, and had put much work into editing the English Hymnal.

His first compositions to attract attention were in the choral tradition with which he was familiar (*Toward the unknown region*, *A sea symphony*) and reveal a cultivated literary taste: it is notable that the sources which were chiefly to inspire him were the Bible, Shakespeare,

Bunyan and Blake. Among other English poets, Rossetti, Stevenson and Housman were put under contribution in the song *Silent noon*, the *Songs of travel* and the cycle *On Wenlock Edge* respectively. A third powerful formative influence, besides folksong and literature, was the polyphonic church music of the Tudor period—which brought into being his most famous work, the *Fantasia on a theme of Tallis*. The year 1914 saw the composition of the *London Symphony*, which combines Elgarian extroversion with poetic meditation, *Hugh the drover*, which attempted to do for English opera what Smetana ≫ had done for Czech, and *The lark ascending* for violin and orchestra, an imaginatively rhapsodic work of a delicacy rare in his output.

After returning from war service he became a professor of composition at the RCM and for six years conducted the Bach Choir; but he accepted very few other appointments (though he was a generous supporter of younger musicians), and the focus of interest became purely his compositions. Apart from his ballet *Job* (1930), his stage works, whatever their lyrical qualities, lacked a sense of movement—he in fact termed his most ambitious, *The Pilgrim's progress*, a "morality": artistically the most

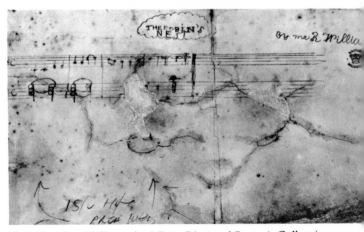

Top: *Vaughan Williams by J Finzi (National Portrait Gallery).*
Above: *The six-year-old Vaughan Williams's first composition.*
Left: *During rehearsals for* The Pilgrim's Progress *in 1951.*

successful opera was the one-act *Riders to the sea*. But central to his output were his symphonies, which cover an extraordinary variety of styles and, despite a tendency to thick colour and galumphing rhythm, include three indisputable masterpieces—the prophetically grim and violent Fourth, written in 1935, the gravely contemplative Fifth, which is cognate with *Pilgrim's progress*, and the restless Sixth, whose desolate Epilogue, drained of all emotion, is one of the most remarkable pieces of music ever written. At the start of World War II, when he was nearing 70, he began writing for films; and from his score for *Scott of the Antarctic* (1949) was later drawn his Seventh Symphony, in which the sequences of block chords which had always been a fingerprint of his took on on a new significance.

The other main field of his creative work was his choral music—liturgical (the Mass), sacred (*Sancta civitas, Magnificat)* and secular (the racy *Five Tudor portraits* and the exquisite *Serenade to Music*). Record collectors are fortunate that so many of Vaughan Williams's works are available in performance by one of his earliest, and finest, interpreters, Sir Adrian Boult.

Above: *Vaughan Williams considers a knotty point in one of his scores.*

CONCERTO ACCADEMICO IN D MINOR FOR VIOLIN AND ORCHESTRA
☐ Grumlikova, Prague SO/Maag/ *Britten: Vln. Conc.*
SUAST50959 (10/69) Supraphon
CONCERTO FOR BASS TUBA AND ORCHESTRA IN F MINOR
☐ Fletcher, LSO, Previn/*Sym. 3*
SB6861 (9/72) RCA
LSC-3281 RCA
CONCERTO IN A MINOR FOR OBOE AND STRING ORCHESTRA
☐ Williams, Bournemouth SO/ Berglund/*Sym. 6*
ASD3127 (10/75) EMI/HMV
DONA NOBIS PACEM—CANTATA
☐ Armstrong, Carol Case, LPO and Ch./Boult/*Towards the unknown*
ASD2962 (5/74) EMI/HMV
FANTASIA ON A THEME OF THOMAS TALLIS
☐ LPO/Handley/*Tippett: Concerto for double string orchestra*
CFP40068 (6/74) Classics for Pleasure
☐ ASMF/Marriner/*Greensleeves; Lark Ascending; Dives and Lazarus*
ZRG696 (10/72) Decca Argo★
☐ Sinfonia of London/Barbirolli/ *Greensleeves; Elgar; Introduction and Allegro for strings; Serenade for strings*
ASD521 (5/63) EMI/HMV
S-36101 Angel
☐ Bournemouth SO/Silvestri/*Elgar*
ESD7013 (10/76) EMI/HMV
☐ LPO/Boult/*Conc. Grosso; Partita*
ASD3286 (11/76) EMI/HMV
S-37211 Angel
FLOS CAMPI FOR VIOLA, VOICES AND ORCHESTRA
☐ Aronowitz, King's College Choir, Jacques Orch./Willcocks/*Dives and Lazarus; Oxford Elegy*
ASD2487 (2/70) EMI/HMV
S-36699 Angel
GREENSLEEVES
☐ LPO/Handley/*Tallis: Fant.; Tippett: Conc. for dble. string orch.*
CFP40068 (6/74) Classics for Pleasure
☐ ASMF/Marriner/*Tallis: Fant.; Lark Ascending; Dives and Lazarus*
ZRG696 (10/72) Decca Argo
☐ LSO/Boult/*Elgar: Enigma Vars; English Folk Songs Suite*
ASD2750 (11/71) EMI/HMV
S-36799 Angel

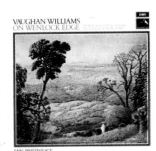

VAUGHAN WILLIAMS
ON WENLOCK EDGE

IAN PARTRIDGE
The Music Group of London
Janet Craxton, ... · Jennifer Partridge, ...

VAUGHAN WILLIAMS
A LONDON SYMPHONY

London Philharmonic Orchestra
SIR ADRIAN BOULT

☐ Sinfonia of London/Barbirolli/*Tallis: Fant.; Elgar: Introduction and Allegro for strings; Serenade for strings*
ASD521 (5/63) EMI/HMV
S-36101 Angel
JOB—BALLET
☐ LSO/Boult
ASD2673 (4/71) EMI/HMV
S-36773 Angel
MASS IN G MINOR
☐ Eaton, Perrin, Doveton, van Asch, King's College Choir/Willcocks
ASD2458 (5/69) EMI/HMV
O CLAP YOUR HANDS
☐ King's College Choir, ECO/Willcocks/ *Mass in G minor etc.*
ASD2458 (5/69) EMI/HMV
ON WENLOCK EDGE—SONG CYCLE
☐ I. Partridge, Music Group of London/ *Water mill; 10 Blake Songs; The new ghost*
HQS1236 (2/71) EMI/HMV

VAUGHAN WILLIAMS
THE NINE SYMPHONIES
LONDON PHILHARMONIC ORCHESTRA
New Philharmonia Orchestra
SIR ADRIAN BOULT

VAUGHAN WILLIAMS
SINFONIA ANTARTICA

NORMA BURROWES
LONDON PHILHARMONIC CHOIR
LONDON PHILHARMONIC ORCHESTRA
SIR ADRIAN BOULT

(The) PILGRIM'S PROGRESS
☐ Cpte. Noble, Herincx, Case, Evans, Keyte, Shaw, Dickerson, Partridge, Shirley-Quirk, LPO and Ch./Boult
SLS959 (2/72) HMV
S-3785 Angel
SERENADE TO MUSIC; IN THE FEN COUNTRY; THE LARK ASCENDING; NORFOLK RHAPSODY
☐ LPO, NPO/Boult
ASD2847 (11/72) EMI/HMV
SONGS OF TRAVEL; TEN BLAKE SONGS
☐ Tear, Ledger
ZRG732 (3/73) Decca Argo★
SYMPHONIES 1-9
☐ Soloists/LPO/New Philh./Boult/ *Orchestral pieces*
SLS822 (4/72) HMV
☐ Soloists, LSO/Previn
SER5649-55 (10/72) RCA

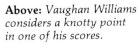

(A) SEA SYMPHONY
☐ Armstrong, Case, LPO and Ch./ Boult/*The Wasps incid. music*
SLS780 (12/68) HMV
☐ Harper, Shirley-Quirk, LSO/Previn
SER5585 (4/70) RCA
A LONDON SYMPHONY
☐ LPO/Boult
ASD2740 (10/71) EMI/HMV
☐ LSO/Previn
SB6860 (8/72) RCA
PASTORAL SYMPHONY
☐ Price, NPO/Boult/*In the Fen Country*
ASD2393 (9/72) RCA
☐ Harper, LSO/Previn/*Tuba Concerto*
SB6861 (9/72) RCA
SYMPHONY NO. 4 IN F MINOR
☐ NPO/Boult/*A Norfolk Rhapsody*
ASD2375 (6/68) EMI/HMV
SYMPHONY NO. 5 IN D
☐ Philharmonia/Barbirolli/*Tallis Fantasia*
ASD2698 (9/71) EMI/HMV
SYMPHONY NO. 6 IN E MINOR
☐ NPO/Boult/*The Lark Ascending*
ASD2329 (10/67) EMI/HMV
☐ LSO/Previn/*Sym. 8*
SB6767 (10/68) RCA
SINFONIA ANTARTICA
☐ Burrowes/LPO/Boult
ASD2631 (11/70) EMI/HMV
SYMPHONY NO. 8 IN D MINOR
☐ LSO/Previn/*Sym. 6*
SB6767 (10/68) RCA
☐ LPO/Boult/*Partita for Double String Orch.*
ECS644 (7/72) Decca Eclispe
STS-15216 London
TOWARD THE UNKNOWN REGION
☐ LPO and Choir/Boult/*Dona nobis*
ASD2962 (5/74) EMI/HMV
S-36972 Angel
THE WASPS—OVERTURE AND SUITE
☐ LPO/Boult/*Sea Symphony*
SLS780 (12/68) HMV

GIUSEPPE VERDI
(b. Le Roncole, nr. Busseto, 1813; d. Milan 1901)

By a strange coincidence, the greatest figures in Italian and German opera respectively, Verdi and Wagner », were born in the same year and first made their name at much the same time. Verdi, the son of a humble tavern-keeper, received his musical education from the cathedral organist in Busseto, where in his teens he made himself generally useful musically, and was enabled to continue his studies in Milan (privately with a member of the staff of La Scala, since he was not accepted for the Conservatorio) through the generosity of a local merchant, whose daughter he married on his return. His first opera, *Oberto*, was produced at La Scala in 1839 with sufficient success for him to be offered a contract for three more: of these, the comedy *Un giorno di regno* was a total failure (but during its composition the death of his wife, after that of his two children, had been a shattering blow), but the biblical *Nabucco* (1842) was a triumph. His next two, *I Lombardi* and *Ernani*, spread his fame wide. In all these works Verdi's vigorous, full-blooded style contrasted sharply with that of his predecessors Bellini » and Donizetti »; if his orchestration was crude, the operas made their effect by their sense of theatre (on which Verdi set much store) and robust melodic gift.

He then turned out four operas in only 15 months before *Macbeth* (1847), which marked a great advance in characterisation and formal construction, and whose libretto was distinctly superior to most of those he too uncritically accepted. The early 1850s saw the production of three romantic works that have become the mainstay of opera companies ever since: *Rigoletto*, noteworthy for its greater continuity, the number of its ensembles and its characterisation, *Il Trovatore*, a wildly melodramatic blood-and-thunder whose excesses can be forgotten in the excitement of the music, and the lyrical *La Traviata*, in which a new delicacy of scoring underlines the pathos. After this came *Les vêpres siciliennes* for Paris, in the five-acts-with-ballet "grand opera" tradition favoured there, *Simone Boccanegra*, initially a failure, and the richly-scored *Un ballo in maschera*, which like several other of Verdi's operas fell foul of the censor, obliging the action (originally about the assassination of Gustavus III of Sweden) to be implausibly transferred to Boston, Massachusetts.

Verdi's ardently patriotic feelings had frequently found outlet in his music, and Italian audiences smarting under Austrian rule had been quick to respond to such things as the chorus of exiled Israelites in *Nabucco*, the anti-monarchist sentiments in *Rigoletto* and *Ballo in maschera*,

Above: *The 'hurdy-gurdy' gibe was most unjust by the time of Verdi's* Don Carlos *(1867).*

Left: *Verdi in later life, an acknowledged musical giant.*

and the openly nationalist propaganda of *La battaglia di Legnano*. After the triumphal political upheavals of 1860 Cavour persuaded Verdi to become a deputy in the new parliament, which he did for five years. It was not only on this account that larger intervals occurred between his operas: they were increasing in complexity and sensitivity. *La forza del destino* was written for St Petersburg, the expansive *Don Carlos* for Paris, and *Aida* (a great spectacular work which also contains some of his most lyrical invention, imaginative scoring and colourful harmony) for Cairo.

In 1873 Verdi composed one of his few non-operatic works, the *Requiem* for the writer Manzoni, whom he venerated: though much criticised for its theatricality at first, its intensely dramatic force and sincerity have ensured its place in the repertoire. With the encouragement and collaboration of Boito, a librettist of genius and himself a more than competent composer, *Otello* was produced in 1887, and (when Verdi was 80) *Falstaff*, his only comedy for more than half a century. These two masterpieces represent the peaks of Italian tragic and comic opera, and their subtlety of construction, their matching of invention and technique, reveal how far Verdi had travelled in his artistic journey. His last compositions were the unexpectedly austere *Four sacred pieces* for chorus.

Above: *Verdi's picture, signature and a line from* La Traviata.

AIDA
☐ *Cpte.* Tebaldi, Simionato, Bergonzi, Mill, MacNeill, Corena, Friends of Music Choral Society, VPO/Karajan
SXL2167-9 (12/59) Decca
1313 London
☐ *Cpte.* Caballe, Cossotto, Domingo, Cappuccilli, Ghiaurov, Roni, Royal Opera Chorus, New Philh., Muti
SLS977 (2/75) HMV
SX-3815 Angel

UN BALLO IN MASCHERA
☐ *Cpte.* Arroyo, Cossotto, Grist, Domingo, Cappuccilli, Covent Garden Chorus/New Philh./Muti
SLS984 (12/75) HMV
SX-3762 Angel
☐ *Cpte.* Price, Grist, Beronzi, Verrett, Merrill, RCA Italiana Chorus and Orch./Leinsdorf
SER5710-2 (2/75) RCA
6179 LSC

DON CARLOS
☐ *Cpte.* Caballe, Verrett, Domingo, Milnes, Raimondi, Foiani, Ambrosian Opera Chorus, Covent Garden Orch./Giulini
SLS956 (7/71) HMV
S-3774 Angel

FALSTAFF
☐ *Cpte.* Gobbi, Schwarzkopf, Moffo, Barbieri, Merriman, Alva, Panerai, Chorus/Philh./Karajan
SLS5037 (1/76) HMV
S-3552 Angel

LA FORZA DEL DESTINO
☐ *Cpte.* Arroyo, Casoni, Bergonzi, Cappuccilli, Evans, Raimondi, Ambrosian Opera Chorus, RPO/Gardelli
SLS948 (3/70) HMV
S-3765 Angel
☐ *Cpte.* Price, Cossotto, Domingo, Milnes, Bacquier, Giaiotti, Alldis Ch./LSO/Levine
RL01864 (8/77) RCA*

FOUR SACRED PIECES
☐ Baker, Philh. Chorus and Orch./Giulini
SAN120 (10/63) EMI/HMV Angel

(Un) GIORNO DI REGNO
☐ *Cpte.* Cossotto, Norman, Carreras, Wixell, Sardinero, Ganzarolli, Ambrosian Singers, RPO/Gardelli
6703 055 (9/74) Phonogram*

LUISA MILLER
☐ *Cpte.* Caballe, Pavarotti, Milnes, Reynolds, Giaiotti, van Allen, Celini, London Op. Ch., Nat. PO/Maag
SET608-8 (5/76) Decca
13114 London

MACBETH
☐ *Cpte.* Cappuccilli, Ghiaurov, Verrett, Malagu, Domingo, La Scala/Abbado
2709 062 (10/76) DG*

MESSA DA REQUIEM
☐ Schwarzkopf, Ludwig, Gedda, Ghiaurov, Phil. Chorus and Orch./Giulini
SLS909 (7/64) HMV
S-3649 Angel

☐ Sutherland, Horne, Pavarotti, Talvela, Vienna State Opera Chorus, VPO/Solti
SET374-5 (10/68) Decca
1275 London

OPERATIC CHORUSES:
Il trovatore: Vedi le fosche; Squilli echeggi. **Nabucco:** Gli arredi festivi; Va pensiero. **I Lombardi:** O Signore dal tetto natio. **Aida:** Gloria all Egitto. **La battaglia di Legnano:** Giuriam d'Italia. **Attila:** Prelude, Urli rapine. **Otello:** Fuoco di gioia.
☐ Santa Cecilia Chorus and Orch./Franci
SXL6139 (1/65) Decca
25893 London
Nabucco: Gli arredi festivi; Va pensiero; **Il Trovatore:** Vedi le fosche; **Otello:** Fuoco di gioia; **Ernani:** Si ridesti il leon di oppressa; **I Lombardi:** Gerusalem; O Signore; **Don Carlo:** Spuntato ecco il di.
☐ La Scala Op. Chorus and Orch./Abbado
2530 549 (11/75) DG*

OTELLO
☐ *Cpte.* Tebaldi, Del Monaco, Romanato, Protti, Corena, Vienna State Opera Chorus, Vienna Grosstadtkinderchor, VPO/Karajan
D55D3 (8/77) Decca
1324 London

RIGOLETTO
☐ *Cpte.* Sutherland, Tourangeau, Pavarotti, Milnes, Talvela, Ambrosian Opera Chorus, LSO/Bonynge
SET542-4 (5/73) Decca
13105 London

☐ *Cpte.* Sutherland, Cioni, MacNeill, Santa Cecilia Chorus and Orch./Sanzogno
GOS655-7 (9/75) Grosvenor
1332 London

SIMON BOCCANEGRA
☐ *Cpte.* Cappuccilli, Freni, Ghiaurov, van Dam, Carreras, La Scala/Abbado
2709 017 (11/77) DG*

LA TRAVIATA
☐ *Cpte.* Caballe, Bergonzi, Milnes, RCA Italiana/Pretre
SER5564-6 (2/68) RCA
LSC-6180 RCA
☐ *Cpte.* Cotrubas, Domingo, Milnes, Bavarian State Op./C. Kleiber
2707 103 (11/77) DG*

IL TROVATORE
☐ *Cpte.* Price, Cossotto, Domingo, Milnes, Ambrosian Opera Chorus/New Philh./Mehta
SER5586-8 (7/70) RCA
LSC-6194 RCA

(I) VESPRI SICILIANI
☐ *Cpte.* Milnes, Raimondi, Domingo, Sharpe, van Allen, Collins, Morris, Arroyo, Ewing, Alldis Choir, New Philh./Levine
ARL4 0370 (9/74) RCA*

HEITOR VILLA-LOBOS
(b. Rio de Janeiro 1887; d. there 1959)

The first, and almost the sole, Brazilian composer to achieve international status, Villa-Lobos has with justice been called a cataloguer's nightmare. Of the works that tumbled out of him in wild profusion, many are still in manuscript; others, though published, are unavailable; some are lost and others prove to have been left unfinished; many more were revised, adapted for other instruments, raided to provide material for other works, or merely re-titled. Like the extravagantly luxuriant giant vegetation of his native country, the uninhibited exuberance of his music suggests some force of Nature that defies control. The confusion extends even to the facts of his early life: he certainly started to learn the cello, and then other instruments, when very young at home, but accounts differ about whether, at 11, when his father died, he supported his family by playing in cafes and street bands or whether, after a period of frustrated Bohemianism, he ran away from home. It is established, however, that he undertook extensive trips into various parts of the country, playing and collecting Indian folk music, in which he became passionately interested; and despite somewhat exiguous tuition he gave a concert of his own works in 1915. He had already written an opera, *Izaht*, a set of Indian mestizo dances, and a quantity of instrumental and chamber music; and shortly afterwards he composed the ballet *Uirapurú*, in which the central role is a jungle bird with magical properties, and five programmatic symphonies for large orchestra (No.3 calling for an extra 37 brass instruments!)

Acquaintance with Milhaud ≫, then in Rio, led to Villa-Lobos spending the years 1923-6 in Paris, where he was much influenced by Debussy ≫, Ravel ≫ and Stravinsky ≫, though asserting his own flamboyant personality. During the 1920s he composed a series of 14 *Chôros* (street serenades) for diverse forces ranging from solo guitar (No.1) or piano (No.5) to gargantuan orchestras featuring native percussion instruments: these had the avowed intention of synthesising various types of Brazilian music. A still more ambitious later series was the nine *Bachianas Brasileiras*, which claimed to pay homage to Bach ≫—each movement has a classical and a Brazilian title—without in fact reflecting his style at all: these also were for various combinations (No. 8, the most popular, for soprano and eight cellos). Like all his music, these are full of exotic rhythms and colours, often introducing novel instrumental effects. Sometimes his appellations for his chamber music are Humpty-Dumptyish, as when one quartet proves to be for four instruments plus female chorus, or his Nonet to include a mixed-voice chorus as one of its nine elements. A constant preoccupation with him was his evocation of his country's tropical forests, which found expression particularly in the four orchestral suites drawn from his score to the film *Descobrimento do Brasil*. He exercised a powerful influence on Brazilian musical education and its musical life generally, frequently conducting mammoth choral concerts. His lavish output for piano and his solo guitar music have done much to keep his name alive.

BACHIANAS BRASILEIRAS NO. 3
□ Ortiz, New Philh./Ashkenazy/
  Momoprecoce
  ASD3492 (2/78) EMI/HMV
  S-37439 Angel
GUITAR CONCERTO
□ Bream/LSO/Previn/*Preludes 1-5 etc.*
  SB6852 (2/72) RCA
□ Williams/ECO/Barenboim/*Rodrigo:*
  Concierto de Aranjuez
  76369 (1/75) CBS
  M-33208 Columbia
GUITAR STUDIES NOS. 1-12;
PRELUDES NOS. 1-5
□ Yepes
  2530 140 (3/73) DG
PIANO PIECES
  Prole do bebe 1; Bachianas Brasileiras
  4; Tres Marias; Rudepoema
□ Nelson Freire
  AS6 41299 (9/74) Selecta/Telefunken*

Left: *Heitor Villa-Lobos, the only Brazilian composer to have made any real impact on the international scene.*

ANTONIO VIVALDI
(b. Venice 1678; d. Vienna 1741)

Not so long ago a wit could safely jeer that Vivaldi had written not 450 concertos but the same concerto 450 times; but now that well over a third of that number are in the current record catalogues we can hear for ourselves how great in fact was his variety—and not only of instrumental colour, for he catered for practically all instruments then in use. It is undeniable that he sometimes fell into conventional formulas or produced mechanically-constructed works; but his best have an extrovert vitality—which clearly commended itself to Bach », who transcribed several. He himself was a noted violinist who had been taught by his father, a violinist at St Mark's; he took minor orders, but had scarcely been ordained in 1703 when he was given a dispensation, apparently on health grounds, and began a long association with the Ospedale della Pietà, one of Venice's four music academies for foundling girls, which gained a great reputation for its high standards.

Most of his concertos, which are in three-movement form, with solo episodes alternating with ritornelli, were written for the Pietà. A set of twelve published in 1712, entitled *L'estro armonico* (Harmonic imagination), brought him widespread fame; but today by far his best known are the first four from another set of twelve published in 1725. *The four seasons*, as these are called, vividly illustrate a sequence of descriptive sonnets: also programmatic are some of the flute concertos of his Op. 10. For the Pietà Vivaldi also wrote church music and his oratorio *Juditha triumphans* (remarkable for the scope of its instrumentation); but he was allowed considerable time away from the Ospedale, on condition that he maintained his supply of works for it. He produced over forty operas in various Italian cities and in Munich, sometimes acting as his own impresario (he was still familiarly known as the "red priest", from the red hair which ran in his family), he spent three years in Mantua as musical director to the Margrave of Hesse-Darmstadt, and after 1724 toured very extensively in Europe. In 1735 he returned to Venice, sold much of his property and moved to Vienna, where, however, he died in poverty. Although he is chiefly remembered for his concertos and sonatas, some of his church music that has been revived has proved to be of outstanding quality, such as the *Gloria*, *Stabat Mater* and *Magnificat*.

Above: *Antonio Vivaldi, from an engraving of 1725 by La Cave.*

12 CONCERTI, OP. 4
☐ Cpte. ASMF/Marriner
ZRG800-1 (4/75) Decca Argo
CONCERTOS FOR VIOLIN AND STRINGS
RV277 in E minor—Il favorito; RV271 in E—Il riposo; RV199 in C minor—Il sospetto; RV234 in D—L'inquietudine; RV270 in E—L'amoroso
☐ I Musici
6580 007 (1/73) Phonogram
CONCERTOS FOR VIOLIN AND STRINGS
RV277 in E minor—Il favorito; RV353 in A minor; RV317 in G minor; RV271 in E—L'amoroso
☐ Grumiaux, Dresden Staatskapelle/Negri
6500 690 (2/75) Phonogram
CONCERTOS
RV158 Concerto in A for Strings; RV177 Sinfonia in B minor; RV524 Concerto in B flat for 2 Violins and Strings; RV569 Concerto in F for 3 Violins and Strings; RV151 Concerto in G for Strings; RV531 Concerto in G minor for 2 Cellos and Strings.
☐ Lucerne Festival Strings/Baumgartner
SXL6628 (7/74) Decca
CONCERTOS
RV94 Concerto in D for Recorder, Oboe, Violin, Bassoon and Continuo; RV92 Concerto in D for Recorder, Violin and Cello; RV105 Concerto in G minor for

Recorder, Oboe, Violin, Bassoon and Continuo; RV87 Concerto in C for Recorder, Oboe, 2. Violins and Continuo; RV108 Concerto in A minor for Recorder, 2 Violins and Continuo.
☐ Bruggen, Harnoncourt, Leonhardt, Ens.
AW6 41239 (2/70) Selecta/Telefunken
CONCERTOS
RV500 Oboe Concerto in A minor; RV484 Bassoon Concerto in E minor; RV107 Concerto in G minor for Violin, Flute, Oboe, Bassoon and Continuo; RV157 Concerto in G minor for Strings and Continuo.

☐ VCM/Harnoncourt
AW6 41961 (12/76) Selecta/Telefunken
L'ESTRO ARMONICO, OP. 3
(12 concerti)
☐ ASMF/Marriner
ZRG733-4 (4/73) Decca Argo*
☐ No. 10 only. ASMF/Marriner/*Handel, Telemann, Gabrieli*
SOL276 (3/65) L' Oiseau-Lyre
☐ Nos. 10 and 11 only. Moscow CO/Barshai/*Bartok*
SDD417 (7/74) Decca Ace of Diamonds
STS-15364 London
THE FOUR SEASONS, OP. 8, Nos 1-4
(RV269, 315, 293, 297)
☐ Sillito/Virtuosi of England/Davison
CFP40016 (6/73) Classics for Pleasure
☐ Loveday/ASMF/Marriner
ZRG654 (9/70) Decca Argo*
☐ Michelucci/Musici
6500 017 (12/70) Phonogram*
☐ Szeryng/ECO
6580 002 (7/72) Phonogram
☐ Frasca-Columbier, Kuentz CO/Kuentz
2548 005 (11/75) DG Heliodor
☐ Ferrari/Stuttgart Soloists/Couraud
6530 014 (2/77) Phonogram

GLORIA IN D, RV589
☐ Smith, Staempfli, Schaer, Rossier, Jaccottet, Corboz, Lausanne Ens./Corboz/*Credo; Kyrie*
STU70910 (5/76) RCA/Erato
AGLI1340 RCA
KYRIE, RV587
☐ Smith, Staempfli, Schaer, Rossier, Jaccottet, Corboz, Lausanne Ens./Corboz/*Gloria; Credo*
STU70910 (5/76) RCA/Erato
AGLI-1340 RCA
MAGNIFICAT, RV610
☐ Palmer, Watts, Tear, Roberts, King's College Choir, ASMF/Ledger/*Bach: Magnificat*
ZRG854 (9/77) Decca Argo*
SONATAS FOR RECORDER AND CONTINUO, RV54-9 (IL PASTOR FIDO)
☐ Hans-Martin Linde, Ens.
2533 117 (3/73) DG Archiv Produktion
STABAT MATER, RV621
☐ Bowman, Academy of Ancient Music/Hogwood
DSLO506 (2/77) L'Oiseau-Lyre*

Far left: *Wagner's 1877 London concerts with singers from Bayreuth and a 170-piece orchestra proved disappointing.*

Left: *Luxurious clothes were one of Wagner's weaknesses.*

Below right: *Wagner (seated second left) with his friends at the dress rehearsal in 1865 of Tristan. Von Bülow stands immediately behind his chair.*

RICHARD WAGNER
(b. Leipzig 1813; d. Venice 1883)

To the dismay of moralists in the field of aesthetics, Wagner was both an individual of monstrous egotism, lack of scruples, carnality, ingratitude and dishonesty and at the same time one of the greatest figures in the story of opera, a composer whose influence on others was overwhelming and who was to change the whole course of music. Brought up in a theatrical atmosphere (his stepfather was an actor who had been friendly with Weber »), he studied music desultorily, composed some youthful orchestral and piano pieces (influenced by Beethoven »), and after a year as a répétiteur in Würzburg secured conductor's posts successively in Magdeburg (where he married an actress), Könisberg and Riga. He had already tried his hand at two early operas, and now began work on *Rienzi*, written in the French "grand opera" style; but efforts to get it produced in Paris (whither he had fled in 1839 to escape his creditors) proved vain, even despite the friendly backing of Meyerbeer, then the most popular musician there; and Wagner spent three years scraping a living by journalism and musical hackwork. Then, borrowing money from all sides as usual, he went to Dresden for the triumphal première of his *Rienzi*, which was followed a year later by *The flying Dutchman*, as a result of which he was offered the post of music director in Dresden, which he carried out efficiently if not tactfully or without a lot of friction. An interest in mediaeval legends led to *Tannhäuser* (1845) and the Weber-influenced *Lohengrin*—which, since Wagner had been heavily involved in the abortive 1848 revolution and forced to flee to Switzerland, was produced (thanks to Liszt ») only in 1850, in Weimar.

In Switzerland he worked out his personal theories of music drama (following in Gluck's » steps in attempting to recapture opera's first ideals) and embarked on the planning of a monumentally ambitious setting of *The Nibelung's ring*: by 1852 he had written the libretti of what had initially been a single drama, *Siegfried's death*, but had expanded into three plus a further one preliminary to the action proper. Having completed the composition of the first two, he interrupted the sequence to write *Tristan and Isolde*—inspired by the latest of his endless amours, the wife of a generous benefactor named Wesendonk. He received an amnesty from arrest in Germany and returned to Dresden, but had little success with performances of his works (though by now he had a host of ardent admirers), and had piled up huge debts.

At this point a fairy godfather appeared in the person of the young King Ludwig II of Bavaria, who invited him to Munich, where *Tristan* was staged in 1865, made much of him and settled his finances. However, Wagner's imprudent meddling in politics, his extravagance and the scandal caused by his seduction of Liszt's daughter Cosima (wife of his disciple von Bülow) forced him once more to go into exile in Switzerland. There he wrote his only comedy, the humane and lyrical *Mastersingers of Nuremberg*, which, together with the the first half of the *Ring* cycle, was given in Munich. But Wagner's visionary ambition was to have his own opera-house where his ideal of a "union of the arts" (music, drama, verse and staging) could be realised; and incredibly enough, this colossal enterprise was brought to fruition by the building of the festival theatre in Bayreuth, which

opened in 1876 with the complete *Ring*, and where his last stage work, the erotico-religious *Parsifal*, was produced six years later.

Wagner made three great contributions to opera. The chief was the new kind of continuity in all his works after *Lohengrin*, which rested on a symphonic conception of drama in which the orchestra was a principal exponent and in which characters and dramatic concepts were represented by "leading motives" woven into the texture. In Wagner's hands the orchestra, and the art of orchestration, were hugely developed—even to the extent of bringing into existence special "Wagner tubas". There were also the importance he attached to dramatic action and motivation (which in the *Ring* have been construed with various different kinds of symbolism), and, in *Tristan*, the unprecedented harmonic audacity which in the course of the next half-century was to lead to the breakdown of tonality.

Above: *Wagner at the time of his Bayreuth triumphs.*

Right: *Wagner's manuscript of the* Mastersingers *Prelude.*

A FAUST OVERTURE
☐ LPO/Boult/*Concert of Wagner Overtures*
ASD3071 (4/75) EMI/HMV
DER FLIEGENDE HOLLANDER
☐ *Cpte.* Uhde, Varnay, Weber, Bayreuth Fest./Keilberth
D97D3 (7/78) Decca
63519 Richmond
☐ *Cpte.* Bailey, Martin, Talvela/Chicago SO & Ch./Solti
D24D3 (5/77) Decca
13119 London
LOHENGRIN
☐ *Cpte.* Thomas, Grummer, Ludwig, Fischer-Dieskau, Frick/Vienna St. Op. Ch./VPO/Kempe
SLS5071 (12/76) HMV
S-3641 Angel
DIE MEISTERSINGER
☐ *Cpte.* Adam, Ridderbusch, Evans, Buchner, Kollo, Donath, Hesse, Moll, Dresden St. Op. Chorus, Dresden State Orch./Karajan
SLS957 (10/71) HMV
S-3776 Angel
☐ *Cpte.* Bailey, Bode, Kollo, Weikl, Hamari, Moll, Dallapozza/Vienna St. Op. Ch./VPO/Solti
D13D5 (9/76) Decca
1512 London
☐ *Cpte.* Fischer-Dieskau, Lagger, Hermann, Doningo, Ligendza, Ludwig/Berlin Op. & Orch./Jochum
2740 149 (12/76) DG
2713 011 DG
ORCHESTRAL EXCERPTS
Der fliegende Hollander: Overture; **Lohengrin:** Act 1, Prelude; **Rienzi:** Overture; **Tannhauser:** Overture
☐ Philharmonia/Klemperer
ASD2695 (9/71) EMI/HMV
Gotterdammerung: Funeral Music; **Lohengrin:** Act 3, Prelude; **Die Meistersinger:** Act 1, Prelude; Act 3, Dance of the Apprentices; **Tristan and Isolde:** Prelude and Liebestod

☐ Philharmonia/Klemperer
ASD2696 (9/71) EMI/HMV
Das Rheingold: Entry of the Gods.
Die Walküre—Ride of the Valkyries.
Siegfried: Forest Murmurs.
Gotterdammerung: Siegfried's Rhine Journey. **Parsifal:** Prelude to Act 1.
Tannhauser: Prelude to Act 3.
☐ Philharmonia/Klemperer
ASD2697 (9/71) EMI/HMV
The above three records are collected on **SLS5075** (2/77) HMV
Die Meistersinger: Prelude, Act 1; **Tristan and Isolde:** Prelude; **Tannhauser:** Overture; **Lohengrin:** Preludes, Acts 1 and 3
☐ New Philh./Boult
ASD2812 (7/72) EMI/HMV
S-36871 Angel
Die Meistersinger: Act 1, Prelude; **Tristan and Isolde:** Prelude and Liebestod; **Parsifal:** Act 1, Prelude; **Lohengrin:** Act 1, Prelude; Act 3 Prelude
☐ Concertgebouw/Haitink
6500 932 (11/75) Phonogram
Tannhauser: Overture and Venusberg Music; **Lohengrin:** Prelude to Act 1; **Tristan and Isolde:** Prelude and Liebestod

☐ BPO/Karajan
ASD3130 (12/75) EMI/HMV
Der fliegende Hollander: Overture; **Lohengrin:** Prelude to Act 3; **Die Meistersinger:** Overture; **Parsifal:** Preludes to Acts 1 and 3
☐ BPO/Karajan
ASD3160 (3/76) EMI/HMV
S-37098 Angel
PARSIFAL
☐ *Cpte.* Ludwig, Kollo, Hotter, Frick, Keleman, Fischer-Dieskau, Vienna Boys' Choir, Vienna State Opera Chorus, VPO/Solti
SET550-4 (4/73) Decca
1510 London
DAS RHEINGOLD
☐ *Cpte.* London, Flagstad, Neidlinger, Svanholm, soloists, VPO/Solti
SET382-4 (9/68) Decca
1309 London
☐ *Cpte. (in English)* Bailey, Pring, Hammond-Stroud, Belcourt/ENO/Goodall
SLS5032 (11/75) HMV
SIEGFRIED
☐ *Cpte.* Windgassen, Hotter, Nilsson, VPO/Solti
SET242-6 (4/63) Decca
1508 London

DIE WALKURE
☐ *Cpte.* Nilsson, Brouwenstein, Gorr, Vickers, London, Ward, LSO/Leinsdorf
7BB125-9 Decca
1511 London
☐ *Cpte. (in English)*. Remedios, Hunter, Howard, Bailey, Grant/ENO/Goodall
SLS5063 (9/76) HMV
SX-3826 Angel
GOTTERDAMMERUNG
☐ *Cpte.* Nilsson, Windgassen, Frick, Watson, Ludwig, Fischer-Dieskau, Neidlinger, Vienna Op./VPO/Solti
SET292-7 (5/65) Decca
1604 London
☐ *Exc.* Hunter, Remedios, LPO/Mackerras
CFP40008 (8/72) Classics for Pleasure
☐ *Act 3 Scenes 2 and 3 (in English)*. Hunter, Remedios, Bailey, Grant, Sadler's Wells Chorus and Orch./Goodall
UNS245-6 (7/73) Transatlantic/Unicorn
SIEGFRIED IDYLL
☐ ASMF/Marriner/*Strauss Metamorphosen*
ZRG604 (9/69) Decca Argo*
TANNHAUSER
☐ *Cpte.* Dernesch, Ludwig, Kollo, Sotin, Braun, Bailey, Vienna St. Op. Chorus, VPO/Solti
SET506-9 (12/71) Decca
TRISTAN AND ISOLDE
☐ *Cpte.* Nilsson, Windgassen, Talvela, Waechter/Bayreuth/Bohm
2713 001 (1/66) DG*
☐ Nilsson/Resnik/Uhl, Krause, van Mill, Vienna Singverein/VPO/Solti
D41D5 (8/77) Decca
1502 London
WESENDONK LIEDER
☐ Baker/LPO/Boult/*Brahms; R. Strauss*
ASD3260 (9/76) EMI/HMV
S-37199 Angel

SIR ADRIAN CONDUCTS WAGNER
LOHENGRIN-Preludes to Acts 1 & 3
DIE MEISTERSINGER VON NÜRNBERG-Overture and Prelude, Act 3
TRISTAN UND ISOLDE-Prelude, Act 1
TANNHÄUSER Overture
New Philharmonia Orchestra
Sir Adrian Boult

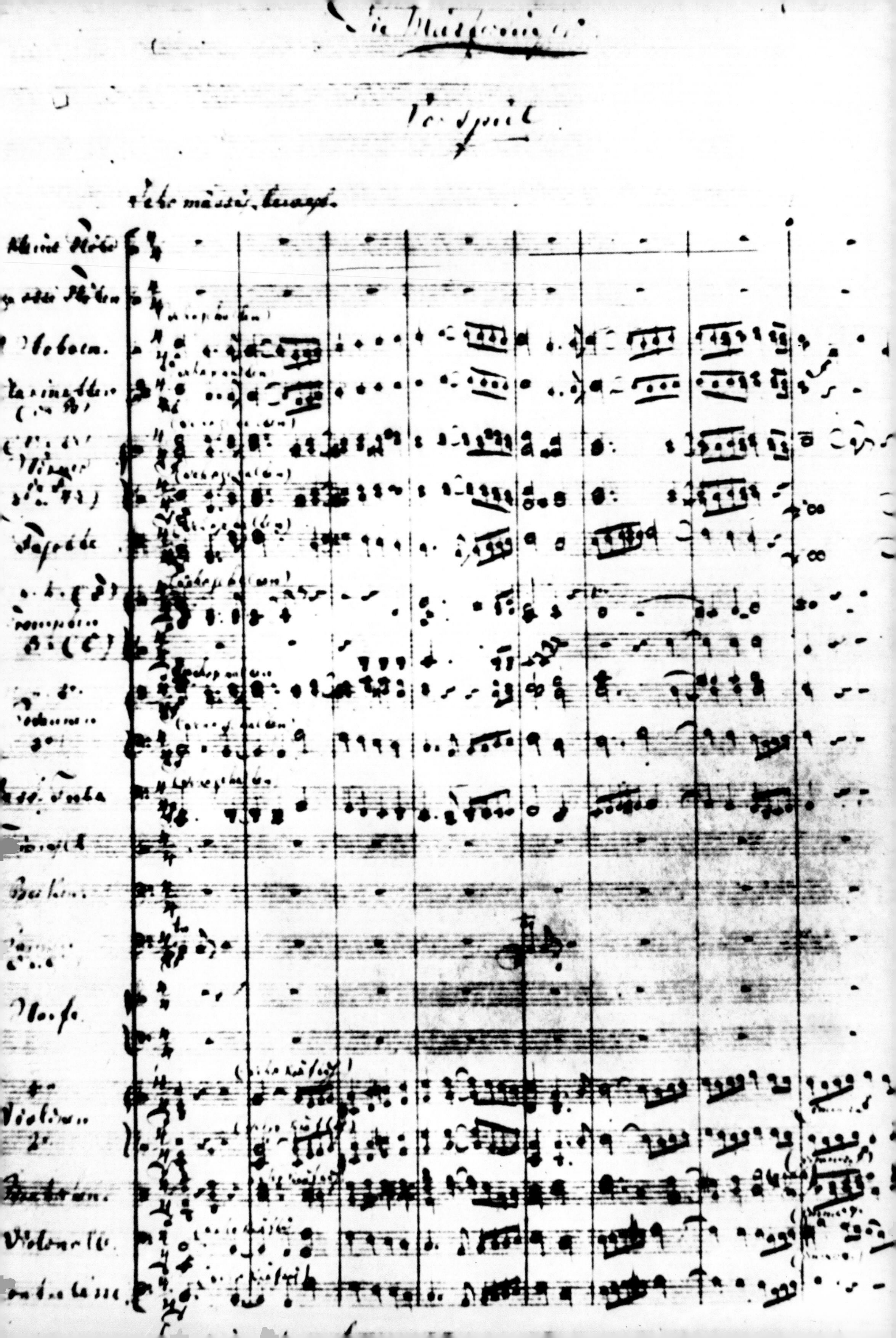
Vorspiel

WILLIAM WALTON
(b. Oldham 1902; d. Ischia 1983)

Though he was a chorister at Christ Church Cathedral, Oxford, whence he entered the university at the exceptionally early age of 16, Walton was largely self-taught as a composer. He first attracted notice when a youthful string quartet (later withdrawn) was played at the first International Society for Contemporary Music festival in 1923; but chamber music was of little significance in his output, save for *Façade* the same year, a coruscatingly witty and satiric setting for reciter and six players of surrealist poems by Edith Sitwell (with whose family he lived for a time after Oxford)—even this is more familiar in a later arrangement for orchestra alone. Its ebullience represented one of the constant threads in Walton's make-up, from the breezy bustle of the 1925 overture *Portsmouth Point* to the *Partita* thirty years later and the one-act comic opera *The Bear* (1967). It was often coloured by a nervous tension that manifested itself in irregular twitching rhythms, as in the scherzo of his First Symphony (uniquely marked *con malizia*); in his large-scale oratorio *Belshazzar's feast*, a work that upset some cathedral authorities by its bloodthirsty exultation, it was transmuted into a vividly barbaric splendour.

Alongside this extrovert and sardonic humour, and in complete contrast, ran a vein of nostalgic romanticism, first apparent in 1929 in the bitter-sweet Viola Concerto (not merely, by common consent, the finest for the instrument but Walton's most intimately revealing composition). It was also exemplified in the opera *Troilus and Cressida*, the Cello Concerto and the *Variations on a theme of Hindemith* (», a composer he always admired, and who was the soloist in the first performance of his Viola Concerto); the Violin Concerto combined lyrical yearning with dazzling technical display, having been written for Heifetz.

A third facet of Walton's music was found in his "occasional" manner: in his works for two coronations—the marches *Crown imperial* and *Orb and sceptre*, and to some extent in the *Te Deum*—he wore the mantle of Elgar ». Mention should be made of his extremely skilful incidental music, particularly for films, notably *Henry V* and *Hamlet*. Apart from his "applied" music he was generally a slow writer because of his acutely self-critical sense (the First Symphony had originally to be performed without its finale, about which he was unhappy); and since about the time of his knighthood, in 1951, he showed little interest in breaking new ground.

BELSHAZZAR'S FEAST
- ☐ Shirley-Quirk, LSO and Chorus/ Previn/*Improvisations on an Impromptu of Benjamin Britten*
  SAN324 (11/72) EMI/HMV
  S-36861 Angel
- ☐ Rippon, Halle Choir & Orch./Loughran
  CFP40063 (12/74) Classics for Pleasure
- ☐ Bell, Philh. & Chorus/*Partita*
  SXLP30236 (3/77) EMI/HMV
  Concert Classics
  S-35681 Angel

CELLO CONCERTO
- ☐ Tortelier, Bournemouth SO/Berglund/ *Shostakovich: Cello Concerto*
  ASD2924 (12/73) EMI/HMV
FACADE—AN ENTERTAINMENT
- ☐ Laine, Ross/Ens./Dankworth
  6382 037 (2/68) Phonogram
- ☐ Orch. Suites. Covent Garden Orch./ Fistoulari/*Lecocq: Mam'zelle Angot*
  ECS586 (9/71) Decca Eclipse
  S-15191 Angel
- ☐ Orch. Suites. CBSO/Fremaux/*Wise virgins*
  ASD3317 (3/77) EMI/HMV
SINFONIA CONCERTANTE FOR ORCHESTRA WITH PIANO
- ☐ Katin, LSO/Walton/*Scapino; The Quest; Capriccio*
  SRCS49 (6/71) Lyrita
SONATA FOR STRINGS
- ☐ ASMF/Marriner/*Prokofiev: Visions*
  ZRG711 (10/73) Decca Argo★
SPITFIRE PRELUDE AND FUGUE; CROWN IMPERIAL: ORB AND SCEPTRE; SCAPINO; JOHANNESBURG FESTIVAL; CAPRICCIO BURLESCO
- ☐ Royal Liverpool PO/Groves
  TWO272 (10/68) EMI/Studio 2
SYMPHONY NO. 1 IN B FLAT MINOR
- ☐ LSO/Previn
  LSB4100 (10/73) RCA
SYMPHONY NO. 2
- ☐ LSO/Previn/*Portsmouth Point Ov.; Scapino Ov.; Lambert: Rio Grande*
  ASD2990 (5/74) EMI/HMV
VIOLIN CONCERTO
- ☐ Kyung Wha-Chung/LSO/Previn/ *Stravinsky*
  SXL6601 (5/73) Decca
  6819 London

Right: *A double image of Sir William Walton, live and sculptured. A study taken at the time of the revival of* Troilus and Cressida.

PETER WARLOCK
pseudonym of PHILIP HESELTINE
(b. London 1894; d. there 1930)

Basically of a sensitive, solitary and melancholy nature, Heseltine, who admired and was encouraged by Delius » while he was still a schoolboy at Eton, adopted a different *persona* (along with a new name) around 1916, when under the influence of Bernard van Dieren he began composing in earnest: the dichotomy between his *alter ego*, a swaggering, hard-drinking Bohemian, and his real self is conspicuous in his music and may have led to his suicide after he had been writing for a mere fourteen years. A musicologist and critic of no mean distinction—he edited a great deal of Elizabethan and Jacobean music, was editor of a hard-hitting magazine, *The Sackbut*, for a time, and wrote books on Delius, The English Ayre, and Gesualdo—he composed only spasmodically, the bulk of his output consisting of about 100 songs. These, showing great gifts in their flexible declamation, melodic line and harmonic elaboration, fall into a number of diverse categories: pseudo-Elizabethan, poetic (*Sleep, The contented lover*), light-hearted (*Yarmouth fair*), rollicking (*Captain Stratton's fancy, Rutterkin*) or dark in mood (*The frostbound wood, The Fox*). Apart from these and some short choral pieces, he wrote for orchestra a *Serenade* for Delius's sixtieth birthday and a *Capriol* suite (his most popular work) largely based on a sixteenth-century dancing-master's book. Perhaps his masterpiece, though seldom performed, is the Yeats song-cycle *The Curlew* for tenor, flute, cor anglais and string quartet, whose desolate beauty suggests the loneliness of spirit that was to become intolerable to him.

CARL MARIA VON WEBER
(b. Eutin, nr. Lübeck, 1786; d. London 1826)

Mendelssohn » is credited with having "brought fairyland into the orchestra", but his *Midsummer night's dream* overture dates from the same year as Weber's *Oberon*, which also achieved something of the kind. It was his last opera, written for London, and so stands somewhat apart from his previous stage works, which have earned him the title of founder of German romantic opera (this despite the earlier *Faust* by his contemporary and friend Spohr », the première of which he conducted). He had opera in his blood, for he was the son of a travelling theatre director (the uncle of Mozart's » wife); and because of this unsettled life his musical education was sporadic, though for a short time he was taught by Haydn's » brother Michael. However, he became an excellent pianist and started composing at a very early age. An opera he wrote at 13 was re-worked a decade later as *Silvana*, at 16 he produced his second opera, *Peter Schmoll*, and at only 17, having meantime studied seriously in Vienna, was appointed conductor in Breslau, where his vigorous talent for theatre organisation was somewhat hindered by his youthful tactlessness.

He then entered the service of the Duke of Württemberg (during which time he composed his two symphonies), but the establishment had soon to be disbanded, Weber finding employment as secretary to the Duke's brother, a rake and spendthrift in whose company he fell into dissolute ways. Becoming involved in some shady financial dealings, he was banished by the king, and eked out a living in Darmstadt as a critic and writer and by giving concerts. It was then that he wrote his amusing

CAPRIOL SUITE FOR STRINGS
☐ Bournemouth Sinfonietta/Hurst/ *Elgar; Holst; Ireland*
  RL25071 (9/77) RCA
THE CURLEW—SONG CYCLE
☐ Partridge, Music Group of London/ *Vaughan Williams: Vocal works*
  HQS1325 (5/74) EMI/HMV
PIANO AND VOCAL WORKS
  Capriol Suite—excs; Piggesnie; Hey

troly loly; Fill the cup; In an arbour green; Sweet content; Peter Warlock's fancy; I asked a thief; Gillian of Berry; My ghostly fader; Away to Twivver; Maltworms/*arrangements various and readings*
☐ I. Partridge, J. Partridge, Taylor, Gray (spkr.)
  SHE525 (3/76) Pavilion/Pearl

ABU HASSAN
☐ *Cpte.* Gohler, Schreier, Hallstein, Adam, Dresden Staatskapelle/Rogner
  LRL1 5125 (8/76)
ANDANTE AND HUNGARIAN RONDO FOR VIOLA AND ORCHESTRA IN C MINOR J47
☐ Zukerman/ECO/*Stamitz; Casadesus; Telemann*
  76490 (5/76) CBS

CLARINET CONCERTO NO. 1 IN F MINOR, J114
☐ De Peyer, New Philh./Fruhbeck/ *Concertino; Rossini: Intro. and Vars.*
  ASD2455 (5/69) EMI/HMV
  S-36589 Angel
☐ Leister/BPO/Kubelik/*Invitation; Konzertstuck*
  2538 087 (7/72) DG/Privilege
CLARINET QUINTET
☐ de Peyer/Melos Ensemble/*Mozart*
  HQS1395 (9/77) EMI/HMV

one-act *Singspiel* with dialogue, *Abu Hassan*, and, for a virtuoso with whom he toured extensively, various clarinet works (a quintet and three concertos) which show an affection for, and a complete understanding of, the instrument.

A lucky break came in 1813, when be became conductor of the German theatre in Prague, where he threw himself with great thoroughness into every detail of operatic presentation: three years later he was appointed director of the court opera in Dresden, where in place of the Italian style which had hitherto held sway he established a strong German tradition (which was to pave the way for Wagner » and Strauss »), though none of his new operas was produced there. With *Der Freischütz* in 1821 he scored a major triumph. This *Singspiel*, which combines the naively sentimental and the supernatural elements of German country folklore, makes much of its effect by its evocative orchestral colouring: its Wolf's Glen scene is a landmark in operatic atmosphere.

There is also a "Gothic" element in Weber's next opera, *Euryanthe* (the forerunner of Wagner's *Lohengrin*): despite its melodic grace this was less successful because of its weak libretto, which (like the programmatic *Konzertstück* for piano and orchestra written for himself to play) is set against a background of chivalry.

A confused libretto also flaws the poetic and picturesque *Oberon*, which nevertheless enjoyed a triumph at its first performances in 1826; but two months later Weber, never robust in health, died in London of consumption.

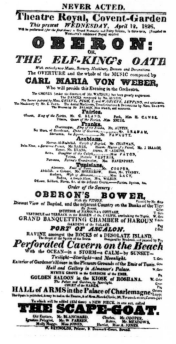

Above: *Weber just before his death in 1826, painted in London by John Cawse.*
Right: *Covent Garden playbill for the première of* Oberon, *directed by the composer.*

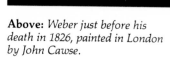

OBERON
☐ *Cpte.* Grobe, Nilsson, Domingo, Prey, Hamari, Bavarian RSO and Ch./Kubelik
2726 052 (1/76)
OVERTURES
Der Freischutz; Preciosa; The Ruler of the Spirits; Oberon; Euryanthe; Abu Hassan; Jubel
☐ SRO/Ansermet
ECS645 (7/72) Decca Eclipse
STS-15056 London
Oberon; Abu Hassan; Der Freischutz; Euryanthe; Preciosa; Jubel
☐ Bavarian RSO/Kubelik
2535 136 (3/76) DG Privilege
Der Frieschutz; Ruler of the Spirits; Oberon; Euryanthe; Abu Hassan; Peter Schmoll
☐ BPO/Karajan
2530 315 (5/73) DG*
SONGS
The four temperaments—Song cycle, Op. 46; Meine Lieder, meine Sange; Klage; Der kleine Fritz; Was zieht zu deinem Zauberkreise; Ich sah ein Roschen er An sie; Wiedersehn; Es sturmt; Unbefangenheit; Minnelied; Reigen; Sind es Schmerzen; Meine Farben; Uber die Berge; Die gefangenen Sanger; Die freien Sanger; Die Zeit; Das Veilchen im thale; Mein Schatzerl ist

EURYANTHE
☐ *Cpte.* Norman, Hunter, Gedda, Krause, Vogel, Krahmer, Neukirch, Dresden Staatskapelle/Janowski
SLS983 (10/75) HMV
S-3764 Angel
DER FREISCHUTZ
☐ *Cpte.* Janowitz, Mathis, Adam, Schreier, Leipzig Radio Choir, Dresden Staatskapelle/Carlos Kleiber
2720 071 (11/73) DG
2709 046 DG

INVITATION TO THE DANCE—RONDO BRILLIANT IN D FLAT, J260
☐ BPO/Karajan/*Berlioz; Liszt; Smetana; Dvorak*
2530 244 (10/72) DG*
KONZERTSTUCK IN F MINOR FOR PIANO AND ORCHESTRA, J282
☐ Gulda, VPO/Andreae/*Bsn. conc.; Clar. concs. 1 and 2*
ECS807 (12/77) Decca Eclipse

hubsch; Ich denke dein; Elfenlied
☐ M. Hill, C. Hogwood (fortepiano)
DSL0523 (1/77) L'Oiseau-Lyre
SYMPHONIES NOS. 1 AND 2
☐ LSO/Schonzeler
LRL1 5106 (4/76) RCA
TRIO IN G MINOR FOR FLUTE, CELLO AND PIANO, J259
☐ Melos Ens./*Beethoven: Serenade*
SOL284 (12/65) L'Oiseau-Lyre
☐ Musica Viva Trio/*Dusík: Trio*
TV34329S (6/73) Decca Turnabout

KURT WEILL
(b. Dessau 1900; d. New York 1950)

The recent popularity of *Mack the knife*, though in one way it would have gratified Weill, would also have saddened him, since the socio-political bitterness underlying it and most of his works written in Europe was largely overlooked. He had grown up during the First World War, studying with Humperdinck », and, after a spell as an opera répétiteur, with Busoni », and his first compositions were in the turgid expressionist style then current in Berlin—the First Symphony, which is headed by a revolutionary slogan, and the opera *The Protagonist* (which, like Hindemith's » *Cardillac* produced in the same theatre eight months later, includes an important scene in mime). With the same librettist, Georg Kaiser, he wrote the topical black comedy *The Tsar has his photograph taken*, before hitting the jackpot in 1928 with *Die Dreigroschenoper* (The Threepenny opera), which enjoyed a sensational success. For this updated version of the eighteenth-century *Beggar's opera*, which marked the start of Weill's collaboration with Brecht, he adopted a *Singspiel* style with dialogue and expressed the work's savage social criticism in a cynical "wrong-note" jazz idiom (scored for jazz band) that, like Georg Grosz's drawings, perfectly caught the sour smell of disillusion, defeat and corruption in post-war Germany.

This style was further developed two years later in *Mahagonny*, another acid social satire by Brecht, with whom Weill also worked on *Happy end* and the cantata *The Lindbergh flight*. The Nazis, infuriated by the success of this Jewish composer's subversive works, had declared his music "decadent"; and after producing *Die Bürgschaft* (The Surety) in 1932 he was forced to flee the country. In Paris he wrote the sung ballet *Seven deadly sins* and his Second Symphony, whose Haydnesque clarity and economy stand in the greatest contrast to his First; then, after a brief stay in London, he settled in the USA in 1935. There the musical climate offered him no opportunity for the kind of works he had hitherto written, and he turned to "musicals" (of which *Lady in the dark* was the most successful), though in his last three years he aimed a little higher with the "Broadway opera" *Street scene*, the folk opera (for college students) *Down in the valley* and the musical drama *Lost in the stars*. The recordings by his widow, Lotte Lenya, while preserving the period style, are not always the most faithful interpretations of what he wrote.

BERLINER REQUIEM
☐ Langridge, Luxon, Rippon, London Sinfonietta/Atherton/*Choral and Orch. works*
2740 153 (11/76) DG
KLEINE DREIGROSCHENMUSIK FOR WIND ORCHESTRA
☐ Philh./Klemperer/*J. Strauss II; Klemperer*
SXLP30226 (1/77) EMI/HMV Concert Classics
☐ London Sinfonietta/Atherton/*Mahagonny Songspiel*
2530 897 (2/78) DG
2709 064 DG
MAHAGONNY SONGSPIEL
☐ Dickinson, Thomas, Langridge, Partridge, Luxon, Rippon, London Sinfonietta/Atherton/*Kleine Dreigroschen*
2530 897 (2/78) DG
2709 064 DG
THE THREEPENNY OPERA
☐ *Cpte. in German.* Lenya and soloists/ Berlin RO/Bruckner-Ruggeberg/

Weill: Theatre Songs
78279 (4/75) CBS

Above & above right: *Weill, whose black comedies and bitter social satires were anathema to the Nazis.*

HENRYK WIENIAWSKI
(b. Lublin 1835; d. Moscow 1880)

Violin virtuosi who write for their instrument take a natural delight in exploiting its possibilities; but the results are sometimes more notable as pyrotechnics than as music. An honourable exception was Wieniawski, whose melodic sense and sound musicianship ensured that his compositions, though certainly designed to provide opportunities for his own dazzling gifts, rarely fall into vulgar exhibitionism. His Second Concerto (his most frequently played work) and *Légende* in particular bear witness to his romantic warmth and poetic refinement.

He was indeed one of the greatest virtuosi of the last century, famous for his phenomenal technique and beauty of tone. Taking up the violin at a very early age, he made such extraordinary progress in Poland that his teacher (who also taught Joachim) advised that he should be taken to Paris when he was only eight. He was immediately accepted for the Conservatoire and completed his course there three years later, carrying off the *premier prix* and also being awarded a Guarnerius violin. At 13 he made his first extensive tour, and then made a name for himself throughout Europe with his younger brother as accompanist. At the age of 25 he was appointed solo violinist to the Tsar, a post he held for twelve years, during which time he taught in St Petersburg and also continued his public concert career. He toured the USA with Anton Rubinstein (Tchaikovsky's » teacher)— though it is related that after a disagreement over the respective size of their names on a poster they gave 70 concerts together without speaking—and in 1874 went to the Brussels Conservatoire as successor to another great virtuoso, Vieuxtemps, who had showered praises on him a quarter of a century earlier. His spectacular career was cut short by heart disease.

LEGENDE, OP. 17
☐ Grumiaux, New Philh./De Waart/
*Romance; Beethoven; Berlioz;
Tchaikovsky*
6580 047 (11/71) Phonogram*
SCHERZO-TARANTELLE, OP. 16
☐ Dicterow, Los Angeles PO/Mehta/
*Polonaise; Concerti by Haydn,
Vivaldi and Weber*
SXL6737 (2/76) Decca
VIOLIN CONCERTO NO. 1 IN F MINOR
VIOLIN CONCERTO NO. 2 IN D MINOR
☐ Perlman/LPO/Ozawa
ASD2870 (5/73) EMI/HMV
S-36903 Angel

Left: *An Amsterdam cartoonist's humorous reaction to Wieniawski's spectacular playing. Sparks fly from his bow and the animal kingdom is set capering.*

Below: *A more sober view of the Polish violinist at the period of his appointment to the Russian court.*

HUGO WOLF

(b. Windischgraz 1860; d. Vienna 1903)

If ever a composer was marked out to be one of Nature's losers, it was Wolf, whose genius seemed to be star-crossed. An unsatisfactory and difficult pupil at three schools and at the Vienna Conservatory, from which he was expelled, he led an impoverished existence in Vienna as a teacher (for which he was temperamentally unfitted), drinking in the music and literature around him, and subsisting only through the help of musical friends. Nobody showed interest in his compositions—in fact, a snub administered by Brahms » probably engendered Wolf's violent hatred of his music, quite apart from the fact that he was already an idolator of Wagner »—and though he secured a job as an assistant conductor in Salzburg, within two months he lost it because of his quarrelsome nature. Some encouraging words from Liszt » led him to write a symphonic poem, *Penthesilea*, which was, rather unfairly, laughed to scorn by the Vienna Philharmonic at a trial run-through. This humili-ation—like an even more brusque dismissal of his string

quartet—undoubtedly sprang in part from the hostility Wolf had aroused as a critic for the *Wiener Salonblatt*, in which he had extolled Wagner and lashed Brahms and his followers with vitriolic abuse.

But suddenly from about 1876 he was gripped with wild urges to compose. After the mercurial and high-spirited *Italian serenade* for string quartet, his only instrumental work to have established itself, he plunged into song-writing with a superhuman intensity, composing 43 settings of poems by Mörike within three months. Even he was taken aback by the incandescent heat of an inspiration which drove him to write two, or even three, masterly *lieder* in a single day. In similar bursts of creative frenzy he dashed off settings of Eichendorff and Goethe poems and the collection known as the *Spanish songbook*; and these at last began to attract attention. There were despairing intervals of exhaustion and barreness, but then another ecstasy would possess him: the *Italian songbook* was brought out in two instalments

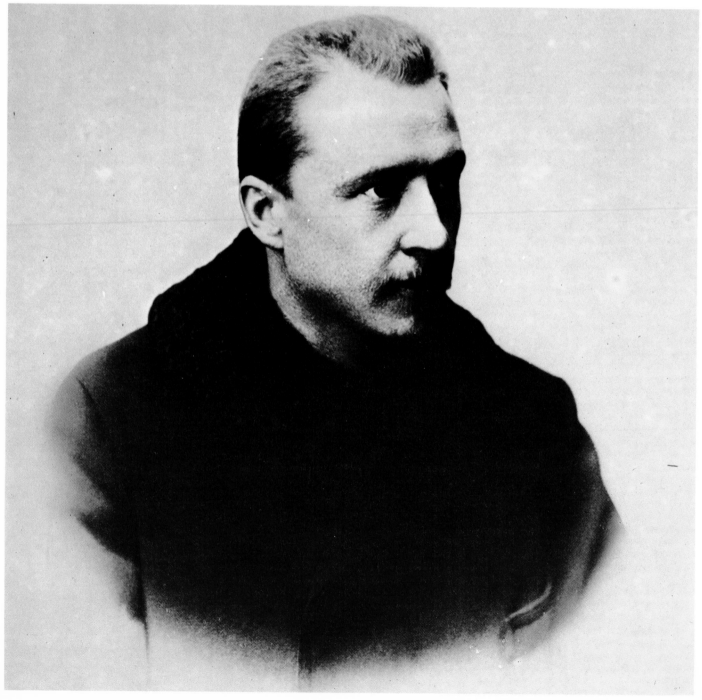

(the 24 songs of the second half taking him 36 days). In 1897, Mahler's » elimination from the Vienna Opera's production schedule of his only completed opera *The Corregidor* (which because of its static nature had been coolly received at its première the previous year) suddenly turned his brain. He was taken to a mental home, but after his release he attempted suicide and was removed to an asylum, where he died insane four years later.

Wolf's reputation rests on his nearly 300 *lieder*, which represent the peak of that art form. His evocative and often technically brilliant piano parts—"accompaniments" would be an inadequate term—frequently bear the main weight of the musical thought (as Wagner's orchestra does), with the voice adding a melodic obbligato, as it were. Without having Schubert's » uncomplicated melodic gift, his work shows the utmost sensitivity to verbal nuance, a remarkable sense of mood and character, and more harmonic subtlety than had ever been known in the sphere of song.

ITALIAN SERENADE
☐ Stuttgart CO/Munchinger/*Suk: Serenade; Strauss: Capriccio*
SXL6533 (2/72) Decca
ITALIAN SONGBOOK
☐ *Cpte*. Mathis, Schreier, Engel
2707 096 (8/77) DG
LIEDER RECITAL
Der Harfenspieler 1-3; Spottlied; Der Sanger; Der Rattenfanger; Ritter Kurts Brautfahrt; Gutmann und Gutweib; Cophtisches Lied 1 and 2; Frech Und Froh 1 and 2; Beherzigung 1 and 2; Prometheus, Ganymed; Grenzen der Menschheit; Epiphanias; St Nepomuks Vorabend; Genialisch Treiben; Der Schafer; Der neue Amadis; Blumengruss; Gleich und gleich; Fruhling ubers Jahr; Anakreons Grab; Dank des Paria; Koniglich Gebet; Phanomen; Erschaffen und Beleben; Ob der Koran von Ewigkeit sei; Trunken mussen wir alle sein; Solang man nuchtern ist; Was in der Schenke waren heute; Nichte Gelegenheit macht Diebe; Dies zu deuten bin erbotig, Hatt ich irgend wohl Bedenken; Komm Liebchen, komm; Wie sollt ich heiter bleiben; Wenn ich dein gedenke; Locken, haltet mich defangen; Wanderers Nachtlied; Madchen mit dem roten Mundchen; Du bist wie eine Blume; Wo wird einst; Wenn ich in deine Augen Seh; Spatherbstnebel; Mit schwarzen Segein; Wie des Mondes Abbild zittert; Frage nicht; Nerbst; Abendilder; Herbstenschluss.
☐ Fischer-Dieskau, Barenboim
2740 162 (8/77) DG
MOERIKE LIEDER
☐ Luxon/Willison
3BBA 1008-10 (5/74)
☐ Fischer-Dieskau/Barenboim
2709 053 DG

Left: *Hugo Wolf's frenzies of creativity produced superb songs, but left him exhausted.*

ERMANNO WOLF-FERRARI
(b. Venice 1876; d. there 1948)

Had Wolf-Ferrari followed in the footsteps of his father, a distinguished German painter, the world would have been the poorer without the neat skilfully written, attractive light comedies he composed—though with only occasional exceptions it shows little urge to know much more than the liltingly tuneful intermezzos which were a feature of his operas. He had in fact been sent to Rome to study art, but his response to music was so passionate that in his middle teens he was allowed to change course and go to Munich to acquire a musical education. Returning to Venice, he wrote an oratorio which was well enough received for him to produce an opera, which however fell flat until it was given in Germany, in translation.

It was perhaps this which was responsible for the curious situation that, though five of his operas were based on plays by Goldoni (a Venetian, like himself) and all twelve were written in Italian (or Venetian), the majority of them received their premières in German opera-houses. Of these, *Le donne curiose, I quattro rusteghi* ("The four curmudgeons", performed in England under the title "School for fathers") and the one-act *Susanna's secret* were all successes in the first decade of this century, during which time Wolf-Ferrari directed—extremely efficiently—Venice's chief conservatory, the Liceo Marcello. He made one excursion into heavily melodramatic realistic opera with *The Jewels of the Madonna* (1911) (the catchy popular intermezzo from which is associated, in the play, with a gang of terrorists!) This had a temporary vogue, but after it he returned to his preferred style of graceful, melodious, rhythmically vital comedies with a touch of the 18th century about them.

SUSANNA'S SECRET—OVERTURE; IL CAMPIELLO—INTERMEZZO; RITORNELLO; LA DAMA BOBA—OVERTURE; SCHOOL FOR FATHERS —PRELUDE; INTERMEZZO. JEWELS OF THE MADONNA—ORCHESTRAL SUITE
☐ Paris Conservatoire/Santi
SDD45 (9/75) Decca Ace of Diamonds
STS-15362 London
SUSANNA'S SECRET
☐ Weikl, Chiara, Cov. Gdn./ Gardelli
SET617 (11/76) Decca
1169 London

Below: *Wolf-Ferrari, pictured in his last year.*

GLOSSARY

Abbreviations: Fr. = French; G. = German; It. = Italian; R. = Russian

Absolute music Music complete in itself, i.e., without words or illustrative "programme", and not designed to support any other art.

Absolute pitch Instinctive ability to identify notes by their sounds alone.

A cappella (ah kapel' ah) (It.). Unaccompanied choral (singing).

Accelerando (acheleran'doh) (It.). Getting gradually quicker.

Acciaccatura (achakatoo'rah) (It.). A short appoggiatura.

Accidental Sign raising or lowering a note chromatically by a semitone or tone.

Adagio (adah'jioh) (It.). Slow.

Ad lib (1) Optional; (2) in free rhythm; (3) as often as required (of repeats).

Aeolian mode Old scale in which, irrespective of the starting pitch, the intervals correspond to those of the scale A-A on the white notes only of the pianoforte.

Affettuoso (afetoo-oh'zoh) (It.). Affectionately.

Affrettando (It.). Hastening.

Agrément (agraymo[ng]) (Fr.). See *ornament*.

Alla (It.). In the style of, e.g., *alla marcia* (mar'cha): in march style.

Alla breve (alahbray'vay) (It.). Indication that a four-beat bar is taken so fast as to appear to consist of two beats.

Allargando (It.). Broadening and slowing down.

Allegretto (It.). Not quite as fast as *Allegro*

Allegro (alay'groh) (It.) Fast.

Allemande (al-mahnd') (Fr.) or **Alman** Moderate-speed dance in common time found in the eighteenth-century suite.

Alto (1) The second highest voice in four-part writing; (2) the highest male-voice register, produced by falsetto; (3) Fr. for Viola.

Andante (andan'tay) (It.). At a moderate speed.

Andantino (andantee'noh) (It.). Slightly quicker than Andante.

Answer In fugue, the entry of the subject in the dominant key.

Anthem A composition for church choir, not forming part of the liturgy, sung in Anglican Protestant services.

A piacere (ah piachair'ay) (It.). See *ad lib* (2).

Appoggiatura (apojatoo'rah) (It.). An adjacent introductory note suspending or delaying a melody note.

Arabesque (1) A florid melodic decoration; (2) a fanciful title used to describe an essentially decorative piece.

Arco (It.). With the bow; the opposite of *pizzicato*.

Aria (ah'riah) (It.). An extended vocal solo in an opera or oratorio.

Arietta (It.). A shorter and usually lighter aria.

Arioso (ahrioh'zoh) (It.). (1) Aria-like fragment interpolated in a recitative; (2) instrumentally, "in a song-like style."

Arpeggio (ahrpej-'ioh) (It.). Chord played harp-style, i.e., with the notes sounded successively instead of simultaneously, either upwards or downwards.

Assai (asah'ee) (It.). Very. Not the same as *Assez*.

Assez (asay') (Fr.). Fairly.

Atonal Not in any tonal system or key.

B (G.). The note B flat.

Balalaika Triangular-shaped Russian instrument of the guitar type, made in several sizes.

Ballad (1) An old popular narrative song; (2) a nineteenth- or early twentieth-century sentimental salon-song.

Ballad opera Eighteenth-century English entertainment with spoken dialogue interspersed with songs set to popular tunes.

Ballett A light, dance-like madrigal, often with the refrain "Fa-la".

Bar The unit of metrical grouping of beats in a composition. *Bar-line*. Vertical line through the stave separating bars. *Double-bar*. A double vertical line through the stave denoting the end of a section or of a complete work.

Barcarolle (Fr.). Boating-song in six-in-a-bar swaying rhythm.

Baritone Male voice midway between tenor and bass.

Baroque Term borrowed from architecture to denote the musical style of the 17th and early 18th centuries.

Baryton Obsolete instrument like the *gamba* but with sympathetic strings like the *viola d'amore* which could also be plucked.

Bass (1) The lowest musical strand in a composition; (2) the deepest type of male voice; (3) the double-bass (largest instrument of the violin family).

Bass drum. Large drum of indefinite pitch, placed vertically and struck sideways.

Basset horn Obsolete instrument. slightly deeper in pitch than a clarinet but of the same family.

Basso ostinato (bas'oh ostinah'toh). (It.). See *ground*.

Beat (1) One of the pulse-units which constitute a bar; (2) the conductor's indication of these units; (3) a seventeenth-century English ornament.

Bel canto (It.). A traditional Italian method of producing beautiful vocal tone.

Bémol (bay'mol') (Fr.). See *flat*.

Ben (It.). Well.

Berceuse (It.). (bairse[r]z) (Fr.). Cradle song.

Binary form Musical design in which two sections balance each other, the first moving out of its original key, the second returning to it.

Bitonal In two keys simultaneously.

Bolero A lively three-in-a-bar Spanish dance.

Bouffe (boof) (Fr.). See *buffo*.

Bourrée (booray') (Fr.). Dance of the eighteenth-century suite in *alla breve* time and starting on the fourth beat.

Brass band Band consisting of brass instruments (and percussion) only. Not the same as *military band*.

Bravura (bravoo'rah) (It.). Skill and brilliance of execution.

Breve (breev). Almost obsolete note-value equivalent to two semibreves. Not the same as *alla breve*.

Bridge (1) Wooden support over which strings of members of the violin and guitar families are stretched; (2) passage linking two subjects or two sections of a composition.

Brio (bree'oh) (It.). Animation.

Broken chord Like an arpeggio, but with the notes of the chord played in a different order.

Buffo (boof'oh) (It.). Comic.

BWV Abbreviation for the German numerical index of Bach's works.

Cabaletta (It.). (1) The quick concluding section of an operatic scena; (2) short operatic song in popular style.

Cadence (1) Harmonic progression closing a phrase, a section or an entire work; (2) French seventeenth-century name for a trill.

Cadenza Flourish (possibly improvised) by a soloist, especially in a concerto.

Canon A device in composition by which one or more melodic lines exactly imitate another at a set interval of time and pitch, making counterpoint together.

Canon cancrizans a canon in which one voice proceeds note for note backwards.

Cantabile (kantah'beelay) (It.). As if sung.

Cantata (It.). A vocal work in several movements based on a narrative text, secular or religious.

Cantilena (kanteelay'nah) (It.). A smoothly flowing melody.

Canto fermo (kan'toh fair'moh) (It.). An unembellished and usually pre-existent melody round which decorative strands of counterpoint are woven.

Cantor (1) Chief singer in a church choir; (2) leader of the ritual chanting in a synagogue; (3) musical director in a German Lutheran church.

Canzonet (1) in seventeenth-century England, a light contrapuntal song for several voices, usually unaccompanied, or one voice with lute; (2) today, simply a light lyrical song.

Capriccio (kapree'choh) (It.) or **Caprice** (1) An instrumental piece of fanciful or whimsical character; (2) a seventeenth-century composition of fugal type.

Carol Popular song, usually joyful, associated with a religious festival, especially Christmas.

Cassation Eighteenth-century divertimento, usually for open-air performance.

Castanets Spanish instrument consisting of two small pieces of wood clacked together.

Castrato A male singer operated on in boyhood to preserve his soprano or contralto vocal range.

Catch Restoration round for men's voices in which the words by unexpected juxtaposition acquire humorous or bawdy meanings.

Cavatina (It.). A short, simple operatic song, or an instrumental piece of similar style.

Celesta Orchestral keyboard instrument in which hammers strike on steel plates.

Cembalo (chem'bahloh) (It.). Harpsichord.

Chaconne (shakon') (Fr.). Instrumental composition in triple time on a ground bass of four or eight bars' length. Closely related to, and often indistinguishable from, the *passacaglia*.

Chalumeau (shalyoomoh) (Fr.). The lowest register of the clarinet.

Chamber-music Concerted music for two or more players, one to each part, suitable for performance in intimate surroundings.

Chamber orchestra See *orchestra*.

Chanter The pipe of the bagpipes on which the melody is played.

Choir Vocal group, especially in a church or cathedral, and properly of boys' and men's voices only.

Chorale (korahl'). German Lutheran hymn-tune.

Chorale prelude Organ composition based on a chorale.

Chord The sounding together of three or more notes to produce a point of harmony.

Choreography The art of arranging the dancing and movement in a ballet.

Chromatic Outside the scale of the prevailing key. *Chromatic scale*. Scale in semitones throughout.

Cimbalom (sim'balom). Hungarian variety of dulcimer.

Classical music (1) Music worthy of serious attention, as distinct from Light or Popular; (2) music of roughly the eighteenth century, as distinct from Romantic and Modern.

Clavecin (klav'sa[ng]) (Fr.). Harpsichord.

Clavichord Old keyboard instrument of faint tone, in which metal tangents press on stretched strings.

Clavier (klaveer') (G.). See *klavier*.

Clef Conventional sign determining the pitch of all the notes on a five-line stave.

Coda (It.). Tail-piece of a composition or movement of a composition.

Codetta (It.). Short coda rounding off a section of a composition or of a movement.

Colla parte (ko'lah par'tay) (It.). Indication that the accompaniment should be accommodated to follow the soloist.

Col legno (kol layn'yoh) (It.). With the stick of the bow, not the hair.

Coloratura (kolorahtoo'rah) (It.). Floridly decorated singing.

Come prima (koh'may pree'mah) (It.). As before.

Come sopra (koh'may soh'prah) (It.). As above.

Comique (komeek'). Term applied to opera with spoken dialogue. Not necessarily comic.

INDEX

Common chord Chord consisting of a note with the major or minor third and the perfect fifth above.

Common time Four beats in a bar.

Comodo (kom'ohdoh) (It.). At an easy pace.

Con (It.). With. *con fuoco* (fwoh'koh). Fierily. *con licenza* (leechen'tsah). Freely. *con malinconia* (malinkoh'niah). With melancholy. *con malizia* (malee'tsia). With malice. *con moto* (moh'toh). With movement. *con tutta forza* (toot'ah for'tsah). With all possible force.

Concertante (konchairtan'tay) (It.). Having a prominent solo part in an orchestral composition.

Concertino (konchairtee'noh) (It.). (1) A small-scale concerto' (2) the solo group in a concerto grosso.

Concerto (konchair'toh) (It.). Extended work, usually in three movements, for one or more solo instruments with orchestra.

Concerto grosso (It.). Concerto of the Bach period, in which a solo group of instruments is combined and contrasted with a larger body of players.

Concord Chord satisfying in itself without the addition of a following chord.

Console That part of the organ, containing the keyboards and stops, where the player sits.

Consort Old English term for a group of instruments performing together. *Whole consort.* instruments of the same family. *Broken consort.* A mixed group of strings and wind instruments.

Continuo or **basso continuo** (bas'oh kontee'-noo-oh) (It.). Seventeenth- and eighteenth-century harpsichord or organ part, in a concerted work, completing the harmony, which was indicated only by a bass line, figured or unfigured.

Contralto The deepest type of female voice.

Contrapuntal See *counterpoint*

Counterpoint (1) The combination of melodic lines; (2) a strand from such a combination. (adjective *contrapuntal.*).

Counter-subject In fugue, a musical phrase designed to accompany an entry of the subject or its answer.

Counter-tenor See *alto* (2).

Courante (kooront') (Fr.). Triple-time dance of "running" type, found in the eighteenth-century suite. There are two different varieties, one Italian and one French.

Crescendo (kreshen'doh) (It.). Getting gradually louder.

Crook Detachable joint fitted to a trumpet or horn to alter the length of the tube and thus the pitch.

Cross-rhythm An effect produced by the accentuation of a phrase conflicting with the basic pulse or with the accents of another simultaneous phrase.

Crotchet The most usual one-beat note-value, equivalent to a quarter of a semibreve.

Cyclic form A design in which the same theme recurs in different movements of a work.

Czardas (char'dash). Hungarian dance consisting of a slow section followed by a quick and fiery one.

D

Da capo (dah kah'poh) (It.). Back to the beginning.

Dal segno (dal say'nyoh) (It.). Back to the sign.

Dämpfer (demp'fer) (G.). Mute. *Dämpfer auf* (awf). Put the mute on. *Dämpfer ab* or *weg* (vayk). Take the mute off.

Descant (1) A contrapuntal line added above an existing melody, especially a hymn-tune, for decoration; (2) old English name for highest voice in part music, used also for highest-pitched instrument of a family (e.g., *descant viol*).

Development (1) Elaboration of the component ideas of a musical subject or subjects; (2) the middle section of a movement in sonata form, in which such elaboration occurs.

Diapason(s) Organ stops producing the solid foundation-tone of the instrument.

Diatonic Consisting only of the notes in the scale of the prevailing key.

Diesis (dee-ay'zees) (It.) or **Dièze** (dee-ayz) (Fr.). See *sharp*.

Diminished interval A perfect or minor interval decreased by a semitone.

Diminuendo (diminooen'doh) (It.). Getting gradually softer.

Diminution Compression of a phrase by reducing the note-values.

Discord. A chord not complete in itself, demanding a following chord on which to resolve.

Divertimento (deevairteemen'toh) (It.). A light and entertaining suite in several movements for a chamber ensemble or for orchestra.

Divisi (deevee'zee) (It.). A direction that a body of strings which normally plays in unison should divide and play separate parts.

Division See *double*.

Do (It.). The note C.

Dodecaphony System of composition initiated by Schoenberg in which the twelve notes within an octave are related not to a key centre but only to each other. See also *tone-row*.

Dolce (dol'chay) (It.). Sweetly.

Dominant The fifth note of an ascending diatonic scale.

Dorian mode Old scale in which, irrespective of the starting pitch, the intervals correspond to those of the scale D-D on the white notes only of the pianoforte.

Dot (1) Above a note, means that it is to be played staccato; (2) beside a note, means that its duration is lengthened by half its normal value.

Double (doo'bl) (Fr.). An ornamental variation.

Double-bar See *bar*.

Double concerto. A concerto for two soloists.

Double counterpoint Counterpoint in two strands whose vertical order may be interchanged with equally good effect.

Double fugue Fugue on two subjects simultaneously.

Double-stop The production of two simultaneous notes on a stringed instrument.

Dulcimer Instrument in which strings stretched over a sounding-board are struck with hammers wielded by the performer.

Dumka (doom'kah). A type of Slavonic lament, in Dvořák's music, alternating with animated sections.

Duplet A group of two notes in the normal time of three.

Duple time Two beats in a bar.

Dur (doorr) (G.). Major.

Durchkomponiert (doorshkom-poneert') (G.). Term used of (1) an opera composed as a continuous whole and not in separate numbers; (2) a song in which the music is different for each stanza.

E

Ecossaise (aykosayz') (Fr.). Dance of (doubtful) Scottish origin in quick two-in-a-bar rhythm.

Eight-foot tone Term derived from organ-building denoting the pitch as written.

Embouchure (ombooshyoor') (Fr.). (1) Mouthpiece of a wind or brass instrument; (2) method of applying the mouth to this.

Enharmonic modulation A change of appellation of the same note, e.g., D sharp to E flat.

Ensemble (onsom'bl) (Fr.). (1) Unanimity; (2) a concerted group of players or singers; (3) in opera, a section for several singers together.

Entr'acte (ontrakt') (Fr.). Music performed between scenes or acts of a stage work.

Episode (1) In fugue, a passage separating two entries of the subject; (2) in a rondo, an independent section between entries of the rondo subject.

Equal temperament A system of tuning the notes of the scale on a keyboard instrument so that it can be played in any key, by making all twelve semitones in the octave of equal size.

Eroica (eroh'eekah) (It.). Heroic.

Etude (aytyood') (Fr.). A study (piece developing some technical point).

Euphonium A tuba of tenor range.

Exposition The setting-out of the themes of a work; in fugue, the section containing the first statement of the subject by all the successive voices; in sonata-form, the whole first section before the development.

Expressionism Term for a style of objectivist painting (mainly second decade of the twentieth century in Germany) sometimes applied to the non-expressive music of that period.

Extemporization The art of simultaneously creating and performing music.

F

Fa (It. and Fr.). The note F.

Fagotto (fagot'oh) (It.). Bassoon.

Falsetto (falset'oh) (It.). A method of voice-production by males resulting in notes above their normal range.

Fanfare A flourish of trumpets, alone or with other brass and/or wind instruments.

Fantasia (fantazee'ah) (It.). (1) An instrumental piece of free or fanciful character, sometimes in several sections; (2) a free composition based on an existing theme or themes.

Feldpartita (felt'partee'tah) (G.). Partita for wind band, originally of military character.

Fifth The interval between a note and the fourth note alphabetically above or below it; it contains seven semitones and is termed "perfect," i.e., neither major nor minor.

Figure A characteristic musical fragment.

Figured bass A bass-line for the use of a continuo player, with the harmony indicated by a series of numbers forming a kind of musical shorthand.

Finale (feenah'lay) (It.). Concluding movement.

Finger-board That part of the neck of a stringed instrument against which the strings are pressed by the fingers in the production of notes.

Flamenco or **cante flamenco** (kan'tay flamen'koh). A gipsified form of traditional florid Andalusian folksong with brilliant guitar accompaniment.

Flat Sign lowering a note chromatically by a semitone.

Flutter-tonguing Special effect obtainable on certain woodwind and brass instruments by rolling the tongue.

Folksong Traditional song, handed down orally, whose origin is unknown.

Forte (for'tay) (It.) (abbreviated *f.*). Loud. *Fortissimo* (fortis'eemoh) (abbreviated *ff*). Very loud.

Four-foot tone Term derived from organ-building, denoting a pitch an octave higher than written.

Fourth The interval between a note and the third note alphabetically above or below it; it contains five semitones and is termed "perfect," i.e., neither major nor minor.

Frets Thin strips of wood or metal across the finger-board of certain stringed instruments (not of the violin family) facilitating the correct placing of the fingers.

Fugato (foogah'toh) (It.). A passage, not a complete movement or composition, in fugal style.

Fughetta (fooget'ah) (It.). A short fugue.

Fugue (fyoog). A polyphonic style or form, vocal or instrumental. with a definite number of textural strands, based on a single subject first stated by one voice alone and then by the other voices in turn alternately in the tonic and dominant keys.

Full orchestra See *orchestra*.

Fundamental The note produced by a string or column of air vibrating in its complete length.

Furiant (fooriahnt). Lively three-in-a-bar Czech dance characterized by strong cross-rhythms.

G

Galliard Lively sixteenth-century dance, nearly always following a pavane and usually based on the same theme.

Galop Fast nineteenth-century ballroom dance in two-in-a-bar rhythm.

Gamba or **viola da gamba** (vee-oh'lah dah gam'bah) (It.). The second largest instrument of the viol family, corresponding to the modern cello.

Gamelan, Gamelang Indonesian orchestra of native instruments, mainly percussion.

Gavotte (Fr.). Dance of the eighteenth-century suite in quick four-in-a-bar rhythm, and starting on the third beat.

Gebrauchsmusik (gebrowkhs' moozeek') (G.). "Utility music", written specifically to satisfy a demand.

Giga (jee'gah) (It.), **gigue** (zheeg) (Fr.). Animated dance in three-, six-, nine- or twelve-in-a-bar rhythm, often forming the finale to eighteenth-century suites.

Giocosco (johkoh'zoh) (It.). Humorous.

Giusto (joo'stoh) (It.). Strict, e.g., *tempo giusto*: strict time.

Glee A type of eighteenth- and early-nineteenth-century English unaccompanied part-song for at least three solo voices, not necessarily cheerful in style.

Glissando An effect of "sliding" a scale passage on the piano, harp, trombone or member of the violin family.

Glockenspiel (glok'enshpeel) (G.). Orchestral instrument in which tuned steel bars are struck with hammers.

Gong An Eastern percussion instrument consisting of a round bronze plate which, when struck, emits a definite note.

Gopak A gay two-in-a-bar Russian folk-dance.

Grace-note See *ornament*.

Gran cassa See *bass drum*.

Grand opera Opera without any spoken dialogue.

Grave (grah-vay) (It.). Solemn.

Grazioso (grahtsee-oh'zoh) (It.). Graceful.

Great organ The chief part of the the organ, containing the most powerful stops, and controlled by one of the keyboards.

Gregorian chant See *plainchant*.

Ground or **ground bass** A bass part continually repeating the same phrase.

H

H (hah) (G.). The note B.

Habanera (abanair'ah). A sensuous Spanish dance (from Africa via Cuba) with a pulse of dotted quaver, semiquaver and two quavers in each bar.

Harmonic (1) Relating to harmony; (2) one of the secondary notes produced together with the fundamental by vibrations of aliquot parts of a string or column of air; (3) a special tone-quality obtainable on stringed instruments by the isolated use of one of these secondary notes.

Harmonic minor scale A version of the minor scale conforming to the key-signature, with the exception of the leading-note, which is sharpened.

Harmonic series Acoustical term for a main note, or fundamental, together with the secondary notes produced by a vibrating string or column of air, arranged in the order of their mathematical ratios, the fundamental being termed the first *harmonic* or *partial*.

Harmonica (1) In the eighteenth-century, musical glasses; (2) today, a mouth-organ.

Harmony The organisation of sounds into chords and chord-progressions.

Harpsichord The pianoforte's most important predecessor, a keyboard instrument in which stretched strings are plucked.

Hautbois (ohbwa') (Fr.), **hautboy** (hoh'boy). Oboe.

Heckelphone Instrument of the oboe family an octave lower in pitch than the oboe.

Homophony A style of music in which the voices or parts move together without independent melodic or rhythmic interest; the opposite of *polyphony*.

Hornpipe An English dance,

originally in three-in-a-bar, later in two, usually associated with sailors.

Humoresque An instrumental composition of capricious character.

Hurdy-gurdy Rustic instrument of the south of France whose strings are set in vibration by a wheel turned by a handle. Nothing to do with the barrel-organ.

I

Idée fixe (eeday feeks) (Fr.). A musical phrase representing a person or idea which persists throughout a "programme" work.

Impressionism A term for atmospheric music by composers contemporary with the Impressionist school of painters.

Impromptu A short instrumental piece, the title suggesting, not an improvisatory type of composition, but its casual origin in the composer's mind.

Improvisation See *extemporization*.

Incidental music Music for theatre, radio or film not fundamental to the dramatic development.

Instrumentation The art of writing for instruments in a way suited to their character.

Intermezzo (intairmed'zoh) (It.). (1) See *entr'acte*: (2) a title given to a short instrumental piece, often of a light nature.

Interpretation That part of a musical performance which is concerned with the re-creation and revelation of a composer's musical thought.

Interval The distance in pitch between two notes. In calculating an interval the degrees of the scale are numbered from one to the other inclusively.

Intonation (1) The act of intoning the opening phrase of a plain-song melody; (2) the degree of accuracy of singing or playing in tune.

Introit (1) Music preluding a church service; (2) music sung as the priest advances to the altar.

Invention Short keyboard piece in imitative counterpoint based on a single musical idea.

Inversion (1) The presentation of a phrase upside down; (2) the presentation of a chord with any note other than the root as the lowest.

K

K. or **K.V.** See *Köchel*.

Kapellmeister (kapel'myster) (G.). Musical director.

Key (1) A system of relating notes and chords to one tonal centre; (2) on pianos, organs, etc., that part of the striking action which is touched by the fingers; (3) a small lever facilitating the fingering of wind instruments.

Keynote Principal note of a key, on which the scale starts and finishes.

Key-signature Indication of the sharps or flats proper to a key, placed on the stave immediately after the clef.

Klavier (klaveer) (G.). Keyboard; keyboard instrument.

Köchel (ke[r]'shel) (G.). The numerical index of Mozart's works.

Kuchka (R.). The so-called 'mighty handful' of Russian composers which included Balakirev, Borodin, Cui, Mussorgsky and Rimsky-Korsakov.

L

La (It. and Fr.) The note A.

Ländler (lend'ler) (G.). Fairly slow Austrian country-dance in triple time, precursor of the waltz.

Langsam (lang'zam) (G.). Slow.

Larghetto (It.). Slightly less slow than *Largo*.

Largo (It.). Broad, slow.

Leader (1) Principal first-violin player of an orchestra; (2) in the U.S.A., conductor.

Leading note seventh note of an ascending diatonic scale, a semitone below the tonic.

Lebhaft (layb'haft) (G.). Lively.

Ledger-lines Short lines accommodating notes above or below the stave.

Legato (Laygah'toh) (It.). Smoothly connected.

Leggiero (lejiair'oh) (It.). Light.

Legno See *col legno*.

Leit-motiv (lyt' mohteef) (G.). A theme or figure, especially in Wagnerian opera, associated with a person or idea, and quoted or adapted at relevant moments.

Lento (It.). Slow.

Lesson Seventeenth and eighteenth-century English name for a

keyboard suite or a separate piece.

Libretto (leebret'oh) (It.). The verbal text of an opera or oratorio.

Lied (leet), plural **Lieder** (lee'der) (G.) The nineteenth-century German art-song cultivated by Schubert, Schumann, Brahms, Wolf, etc., in which voice and piano are of equal importance.

Liederkreis (lee'derkrys) (G.). *song-cycle*.

Lieder ohne worte (lee'der ohne vor'te) (G.). Songs without words—a title invented by Mendelssohn for short lyrical piano pieces.

Loure (loor) (Fr.). Originally a type of bagpipe found in Normandy, later a dance in fairly slow six-in-a-bar rhythm.

Lute Obsolete plucked stringed instrument.

Lyric Sweet-toned (of voices, as opposed to dramatic).

M

Madrigal (1) Form of polyphonic *a capella* composition flourishing in the sixteenth and early seventeenth centuries, usually one voice to a part and of secular character; (2) a fourteenth-century poetic and musical form bearing little resemblance to its sixteenth-century namesake.

Maestoso (mystoh'zoh) (It.). Majestic.

Maestro di cappella (my'stroh dee kapel'ah) (It.). See *kapellmeister*.

Maggiore (major'ay) (It.), **Major** One of the two present-day key systems, of which the ascending scale runs in tones except between the third and fourth and between the seventh and eighth degrees, which are semitones.

Magnificat The canticle of the Virgin (as it appears in St Luke) which is sung at Vespers (or Evensong).

Major interval The interval of the second, third, sixth or seventh as found in the major scale.

Manual A keyboard of the organ played by the hands, as opposed to the feet.

Marcato (markah'toh) (It.). (1) Well accented; (2) to the force.

Märchen (mair'shen) (G.). Fairy-tale.

Marimba Species of xylophone with a deeper register and a large resonator attached to each note.

Masque Stage production, designed for the entertainment of the nobility in the sixteenth and seventeenth centuries, usually allegorical and mythological in character and involving poetry, music, dancing and elaborate scenic effects.

Mässig (mes'ik) (G.). Moderate. *Mässig bewegt* (bevaykt'). At moderate speed.

Mazurka Polish national dance in moderate three-in-a-bar rhythm, the accent tending to fall on the second or third beat.

Mediant the third note of an ascending diatonic scale.

Melisma (1) A decorative passage; (2) in plainsong, a group of notes sung to a single syllable.

Melodic minor scale A version of the minor scale in which the descending form conforms to the key signature, but the sixth and seventh degrees of the ascending form are sharpened.

Meno (may'noh) (It.). Less. *meno mosso*. Slower.

Metronome A mechanical instrument on the pendulum principle which audibly marks a pulse at any required speed and whose calibration is used as a convenient method of speed indication.

Mezzo forte (med'zoh for'tay) (It.). (abbreviation *mf*.). Moderately soft.

Mezzo piano (med'zoh piah'noh) (It.). (abbreviation *mp*.). Moderately soft.

Mezzo-soprano (med'zoh sohprah'noh) (It.). Female voice midway between soprano and contralto.

Mi (mee) (It. and Fr.). The note E.

Microtone Interval smaller than a semitone.

Military band Band consisting of woodwind and brass instruments (with percussion).

Minim A note-value of two crotchet beats, equivalent to half a semibreve.

Minor One of the two present-day key-systems, of which the scale may be according either to the melodic or harmonic form.

Minor interval The interval of the major second, third, sixth or seventh reduced by a semitone.

Minuet Triple-time stately French dance, nearly always with a contrasting middle section called a trio, after which the minuet is repeated. It was common in the eighteenth-century suite and was a regular movement of the sonata and symphony until Beethoven superseded it by the scherzo.

Mixed voice choir Choir of both male and female voices.

Modes The early scales in use before the establishment during the sixteenth-century of the major and minor systems. *Rhythmic modes*. Thirteenth-century systems of rhythm, involving the consistent repetition of certain simple metrical patterns.

Modulation The movement from one key to another.

Moll (G.). Minor.

Molto (It.). Much, very.

Monody A style of music in one voice or part, or in which the melodic interest is so confined.

Mordent An ornament indicating that the note over which it stands is struck rapidly twice with an adjacent note between.

Mosso (It.). Motion. See also *meno mosso, più mosso*.

Motet A form of sacred poly-phonic vocal composition set to (usually Latin) words other than those of the Mass; the Catholic counterpart of the anthem.

Motif (Fr.), **Motiv** (G.). (mohteef'). Figure. See also *leit-motiv*.

Motto theme A musical phrase which recurs in the different movements of a symphony.

Movement A self-contained subdivision of a larger work.

Musette (myoozet') (Fr.). A short piece in quasi-pastoral style imitating the French cornemuse or bagpipe.

Music drama A term for Wagnerian opera.

Musicology Musical scholarship, embracing all theoretical, stylistic and historical aspects of the art.

Mute Device for damping and softening the tone of an instrument.

N

Nachtmusik (nahkht'mooseek') (G.). See *serenade* (2).

Natural Sign countermanding an accidental.

Naturale (natoorah'lay) (It.). Direction that a voice or instrument, after some special manner of performance, should revert to the normal.

Neo-classical. A style of twentieth-century music deliberately adopting the impersonality and formal style of the "classical" period, and concerned with craftsmanship rather than emotion.

Nobilmente (nobeelmen'tay) (It.). Nobly.

Nocturne A romantic piece or movement suggestive of night thoughts.

Notturno (notoor'noh) (It.). See *serenade* (2).

Nonet (1) A composition for nine instruments; (2) a movement for nine voices.

Note (1) Sound of definite pitch; (2) symbol by which this sound is represented.

Novelette Fanciful title for a piano piece introduced into music by Schumann to denote "a romantic story in music".

O

Obbligato (obleegah'toh) (It.). An essential instrumental part of solo character. Often wrongly used as meaning an optional part.

Oboe d'amore (damor'ay) (It.). Rarely used instrument slightly lower in pitch than an oboe, but of the same type.

Occasional music Music written for some definite occasion.

Octave The interval between a note and another of the same name (with half, or twice, the number of vibrations) eight degrees of the diatonic scale away.

Octet (1) A composition for eight instruments; (2) a movement for eight voices.

Open fifth One without an intermediate major or minor third.

Opera A sung drama with orchestral accompaniment acted with costumes and scenery on a stage.

Operetta A light comedy opera, usually with some spoken dialogue.

Ophicleide Obsolete bass brass instrument, superseded by the tuba.

Opus number (abbreviation Op.). Enumeration of a composer's work, properly based on the order of composition or publication, for the purposes of identification.

Op. posth. A posthumous work, i.e., one published after the composer's death.

Oratorio Extended composition for solo voices, chorus and orchestra on a religious subject but not liturgical; dramatic in style but not intended to be acted.

Orchestra A body of instrumental players combining to form an ensemble, differing from a chamber group by having more than one instrument to each string part. *Chamber orchestra*. A small orchestra. *Full or symphony orchestra*. An orchestra of at least sixty players, including strings, woodwind, brass and percussion. *String orchestra*. An orchestra consisting entirely of stringed instruments.

Orchestration The art of writing music laid out for the instruments of the orchestra.

Ordre (Fr.). An old word for *suite*.

Ornament A melodic decoration.

Ossia (It.). A term denoting an alternative, sometimes simpler, passage.

Ostinato (ostinah'toh) (It.). A persistently repeated figure or phrase.

Ottavino (otahvee'noh) (It.). The piccolo flute.

Overtone See *harmonic* (2).

Overture (1) Piece of instrumental music properly preceding an opera, a play, etc., but also sometimes an independent orchestral composition for concert performance; (2) in eighteenth-century music, a suite.

P

Pantonal Schoenberg's preferred term instead of *atonal*.

Partial See *harmonic series*.

Partita (partee'tah) (It.). (1) The eighteenth-century suite; (2) occasionally, in early organ music, a set of variations.

Partition (partee'sio[ng]) (Fr.), **Partitur** (partee'toor) (G.). See *score*.

Part-song A nineteenth- and twentieth-century type of short secular composition for several voices with piano accompaniment, usually homophonic and strophic in style.

Part-writing The disposition of the "parts" or melodic strands in the texture of a composition.

Passacaglia (pasakah'liah) (It.). Instrumental composition on a ground (which can recur in any voice) of four or eight bars length. See also *chaconne*.

Passepied (paspiay') (Fr.) Breton dance like a faster minuet sometimes found in the eighteenth-century suite.

Passing-note Note not forming part of the harmony serving as a link, in any one strand of the texture, between two chords.

Passion music Musical presentation of the Gospel story of the Passion.

Pastorale (pastorah'lay) (It.). Composition in rustic style, sometimes on a drone bass, imitating a shepherd's pipe, and with six, nine, or twelve beats in a bar.

Pavane (pavahn') (Fr.). Stately two-beats-in-a-bar sixteenth-century dance, often followed by a galliard on the same theme.

Pedal (1) A lever raising or shifting the dampers on the pianoforte, setting a tone-colour on the harpsichord, altering the pitch of a note on the harp and the kettle-drum; (2) an organ keyboard played by the feet; (3) on the trombone, the just-playable fundamental note of the tube; (4) a device, especially in fugue, of holding one note through a number of changing harmonies or moving parts.

Pentatonic scale The five-note scale, widely current in folk-music, which is most easily represented by the black notes of the pianoforte.

Perfect cadence Cadence consisting of the chord of the dominant followed by the tonic chord.

Perfect interval The interval (neither major nor minor) of the fourth, fifth or octave.

Phrase Musical "sentence" or "clause," usually a few bars long.

Phrasing The shaping of phrases in performance.

Piano (piah'noh) (It.) (abbreviation *p*.). Soft. *Pianissimo* (piahnis'eemoh) (abbreviation *pp*.). Very soft.

Pianoforte (piah'nohfortay) (It.). The most common keyboard instrument of today, in which hammers strike on stretched strings. Most frequently abbreviated to "piano".

Pitch The "height" or "depth" of a musical sound according to the greater or lesser number of vibrations producing it.

Più (peeoo') (It.) More. *Più mosso*. Faster.

Pizzicato (pitzikah'toh) (It.). Plucked (of a stringed instrument).

Plagal cadence Cadence consisting of the chord of the subdominant followed by the tonic chord.

Plainchant, plainsong The ancient modal music of the Church, sung in unison, in free rhythm and

---

unaccompanied, which still survives in the Roman Catholic ritual.

Player-piano Mechanical piano worked by the action of air through perforated paper rolls.

Poco (It.). Little. *Poco a poco* (It.). Gradually.

Polacca See *polonaise*.

Polka Lively Bohemian dance in moderate three-in-a-bar rhythm.

Polychoral For several choirs, usually spatially separated.

Polyphony A style of music in which the textural strands, though combining to form a satisfactory whole, move independently and are of equal melodic interest.

Polytonality The system of writing music in two or more keys at once.

Ponticello (sul) (sool pontee-chel'oh) (It.). Direction to play near the bridge of a stringed instrument.

Portamento (It.). Slurring from one note to another vocally or on a bowed instrument.

Postlude Organ piece played after a church service while the congregation is leaving.

Prelude (1) An introductory piece to an opera or act of an opera, an oratorio, church service, suite or fugue; (2) sometimes merely a separate short piano or orchestral piece without anything following.

Presto (It.). Rapidly. *Prestissimo* (It.). Very rapidly.

Prima donna (pree'mah don'ah) (It.). "Leading lady" of an opera.

Programme music Music illustrating some literary, pictorial or extra-musical subject.

Progression Motion from note to note or from chord to chord.

Q

Quarter-tone Half a semitone, an interval not normally used in Western music.

Quartet (1) A composition for four instruments, especially a string quartet; (2) a movement for four voices. *String quartet.* Ensemble consisting of two violins, viola and cello. *Piano quartet.* Ensemble consisting of piano, violin, viola and cello, or a work for such an ensemble.

Quaver Note-value equal to half a crotchet.

Quintet (1) A composition for five instruments; (2) a movement for five voices. *Piano quintet.* Ensemble consisting of a piano and a string quartet, or a work for such an ensemble.

R

Rallentando (It.). Gradually slowing down.

Re (ray) (It. and Fr.). The note D.

Realisation The filling-up of a continuo part.

Recapitulation The last main section of a movement in sonata-form, restating the original themes.

Recital Properly, a concert given by a single performer (with piano accompaniment if necessary) or a single group such as a string quartet. Nowadays recitals are sometimes shared by two artists.

Recitative Narrative declamation in opera or oratorio, sung to definite notes but following speech-rhythm.

Recitativo secco (recheetahtee'voh sek'oh) (It.). Recitative accompanied only by simple chords on the harpsichord.

Recorder Type of flute, blown downwards and not sideways.

Reed Thin vibrating tongue (of wood in woodwind reed instruments, of metal in organ pipes) causing an instrument to "speak".

Registration The choice and use of tone-colours on the organ or harpsichord.

Relative major Major key based on the mediant of a minor key and having the same signature.

Relative minor Minor key based on the sub-mediant of a major key and having the same signature.

Répétiteur (raypaytiter') (Fr.). Musician in an opera-house who teaches singers their roles.

Requiem Mass for the dead.

Resolution Progression from a discord to a concord which relieves its harmonic tension.

Rhapsody Impassioned or declamatory piece of no fixed form.

Ricercare (reechairkah'ray) (It.). (1) Seventeenth-century term for a fugue employing as many technical devices (e.g., augmentation, diminution, inversion, stretto, etc.) as possible; (2) sixteenth-century term for a fantasia on a popular song.

Rigaudon (reegohdo[ng]') (Fr.). Old Provençal dance in lively two-in-a-bar rhythm.

Ritardando, ritenuto (It.). See *rallentando.*

Ritornello (It.). An introductory, intermediate or closing instrumental passage in a vocal composition. Modern writers also use the term to describe the recurrent tutti portions in a concerto grosso.

Romantic music Subjectively emotional music of roughly the nineteenth-century, as distinct from Classical.

Rondo Musical form in which one principal subject recurs several times, with different episodes between.

Root Bass note of the triad from which a chord is derived.

Round Vocal canon at the unison or octave in more than two parts, continuously returning from the end to the beginning.

Rubato (roobah'toh) (It.). Expressive elasticity of rhythm.

S

Sackbut Obsolete instrument, the predecessor of the trombone.

Saltarello (It.). An animated Roman dance similar to the Neapolitan tarantella, but with a leaping rhythmic figure.

Sarabande (sarabahnd') (Fr.). Dance in slow triple time found in the eighteenth-century suite.

Satz (zahts) (G.). Movement.

Scale (1) The notes of a key in order of pitch; (2) a succession of ascending or descending notes in some conventional order, e.g., by semitones (chromatic) or tones (whole-tone), or with gaps (e.g., pentatonic).

Scena (shay'nah) (It.). Operatic movement of dramatic character, usually in two or more sections, for solo voice.

Scherzando (skairtsan'doh), **Scherzoso** (skairt-so'zo) (It.). Playful.

Scherzo (skair'tsoh) (It.). A fast piece or movement, generally in triple time, very frequently found in the symphony since Beethoven's time, when it replaced the earlier minuet movement, whose contrasting trio it usually retains.

Schottische (shot'eesh) (G.) Nineteenth-century ballroom dance like a slower polka. Not the same as an *écossaise.*

Scordatura (It.). An abnormal tuning of a stringed instrument in order to produce some special effect.

Score Copy of a work showing on separate staves, one above the other, the music performed by all the instruments or voices taking part, so that they may be easily seen together. *Full score.* Score of an opera, oratorio, or orchestral or choral work. *Vocal score.* Score showing vocal parts in full, but with the orchestral parts reduced to an arrangement for piano.

Scoring The art of writing music laid out for orchestra and/or chorus.

Second The interval between two notes alphabetically adjacent: a minor second is a semitone, a major second a whole tone.

Segue (say'gway) (It.). Direction meaning "straight on."

Seguidilla (segeedil'yah). Popular Spanish dance in three-in-a-bar rhythm, dating back at least to the sixteenth century.

Semibreve The longest note-value now in use, equivalent to four crotchet beats.

Semiquaver Note-value of a quarter of a crotchet, equivalent to a sixteenth of a semibreve.

Semitone Smallest interval in use in Western music, one-twelfth of an octave. On the piano it may be exemplified by the interval between a white note and the adjacent black note (e.g., C to C sharp).

Semplice (sem'pleechay) (It.). Simply.

Sempre (sem'pray) (It.). Always.

Senza (sen'dza) (It.). Without.

Septet (1) A composition for seven instruments; (2) a movement for seven voices.

Sequence Repetition of a phrase or figure, starting on successive degrees of the scale.

Serenade (1) Evening vocal or instrumental music by a lover under his lady's window; (2) a type of cassation or divertimento.

Serialism Dodecaphony or an extension of its principles.

Serpent Bass wind-instrument of wood covered with leather played with a cupped brass mouthpiece: it fell out of use during the nineteenth-century.

Seventh The interval between a note and the sixth note

alphabetically above or below it: a major seventh is a semitone short of an octave, a minor seventh a whole tone short.

Sextet (1) A composition for six instruments; (2) a movement for six voices.

Sforzando (sfortsan'doh) (It.). Sudden emphasis on one note or chord.

Shake Ornament consisting of rapid alteration of a note with the note above.

Shanty Working-song on sailing-ships assisting rhythmic unanimity for collective tasks.

Sharp Sign raising a note chromatically by a semitone.

Si (see) (It. and Fr.). The note B.

Siciliano (seecheeliah'noh) (It.). Slow pastoral Sicilian dance in dotted six-in-a-bar rhythm.

Sinfonia concertante (sinfonee'a konchertan'tay) (It.). A symphonic work with one or more solo instruments: almost indistinguishable from a concerto.

Sinfonietta A small symphony.

Sixteen-foot tone Term derived from organ-building denoting a pitch an octave lower than written.

Sixth The interval between a note and the fifth note alphabetically above or below it: a major sixth contains nine semitones, a minor sixth eight.

Slide (1) See *portamento;* (2) mechanism on a trombone changing the length of tube and hence the pitch of the harmonic series produced.

Sol (It. and Fr.). The note G.

Sonata Extended composition for one or two instruments, normally in four (less often three) movements—the first in sonata form, the middle two a slow movement and a minuet or scherzo, the last often a rondo—though there have been many modifications of this pattern. The sonatas of D. Scarlatti and other early eighteenth-century composers are mostly single-movement pieces in binary form.

Sonata form Musical design normally employed in the first movement (and sometimes others) of a symphony, sonata, quartet, etc. As generally found, it has three sections—an exposition in which two main subjects in contrasted keys are introduced, a development section and a recapitulation in which the subjects are restated in the same key; there may be a coda to round it off.

PICTURE CREDITS

Sonatina A small, sometimes easy, sonata.

Song-cycle A group of songs linked by some poetic idea and intended to be sung as a set.

Soprano The highest-range female voice.

Sordino (sordee'noh) (It.). Mute.

Sostenuto (sostenoo'toh) (It.). Sustained to the full value of the note.

Sotto voce (sot'oh voh'chay) (It.). In an undertone.

Soubrette (soobret') (Fr.). A light soprano who undertakes a certain type of stock character in opera, usually a young, chattering servant.

Spinet A smaller and simpler harpsichord, sometimes without legs so that it could be laid on a table.

Spiritual Religious song of negroes of the southern states of the U.S.A.

Staccato (stakah'toh) (It.). Detached: the opposite of *legato*.

Staff notation The normal universal method of musical notation, as distinct from *tonic sol-fa*.

Stave The five parallel horizontal lines on which music is written.

Stretto (It.). Device in fugue whereby entries of the subject overlap.

Stringendo (strinjen'doh) (It.). With increasing speed and excitement.

String orchestra See *orchestra*.

Study See *étude*.

Subdominant The fourth note of an ascending diatonic scale.

Subito (soo'beetoh) (It.). Suddenly.

Subject Musical passage forming a basic idea or group of ideas in a composition.

Submediant The sixth note of an ascending diatonic scale.

Suite A set of pieces intended to be performed in succession; in the eighteenth-century a series of various dance-forms.

Sul (sool) (It.). On the *sul G*. On the G string.

Supertonic The second note of an ascending diatonic scale.

Suspension Device in harmony whereby a note of a chord is held up by the persistence of a predecessor not forming part of that chord.

Swell An organ manual whose pipes are enclosed in a box fitted with shutters which can be opened by means of a pedal.

Swell pedal Mechanism on an organ producing a crescendo and diminuendo.

Symphony A sonata for orchestra.

Symphony orchestra See *orchestra*.

Syncopation Temporary displacement of accent from a strong to a normally weak beat.

T

Tablature Special system of musical notation employing letters, figures and other symbols. Used chiefly for lute, guitar, etc., and already obsolescent by the eighteenth century.

Tacet (tas'et). Direction in an instrumental or vocal part indicating that there is nothing to perform for a period or that the performer should remain silent.

Tam-tam Like a gong, but emitting an indefinite note.

Tarantella Six-in-a-bar dance from southern Italy in alternating major and minor sections, fast and gaining in speed towards the end.

Tasto solo Direction in a continuo part that the bass line is temporarily to be played without added harmonies. *Sul tasto*. Direction to play towards the fingerboard of a stringed instrument.

Temperament A system of tuning the notes of the scale on a keyboard or on woodwind instruments so as to produce a satisfactory musical result.

Tempo (It.). Pace. *A tempo*. Up or back to speed *L'istesso tempo*. The same speed. *Tempo ordinario*. Handelian term for moderate-paced common-time. *Tempo primo*. At the initial pace. *Tempo rubato*. See *rubato*.

Tenor The highest-range male voice produced naturally, i.e., not falsetto.

Tenuto (tenoo'toh) (It.). Sustained to the full value of the note, or even slightly beyond.

Ternary form Musical design of three sections, of which the second contrasts with, and the last is a repetition of, the first.

Tessitura (tesitoo'rah) (It.). The average level of pitch in a given part in relation to the compass of the voice or instrument for which it is written.

Theme Synonymous with subject, but also used for the longer and completely self-contained basis of a set of variations.

Third The interval between a note and the second note alphabetically above or below it: a major third contains four semitones, a minor third three.

Thorough-bass See *continuo*.

Timbre (tambr) (Fr.). Tone-colour.

Time signature Indication of beat groupings in each following bar of a movement or piece, initially placed on the stave immediately after the key-signature and thereafter at each change of rhythmic grouping.

Timpani (tim'panee) (It.). Kettle-drums.

Toccata (tokah'tah) (It.). A brilliant piece of keyboard music designed to show off the instrument and the performer's skill.

Tonality Synonymous with key, but also meaning the feeling of one tonal centre suggested throughout a movement or piece.

Tone (1) Interval of two semitones; (2) quality of sound; (3) a pure note without any secondary harmonics; (4) one of the fixed psalm chants in the Gregorian system of modes; (5) in the U.S.A., a note.

Tone-poem See *symphonic poem*.

Tone-row The twelve semitones of an octave arranged in some predetermined order for use as the basis of a composition in Schoenberg's twelve-note system.

Tonguing Method of articulation by using the tongue in playing wind-instruments.

Tonic See *keynote*.

Tonic sol-fa System of musical notation, by letters and not notes on staves, used in Britain (and the Commonwealth) by some schools.

Transcription Arrangement of a composition for a medium other than that for which it was intended.

Transposing instrument Instrument whose part, for convenience of playing, is written in a key or at a pitch other than that in which it will sound.

Transposition Process of performing a part, passage or piece in a key or at a pitch other than that in which it is written.

Trautonium An electronic instrument invented in Berlin in 1930.

Treble (1) Boy's voice equivalent in pitch to the soprano; (2) the highest voice or part in a composition.

Tre corde (tray kor'day) (It.). Direction to release the left pedal of the piano, countermanding *una corda*.

Tremolo (tre'mohloh) (It.). (1) Rapid alternation of two unadjacent notes; (2) rapid and agitated up-and-down movement of the bow on the strings of an instrument of the violin family; (3) see *vibrato*.

Triad Three-note chord consisting of a note with the major or minor third and a perfect, augmented or diminished fifth above.

Trill See *shake*.

Trio (1) A composition for three instruments; (2) a movement for three voices; (3) the middle section of a minuet or scherzo.

Triplet A group of three notes in the normal time of two.

Triple time Three beats in a bar.

Tritone The interval of the augmented fourth, containing six semitones.

Troppo (It.). Too, too much.

Tubular bells Metal tubes tuned to the notes of the scale, suspended in a frame and struck with a hammer to produce the effect of bells in orchestral music.

Turca, alla (ala toor'kah). (It.). In the Turkish style, i.e., as if with the drums, cymbals and triangle (of the regiment of Turkish Janissaries).

Turn Type of ornament which twists around one main note.

Tutti (toot'ee) (It.). (1) The combined performance by the entire forces called for in a composition; (2) a passage for orchestra without the soloist; (4) direction that all the instruments of a string section should play, countermanding the direction "solo".

U

Una corda (oo'nah kor'dah) (It.). Direction to apply the left pedal of the piano.

Unis Direction that a body of strings which has been playing divisi should now revert to playing in unison.

Unison Simultaneously sounding of notes of the same pitch.

Ut (eet) (Fr.). The note C.

V

Valse See *waltz*.

Valves Mechanisms on all brass instruments but trombones changing the length of tube and hence the harmonic series produced.

Variations Varied presentations, treatments or elaborations of a theme.

Verset A short organ piece based on plainsong, replacing a verse of a psalm, etc.

Vibrato (veebrah'toh) (It.). A slight continuous oscillation of pitch, improving and giving warmth to string playing, and being acceptable on certain wind-instruments, but intolerable in singing unless under control.

Villanelle Musical setting of a type of French poem in three-line stanzas.

Viol (vy'ol). Family of bowed stringed instruments preceding, and slightly overlapping, the violin family.

Viola da'gamba (It.). See *gamba*.

Viola d'amore (vioh'lah damor'ay) (It.). A special variety of tenor viol with a second set of strings not touched by the player but vibrating in sympathy with the main strings.

Virginal, virginals Elizabethan keyboard instrument like a spinet.

Virtuoso Performer with out-standing technical mastery of his instrument.

Vivace (veevah'chay), **vivo** (vee'voh) (It.). Lively.

Vocalise (vohkahleez') (Fr.). A vocal study or piece without words.

Volta, prima (It.). First time. *Seconda volta*. Second time.

Voluntary Organ piece played as the congregation assembles or leaves the church.

Vorspiel (for'shpeel) (G.). See *prelude* (1).

W

Waltz Ballroom dance in triple time descending from the Ländler and coming into fashion in the early nineteenth century.

Whole-tone scale Scale proceeding exclusively in whole tones.

Wiegenlied (vee'genleet) (G.). Lullaby.

X

Xylophone Instrument in which tuned wooden bars are struck with hammers.

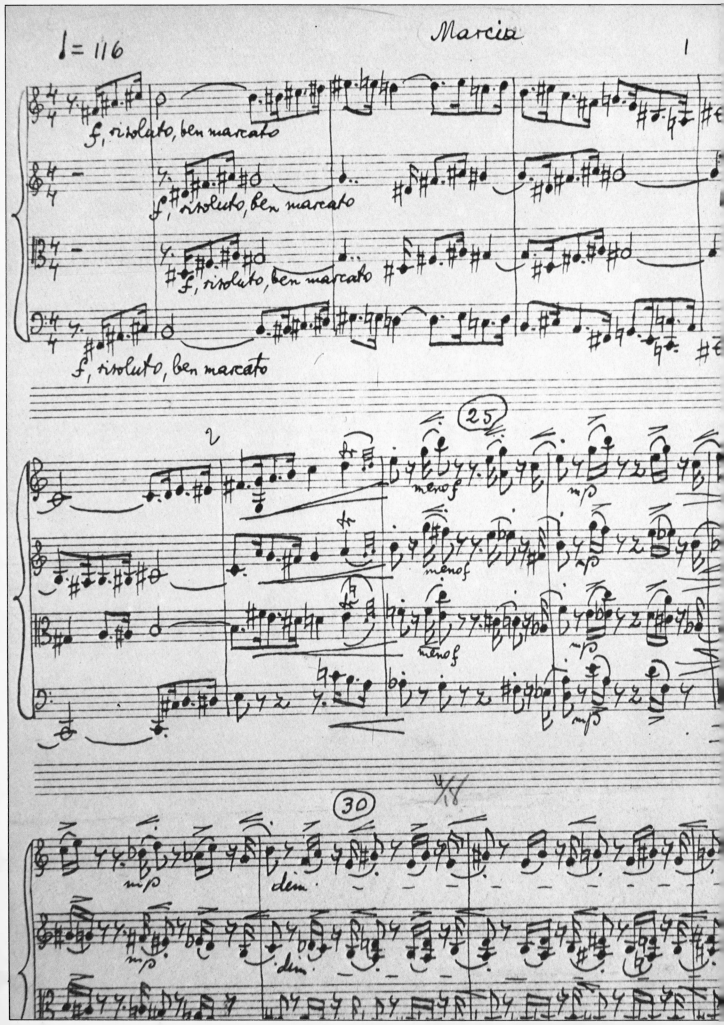